THE YEAR OF DISAPPEARANCES

Political Killings in Cork, 1921–1922

SECOND EDITION

THE YEAR OF DISAPPEARANCES

Political Killings in Cork, 1921–1922

SECOND EDITION

GERARD MURPHY ~

Gill Books

Gill Books
Hume Avenue, Park West, Dublin 12
www.gillbooks.ie

Gill Books is an imprint of M.H. Gill & Co.

978 07171 5101 1
First published in hard cover 2010
First published in paperback 2011

Index compiled by Cover to Cover
Typography design by Make Communication
Print origination by O'K Graphic Design, Dublin
Printed by Sprintprint, Dublin

This book is typeset in 11/13 pt Minion.

The paper used in this book comes from the wood pulp
of managed forests. For every tree felled, at least one
tree is planted, thereby renewing natural resources.

A CIP catalogue record for this book is available from the
British Library.

5 4

Dedicated to the memory of Eugene Turpin (1926–2006)

CONTENTS

PREFACE TO THE SECOND EDITION

O n its publication in 2010 *The Year of Disappearances* was the subject of significant controversy. This is not surprising given that the War of Independence period, though 90 years in the past, is still a contentious subject and there are many people both inside and outside of academic circles with strong views on how this period of Irish history is portrayed and interpreted. Much of the criticism directed at the book thus far was either of a peripheral or semantic nature and had little bearing on the main contents of the book—at least not in the eyes of reasonable persons reading it. However, history is a collaborative process and proceeds by a process of correction. I have, therefore, in this edition corrected any errors in the text that have been brought to my attention since the book was first published. I have also, insofar as I could, addressed various issues raised by providing additional information which I had not included in the first edition. Since the book originally went to print I have uncovered new material that I hope helps to clarify some issues which, due to pressure of deadlines, I was not able to include at the time.

Gerard Murphy
14 April 2011

PREFACE TO THE FIRST EDITION

In the autumn of 2003 I submitted a novel to several Irish publishers. The book, which detailed the operation of a sort of killing field operated by the IRA on the outskirts of Cork during the War of Independence, was well received, yet did not find a publisher. However, one well-respected publisher called me up and asked to meet with me. 'Surely,' she said, after she had established that the story was true in its essentials, 'you don't expect to get away with this?' By this she meant that, though she liked the novel, it was none the less a work of fiction and would lead to as many questions as it would answers. 'Was it true that the IRA was rounding up teenagers on the streets of Cork in 1921 and executing them as spies?' When I said that, as far as I could establish, it was true, she said I had little choice but to write a non-fiction account of these events.

This entailed a lot of further research—the novel had been based on the version of events left by old Cork IRA men who had lived into the 1960s and 70s. I had no independent verification of these events at the time. The result of this search is what is to be found within the covers of this book. It does not claim to be the last word on these events. It is rather a summary of the evidence for the secret killings that took place in Cork city during the years of the revolution, not just during the War of Independence but right through the Civil War. It is the best I could do with what I uncovered, and some conclusions may turn out to be incorrect when more evidence becomes available. It is at best a theory or, rather, a series of interrelated theories. These may be refuted by future scholars. If so, good luck to them.

This is a dark part of Irish history and it has suited various interests to keep quiet about it for the best part of a century. However, all the events described here took place, some of them in the area in which I myself was brought up. What is less certain is the precise motivation behind many of the killings. History at a microscopic level is always a lot more complex than it might appear on superficial examination. War, even a war as limited and circumscribed as the Irish revolution, is an environment in which men (and occasionally women) are capable of doing almost anything. Hate is something that cannot be measured and is often unfathomable to those of us who are lucky enough to live in times and environments that are free of conflict. It is therefore difficult and probably unfair to judge what people did in times when extreme behaviour was the order of the day. War is a phenomenon from which very few protagonists emerge smelling of roses. None the less, whether we like it or not, to write history is in effect to sit in judgment on the past. History is not a chemical that can be assayed in a lab; it is made of human failure and pettiness, just as it can sometimes be made of the most extraordinary acts of self-sacrifice and bravery.

There were many times during the writing of this book when I felt that it might be better to let sleeping dogs lie—often in this instance in their anonymous and unmarked graves. There will be people who will be unhappy with this book because it opens up some of the deep divisions inherent in this as in any society. For people in conflict situations do things for all kinds of complex motivations. There is only one reason for publishing a book like this one: it is what happened; these are the facts, even if the truth is a much more elusive quarry than what can be reconstructed from mere facts. It was a very difficult book to write mainly because it suited everybody concerned to either lie about what happened, or cover it all up.

The reality is that during the early 1920s scores of people—at least 50 and probably many more—went missing in Cork city and the surrounding areas, executed by the IRA for various 'crimes against the Republic'. In most of these cases their families were never to receive any information as to the fate of their loved ones. In many instances the families themselves colluded in the silence out of fear because to do otherwise would bring the ultimate sanction on other family members, as indeed sometimes happened. These killings were in most cases forgotten about eventually because in order to live in the new order of the Free State it was best to say nothing about the past and bury it along with the dead. Even the nascent state colluded in this silence since it was often less than helpful, for reasons of respectability and not 'wanting to let the side down', when relatives wrote concerning what had happened to the victims. 'And some there be, which have no memorial; who are perished, as though they had never been.' (*Ecclesiasticus*) This is the story of a few of them.

ACKNOWLEDGMENTS

This project would not have been started, let alone finished, without the help and encouragement of the following people: the late Eugene Turpin who first told me of the events in east Cork, Jim Fitzgerald who generously gave of his time and granted me permission to quote unreservedly from his book dealing with Sing Sing, and Jo O'Donoghue who suggested I undertake the work in the first place. But the most important source of encouragement was Dick Kenny who took many dozens of phone calls over the years, cross-checked details and proof-read the manuscript several times and shared his in-depth knowledge of events in Cork city during the War of Independence. Others who deserve special mention for helping beyond the call of duty during the research for this book were Gef Dickson of the Cork YMCA for kindly giving me access to Cork YMCA records, the indispensable Gregory O'Connor and his staff of the National Archives in Dublin, Comdt Victor Laing of the Irish Military Archives and his staff, Brian McGee and his staff at the Cork Archives Institute and Seamus Helferty and his staff at the Department of Archives, UCD. Another person who gave a lot of encouragement and help over a long period was Julian Putkowski, who made several very useful suggestions that proved invaluable. I also want to acknowledge the input of my brother Mike who, with his usual diligence and attention to detail, drew the maps that accompany the text.

Work of this kind cannot be done without the courtesy and help of the staff of many libraries and archives throughout Ireland and Britain: the National Library of Ireland, the National Archives at Kew, Trinity College Library, Cork County Library, in particular the Ballincollig and Bandon branches, Carlow County Library, Cork City Museum, the Boole Library, UCC, the Representative Church Body Library, Dublin, the Imperial War Museum, the British Museum of Military History, the Liddell Hart Centre for Military Research and the following British regimental museums: the Cameron Highlanders, the Royal Engineers, the Royal Artillery and the Hampshire Regimental Museum. Special mention should be made of the staff of the Department of Local Studies, Cork City Library who dug out material for me that is not available anywhere else, Ivana Frlan of the Special Collections department of the Library of the University of Birmingham who did several searches through their YMCA records for me, and also Rebecca Hayes of the

Library of the Grand Lodge of Freemasons of Ireland who gave me access to the lodge's membership rolls and annual reports. Also my thanks to the staff of the Registry of Deeds, Dublin, the General Registers Office, Dublin, and the Irish Valuation Office.

I am also grateful for the kind words and the sharing of information from my two predecessors in this field, the late Peter Hart and John Borgonovo, both of whose work in different ways shine light into this particularly murky area of history. I also wish to acknowledge the help of the following: Jim Herlihy for his expertise on the RIC, Gerry White, Pat Cremin and Lar O'Brien for their knowledge of events in Cork city, Nick Hiley for his intelligence expertise, Alicia St Leger for her background knowledge of the families of Cork, James Donnelly and Laurence Geary for their suggestions on matters relating to the Cork Defence Union, Graham Walker for giving me access to the 'Notes from Ireland' series, and Sarah Barratt and Liz Evans, my occasional eyes in the National Archives, Kew.

The following chipped in with help and encouragement over the years: Ollie Ryan, Brian Scannell, Meda Ryan, Christeoir de Baróid, Donal O'Flynn, Alan Stanley, Brian Murphy, Fred Rosehill, Trevor West, Martin Cherry, Alan Brown and Karen Egan. My neighbours and friends from east Cork and the area I grew up in: John Arnold, Paddy Forde, the late Bina Dunlea, Jim Healy, Matt Healy, Tomás O'Riordan, John C. Garde, Jim O'Connor and Dick Barry.

I also wish to acknowledge the help and encouragement I received from my colleagues at the Institute of Technology, Carlow, from my boss David Ryan, from Barbara Kinsella and Richard Lennon of the ITC Library, from Pádraig Ó Murchú, Jim Walsh, Brian O'Rourke and Thelma Keegan.

I am grateful to Fergal Tobin and the staff of Gill & Macmillan, in particular Deirdre Rennison Kunz, Jennifer Patton, Nicki Howard and Teresa Daly, who helped in various ways in the production of the book.

I wish to thank my agent, Jonathan Williams, for his attention to detail and for believing in me over many years.

Of course, while all this was going on, someone had to keep the show going on the home front and, for her forbearance and tolerance and for putting up with me through all the twists and turns of this apparently endless task, I wish to express my utmost gratitude and love to my wife, Mary. And of course thanks to my children, Áine, Grace and James, for providing normality and helping to keep me sane. In a book of this length and difficulty it is inevitable that there are very many people who helped in various ways to bring it to fruition. It is equally inevitable that I will neglect to thank all of them. So to you, my apologies and my thanks.

Gerard Murphy
24 July 2010

ABBREVIATIONS

ACRI	American Commission for Relief in Ireland
ADRIC	Auxiliary Division, Royal Irish Constabulary
AFIL	All For Ireland League
ASFL	Anti-Sinn Féin League
ASU	Active Service Unit
Bde	Brigade
Bn	Battalion
CDU	Cork Defence Union
CI	County Inspector
DI	District Inspector
DMP	Dublin Metropolitan Police
GHQ	General Headquarters
GOC	General Officer Commanding
GPO	General Post Office
IGC	Irish Grants Commission
IO	Intelligence Officer
IRA	Irish Republican Army
IRB	Irish Republican Brotherhood
IUA	Irish Unionist Alliance
MGC	Machine Gun Corps
MLA	Martial Law Area
O/C	Officer in Command
QOCH	Queen's Own Cameron Highlanders
RAF	Royal Air Force
RAMC	Royal Army Medical Corps
RASC	Royal Army Service Corps
RE	Royal Engineers
RFA	Royal Field Artillery
RGA	Royal Garrison Artillery
RIC	Royal Irish Constabulary
UVF	Ulster Volunteer Force
WS	Witness Statement
YMCA	Young Men's Christian Association

Archives

BMH	Bureau of Military History, Dublin
BU	Birmingham University
CAI	Cork Archives Institute
CCM	Cork City Museum
MA	Military Archives, Dublin
NA	National Archives, Dublin
NLI	National Library of Ireland
TNA	The National Archives, Kew (formerly the Public Records Office)
UCC	University College Cork
UCD	University College Dublin

Records

ADM	Admiralty
BMD	Births, Marriages, Deaths Register, UK
CAB	Cabinet Papers, UK
CCPO	Cork Crown and Peace Offices Records
CO	Colonial Office Papers, UK
DOD	Irish Department of Defence
DOJ	Irish Department of Justice
Fin	Irish Department of Finance
GRO	General Registration Office, Dublin
HO	Home Office, UK
IWM	Imperial War Museum
ROD	Registry of Deeds, Dublin
T/-	Department of the Treasury, UK
Taois	Department of the Taoiseach
VO	Valuation Office, Dublin
WO	War Office

'We buried the bodies in Carroll's Bogs. Every spy who was shot in Cork was buried so that nothing was known about them. They just disappeared.'

MICK MURPHY O/C 2ND BATTALION, CORK NO I BRIGADE, IRA

PART I

Chapter 1 ∾

THE MYSTERIOUS DEATH
OF GEORGE TILSON

On 19 February 1921, as the mail train from Fishguard pulled into Paddington, a man called Fred Jones, an electrician employed by the Great Western Railway Company, was surprised to find one of the toilet doors locked. He heard groans coming from inside and then he heard a thud as if someone had fallen. When the door was finally forced open, he found a dying man slumped against the toilet. There was blood all over the floor. The man's throat had been cut. He was still alive, though unable to speak. He pointed towards his coat pocket, indicating to Jones to take out what was inside. In the pocket Fred Jones found a note that read: 'I have been shadowed all the way from Cork, but they shall not get me.' The man was taken to St Mary's Hospital where he died without making a statement.[1]

The man's name was George Frederick Tilson, a 36-year-old pawnbroker from Cork and, though there was a suggestion that he had been murdered, the inquest into his death found that he had slit his own throat and the reason was stated in the envelope in his pocket: 'not to be done in by them'. For 'them', the men who he believed had followed him from Cork, were members of the Cork NO. 1 Brigade of the IRA, though there is no evidence that they had actually done so.

Tilson had received a threatening letter a few days earlier warning him that his life was in danger and he was 'going to be next'. The letter was written in capitals in pencil and was unsigned. As a result he decided to leave immediately to stay with friends in the south of England. As his brother saw him off from the Cork docks on the Friday evening, he gave 'the impression that he was being pursued' and was terrified of what he called 'the overshadowing danger'.

Such was his terror of the men who were then in the process of waging war to wrest political control of Ireland from Britain that he would rather take his own life than fall into their hands, even though at that point he was probably safe from whatever punishment he believed the IRA might have had in store for him. A police sergeant who arrived on the scene asked Tilson if he had done the deed himself. Tilson nodded. When the policeman suggested that he had been very foolish, Tilson 'shook his head in a negative manner'. He also shook his head to indicate that he was not a member of the RIC. It is assumed by many people acquainted with the case that Tilson had been a British agent and that he was on the run from IRA retribution. Yet he denied that too. His own brother Richard Tilson, a former Cork Nationalist politician and JP,[2] cross-examined Jones at the coroner's inquest a week later. He said his brother was a man of private means and had taken no part in local politics.

'You are certain he did not make a statement to the effect that he was a secret service agent?'

'Perfectly certain.'

The second witness, a time-keeper in the railway, also said in reply to the coroner that the dying man did not say anything to him about being in the secret service. The coroner concluded that he was quite sure the dead man had no connection with police work of any kind, 'nor apparently had he any connection with political matters'. The jury returned a verdict of 'suicide, whilst temporarily insane, as the result of receiving the letter'. Curiously, the *Cork Examiner* account of the inquest also carried a retraction, headed:

UNFOUNDED STATEMENT

In our issue of Monday, a paragraph was quoted from the *London Star* which read the deceased had said he was a secret service agent. If such a statement had been made by the unfortunate gentleman, it would of course be regarded as a delusion, but it is evident from the above report that in point of fact he made no such statement.[3]

Writing years later, several IRA survivors of the conflict claimed that Tilson was a member of a group calling itself the Anti-Sinn Féin League, a shadowy civilian counter-revolutionary organisation consisting of a cabal of loyalist businessmen in Cork city who, the IRA men claimed, were dedicated to retaining the British link and were employed by the British military establishment to gather information on IRA personnel and operations. The notion that such an organisation existed runs through the accounts of many Cork IRA men. Tilson, so the theory goes, was one of six members of this organisation to die, though the only one to die by his own hand; the others were either executed or assassinated by the IRA. As a result of the assassination campaign, in this version of events, the 'League' was frightened into silence and the IRA had won a major victory against one of its most serious enemies. Tilson was supposedly the last of this group to be targeted.

While this all appears perfectly plausible, it is not quite the full story. For a start, Tilson's brother was a Home Rule politician, not a Unionist, and was all his life a very popular figure in Cork. George Tilson died by his own hand largely because he was mentally unstable. There was no question that he was terrified and that he had received a threatening letter; he may even have been some sort of 'spy'. But he was not a member of a loyalist cabal of counter-revolutionaries dedicated to reversing the Irish revolution, for the simple reason that there is no firm evidence that such a cabal actually existed.[4] Yet the accounts left by up to a dozen members of the Old IRA subsequently claim that such an organisation did exist. One of the aims of this book is to look at this thorny question and to show where the notion of a so-called loyalist 'spy circle' came from. This is of more than academic interest because it led to dozens of deaths as members of this society were pursued across the county of Cork and in many cases shot dead in cold blood with little more than suspicion acting as 'evidence'. It is a story of some complexity and takes in what has since been called the intelligence war or the 'dirty war' fought between the IRA and a variety of British forces in Cork city and surrounding areas. It can justifiably be called one of the murkiest aspects of Irish history. It has largely been neglected until recently and it is a topic that many people in Cork do not want to talk about almost a hundred years later.

Chapter 2 ❧

| THE STORY OF SING SING

I f you travel the main Cork-Dublin road heading north out of Cork city and you look to your right as you approach the village of Watergrasshill, you will see a broad stretch of upland consisting mostly of pine forest and unreclaimed moorland. This area, lying between the parishes of Knockraha and Watergrasshill of around five or six square miles and around 700 ft above sea level, is known locally as the Rea. It looks like any other hillside, isolated, lonely, a piece of high marginal land with small farms and low bungalows cosying up to its rather bleak forest-covered brow. Once a broad upland bog or moorland, the land is now a forest managed by Coillte and is covered with dense Nordic pine.

But this is no ordinary hill and if you go for a Sunday walk along the many forest pathways signposted on the roadside lay-bys on the road between Watergrasshill and Leamlara, nobody will tell you that this otherwise benign piece of public walkway was once the scene where death was meted out on an almost nightly basis. For the Rea, less than ten miles from Cork city and therefore the nearest piece of isolated land to the city, was the killing field where the Cork IRA No. 1 Brigade carried out most of its executions during the Irish War of Independence and the period immediately afterwards. This is the burial ground for at least 20 and perhaps as many as 30 victims of that conflict. Yet virtually nobody under the age of 50 living in the locality knows anything about this now. To them it is just a hill, a place to take the dog for a walk and, for a brief period in the late 1990s, a focus of protest groups as locals tried to block plans by Cork County Council to site a municipal dump there. What very few people realise now is that in the 1920s this was a dumping ground of an entirely different kind.

This was not because it was a secret. Many of the older people knew about it, including my father, though he rarely mentioned these events. It was just that for two generations most people were reluctant to talk about it. And then because it was never mentioned, it just got forgotten about. It is not the only such secret burial ground in County Cork: many bogs throughout the county contain victims of the period, but this is one of the most important, at least in the vicinity of the city.

My father's generation—he was born in 1924—was half-afraid of the generation that came before them, the sometimes brave and sometimes savage men who had fought against the British Empire to secure political autonomy for the southern two-thirds of Ireland. The older men, the revolutionary generation, cast a long shadow over political life and discourse that was still palpable well into the 1960s. Their word was law, not only in the normally accepted sense of that term but also in the political and judicial sense. For politics, both national and local, was still dominated by the denizens of what has come to be called 'the struggle for freedom'. When John F. Kennedy visited Ireland in 1963 and addressed the Dáil, what is striking about the television footage of his speech is the youthfulness and energy of the US president compared to the Muppet-like doze of his ageing audience. Many members of both sides of the Dáil and the Seanad were at that time in their sixties or early seventies. My generation was born, though we did not see it like that at the time, into a gerontocracy. And this was a gerontocracy that liked to guard its secrets. For, though many people knew about them and had heard the rumours, the killings in the Rea and elsewhere were carried out quietly. Only a small number of people knew of them even as they were going on in the 1920s.

It was in the summer of 1994 that I stumbled on the story of the Rea and how it operated. Very quickly I realised that this was one of the grimmest and most neglected untold stories of the period. It was obvious that if what I had been told could be substantiated, it would be a significant unwritten episode of the national struggle. If it were true, and I was initially extremely sceptical that it was, then something bigger was going on here than mere local history.

Yet it was a local historian called Eugene Turpin who told me about it. Eugene, a highly intelligent and engaging man with an interest in everything from the history of machinery to the history of the GAA, the IRA and the Blueshirts, told me this extraordinary tale. But I was quickly able to corroborate from other local sources most of what he told me.

'I presume you've heard about Sing Sing,' he said to me one evening in his kitchen in the spectacularly dull and damp summer of 1994, taking a manuscript about the size of a small masters thesis down off the shelf.

'Sing Sing?'

I had never heard of it, outside of the American prison of that name. The essence of what Eugene Turpin had to say was that the IRA ran a sort of killing field in the bogs north of Knockraha, where prisoners taken by the Cork No. 1 Brigade in the city and surrounding areas were executed. Prior to execution the prisoners were held in an underground vault in a local cemetery at Kilquane, a mile outside the village. The vault with grim Irish humour became known as Sing Sing. If Turpin's story was to be believed, up to 35 individuals were executed in the Rea, north of Kilquane, which lies in the heart of east Cork between the villages of Knockraha, Watergrasshill and Leamlara.

Not only was he able to tell me what had gone on there, but 'the thesis' contained documentary evidence of a lot of the killings of prisoners in the area. This was a monograph written in the 1970s, a Macra na Feirme project entitled *Foras Feasa na Paróiste*,[1] a history of the parish of Knockraha's role in the War of Independence compiled while most of the survivors were still alive. It had been written by a Knockraha man, Jim Fitzgerald.

The intention of the book was to give a detailed picture of Knockraha's role in the War of Independence. One of the more interesting details was that there were two bomb factories in the parish, where local IRA men made iron casings for hand grenades. Some of these grenades can now be seen in the Cork County Museum in Fitzgerald's Park. However, the bulk of the book, which in its original version ran to over 90 pages of dense two-column script, is taken up with the holding and execution of prisoners. The essence of the story was that the Cork No. 1 Brigade used the vault in Kilquane graveyard outside Knockraha as a prison for holding people before taking them up to the Rea for execution. The operation of this prison is given in great detail.

My first reaction to this was one of disbelief. Could executions on this scale have been going on only a few miles from where I was reared? Could I have spent nearly 40 years in the area and have been blissfully unaware that death was dealt out on such a scale in such a small area? Where was this in the history I had been taught, the catalogue of struggle against 'the British oppressor' that had been drummed into us from the very first day at primary school, the centuries of grief that our 'noble' nation had to suffer before 'freedom' was finally achieved? (In the 1960s we were the most noble nation on earth.) Every morning of my young life I could see the Rea across the valley from our house. It formed the south-eastern horizon of my childhood world, where the sun rose every morning. It was seven or eight miles away but it was still within the universe of my childhood. I had never thought of it as anything other than a hill. My mother had been born to the south and east of it and had cycled across the Rea every Sunday of her childhood in the years immediately after the conflict. It was inconceivable that a few years before my mother routinely cycled that lonely road, it was host to a far more grisly form of traffic.

Yet here was an account detailing the execution of dozens of prisoners,[2] as seen from the viewpoint of the men who were involved in the executions and burial of the bodies. These prisoners were a mixture of British soldiers, Black and Tans and civilian 'spies', only three of whom are mentioned by name. Martin Corry, the local IRA captain and later well-known Fianna Fáil TD, who was Jim Fitzgerald's main source, claimed the real number was 35. Fitzgerald went to considerable lengths in the 1970s to corroborate Corry's account of events by talking to other survivors of the time on both sides of the political divide. (His taped interviews with Martin Corry, containing much of the same detail, are now in the possession of the Cork Military Museum.) He was lucky to have gathered his material when he did, while most of the survivors of E Company (4th Battalion, 1st Cork Brigade) were still alive, for by the time I got interested in it some 20 years later, they were all dead. He said he only wrote down what he managed to confirm from more than one source. It was difficult, even for a sceptic like me, to argue with such an approach.

One Sunday in September 1994 Eugene Turpin showed me the vault. It was an underground mausoleum of solid stone right in the middle of the graveyard and had been used apparently for holding dead bodies during the days of the body snatchers. It was about 12 to 15 feet long with an arched roof and a creaking rusted iron door and was about 6 feet high at its highest point. The first time I was shown it, it was covered in briars and scrub and hidden behind a crumbling tomb, almost invisible unless you knew where to look for it. The vault has since been opened up to the public and there is now a plaque near by commemorating its use in the War of Independence. It is a grim cave-like structure, though it looked much worse before it was cleaned out, as no doubt it did in 1920. It is still possible to see the holes in the iron door made by Ned Maloney, the local blacksmith and so-called 'Governor of Sing Sing', who drilled the holes so that the prisoners inside could breathe.

There was only one problem. I had no corroborating evidence that any of this stood up in the broader historical context. If these stories were true, then there would have to have been a lot of disappeared persons from the vicinity of Cork, both military, police and civilians. Evidence of this seemed, initially at least, to be difficult to find.

And there were other problems with it from a historical point of view. Despite a 12-month period when I read every published book and article connected with the War of Independence in Cork, I did not come across a single reference to Sing Sing or to the execution of prisoners in Knockraha. Looking through the newspapers of the time revealed only a picture of general chaos. Such was the mayhem that prevailed, that finding anything connected with these disappearances seemed futile. Either a lot was going on that went unreported in the press, or Corry's account of his 'war' was a gross exaggeration.

As I began to look into the history of the period, all kinds of contradictions began to appear which had the effect of throwing me into years of hopeless confusion. It was in that confusion that I gradually began to untangle the secret operations of the IRA and the various branches of British intelligence as they operated in Cork at the time. It turned out that many of the facts could, with considerable effort, be unearthed. Those facts told of a 'dirty' war, of espionage and counter-espionage, of terror and counter-terror, of episodes so well covered up that no historian had been able to write about them. Here was a tale waiting to be told. It was not a pleasant story and had either been ignored or buried by nationalist historians for two generations. It was time for the first of my many trips to, and contact with, archives and museums all over Britain and Ireland. It gradually began to dawn on me that the truth of the time had never been told; that the received history we had all been taught in school had been full of evasions and even lies. It was not a happy place to be, but I felt if I stayed at it long enough, I might finally dig out the facts as they happened. What I did not realise then was that it would take me the best part of a decade to do so.

Chapter 3 ⌒

| THE WAR IN CORK

From 1919 the Irish Volunteers, the immediate forerunner of the IRA, were organised into three brigades in Cork. The Cork No. 1 Brigade covered the centre of the county and stretched from Youghal in the east to the Kerry border. Including Cork city and several major towns, it was the biggest brigade in the country. It was organised and led initially by Tomás MacCurtain, then by Terence MacSwiney and finally by Seán O'Hegarty. North of this lay the Cork No. 2 Brigade which covered north Cork and was commanded by Liam Lynch. Finally we have what is probably the best-known of all the IRA units of the war, the west Cork Brigade, otherwise known as the Cork No. 3 Brigade, led for most of the conflict by the Hales brothers of Ballinadee outside Kinsale, though its flying column was led from the autumn of 1920 onwards by Tom Barry. Knockraha and Sing Sing were in the area controlled by the Cork No. 1 Brigade.

The 'war', if it can properly be called a war, can be divided into three phases. The first phase ran from late 1919 to the early summer of 1920 and consisted largely of assassinations of RIC men by the IRA. Ireland did not so much 'descend' into violence as it was nudged. As early as 1917, when the city battalion raided the Cork Grammar School in order to snatch the rifles of the Officer Training Corps (one of only three in Ireland where putative officers for the British Army received their first taste of military training), Mick Murphy, later to gain the reputation as one of the most ruthless of the guerrilla leaders in the city, remembered Roibeárd Lankford, who led the raid, ordering his men that 'in the case of such an eventuality [possible opposition], we were not to hesitate to shoot'.[1] Lankford, who had been sworn into the IRB only months earlier by Michael Collins,[2] was itching, like Dan Breen some two years later, for the shooting to start.

The second phase, which began to emerge in the summer of 1920, was what has come to be called the Tan War. The British government, reluctant to allow its army to become involved in what it tried to persuade itself was a domestic matter, decided to unleash a police war on the IRA. The RIC, which had to date borne the brunt of IRA actions, began to lose significant numbers through early resignations. Lloyd George decided to reverse the decline by recruiting ex-soldiers to fill its ranks. These were to become the notorious Black and Tans who were to terrorise the population for the next year. The Black and Tans were themselves augmented in the latter half of 1920 by the Auxiliaries, ex-officers recruited into a separate force for a similar purpose, and were to prove to be one of the worst embarrassments in British political history. Not only did they fail to quell the IRA, they caused moderate opinion in Britain and elsewhere to clamour for a settlement. The Black and Tans and the Auxiliaries are a disgraceful chapter in the history of modern democracy; their tactics would not have been out of place among the ss or the Blackshirts of ten years later. However, their excesses have been more than adequately dealt with elsewhere. But they managed to conjure up the political miracle of making the IRA, which in 1919 had received considerable odium for its policy of assassinating policemen, look respectable. The combined militias of the 'new' RIC inadvertently contributed as much to the cause of Irish freedom as did many brigades of the IRA.

The final phase of the conflict took place from the beginning of 1921 to the Truce of 11 July of that year. In Munster this period was marked by Martial Law and the conflict had become a 'war' in the normally accepted meaning of the term. The Martial Law Area (MLA) was now under the control of the British Army, and the RIC and its various militias became subservient to the army. The war in this period was overshadowed by backroom rumours of a settlement, though on the military front the army was successful enough against the IRA for senior officers almost universally to complain that victory had been snatched from their grasp by the Truce. However, this was almost certainly an illusion as it seriously underestimated the IRA's capacity for survival. The last six months of the conflict were by far the most violent, with both sides shooting civilians and carrying out unspeakable deeds on a daily basis. Death swaggered on the streets of Cork in the first six months of 1921 and no one was immune. While the army limited the excesses of the Tans and the Auxiliaries—the random shootings of civilians by British forces which occurred almost on a nightly basis in the last months of 1920 were greatly reduced with the introduction of the MLA—a military cordon was thrown over the city; all bridges and major intersections were constantly manned; and searches were the order of the day. At the same time, remaining indoors was the order of the night, while undercover army and RIC patrols in Ford cars raided suspect houses and IRA men and others were bombed into oblivion or shot 'while trying to escape'.

The attrition rate—that is to say the number of casualties inflicted and suffered per head of population—did not differ significantly among the three brigades. However, the war was pursued quite differently in each of the three brigade areas. This was partly due to the character of the individual leaderships and partly due to how the British forces fought back in each area.

The fight was cleanest in north Cork, if any war can be described as clean. Liam Lynch and Seán Moylan, who succeeded him, endeavoured wherever possible to fight within the rules of war. Captured prisoners had their wounds bandaged and British soldiers and indeed RIC men rounded up in ambushes were often allowed to walk back to their barracks after attacks. This was to save Moylan's life when in May 1921 he was captured by British forces and would have been shot out of hand had not one of his captors remembered his gallant treatment of prisoners in earlier attacks.[3] Only in the last months before the Truce were prisoners shot, and this was as a result of betrayals by captured British troops of IRA positions; by my estimation only seven civilians were shot as spies by the north Cork Brigade during the Anglo-Irish conflict.

At the other end of the scale was the west Cork Brigade, where the campaign was fought with particular brutality. While it is easy to castigate the likes of Tom Barry at this remove in time and focus on particularly brutal episodes like Kilmichael, the main reason why west Cork descended into savagery was that the other side fought back ruthlessly from the very start. While in north Cork the British Army was almost integrated into the society, having huge barracks and camps in Fermoy, Kilworth, Buttevant, Mallow and Ballyvonaire,[4] and the RIC were 'not tough',[5] in west Cork individual RIC officers such as Sgt Mulvey and Sgt Hussey, and indeed the Essex Regiment when they arrived in the spring of 1920, were particularly assiduous in pursuing known republicans. The methods employed both by the RIC and the army were particularly savage with midnight raids on the homes of known suspects and prisoners being savagely beaten to extract information. While the forces of the Crown drifted sleepily into the conflict in north Cork, apart from the sacking of Mallow and Fermoy in the wake of IRA attacks, they were a lot more savage in west Cork.[6]

In west Cork guerrilla warfare was mutual and reached spectacular depths of depravity: undercover RIC men dressed as farmers flogged suspects with wire until they passed out. While the Essex Regiment stationed at Bandon and Kinsale get most of the blame for the brutality of the British Army, it appears that it was the undercover activities of the RIC and the Intelligence department, led by Major Percival, that carried out most of the torture and shootings. Even a cursory perusal of the newspapers of the time and documents such as those gathered by Flor Crowley[7] give many examples of the violent treatment meted out to suspects in west Cork. Any suspected IRA man, even if he had never been on a route march, was liable to get such a beating that it is no wonder quite a number of them gave away the names of their comrades. Some were themselves shot as informers as a result, though surely the term 'informer' is not quite right for an unfortunate who may have had his nails pulled out or who was flogged to the point of collapse to extract information. The killing and burial of such 'informers' by the IRA says much about the nature of the conflict west of Bandon. The recent description of west Cork as the Gaza Strip[8] of the Anglo-Irish War is not without its justification. Tom Hales, commandant of the brigade, was savagely brutalised himself. In the same month in 1921 that a column of north Corkmen ambushed a British Army convoy at Labbeecallee outside Fermoy, where one soldier was killed and the others allowed to walk back to barracks, Tom Barry and his men opened fire on a group of soldiers playing football near the barracks in Bandon.

But it is the Cork No. 1 Brigade that is the subject of this book and in terms of the known statistics of brutality and counter-brutality the perception is that it lies somewhere between the other two, being neither as cleanly fought as the war in north Cork nor as vicious as the conflict west of Bandon. There are other significant differences: while north and west Cork were led by men who at the time kept to the political shadows, Cork One, as it came to be called, was led by two very public figures. Tomás MacCurtain and Terence MacSwiney were major political figures in Cork city, being senior members of Sinn Féin as well as successive o/cs of the brigade. They were both also successive Lord Mayors of Cork and were to become the great Cork martyrs to the Irish cause.

Another difference is that, while the fighting units of the 2nd and 3rd Brigades were led by men who displayed significant military competence, the 1st Brigade found itself on several occasions at the receiving end of severe military setbacks at the hands of British forces, suggesting that there was more leakage of information from within the ranks than there was in north and west Cork. Also, 1st Brigade guerrilla leaders displayed a lot of carelessness and outright incompetence on several occasions.

The Volunteer movement had been set up in Cork in 1913. After the split with the National Volunteers, it was to keep operating, that is to say, drilling, marching and attempting to arm itself, with increasing membership up to 1916. The Easter Rising found the Cork Volunteers ready to fight in the hills west of Macroom, but in the confusion and countermanding orders between the IRB and the Volunteer command in Easter week not a shot was fired. However, 112 Cork Volunteers were rounded up and interned in 1916.[9]

The fallout of the debacle of the attempted rising in Cork was that it radicalised the leadership. People like MacSwiney and MacCurtain were racked with guilt at the failure of Cork to 'rise' in 1916. And so they were determined that if conflict was to break out again, the Cork Volunteers were not going to be found wanting. This was compounded by the humiliating climbdown mediated by the Catholic Bishop of Cork, Dr Cohalan, and local politicians when the Cork Volunteers handed in their weapons in the belief that they would not be confiscated by the military. Since this was exactly what happened and the guns were passed on to the army, the Cork IRA was even more determined to fight when the opportunity arose again and became deeply suspicious of Nationalist politicians. And so began the running feud with Bishop Cohalan which was to lead to the bishop in late 1920 excommunicating IRA members guilty of murder.

During 1919 there were only a few sporadic shootings of RIC men and soldiers in the county. It was only at the start of 1920 that the conflict began to gather momentum. On the night of 20 March 1920, probably as a result of the killing of a Constable Murtagh of the RIC in the streets of Cork some hours earlier, the Sinn Féin Mayor and o/c of the brigade Tomás MacCurtain was shot dead in his home by RIC men with soot-blackened faces. MacCurtain, who had been a charismatic leader and very popular in Cork, had been commiserating with Murtagh's widow only hours before the assassination. The IRA held District Inspector Swanzy of the RIC responsible for the murder and he himself was in turn assassinated by Cork IRA men in Lisburn, Co. Antrim, the following August.[10]

MacCurtain was succeeded as Lord Mayor and also as o/c of the brigade by Terence MacSwiney, a well-known nationalist playwright. It was MacSwiney, so local lore has it, who decreed that the vault in the graveyard at Kilquane be used as a prison by the IRA. MacSwiney was a more intellectual and ascetic man than MacCurtain, and when he was arrested by the British Army in August 1920 and found guilty of having in his possession a cipher key for decoding RIC messages, he immediately went on hunger strike.

The hunger strike had been a weapon used by many IRA prisoners before MacSwiney. It led to a series of acquittals and climbdowns by the British government and several waves of IRA men were released as a result of the moral pressure inherent in such strikes. But by the time MacSwiney began his strike, the government was not going to back down. And neither was MacSwiney. He died on 25 October after 72 days on hunger strike. His death attracted world attention to the conflict in Ireland and was probably more instrumental than any military successes or otherwise in ultimately persuading the British government that force could no longer be effective in trying to quell unrest in Ireland. The moral force of MacSwiney's martyrdom was felt anywhere in the world that people read newspapers.

MacSwiney was then replaced as commander of Cork No. 1 by Seán O'Hegarty. O'Hegarty, a 40-year-old Fenian of the old school, had been the IRB 'centre' for Cork for many years and as a result had a long history of intimidation and enforced exile imposed on him by the authorities. He was very much a backroom operative and had been restive during the command of MacCurtain and MacSwiney, being in favour of more direct action than they were. A resident of Douglas Road in Cork—he worked as a storekeeper in the local workhouse—he had the reputation of having a fearsome intelligence and being utterly ruthless in everything he did. He has recently been painted as something of a fanatical figure, the *éminence grise* of the revolution.[11] But it is difficult to judge him as he left very little in the way of personal papers or documentary evidence of his actions or his decisions.

Certainly the IRA battalions under his control were ruthless, but that may be due partly to circumstances and partly to some of the men under his command. A fierce ascetic and atheist, O'Hegarty mistrusted Michael Collins and hated Richard Mulcahy, a feeling that appears to have been mutual. His relationship with MacCurtain and MacSwiney had never been easy. The leaders of the Cork Volunteers were too moderate for O'Hegarty and he had his own view of what the IRB should be about.

From his ascension to the leadership of the brigade on the capture of Terence MacSwiney in the summer of 1920 right to the outbreak of Civil War nearly two years later, O'Hegarty was the undisputed leader in Cork city and governed his fiefdom with no small amount of cunning and savagery. He also operated under a habitual cloak of secrecy. It is doubtful, even in the 12 months after the Truce when he was virtual dictator of the 'republic of Cork', that he would even have been recognised in the street. No photographs of him as a young man exist and he was not photographed until many years later. He had a sharp, rapier wit, his faithful deputy and right-hand man Florrie O'Donoghue wrote of him. He had a tongue that flayed, according to the much younger Ernie O'Malley. A 'surly gob' was what Richard Mulcahy called him.

If MacCurtain and MacSwiney were public figures, then O'Hegarty was the opposite. For two years he was probably the most significant republican leader outside of Collins and Mulcahy in charge of the biggest IRA unit in the country. Yet he is almost a forgotten figure. The main reason for this is that he shunned the limelight, perhaps out of habit; after all, he had spent over 20 years as a Fenian outlaw. He refused to take sides during the Civil War, being republican by inclination and thus anti-Treaty, while on the other hand as a member of the Collins-led IRB and a pragmatist, he recognised that Ireland had got as good a deal as it could expect in the circumstances. Thus the Civil War grieved him immensely and it has to be said to his credit that he made many efforts to bring the two sides together. He was notoriously reclusive and lived the last decades of his life in Gretta Garbo-like seclusion in a south Cork suburb. He drifted into the background after the Civil War but was held in the highest regard by Cork republicans until his death in 1963.[12]

Martial Law had been introduced into Munster on 5 January 1921 and was to run until the Truce of 11 July. While there were very few major operational successes on the part of the IRA in Cork city and the surrounding area during the first half of 1921, the period was marked by a descent into unprecedented savagery: the shooting of civilian 'spies and informers', the execution of military prisoners and the burning of loyalist houses in response to the 'official' reprisals by British forces, a euphemism for the destruction of property in the vicinity of IRA operations.

Most of the events described in this book took place in those final six months of the conflict and they prove that, when it comes to brutality, the

Irish can mete it out as well as anybody else. What youthful Volunteer after allowing a group of Cameron Highlanders disarmed in east Cork in the summer of 1920 to cycle back to their barracks could envisage that in under a year he might be asked to execute 15-year-old boys? What idealistic young patriot could imagine, while on a route march to Blarney on a Sunday morning in the autumn of 1919, that a year and a half later he would pick up four unarmed young soldiers who had gone out to buy sweets in view of the impending Truce, when all IRA units had been informed of the ceasefire, take them to a field in Togher, shoot them and leave their bodies, in the sad rigour of death, to be found the next morning? For once shooting begins, a conflict can only intensify, and both sides find themselves in ever-widening cycles of degradation until one side or the other calls a halt.

The Anglo-Irish conflict of 1919–1921 was a very minor war in relative terms, as the memoirs of serving British officers attest. A 'side-show in Southern Ireland' is a term often used—a small war, but utterly vicious. I was once told that the worst peace is better than the best war. Ireland could be described as one of the 'better wars' in that casualty numbers on all sides were comparatively low. But for all that it was a squalid little conflict and very few emerge from it with their reputations enhanced. But some did, Seán Moylan and Liam Lynch among them, as well as minor players like the unnamed RIC man, a noted high-jumper, who recognised Connie Neenan, a senior IRA activist in the city, at a roadblock in Cork but waved him through, or the Auxiliary who told an IRA prisoner in west Cork to feign illness to avoid being summarily executed in his cell.[13] In this story there are many tales of gallantry interspersed with the violence. But humanity is capable of great savagery as well as gallantry.

THE POLITICAL
LANDSCAPE

The political landscape of north-east Cork from the late 1920s to the 1970s was dominated by Martin J. Corry. Corry was a Fianna Fáil TD from 1927 to 1969 and usually topped the polls as well as being the longest-serving member of Cork County Council. In the late 1960s he was a small, benign-looking old man in a soft felt hat who knocked on doors surrounded by supporters canvassing for votes in the run-up to general elections.[1] He was a colourful character, popular even with his political opponents, and was seen as a 'great man to get things done'. It is said that when he emerged from the county council offices there would be queues around the corner of people waiting to ask political favours of him. If you wanted your road tarred or an outside toilet installed or a sewerage system put in place for a terrace of cottages then, as all my neighbours put it, 'Martin was your man.'

Corry was also an unreconstructed republican of the old school and was frequently in the wars with Fianna Fáil and with de Valera.[2] On several occasions he threatened to leave the party when he felt they were not 'Republican' enough on various issues. He was noted for his pronouncements in the Dáil and for his extreme anti-British views. In a debate on exporting food to Britain in 1942, Corry remarked on British food shortages that 'they have no more rabbits to get and now they are on the crows. I would not like to see too many crows going out to feed them. I think the crows are too good for them.' On Northern Ireland he suggested that 'I am personally in favour of storing up sufficient poison gas, so that when you get the wind in the right direction you can start at the border and let it travel.' This could all be dismissed as bombast were it not for the fact that, if Jim Fitzgerald was correct, when Corry got the opportunity, he killed as many 'Britishers' of various types as he could get his hands on. All the evidence suggested that his public utterances were backed up with private deeds.[3]

However, in our part of the country, Corry was never referred to as anything other than 'Martin' and was lionised by Fianna Fáil supporters in all the hill parishes of east Cork. Noted for his acerbic wit and his cutting remarks in the Dáil, he is one of the most frequently quoted public representatives in the history of the Dáil and Cork County Council.[4]

What I didn't know, when I first saw the apparently rather mild-mannered old Corry of the 1960s, was that he had been, at least in his own estimation, a major figure during the War of Independence. On the face of it, this did not appear to be a matter of any great significance. After all, half the old men I grew up among had been in the IRA in some capacity or other and had all kinds of hair-raising stories to go with it, usually involving attempted ambushes and narrow escapes from the Black and Tans, even though as I found out much later, most of the activity in my area, such as it was, involved the British Army and not the Black and Tans. But these old men had made history and this was part of the fascination they held for us children. When these men died, their stories died with them because, with the exception of people like Eugene Turpin, nobody of the later generation cared.

But the past does not go away: it is there under the stones and in the bogs; it is in the unspoken fear and suspicion that lurks in certain communities; it is in the silence of a family whose ancestor may have been on the wrong side; it is in the strange invisibilities of the historical narrative, the people who 'vanished' or the others who had to depart as a result of the revolution or who had to remain invisible because one of their members had once been branded a 'spy'. It is also in the well-preserved records of the RIC, as well as the recently available accounts of the IRA survivors of the conflict. For the Irish revolution is probably one of the best recorded of all revolutions. This is because the civil administration managed more or less to keep going during the conflict, as did the newspapers. The war was not total enough to stop normal everyday activities. The past is also to be found in stacks of mouldering documents held in archives all over Ireland and Britain.

Chapter 5 ~

| MARTIN CORRY'S IRELAND

British soldiers? I planted oats on British soldiers, and 'twas good oats!
MARTIN CORRY TD

Martin J. Corry was born in 1889, the son of an RIC head constable, and joined the Irish Volunteers in his twenties while the family still lived in Mourneabbey near Mallow in north Cork. This was the native parish of Tomás MacCurtain, the first republican Lord Mayor of Cork, and it was a hotbed of Volunteer activity. Corry joined the Volunteer movement in the years before World War I and was very active in the Mourneabbey company. In 1916 his father, who had by then retired from the RIC, moved from Mourneabbey to Glounthaune, about seven miles east of Cork city. It is said that the move was to take Martin away from the more radical element he was associating with in north Cork. In the event, it made little difference because in 1917 Corry, by that time nearly 30, was a founding member of the Knockraha Company of the Volunteers.

He was imprisoned several times before and during the War of Independence: in 1917 when he was arrested on suspicion of raiding for arms; in 1918 when he was sentenced to three months in Crumlin Road Jail in Belfast; and early in 1920 when he found himself in jail in Cork, Crumlin Road and Wormwood Scrubs where, along with 51 others, he underwent a 21-day hunger strike that ultimately led to a climbdown by the British government and the men's release. Thereafter he went 'on the run' from the latter half of 1920 to the Truce of July 1921, while managing somehow to get married in the meanwhile to a local girl, Margaret Fenton.

The Corry home, he always claimed, was raided no less than 70 times by British forces during the conflict and was to be raided again during the Civil War when Martin, who took an anti-Treaty stance along with most of the Cork IRA, was captured and interned in the Curragh from December 1922 to January 1924.[1]

On his death in 1979—in his 90th year—Corry was described as a 'tough, aggressive and uncompromising politician and a man of strong views, who spoke his mind in a forceful and often colourful fashion and cared little whether his viewpoint was a popular one or not'. A typical example was the comment at the top of the chapter which he made at a Fianna Fáil Cumann dinner in Fermoy in 1970 after British troops had been sent in to Northern Ireland. However, Corry was also known to make another, more interesting, variation on that statement: 'I planted oats [or barley, depending on who you speak to] on members of the Anti-Sinn Féin League.'

If you were sceptical, like I was, this was the kind of oats (or barley) you were inclined, like good porridge, to take with a grain of salt. Another comment I heard from a man in Glounthaune, where Corry lived, served only to heighten my incredulity. 'Sure, if Corry was to be believed, he had his own private graveyard up around the yard.' Was the private graveyard full of Anti-Sinn Féin Leaguers? It seemed to me at the time to be highly improbable. For what manner of man could live among the graves of his enemies and raise a family surrounded by their ghosts?

My doubts only increased when I looked up the command structure of the 4th Battalion of the Cork No. 1 Brigade.[2] This was the east Cork section of the IRA. There was no mention of Corry anywhere in the command structure. Even the Knockraha company is described as having been commanded by one Tommy Sullivan, who is not even mentioned in Jim Fitzgerald's book. Yet on the flyleaf of that book, there Corry stands, proud as a peacock, his face in Pearse-like profile, with his IRA captain's uniform and cocked hat. In the battalion lists, however, it was as if he had been completely removed from its official history. Through all the changes in personnel brought about by capture, death and changing political allegiances from 1918 to the spring of 1923, there is no mention of Martin Corry. The only specific reference to Knockraha is a comment that 'the bomb factory in E Company area [was designated] as a Special Brigade Unit under arms continuously from Jan 1920 to the Truce'.[3]

As far as I was concerned, the last nail in the coffin of the authenticity of Corry's war was driven home when I contacted the regiment of some of the missing soldiers he claimed to have killed. According to Corry, 17 of his victims were members of the Cameron Highlanders and Manchester regiments who were stationed at Cobh and Ballincollig respectively. Seven were Black and Tans and the 11 others were loosely defined as spies and informers. There is no mention, however, of any Cameron Highlanders or Manchesters disappearing off the face of the earth in published accounts of the casualty lists of the conflict or in regimental histories.[4] Nor is there anything in the published histories of the war in Cork to suggest that this might have been the case. There is, however, one hint of what Corry may have been up to in Ernie O'Malley's classic account of the War of Independence,

On Another Man's Wound, which is set largely in Cork: 'East Cork had shot many spies. Hegarty had the name of not being very particular about evidence, but that might be talk.'[5]

This was the only hint I found in any published work or history of the War of Independence that suggested there might have been a significant amount of killing, at least of 'spies' in east Cork. It was only a hint and it might well have referred to the revenge killings of civilians that came about as a result of the Clonmult encirclement where, in February 1921, 12 IRA men, members of the east Cork column, were wiped out by a combination of British Army and police forces. What is interesting though is that the connection is with Seán O'Hegarty, the brigade commander, not with the east Cork leadership. This suggests that the executions mentioned by O'Malley were not just an east Cork phenomenon but were carried out by the brigade itself. It is also worth noting that O'Malley wrote this in the early 1930s while the stories of the war in Cork were still fresh in his mind. Other than that one comment, there is silence. But in 1998 at least some of this historical silence was about to change.

Chapter 6 ∾

HELP COMES FROM AN UNEXPECTED SOURCE

In 1998 Peter Hart, a young Canadian historian, published his seminal work on the revolution in Cork, *The IRA and its Enemies*.[1] This was at the time the most detailed and exhaustively researched book on the war in Cork, and because it is confined to Cork, it did not suffer from the need to generalise which limits the value of many histories of the period. In Cork, Hart had an almost open field of inquiry, as most previous academic histories confined themselves to what records could be found in London and in the Dublin newspapers. *The IRA and its Enemies* is not mainly concerned with the political issues between Dublin and London, nor does it suffer from being overly concerned with the events surrounding Dublin Castle and Bloody Sunday, and Michael Collins is not, for once, the dominant personality in it.

Hart's work was also a first in that it looked at the conflict from the victims' point of view, though it made no effort to distinguish between genuine 'spies and informers' and innocent victims. The book's huge advantage, however, was its mastery of sources. The book is worth the cover price for the sources alone.[2] With Hart's sources as a starting point I gradually built up a picture of what had gone on in Cork city in the grim months of 1920 and 1921. It also allowed me to establish the essential veracity of the story of Sing Sing.

So what independent verification is there that Knockraha might have been used as an execution area for those captured in Cork city? As we have seen, Corry himself claimed that the British Army raided his home more than 70 times during the conflict.[3] While this may have been exaggerated, Corry was a well-known IRA activist, so the military would be expected to have devoted considerable resources in trying to capture him. Indeed, there is some evidence that by the end of 1920 the British knew there was something odd going on in the area. On 8 December, a Church holiday, a search cordon was thrown around the Catholic church in Glanmire during Mass; the men were segregated, searched and questioned.[4] The military then proceeded from Riverstown to Knockraha where they continued their searches. This may account for one of the rare incursions by the British mentioned by Jim Fitzgerald, when they got near enough to Sing Sing but did not find it.[5]

Then on 6 January 1921, the feast of the Epiphany, a similar series of searches took place, this time on a larger scale, when the churches at Glanmire, Watergrasshill, Carrignavar and Knockraha were all surrounded at the same time during Mass and the men were again searched and questioned.[6] While there is no evidence of what was being searched for, bearing in mind that the parish was deliberately kept 'quiet' and no overt activities were to take place there (nor did they), the operations suggest that the military may have had some inkling of what was going on, particularly since the first search followed quickly on the heels of a series of kidnappings by the IRA of civilians in the city.[7] While the searches caused little more than annoyance on the part of the parishioners, the military may have had some information that there was more than meets the eye in this, 'the quietest area in Cork'.

But the biggest piece of circumstantial evidence comes from the ranks of the IRA itself. In the Knockraha area, 'a Leahy fellow from Cobh' is often cited as the most ruthless of all the IRA men who carried out executions in the area. This was Mick Leahy, the commander of the 4th Battalion, who would be expected to have a major role in anything that went on there. But Leahy was more than just the commander of the east Cork IRA. He was also deputy commander of the entire No. 1 Brigade after the capture of Terence MacSwiney in August 1920. This makes him, along with O'Hegarty and Florence O'Donoghue, one of the three most important men in the brigade from the summer of 1920 right up to the Truce. And while he was abroad for several months at the start of 1921, because he was the only one of the leadership with roots outside the city, it would make sense that secret functions such as the manufacture of grenade casings and the execution of prisoners might take place in his area.

There are also several mentions of Seán O'Hegarty[8] spending significant lengths of time in the Knockraha area, particularly in May 1921. In one account he even found himself imprisoned in Sing Sing when the overzealous guards, literally 'guarding the tomb', captured him and locked him up, suspecting he was a spy.[9] In Corry's words: 'Seán Hegarty was a gentleman. He never asked awkward questions. He sent us on [prisoners] to be shot . . .'[10] Clearly Knockraha was an important part of O'Hegarty's fiefdom, and not just for the making of bombs. It is equally clear that Corry, though not highly regarded by some of his former comrades on account of his subsequent political career, was O'Hegarty's chief executioner.

But the most important details can be found in the Ernie O'Malley notebooks in the Archives Department of UCD. O'Malley spent several years in the late 1940s travelling from place to place, sometimes sleeping in his car, interviewing survivors of the revolutionary period for a book he never got around to writing.[11] The text of these interviews lies in a series of hardback notebooks now housed in UCD. (It is important to note that these interviews had no bearing on the writing of *On Another Man's Wound*, which was written 20 years earlier, so O'Malley's comment on the killing of innocent 'spies' in east Cork was not derived from these interviews but was a view he had picked up from his time in Cork during the actual War of Independence itself.)

Several of O'Malley's interviewees remember Sing Sing being used as a prison for holding prisoners prior to execution. Based on the evidence of the survivors of Cork One, there was a significant number of individuals executed and buried in the Rea. But who were they? To find out, I had to virtually turn over the entire rotten corpse of the revolutionary period in Cork. Very few on either side come out of it smelling of roses. But that is the nature of war.

Chapter 7

KNOCKRAHA WAS THE PLACE FOR SPIES

Mick Leahy's papers held in Cork City Museum contain no reference to Sing Sing or to executions in the Rea. However, he was not quite so reticent when he spoke to Ernie O'Malley: 'Knockraha was an excellent spot . . . [There were] no Protestants in the village . . . [There] were a bloody pile of spies . . . The spies came from Cork city and Martin Corry was Chief Executioner . . . There was a graveyard in Knockraha and a vault there called Sing Sing. The vault had been used in the time of the body snatchers . . .'[1]—exactly the same story as I had heard locally.

Other east Cork IRA men also referred to it: 'Knockraha, some five miles from Glanmire, was the place for the spies. They were kept in a vault in the old graveyard at Kilquane.'[2] The British also noticed how quiet the area was. 'The area for which the Battalion is responsible has been one of the quietest in Ireland', the Cameron Highlanders, who were based in Cobh, reported around the time of the Truce.[3] It was quiet for good reason.

So there had been a lot of executions in the area, and no shortage of evidence for it; the prisoners were kept in a vault in the graveyard before their execution and Corry was the principal executioner, despite the more bland assertions by Corry himself that prisoners were killed by 'firing parties'. Mick Leahy describes one execution: 'The first I personally executed was an RIC man named Dinny Lehane.' What follows is a long, almost indecipherable account of what this Dinny Lehane did to justify his execution, then the line, 'I'll put you where no one will ever find you again. . . . We knelt down and said the Rosary before we shot him.'[4] This account, while it sounds authentic, also illustrates one of the biggest problems facing someone writing a story where motivations are complex and human memory is fallible. For there was nobody called Dinny Lehane in the RIC at that time. So either Dinny Lehane, whoever he was, was a civilian or he did not exist or the name was used for somebody else by Leahy years after the event.

However, there are many connections with the city battalions. One of these is the account of Seán Culhane, a young intelligence officer in the city: 'It was a tomb he was in, a mausoleum, Sing Sing. Corry had several prisoners in it and they used to shoot them at night.'[5] But perhaps the most chilling statement of all is that of Mick Murphy, commander of the Cork No. 2 Battalion that operated on the south side of the city. 'We buried the bodies in Carroll's Bogs. Every spy who was shot in Cork was buried so that nothing was known about them. They just disappeared.'[6] The eastern end of the Rea is sometimes referred to as Carroll's Bogs, where some executions took place.

There could now be little doubt that the Rea was an area where a large number of killings were carried out during the War of Independence. The area was chosen because of its proximity to Cork city, because there were no loyalists in the area who might betray it to the authorities and because the wretched vault in the graveyard was a secure prison. Clearly the 'Special Brigade Unit under arms continuously from Jan 1920 to the Truce' was doing more than just operating bomb factories.

But is it possible that up to 35 people could disappear off the face of the earth in a 12-month period and that no history book mentions this? That is three times more than disappeared in the entire 30 years of the Northern Ireland conflict. Only for Jim Fitzgerald, it would never have been recorded. But who were the victims? Where were their families? What had happened to them? It was as if a mist of silence had moved up from Cork Harbour and enshrouded the place for ever in a fog of damp quiet. The people who were buried in the Rea, whoever they were, were 'the enemy', whether they took the form of British soldiers, RIC men, Black and Tans or 'spies and informers'. The community silence made it clear that these people were outside the Pale of the 'national right to self-determination'. Another local told me he had been told that these were 'bad people'. They were the enemy, so nothing could be said or known about them. 'Spies and informers', of course, were particularly loathed. As one IRA man who operated both in the city and in east Cork put it: 'Spies and informers are about the most loathsome persons that ever existed and deserve to be exterminated in the same manner as rats or snakes.'[7] So it should come as no surprise that anyone suspected of belonging to such a category could be shot and disposed of with impunity. They were on the 'other side' so they had to be dumped and forgotten about. It is clear that the men running Sing Sing knew little or nothing about their victims. They were simply doing a job; the orders were coming from higher up.

Yet some locals were prepared to talk about Sing Sing, even if they did not know the names of its victims. In fact the vault is now open to the public and is commemorated by a plaque unveiled in July 2001 where the souls of all those buried in the bogs were remembered and prayed for. It was a sad and moving spectacle; perhaps it was closure of a kind.

The general view was that the individuals killed and buried in the Rea were guilty of spying for the British authorities, if they were not actually army and police personnel themselves. But one man I met at the commemoration that evening muttered darkly: 'They put a lot of innocent fellas into the Rea there too.' Another man told me a story of a German who was found guilty by a Sinn Féin court of having stolen a watch from Fr Shinquin, the parish priest of Glanmire. This German—what he was doing in Cork nobody can remember—was sentenced to be deported from Ireland. The local IRA men detailed to escort him to Cobh for that purpose simply took him up to the bogs and instead shot him and buried his body. These accounts suggest that, in local eyes at least, not all that went on in the Rea could be justified by the exigencies of war.[8]

With one notable exception, the interrogation of prisoners appears to have gone on elsewhere, prior to their arrival at Sing Sing. The dungeon was the end of the line. To judge from internal inquiries carried out during the Truce into the killing of civilians, abducted 'spies and informers' could expect to live from two days to a week between their abduction and execution.[9] What their experience was during that week doesn't bear thinking about. In some cases they may have been interrogated and possibly tortured, depending on which group got their hands on them.[10] They would then be removed to Sing Sing for execution. If they talked, they would have been executed; if they didn't talk, they probably would have been executed anyway. The only people, to my knowledge, who lived to tell the tale of having been incarcerated in Sing Sing were three RIC men who promised to act as double agents, and one or two women spies who were immediately deported.[11]

One of the main reasons for the lack of any reference to Sing Sing in the history books has got to be the longevity and political clout of Martin J. Corry. Corry, on his IRA pension application form, said he had executed 27 individuals in Knockraha. While he had no trouble boasting about his executing exploits himself when the mood took him, he didn't want anyone else writing about it or making unwanted enquiries, though he was able to make the following statement in the Dáil in the 1930s:[12]

Corry to James Dillon: 'Come down and I will show you. I will show you a lot of things you never saw before. I would nearly show you Sing Sing if you came down.'
Mr Dillon: 'What a fascinating creature!'
Mr Corry: 'I am sure the Deputy would have to be very fascinating before he would get out of it . . .'

Yet surely if this level of killings had gone on, some physical evidence of it would have turned up in the intervening years between 1921 and the early 1960s when the entire area was planted with forest. In other words, where are the bodies? Well, some of that evidence did appear from time to time.

In 1963 a local farmer purchased part of the Rea and was reclaiming it when he came across several skeletons. These were removed to Watergrasshill garda station for reburial. This created quite a stir and was covered in the newspapers of the time. In the late 1970s when Fitzgerald's book appeared, a lady from east Cork tried to authenticate his claims. Enquiries at Watergrasshill garda station about the skeletons of a dozen years earlier found that there was no record of them. This looks suspiciously like what would now be called 'political interference'. Corry would certainly have had enough influence to make such a record 'disappear' in the heart of his own constituency. Another family found two skeletons on their land. When they reported it, the gardaí simply took the bones and buried them elsewhere.

Then there was the story of how ESB workers laying an electricity line across the Rea in the 1950s came across another pair of bodies when they were digging for the positioning of poles. The bodies were in uniform—the ESB men found buttons first—and had been thrown head first into a narrow hole. The chances of electrical erectors finding bodies in the occasional hole dug for poles in such a large area would appear to be slim. Yet they found them.

Then there is the even grimmer story, authenticated by people who worked there, of the exhumation of a body by Free State forces from under the floorboards of Corry's house in Sunville, Glounthaune, sometime during or after the Civil War, a house that is now deserted with ash trees as big as your thigh growing out through the walls (see photo). Eugene Turpin remembers seeing one of the buttons belonging to the uniform of that officer or soldier. Indeed there is a confidential dossier on Corry in the Department of Defence files[13] which is not open to the public. This is likely to be in connection with this exhumation since it is the only reference I have been able to find that links Corry's address and the forces of the National Army during the post-Civil War period.

Which finally brings us to the biggest question: if all these people were killed and buried there, what are their names and when did they disappear? We know it must have happened between 1919 and 1923. We know the historical record of the war is, as wars go, pretty complete. Thirty-five people could not have simply vanished off the face of the earth. So who were they? Many appear to have been either soldiers, RIC men or Black and Tans. These were, presumably, simply casualties of war. This still leaves over a dozen civilians inevitably described as 'spies and informers'.

And then there is the question of culpability. What had these people done to deserve such a fate? Were they all spies? These are questions we need to make some attempt, however inadequate, to answer, if indeed they can be answered. So the next thing we must do is try to establish, if that is possible at this remove, exactly who is buried in the Rea and elsewhere in the area. This is not an easy task and will, by definition, be incomplete. It will also mean establishing best-fit theories to suit individual cases, depending on the evidence. We will also look, in so far as that is possible, at the reasons why some of these people were killed, and try and understand the events that led to their deaths. The balance of evidence in some cases suggests culpability for passing on information to the British authorities on IRA activities; in other cases the evidence suggests otherwise. The theories forwarded as to the guilt or otherwise of various individuals are the best I can do with the information I have been able to uncover. Further evidence may ultimately suggest that even my most closely argued theories are wrong. But if there is better evidence out there, someone else can find it.

PART II

Chapter 8

THE DEAD OF THE REA— TRUTH OR EXAGGERATION?

Given that the Civil War was not fought in the area, those who were allegedly shot and buried in the Rea must have been killed during the War of Independence or in the 13 months from the Truce to the Civil War. Is it possible that up to 35 persons,[1] subdivided into British Army personnel, RIC men/Black and Tans and what might loosely be called civilian 'spies and informers' could have been shot and buried there during this time?

According to Corry, two undercover British Army agents dressed in mufti were apparently apprehended by Corry himself, disarmed and immediately executed. This account is authenticated by Mick Murphy of the city IRA who said two intelligence officers were picked up while nosing around Corry's area.[2] Another undercover agent appears to have met the same fate. There is also a mention of two 'deserters' from the British Army base in Cobh. It was common for army intelligence to send false 'deserters' into the field in the hope that they would join the IRA and pass on information on its operations. There are several accounts of this kind of intelligence-gathering from different parts of Cork.[3] A number of successful British Army operations against IRA units were due to this kind of intelligence-gathering.

Two other British soldiers, this time in uniform, are mentioned as having been picked up and shot, and another, a Sergeant Major Mackintosh of the Cameron Highlanders, was, it is claimed, shot after the Truce. How much of this can be authenticated? Did Corry exaggerate the number of Crown forces he claimed to have killed? The British government published a missing persons list on 22 August 1921.[4] This contained the names of eight military personnel, six of whom had gone missing in County Cork. These were all relatively well-known cases. I have tracked down the fate of all of them. Not a single one ended up in east Cork.

In the case of RIC men and Black and Tans, a similar disparity exists between what Corry claimed and what can be verified from historical sources.

However, a few can be authenticated. One of the better-known abductions carried out by the city IRA was the kidnapping of two Black and Tans from Johnson and Perrott's garage in Ely Place where they had brought a Crossley tender for repair. This was done by Jim Gray, one of the city's most notorious gunmen, with the help of (accounts vary) either his brother Miah or Jack Cody of the 2nd Battalion. In any event, they forced the two Tans to drive to Knockraha, where they were disarmed and executed the same day and buried in the Rea. This well-known incident occurred in mid-November 1920 and can be authenticated from a number of sources.[5] Two Auxiliaries, Cadets Mitchell and Agnew, also disappeared in November 1920. They had been staying overnight in the Imperial Hotel in Cork. They left the following morning and went up the South Mall. They were never seen again.[6] It is difficult to authenticate the disappearance of RIC men and Black and Tans for some who were abducted were subsequently described as having been dismissed from the force, presumably because they were believed to have deserted. There are several other accounts by Cork city IRA men of the abduction and killing of Tans but none of these can be authenticated either, though two, perhaps Mitchell and Agnew, are said to have been killed in the Whites Cross area just north of the city. Corry reports the killing of two others captured by Cobh IRA man Daithi O'Brien at Carew outside Carrigtwohill. These deaths cannot be authenticated either.

One that has been recently authenticated was the trial and execution of an RIC man called Williams for his part in the assassination of Tomás MacCurtain. Williams was court-martialled by the top brass of the city brigade in Corry's own living room. He allegedly admitted to being the third officer up the stairs on the night of MacCurtain's killing.[7] He was sentenced to death and executed. His confession was kept in the Corry family for many years afterwards.[8]

Richard Abbott in his book *Police Casualties in Ireland 1919–1922* lists 18 missing RIC men for the entire island for the period, while the 1921 British list names 19. These include Mitchell, Agnew and T. J. Walsh, who was captured and executed near Blarney.[9] There are no other missing RIC personnel listed for the Cork city or east Cork areas in these published lists.

In all, five RIC men/Tans are mentioned in *Foras Feasa na Paróiste* as having been killed in the area. Add to this the eight soldiers supposedly killed (for which there appeared to be no independent evidence) and you still only come up with 13 possible killings. This is a long way short of the 23 or 24 military personnel claimed by Corry. Either his numbers are grossly exaggerated or else the number of civilian casualties in the Rea is much higher.[10]

Corry also listed some 11 'spies' as having been killed in the Knockraha area. These include a man referred to only as 'Paddy the Painter', who appears to have been a tramp. His death cannot be authenticated anywhere, though it is likely to have taken place. Peter Hart has found at least ten cases of tramps and tinkers who were killed by the IRA in County Cork. The Midleton IRA boasted that the entire tramp and tinker class had been driven out of the town, so this at least fits into the general picture of the targeting of tramps and tinkers.[11]

The first genuine spy killed out of Sing Sing appears to have been an agent sent from Dublin to infiltrate the Cork IRA. He was caught and held in Sing Sing for several weeks while his fate was being decided by HQ in Dublin.[12] This took place in the autumn of 1920 just as the vault was being made ready as a prison. This man appears to have been one James Gordon, an RIC undercover agent who arrived in Cork from Thurles and who was picked up while drunk in a pub in the city centre. Gordon was moved north of the city and held for interrogation before being moved to Sing Sing.[13]

There is also a suggestion that at least one woman was among those killed out of Sing Sing.[14] This may have been the middle-aged woman abducted on Cork's north side during the first week of June 1921 and taken 'to a destination unknown'.[15] As we shall see, there were at least two girls who may have been held in Sing Sing, one of whom, a Miss McGrath, who was taken off the Cork to Cobh train late in 1920, was released, while another girl was deported for spying.[16]

How does all this compare with the actual list of missing persons published in August 1921? The list contains the names of ten missing civilians for the Cork East Riding area (the missing military personnel will be dealt with later in the book):

Table 1. List of missing civilians, Cork city and East Riding[17]

John Coughlan	14/8/20
James Blemens	29/11/20
Fred Blemens	29/11/20
George Horgan	11/12/20
Patrick Ray	22/1/21
Thomas Downing	24/4/21
Francis McMahon	19/5/21
Eugene Swanton	5/6/21
W. J. Nolan	11/6/21
James Begley	11/7/21

This is from the civilian portion of the list published on 22 August 1921. It is noteworthy that there are a number of errors in it: Downing disappeared on 28 November 1920, not in April 1921; Begley's name was John, not James; and the date of Nolan's disappearance is also incorrect.

Did some or any of these individuals end up in Knockraha? We can exclude at least three: John Coughlan died while in IRA custody and was buried in a pauper's grave in Knockgriffin outside Midleton. George Horgan was executed and buried in Lakelands near Blackrock—it appears that his family got his remains back after the Civil War. This is the only one of these cases where, to my knowledge, the family of the missing person retrieved the remains. Patrick Ray, an ex-soldier suffering from shell-shock and apparently 'not right in the head', was abducted in Passage West and shot dead and buried near by. He received the last rites before being killed.[18]

On the other hand, there is a very high possibility that Eugene Swanton ended up in the Rea. Swanton, a Catholic from Ballinhassig and an ex-soldier from the Canadian Army who had fought in World War I, was working for a farmer in Ballinacurra near Midleton when he was abducted by masked men on 5 June 1921 and never seen again.[19]

We know a few more things about people on the list. Downing was head of the ex-servicemen's association in Cork, Francis McMahon worked in the War Pensions office and Nolan was killed allegedly because he applied to join the RIC.[20] However, this list represents only half of the total number of disappearances that can be put together from other sources.[21] And it is almost certain that there were still other abductions that went unreported.

Table 2. Missing persons not on the August 1921 list

James Herlihy	20/8/20
James Gordon	August 1920
John O'Callaghan	15/9/20
Din Din Riordan	December 1920?
Michael O'Brien	11/4/21
'Saunders'	31/5/1921
John Lynch	25/6/21
Duggan?	July 1921

Herlihy and Riordan were Volunteers. All but Riordan were ex-soldiers and he may have been one also. Little or nothing is known about Duggan. At least two others are believed to have been shot and buried as fallout from the Broad Lane killings of November 1920 (see Hart, *The IRA and its Enemies*).

Again, we can exclude some of these: Herlihy was executed and buried in the bogs at Farmer's Cross, where Cork Airport now stands. O'Callaghan was killed in Pouladuff. Lynch, a railway clerk in the parcel office at Carrigrohane, was killed to the west of the city and Riordan was executed at the viaduct on the Bandon road. 'Saunders' was shot and buried in the 6th Battalion area north of Carrignavar.[22]

How many ended up in the Rea? Downing and Gordon certainly did. It is probable that some of the others also ended up there.[23] However, it also has to be said that there are reports of bodies being buried in other bogs in the general area north of Cork city. Bogs north of Carrignavar and west of Glenville contain at least four bodies, while farther west at Rylane lies the IRA's other major burial ground where a dozen more executions took place. There are also several reports of bodies being buried in the vicinity of what is now Cork Airport to the south of the city and also at Killumney to the west.

However, there is one other group of 'spies' mentioned in *Foras Feasa na Paróiste* who do not appear on either of the above lists; nor indeed do they get a mention in any British source or anywhere else in the published historical record. This, if Corry is to be believed, was the apparent killing of teenagers, members of the Cork YMCA. When I first read it, I was inclined to dismiss it as yet another of Corry's exaggerations. However, if it were true, it would be a catalogue of killings far worse than any of the above, if only because the victims appear in some cases to have been 15- and 16-year-olds. Some of them also appear to have been Evangelical Christians. Yet there was no mention of the disappearance of YMCA members anywhere in the newspapers or in any history book, not even in Peter Hart's *The IRA and its Enemies*, which details the killing of Protestants by the IRA. It seems inconceivable that well-connected, middle-class Protestant boys could simply vanish and that there would be no record of it. It appeared so much at odds with the standard histories of the time that it is worth quoting in full.[24]

THE EXECUTION OF MEMBERS OF THE YOUNG MEN'S CHRISTIAN ASSOCIATION

During the latter part of 1920 the Intelligence Section of the First Cork Brigade of the IRA came to know that there existed an organization which called itself the Junior Section of the Young Men's Christian Association. It came to the IRA's attention that members of this Organization were engaged in spying on the activities of the IRA, and that, as a result of that work that [sic] many of the organization's personnel had been arrested and some had been executed and more had been jailed. It further came to their notice that a Mr. Parsons was actively engaged in the work of this movement.

At that period none of the names of the other members of this Organization were available so Peter Donovan who was the OC of the Cork Number One Brigade Column did mount a trap in the city and succeeded in arresting this man Parsons. After his arrest he immediately brought him out to Corry's in Glounthaune and handed him over to Martin Corry for questioning. They were particularly interested at this stage in getting the names of other members of his organization who were also engaged in spying work.

The first efforts to cross-examine him proved fruitless and no information was extracted from him. This eventually irritated the people who were conducting the questioning so Martin Corry said 'Look, you're not going to get out of this place alive, but there are a number of ways an execution can be performed.' At this stage he took Parsons up into a loft in the yard and asked one of his men to get a rope and bring it up. When this rope was procured, Martin told the man to put one end of it over the rafter in the roof of the loft. When this was done, a noose was then placed at the end of the rope. Martin then addressed Parsons and he said that 'if you're not going to give us the information then we are going to execute you by hanging. But if you will give us the information we desire, you will be executed by a firing party.' Then he said to Parsons 'When we will pull the rope around your neck and when the man will be pulling it up, if you want to give information, put your hand up and we will let you down.' With that Parsons' head was put into the noose and Martin Corry instructed the man at the other end to pull the rope to raise him from the ground. However, he had not raised the rope very far and it had hardly come tight on Parsons' neck when he [Parsons] put up his hand indicating that he wished to give information. The rope was then slackened. Parsons then explained the workings of this 'Young Men's Christian Association'. Basically the information he gave them was that the members of this organization were being paid a basic rate of £10 per week while they were being engaged in spy work. As well as this there was a reward of £40 for information leading to the capture of prominent IRA personnel. However, over all this was a reward of £50 for information leading to the capture of Seán O'Hegarty who was commanding officer of the Cork Number One brigade. As well as this information Parsons also gave the names of six other members of the YMCA which was the important information that the IRA wished to extract. Following on his word that on giving this information he would be executed not by hanging, Martin Corry had Parsons taken outside and executed by a firing party [after] which he was buried in Corry's farm.

After this the column of the Cork Number One Brigade did seek to capture the other names that had been given by Parsons and eventually they succeeded in doing this and all other individuals on being captured in Cork [were] also brought down to Martin Corry's and executed in Corry's and buried in the farmyard. As a result of the work of members of the flying column this spying section of the British Establishment was completely eliminated.[25]

Apart from its casual brutality, this incident is interesting from a number of points of view. For a start the execution took place at Corry's farm. The level of detail suggests that it is true. Even Corry's imagination could not have made up such a story. Corry repeated the essential details of the story to Ernie O'Malley, though in this instance he claimed it happened after the Truce rather than during the War of Independence.[26] A neighbour who worked at Corry's and who was present when the 'hanging' and execution took place told a similar story to Eugene Turpin. His description of what happened on the day of Parsons' execution was more or less the same as what is in the book. If Parsons was indeed a member of the junior section of the YMCA, he could not have been more than 15 or 16 years old. And what of the other half-dozen or so members of the YMCA who were supposedly rounded up on the basis of evidence extracted from Parsons? Who were they? Were they adults or teenagers? Could these be the members of the mythical Anti-Sinn Féin League over which Corry boasted he had planted oats (or barley)? Could half a dozen such people simply disappear? Were their families still in Cork? Why was there no record of their disappearance? Why were British sources completely silent on the matter? Why were there not half a dozen families writing to the British and Free State governments in the post-conflict period trying to find out what had happened to their children? Was there anything in the broader historical record to authenticate any of this? Indeed, did it happen at all?

This turned out to be one of the more intractable puzzles of the entire period. It meant I had to go through virtually the entire day-to-day history of the conflict in Cork city and the year-long subsequent 'peace', uncovering in the process dozens of unknown and forgotten tales that had never been written about.

As we'll see in the next section, the disappeared—and these were the truly disappeared, since with one exception no body was ever found and none of the families was ever to receive any information as to what had happened to their dead—were only a fraction of the total number of civilians killed in Cork city during the conflict. But before we look at the reasons why some of those in Tables 1 and 2 disappeared, we will first have to look at the broader picture of the killing of alleged spies and informers in the city. And we will have to look in depth at the intelligence war between the IRA and British forces before we can even hope to deal with the more mysterious issue of disappeared teenagers.

Chapter 9 ～

A CITY OF SPIES

Cork is, or rather was until recently, a city of spies.[1]

Accoring to the Hague Convention, a spy may be defined as a person who, 'acting clandestinely or on false pretence, obtains or endeavours to obtain information in the zone of operation of a belligerent, with the intention of communicating it to the hostile enemy.'[2] At the outbreak of World War I the number of German spies caught in Britain was 21 of the 22 known agents. During the war itself the total number of spies arrested and convicted in Britain was 12 executed and 13 sentenced to various terms of penal servitude.[3]

This statistic is worth bearing in mind when analysing the number of civilians shot as spies by the IRA during the War of Independence. In his recent history of the conflict, Michael Hopkinson estimated that around 200 civilians were killed in the conflict on all sides and contrasted this with the more recent Troubles in Northern Ireland where, relatively speaking, civilian casualties were much higher.[4] Peter Hart, on the other hand, has estimated that the Cork IRA alone shot 204 civilians over the period from 1918 to the end of the Civil War.[5] These figures are not mutually exclusive: the War of Independence is only part of the story. As Hart pointed out, a lot of the civilian casualties and much of the intimidation suffered, in particular by Protestants, occurred after the Truce and during the Civil War.

From the public record and the (less reliable) accounts of Old IRA men, around 40 civilians were shot dead as alleged spies by the IRA in Cork city and the immediate area during the War of Independence, and at least as many more were shot and maimed. While the period covered was from the first shooting in February 1920 to the Truce of July 1921, the vast majority of the killings occurred in the spring and early summer of 1921.

In fact, many of the civilian casualties of the war occurred in Cork city in the first half of 1921. While for the country as a whole the chief casualties on the British side were soldiers and RIC men, in Cork city it was the other way round. This means that the war in Cork city was exceptional. This was not the history we had learned in school, though it did correlate with what I had learned from neighbours as a child when I'd be told: 'Well, there was a fella buried in this bog, and there was a fella buried in that bog, and there was another fella tied to a gate and shot in Glashaboy.'

The 40-odd civilians shot as 'spies' by the Cork IRA during the War of Independence is likely to be an underestimation, because tramps and those in the margins of society disappeared leaving no record.[6] Spies from within the IRA's own ranks also tended to disappear without trace. I was able to find reliable information on only a few of these. Anecdotal evidence suggests there were others. All in all, whatever the total numbers, the evidence suggested that the executions out of Sing Sing are just part of an overall picture. This suggests that up to a quarter of all civilian casualties for the entire War of Independence were in Cork city during this period. A closer examination of the individual cases throws up another striking statistic: over three-quarters of these killings occurred on the south side of Cork.[7] What this implies is that the majority of these killings were carried out in the 2nd Battalion area which operated south of the River Lee.[8] It is no wonder that IRA men from other Cork brigades regarded the city men as 'a tough crowd'.[9] When viewed in the context of the overall number of activities carried out by the two Cork city battalions, the killing of 'spies' and attempts to kill others constituted a significant deployment of resources by the city IRA, far in excess of all attempted ambushes of military and police put together. In terms of the number killed and the number of 'successful' operations, the killing of civilians outstripped all other operations in the city.

But who were these people? From the lists in the previous chapter and in Table 3 we have many of the names. Were they all spies? If so, the city battalions shot over three times more spies in 12 months than did the entire British military in the four years of World War I. Or were they, as has recently been suggested, merely soft targets, those perceived to be pro-British, such as ex-soldiers, various forms of 'low life' and Protestants?[10] Was this counter-espionage or merely the need to hit back for British successes, particularly in 1921? Was it espionage or was the IRA merely retaliating by targeting any available individuals who could be regarded as enemies? In order to come to some conclusion about this complex issue, we need to look at who was killed, where, and if possible why they were killed.

Table 3. List of civilians killed in the environs of Cork city during the War of Independence

Name	Profession	Place of death	Date
Harry T. Quinlisk	RIC agent	Tory Top Rd	20/2/20
James Gordon •	RIC agent	Knockraha	–/8/20
Brady •	Printer	Tory Top Lane	Unknown

John Coughlan•*	ND	ND	14/8/20
James Herlihy •	Ex-soldier	Pouladuff	20/8/20
John O'Callaghan •	Ex-soldier	Farmer's Cross	15/9/20
Thomas Downing •	Ex-soldier	Knockraha	28/11/20
James Blemens •	Horticulture instructor	Carroll's Bogs	2/12/20
Fred Blemens •	Grocer's assistant	Carroll's Bogs	2/12/20
Din Din Riordan •	IRA Volunteer	Viaduct	Dec 1920?
George Horgan •	Ex-soldier	Blackrock	12/12/20
Patrick Ray • *	Ex-soldier	Passage West	22/1/21
Alfred C. Reilly	Company director	Douglas	9/2/21
John O'Leary	Ex-soldier	Peacock Lane	12/2/21
William Sullivan	Ex-soldier	Tory Top Rd	14/2/21
James C. Beal	Accountant	Wilton	15/2/21
Michael Walsh	Ex-soldier	Cork Workhouse	18/2/21
William Mohally	Ex-soldier	South Infirmary Hospital	20/2/21
Finbarr O'Sullivan	Ex-soldier	Found in Douglas river	20/2/20
David Nagle *	Ex-RIC	Waterfall	12/3/21
Cornelius Sheehan	Hospital attendant	Blarney St	19/3/21
John Good	Ex-soldier	Tower St	10/3/21
Michael O'Brien •	Ex-soldier	ND	11/4/21
Denis Donovan	Ex-soldier	Found at Ballygarvan	12/4/21
Stephen Callaghan	Quay labourer	Anderson's Quay	29/4/21
James Purcell	Cattle dealer	Tory Top Rd	7/5/21
Patrick Sheehan	Cattle dealer	Lankford Row	15/5/21
Edward Hawkins	Ex-soldier	Mountdesert quarry	20/5/21
Francis McMahon	Ex-soldier	ND	20/5/21
Christy Sullivan	Ex-soldier	Wilton	26/5/21
'Saunders' •	Army agent	Carrignavar	31/5/21
'Another' •	ND	Turner's Cross	May 1921
John Lucey §	ND	Farrell's Square	11/6/21
Daniel O'Callaghan*	Ex-sailor	——	23/6/21
John Lynch •	Ex-soldier	Ballincollig	25/6/21
George O'Connor	Retired major	Rochestown Rd	10/7/21
William Nolan •	ND	ND	11/7/21
John Begley •	ND	ND	11/7/21
Duggan • *	ND	ND	July 1921?

Names with a bullet (•) denote individuals who were abducted and secretly executed.

* denotes those for whom there is either nothing in the public record or who may have been abducted or killed outside the city limits but in the Cork East Riding area.

§ denotes those who may have been killed by either side.

ND denotes not determined.

List compiled mainly from the Cork Court Registers, Miller-Borgonovo, Peter Hart and from the official list of disappeared persons of 22 August 1921.
(*Cork Examiner*, 22 August 1921)

As can be seen from Table 3, two-thirds of the victims were ex-soldiers and working class. Of the total, seven were Protestants, the rest Catholics, which is broadly in line with the relative proportions of Protestants and Catholics in the population in Cork, suggesting that the IRA campaign in the city, at least up to that point, was not sectarian.[11] Twenty-one were abducted, shot and secretly buried. There were no women among the victims.[12]

Cork was in many ways still a loyal city even as late as 1919. Seán Healy, an activist with the 1st Battalion of the city IRA that operated in the north side of Cork, stated: 'A large percentage of the people in A Company area had connections with British forces and police; vested interests had been established over the years; shopkeepers were handling big military contracts; the soldiers and police had intermarried with the citizens; in fact 90 per cent of the residents in our area could be regarded as being pro-British and hostile to the IRA. Only about one house in every hundred could be regarded as pro-IRA.'[13] Along with the British garrison, 'these factors made our activities very difficult and dangerous, in fact, they could be regarded as behind the line operations'. Michael Kenny, an IRA intelligence officer who lived in the vicinity of Victoria Barracks, was twice betrayed to the police by loyalist neighbours. It took no small amount of bravery to operate in such an area and it comes as no surprise to hear that the general republican view was that 'the area was also infested with British spies and informers and only for taking drastic action against these people we would never have survived'.[14] There are many references to hostility to 'the cause' in the memoirs of old IRA men. In fact it is almost a constant complaint. Thus Florrie O'Donoghue, the IRA's chief intelligence officer for Cork, was able to say: 'The population of Crosshaven is, almost to a man, hostile.'[15]

But before we look at individual cases, we should examine the background in which these killings occurred, in particular at the competing forces in operation in the city at the time. More specifically, we need to look at that most essential ingredient in an intelligence war, the gathering of information. Both sides needed it badly, the IRA in order to be able to predict British troop and police movements, and the military and RIC in order to track down IRA suspects.

Chapter 10 ⌒

HOW INTELLIGENT WAS
BRITISH INTELLIGENCE?

Lieut Koe has on several occasions been responsible for the capture of parties of rebels and large numbers of arms and exposed himself to great danger to obtain valuable information.[1]

Much has been written about the failure of British intelligence during the Irish revolution, from its inability to predict the 1916 Rebellion to the rivalry and infighting that hampered efforts during the 1919–21 period.[2] Much is also made of the ruthlessness and efficiency of Michael Collins's 'Squad' in wiping out successive waves of agents sent to Dublin to infiltrate Sinn Féin and later to try to kill known Sinn Féiners.[3] The words used by British historians to describe the performance of British intelligence in the immediate aftermath of World War I are 'confusion', 'debacle' and 'disaster'. They paint a picture of a secret service on its last legs, where a multiplicity of roles were taken by a number of often colourful individuals of the British spook community who were trying to meddle in Irish affairs.[4]

During World War I, British intelligence in Ireland was so obsessed with potential German intrigues in Ireland (which never materialised) and with trying to find ways to encourage the United States to enter the war that it appears to have grossly underestimated the growing nationalist movement. Brigadier General J. A. Byrne, the Inspector General of the RIC, who advocated negotiating with Sinn Féin and the need to separate the moderate politicians within Sinn Féin from the gunmen, was sent on indefinite leave at the end of 1919 and was not allowed to return to office.[5] This was part of the promotion of Protestant unionists into senior positions in Dublin Castle that took place in 1919 and 1920, what Paul McMahon has recently called the 'Orangification' of Dublin Castle.[6]

Domestically, political intelligence was in the hands of the detective unit (G division) of Dublin Metropolitan Police (DMP) in Dublin and the Special

Crimes Branch of the RIC in the rest of the country. By the beginning of 1920 the G division and the Special Crimes Branch were riddled with Collins's informers, several detectives had been assassinated and both forces appeared to be fighting a losing battle. As Michael Hopkinson has pointed out, probably the most crucial turning point in the entire conflict was the decision, late in 1919, to shut down most of the RIC barracks in rural Ireland and withdraw the police to the larger population centres. This was of course for the police's own protection. However, it meant that whole stretches of the countryside were now without a police presence, areas where the IRA was able to do more or less what it wanted. The void was filled by the Sinn Féin courts which in many areas ran a parallel judicial system that received widespread support, even from loyalists.

However, in the larger towns and cities the RIC still had a significant presence and, while they were boycotted by the population at large under pressure from the IRA, they were still able to operate intelligence-gathering with some efficiency. In Cork city Detective Sergeant Thomas Ryan and Constable John Carroll, both of whom were involved in intelligence work, were captured outside St Patrick's church on the Lower Road in December 1920.[7] They were held in Sing Sing for a short period before being released by Seán Culhane on the promise that they would 'provide me with a few little tit-bits from time to time'.[8] Ryan and Detective Jack Maliff, a rugby inter-pro who played for Munster and was later chairman of Cork Constitution rugby club, ran a string of informants around the city and were lucky to survive a subsequent IRA assassination attempt while returning from a rugby match in the Mardyke in January 1921.

Carroll, however, was not so lucky. A few days before the shooting of Ryan and Maliff, Carroll and an alleged informant, Con Sheehan, an ex-soldier who worked as an attendant in the Cork Asylum, were shot outside the Good Shepherd convent. Both were wounded in the attack. A month later while on a trip to Tipperary to visit his father, Carroll was abducted outside Nenagh. His body was found a few days later; his hands and feet were tied together. He had been shot twice in the head and twice in the body. In one account of the killing, 'Constable Carroll was a witness in an important murder trial that was pending and it was believed that the motive for his killing was to exclude his evidence from that trial.'[9] In 1922 Carroll's brother was murdered in Tipperary and his father's house burnt down. On 21 March Con Sheehan was himself abducted and found shot dead in Bishopstown on the outskirts of the city.[10]

During all previous Irish attempted revolutions Dublin Castle had informers in the rebel camp. Now the Castle found it difficult to recruit informers from within the IRA.[11] As the British Army's Intelligence Report, which summarised the lessons learned from the conflict, stated after the event: 'The bulk of the people were our enemies and were therefore far more incorruptible than has been the case in former Irish movements.' The only place where the flow of information remained undiminished was in Protestant Ulster, though here it was worthless owing to the paranoia of Ulster loyalists who saw 'a Sinn Féiner and a potential murderer in every Catholic'.[12] When Lord French decided at the end of 1919 that secret service work in Ireland should be directed from Scotland Yard by Sir Basil Thompson, Collins reacted by assassinating the new assistant commissioner of the DMP, whose role had been to 'take care of political crime'. Jack Byrnes, the star secret service agent sent in by Scotland Yard to meet Collins, and Alan Bell, who appears to have been the local co-ordinator of Thompson's secret service network, were also quickly dispatched.[13]

In May 1920 the Cabinet then decided that all Irish intelligence should be placed under the control of a single director of intelligence. Much has been written both about and by the new director, Brigadier Ormonde de l'Épée Winter, one of the more colourful imperialists of the period. While he threw himself into his task with gusto, he had no experience of intelligence work. He concentrated his energies on Dublin and failed to co-ordinate intelligence for the country as a whole, preferring the excitement of covert action to the patient collation and analysis of all forms of intelligence on the IRA.[14] He set up a secret recruiting office in London under his friend Major C. A. Cameron. Cameron sent some 60 agents to Ireland in the second half of 1920. Some were trained in a 'school of instruction' in London and sent to Dublin, having been given suitable cover as 'shop assistants, garage hands and similar occupations'.[15] These were the 'spooks' that General Frank Crozier, the commander of the Auxiliaries, appears to have noticed in Dublin, lurking around every corner.[16]

Twelve of them came to a sticky end when Collins decided to assassinate as many of the group as he could on Bloody Sunday morning. This was largely a political stunt, carried out to maximise the effect it would have on public opinion. He wanted the killings to be co-ordinated: all were to be carried out at exactly nine o'clock. 'These hoors,' he insisted, 'have got to learn that Irishmen can turn up on time.'[17] Bloody Sunday had the effect, at least temporarily, of paralysing the Special Branch in Dublin. We don't know what effects it had, if any, in Cork. However, one of the indirect outcomes of Bloody Sunday was that military undercover agents were now discouraged from living in civilian quarters and had to try to operate out of barracks, which was much more difficult.

One of its agents who found his way to Cork has the dubious distinction of being the first civilian shot by the Cork city IRA. Harry T. Quinlisk, a native of Wexford and a former member of Casement's Irish Brigade appears to have been something of a Walter Mitty character.[18] Tall and distinctive in his army greatcoat, he had been noticed by Collins's men touting around Dublin, asking to meet with Collins. Collins, as a ruse, got him sent to Cork, cynically neglecting to tell the Cork IRA who he was. Soon Quinlisk, staying at a city centre hotel, began again to make enquiries about Collins. The IRA became suspicious. When Mick Murphy, commander of the 2nd Battalion, posed as an intermediary and met with Quinlisk in a city centre pub, his suspicions were confirmed. The police raided the hotel where Quinlisk had been told that Collins was staying. On 20 February 1920, Mick Murphy, who gave a detailed account of this killing to the Bureau of Military History, shot Quinlisk at Tory Top Road, just south of the city, after first getting the go-ahead from GHQ. There can be little doubt that Quinlisk was a British agent. It would be five months before another civilian was shot by the city IRA.

One question jumps out of all this: if British intelligence was on its knees by the end of 1920, then why did the IRA killing of 'spies' in Cork get into its stride only in the spring of 1921, with more being killed in an average month between February and July than had been killed in the entire previous year? We're back to the 'war within a war' argument again, where at least within the MLA the British Army replaced the RIC as the IRA's principal enemy. The job of intelligence-gathering fell to junior officers, mostly lieutenants and captains from various support corps who were attached to the main regiments stationed in Ireland. The Royal Army Service Corps (RASC), the Royal Army Medical Corps (RAMC), the Machine Gun Corps (MGC), the Royal Garrison Artillery (RGA) and the Royal Field Artillery (RFA) appear to have supplied most of these officers. This was a job involving the most appalling danger and at least some of these officers lived in civilian quarters and dressed in mufti.[19] The Signals Corps was also involved in the setting up and use of listening sets. Microphones and 'detectaphones' were used to a certain extent in buildings used by IRA personnel, though they were limited by poor technology and were worthless in timber buildings where every sound was magnified.[20] There was, moreover, a distaste for human 'espionage' among senior military personnel. Field Marshal Haig in 1919 refused to have anything to do with Thompson's Secret Service. 'As regards the troops, I said that I would not authorise any men being used as spies. Officers must act straightforwardly and as Englishmen. Espionage amongst our own men was hateful to us army men. . . . Thompson's machinery for getting information on sedition must work independently of the Army and its leaders.' This attitude was not going to get the army anywhere against the IRA.

In the early part of the conflict in Ireland the army had to rely on the police for information. The dated nature of this information is apparent in the fact that right up until the Truce the military were still focused on Sinn Féin while the IRA men on the ground were often unknown to them.[21] The contents of the RIC lists of 'Sinn Féin suspects 1917–21', the so-called 'Black List', is almost laughable in this regard. The list consists mostly of political 'suspects', people like Count Plunkett and Maude Gonne. Only one of the Cork city IRA men gets a mention in the list and that was Fred Murray, who was captured in the spring of 1921. If the RIC was the 'eyes and ears of the Crown', as it is often termed, then it was both deaf and blind as to who the real movers were in the IRA.

The debacle during the arrest of Terence MacSwiney, when virtually the entire command of the Cork No. 1 Brigade was captured, only to be released again, illustrates this.[22] MacSwiney was held; as Lord Mayor he was a well-known Sinn Féin figure. The others captured with him, including Liam Lynch, Sandow Donovan and Mick Leahy, much more dangerous men, were let go. This and the earlier assassination of Tomás MacCurtain illustrates the policy of 'knocking off the heads of the leadership', a mistaken and futile notion that the rebellion could be quelled by taking out the leaders. Meanwhile the men who were carrying out the actual war were released despite in many cases giving their own names in the belief that they were known anyway. Had the British Army held on to the entire IRA command after that raid on the City Hall in August 1920, there would have been little revolution in Cork. This was truly a case of the blind leading the blind.

Senior IRA activists such as Mick Murphy and Sandow Donovan, who were well known in Cork city for their hurling and footballing abilities, were able to wander freely through the city for much of the conflict.[23] It was only a few weeks before the Truce that Murphy was finally captured and that was by the RIC. And even then he was not recognised. Nor was he later when the infamous 'informer' Monkey Mac refused to identify him during his incarceration in Victoria Barracks.[24]

Towards the end of 1920 there was a gradual shift away from police methods and towards a more military strategy, and during the six months up to the Truce constant raiding and searching and the capture of IRA documents were the most effective method of gathering information. Between October 1920 and the Truce, some 6,311 raids and searches were carried out—nearly as many as IRA raids on mails during the same period. Intelligence officers assisted in most raids and searches, usually disguised. This led to several cases where 'spies' were suspected and shot because they were believed to have been these disguised men.[25] 'In the 6th Divisional area (Munster, but centred in Cork) there were 45 agents, of whom 23 were believed to have been active, working for the divisional intelligence officer. These sources were almost entirely dried up in February [1921] when the IRA . . . began a series of murders of persons who they believed might have given information.'[26]

Thompson's secret service in London also appears to have been making its rather limited contribution, at least up to the summer of 1920 when all secret service activity was brought under Winter's command. The army report is scathing about this: 'Another branch of the secret service, based in London, is said to have cost about £15,000 a year. The information which came through this source was always 24 to 48 hours delayed and this militated against its usefulness. Moreover, owing to the police office system it was never clear from what source their secret information came.'[27]

From an operational point of view, however, the best information came from 'IRA deserters and prisoners under interrogation'. The intelligence report gives a lot of detail on how prisoners were to be handled in order to extract information from them. The methods are subtle and only in the case of senior operatives, who were unlikely to break under interrogation, is there a recommendation that force might be used. 'Brutal methods are a mistake', the report states.[28] Though for trying to 'secure a conviction' for a senior figure torture was regularly used, it was acknowledged that it was not a particularly effective method of getting at the truth.[29]

As for classical espionage, only a few Irishmen were prepared to act as agents. For those who were, it was an extremely risky occupation. Women 'were particularly useful, but their employment sometimes involved relations that were more than friendly'. Englishmen were mostly precluded from service because of their accents and because 'no amount of disguise could conceal the stamp of the British officer'.[30] However, some did attempt it and ended up in bog holes throughout the southern counties of Ireland.

In spite of all that, the campaign of the British Army against the IRA, particularly in Dublin and Cork during the period leading up to the Truce, was reasonably effective. The army's intelligence report states that in Cork and Limerick the liaison between the military and police had improved. Local intelligence centres to pool police and military resources were set up in many cities and towns, including Cork, where the centre was in operation by April.[31] 'In the area that was to become the Martial Law area, from June 1920 to July 1921, 85 per cent of the operations carried out were based on military information. It must be admitted, however, that in this area, the Divisional Intelligence Officer had exceptional local knowledge.'[32]

'Secret services in a small city like Cork presented very considerable difficulties. Everyone knew everyone else and of secret service in the strict sense there was none. There were numerous informers, however, and most of them were procured by and gave their information to military intelligence.'[33] Informers were paid on a sliding scale, up to £50 for a given piece of information, depending on the value of what they had to impart.[34]

How widespread was the use of ex-soldiers in the procurement of information? Was there any justification for the sudden upsurge in the assassinations of ex-soldiers that began in the city in February 1921 and was to last until the Truce? Well, ex-soldiers were the obvious place for the army to begin the recruitment of informers. Many were out of work and almost destitute; many would have allegiance to the Crown. They were one potential source of information, though their information would, by definition, be of limited value. Their knowledge of IRA activities, though, as was the case with loyalists, was minimal, unless they managed to infiltrate IRA units, as a few tried to do.

An example of this comes from the confession of the spy codenamed

Saunders, who was captured outside the city in late May 1921: 'Saunders' was the brother of a north Cork IRA man and did most of his spying activities in the Mallow area, being one of the chief informants in the round-up in Mourneabbey which led to the killing of four Volunteers and the execution of two others. He was recruited by an undercover ex-British Army man, Dan Shields. 'We were on a military lorry. We came straight to Cork. We remained about a fortnight knocking around Cork. We were told to knock about the city and go into the countryside now and then. We were to stay in the Salvation House in the nights while we were in the city. We were told to go up to Blarney St and we got the names of four men wanted.'[35] Sinn Féin councillor Liam de Roiste reported in mid-1920 in his diary: 'They have for some time been inviting informers and secret agents to send them information. Rewards are offered. What they asked for means that any vile wretch who may be tempted to secure a few pounds for himself . . . will come to the help of the British Empire by informing.'[36] Most anonymous letters, however, were of limited value, being the result of fear or malice. Some informed out of sheer spite, for imagined slights as well as for real ones; others informed for money or loyalty to the Crown. IRA men informed to give themselves immunity and the families of IRA men for the same reason.[37]

However, the usefulness of this approach was limited. 'Early in 1920 it was possible to get some information in this manner, but as time went on and the terror grew more real and was more widely advertised, informers became fewer and fewer. Information was however received through this source right up to July 1921.'[38] A number of those shot as spies in March and April 1921, some of whom were ex-soldiers, were, like 'Saunders', out-of-town visitors to the city.

The army men knew their stuff when it came to cajoling information out of captured IRA men. 'It was then found as a rule that some were ready to tell what they knew, frequently without asking for payment—indeed it was often found that small presents were more acceptable than money.' However, as the IRA killing of suspected spies became more regular and brutal, 'the desire to inform for the sake of informing, which is such a common characteristic among secret service agents, was conspicuous by its absence'.[39] 'I knew [an IRA informer] very well and asked him, the day before he was executed, why he gave us away to the enemy. He said he could give no reason why he did it.'[40] This suggests that some people informed for the very simple reason that they derived some perverse pleasure from it. Begrudgery is probably another name for it.

When Florrie O'Donoghue wrote that many of 'the creatures sent out to spy on us were of a very low calibre', he may have been betraying his distaste for the 'lower class of spies'. He may also have been simply telling the truth. This is borne out by a comment made by the anonymous writer of the army intelligence report who stated that written notes either to or from informants were of limited value because many of the informants could neither read nor write.[41] In Frank O'Connor's story 'Jumbo's Wife', the wife of an informer has to take a cheque for payment received to an IRA man in order to read it—with obvious results.[42]

The biggest challenge facing the security forces was how to place agents within the IRA. 'For many reasons, it was practically impossible to place a man in any inner circle.'[43] However, infiltrating the IRA was attempted, often by ex-soldiers or by army or RIC deserters or soldiers posing as deserters. Some of the most infamous 'spies' of the period, including Dan Shields, Monkey Mac and Cruxy Connors, were all ex-soldiers who managed to attach themselves to IRA units. This was undoubtedly one of the main reasons for the wholesale targeting of ex-servicemen in the city, especially in the months after these men had been 'found out'—Cruxy Connors after the Clogheen episode at the end of March appears to be the last of the above to have been discovered.

There are several accounts of how these 'deserters' disappeared across the county, particularly in active areas. This led to the situation in the spring of 1921 where real deserters, who would have been of significant value to the IRA because of their military experience, and fake deserters were both equally shot out of hand.[44] There were also a number of 'deserters' such as Shields who appear to have got away with it. The north Cork column nearly came to grief on a number of occasions because of the work of these operatives. Classical espionage of this nature was exceedingly difficult when it came to the rural IRA because of the intimate nature of communities and the fact that everyone in a locality knew everyone else. It was very difficult to break into IRA inner circles. Even Tom Barry had difficulty proving his credentials when he tried to become a member of the West Cork Brigade and indeed brigade members were suspicious of him for a long time afterwards.[45] However, infiltration was regularly tried on Cork No. 1 and it was sometimes successful.

Chapter 11 ～

IRA INTELLIGENCE IN CORK

The Intelligence System, as in all twentieth-century colonial struggles, provided the essential precondition for the development of guerrilla warfare.[1]

In a report in *The Times* of London of 18 May 1921 entitled 'Life in Cork', written as part of a series of articles 'by a young Englishman, unconnected to the staff of any newspaper, who determined on his release from military duties, to visit Ireland and form his own opinions', Cork is described as a city of spies.

Cork is—or until lately was—a city of spies and one speedily found that to be a stray Englishman bent upon an apparently aimless mission was to be almost inevitably mistaken for a government agent. Nor is it an over-pleasant sensation to find yourself watched at times through the lace curtains of the hotel window or to realize that walking up a crowded street you are being followed by a hungry-looking individual in brown. The least desirable place to visit in such circumstances is the Victoria Barracks and for prudence sake one is apt to return to one's hotel by a circuitous route.

Sinn Féin Intelligence is extremely keen, and it soon dawns on one that most plain clothes visitors to the barracks are objects of peculiar interest to the various groups of young men who lounge at street corners in that vicinity.[2]

The 'young Englishman' gives external verification to something that had been set up well over a year earlier and was probably the most efficiently run of all IRA activities in Cork city—the gathering of information. Often overlooked in the fascination with Michael Collins's squad in Dublin, the Cork intelligence system was at least as efficient in terms of levels of surveillance and led to many more operations and shootings than did the squad.

And while the British had to contend with several rival intelligence-gathering systems, who vied with each other for credit when it came to successes and tried to lay the blame on each other when it came to failure, the IRA had a centrally controlled system that was both more extensive than its British equivalent and also more efficient and ruthless. Central to its success was the fact that it could call on large sections of the population to supply the snippets of information that are necessary to build up a picture of enemy operations. Many individuals who worked in military and police barracks, including soldiers and RIC men, passed information out to IRA contacts on troop movements, the living quarters of officers and the identity of intelligence officers and agents.[3]

According to Florence (Florrie) O'Donoghue, who organised intelligence in the city, the brigade structure allowed for the organic development of intelligence over the period. The two city battalions each had an intelligence section headed up by an intelligence officer. Each of the 16 companies comprising the two battalions within the city also had an intelligence officer. In addition, the brigade itself set up its own intelligence section at the beginning of 1920. This was known as the brigade intelligence squad and consisted of six men.[4] In contrast to the battalion intelligence sections, these were full-time operatives engaged in observation and surveillance. These men were selected for 'their proven worth in work of a similar nature under ordinary Company organisations. . . . The work which they were called upon to do was extremely dangerous and in the conditions prevailing in the city at the time could only be performed by men of exceptional courage and resource.'[5] They worked individually and in pairs and reported directly to Seán O'Hegarty or O'Donoghue. In March 1921 Michael Collins gave the go-ahead for the Cork 'Squad' to be paid out of a fund of £25 a week, which they began to receive a few weeks later.[6] In O'Donoghue's words: 'The fact that the Intelligence Dept. of Cork No. 1 Brigade was congratulated on several occasions by the DI [Michael Collins] is evidence of the efficient manner in which they carried out their onerous tasks.'[7]

The effect of three intelligence-gathering operations and the executions that often resulted from their activities was to terrorise the community into silence and make life difficult for the military. In the view of British intelligence, 'in addition to the battalions, there was, whatever it may have been called by the IRA, what was neither more nor less than a murder gang organised apparently in three sections'.[8] This most likely refers to the Active Service Unit set up in the city in January 1921 and the 'hit squads' of the two battalions who carried out most of the killings of suspects, though it has to be said that members of the intelligence squad themselves also occasionally carried out killings.[9] The use of the term 'murder gang' is oddly symmetrical, since the British Army, Auxiliary and RIC intelligence-gatherers and their attendant hit squads were also known to the IRA as the 'Murder Gang', from their habit of working undercover at night and carrying out shootings of IRA suspects. One man's hit squad is another man's murder gang.

A flavour of the intelligence-gathering activities of one company may be garnered from the account of Danny Healy, a member of the ASU and one of the men sent by O'Hegarty to New York in 1922 to shoot Cruxy Connors. 'From early in 1920 practically the whole of "C" Company was engaged in watching the comings and goings of the RIC at various barracks in our district. Particular attention was paid to civilians seen to be coming or leaving barracks. Reports of these activities were forwarded to the Battalion Intelligence Officer.'[10] The memoirs of survivors of the campaign in Cork city are full of accounts of the thoroughgoing nature of their spying activities.[11]

The intelligence system meant that O'Donoghue built up a network of informants both in the military and various parts of the civil administration such as the Post Office, the Customs and Excise, the Income Tax office and so on. According to IRA accounts, all strangers arriving in Cork were noted at the ports and railway stations; all military and RIC barracks were watched on a 24-hour basis, despite curfew; newspapers were monitored for coded messages; phones were tapped and police ciphers (used to decode secret police messages sent by telegraph or post) broken.[12]

The 'night shift'—watching barracks all through the night—was one of the most hated of all the jobs carried out by these men. It meant standing around in all kinds of weather watching shadowy figures enter and emerge from barracks; it meant following those individuals to their homes or lodging places and finding out who they were and what they were doing. It also led to an atmosphere of extreme suspicion as well as danger. Bob Ahern, a member of the brigade intelligence squad, remembers getting '£1 entertainment allowance per week from brigade funds . . . to cover my expenses when in the company of British military and Black and Tans whom I met in public houses and hotels in Cork city. It was part of my job to meet such people, engage them in conversation and obtain as much information as possible about their own duties, about the names of the most prominent members of the British Intelligence Service, their movements and anything else which might be useful to us in countering their activities. I need hardly add that the allowance was quite insufficient for the purpose intended.'[13]

The two battalion intelligence sections in the city also gathered information. These were under less control than the brigade squad itself. In fact, as we shall see, in the case of the 2nd Battalion they often acted precipitately and shot people on mere suspicion.[14] Files were compiled on individual suspects by O'Donoghue but also by battalion intelligence officers. While some 'spies' were inevitably shot by members of the intelligence units or by a hit squad of men close to Seán O'Hegarty, the majority of such shootings appear to have been handed over to individual companies to carry out in the areas in which the 'spy' was living. The witness statements of members of the various companies from Cork city gathered in the BMH give credence to the notion that each company was more or less given its 'quota' of 'spies' to be shot. In some cases the orders appear to come from brigade HQ; in others the decision appears to be taken by battalion commanders. Geography often seems to have been the chief factor in determining who actually carried out shootings.

At the core of the war in Cork city was the conflict between the intelligence systems of the British—the military and the RIC—and that of the IRA. Attempts to shoot known British intelligence officers were given the highest priority by the IRA. Many, if not all, the names of the British Army intelligence staff were known to the IRA.[15] For instance, Michael Kenny, the only IRA man who could recognise Captain Kelly, the head of intelligence at Victoria Barracks, by sight, was instructed to be constantly on the watch-out for him.[16] He was ordered to capture or kill Kelly should the opportunity ever arise. In fact, the Dillon's Cross ambush that led to the burning of Cork was set up by Kenny in an effort to shoot Captain Kelly who, it was believed, would be in one of the lorries ambushed.

Over a year later, just before the British left, Kelly saw young Kenny, who by then had been released from jail, watching the gate of Victoria Barracks. 'Come in here, Kenny,' he said, 'and I'll give you something else to do instead of watching me.'[17] Yet for all that, even though O'Donoghue knew where the British intelligence officers were living, only one intelligence officer was killed in the city and that was in 1922. Kelly's home address is listed in Guy's Postal Directory for 1921. Telephone transcripts intercepted by the IRA in the post-Truce period find him living at Bellview Park. Yet he was not shot.

Ironically there were Irishmen on all sides. While the IRA intelligence squad was led by a Kerry man, the draper's assistant Florrie O'Donoghue, the British Army's intelligence corps was led by another Kerry man, for Captain J. O'C Kelly was the son of a Glenbeigh water bailiff. Several members of his staff, including the aforementioned Lieutenant Koe, were also Irish. One of the striking things about British Army correspondence is the large number of Irish names among the junior officer ranks. Of all the little theatres of the Anglo-Irish conflict, Cork city came closest to being an actual civil war.

An idea of the attention to detail given by Florrie O'Donoghue on the matter of intelligence methods used can be seen from the following memo he sent to all battalion o/cs in December 1920. This is one of several such memos in O'Donoghue's papers.

December 22, 1920
Cork No. 1 Brigade Headquarters
To all Battalion OCs:

It is beyond question that the Intelligence Service is of the utmost importance and it is the duty of every Volunteer Commander to see that the lead, which we secured in this matter against the enemy, is properly maintained. The objects of the intelligence service are:
To discover the intention of the enemy. In the present conflict this intention is political as well as military.
To keep in touch with, observe and report at once, the movement of enemy agents seeking information.
(a) in your area and (b) moving from or to your area. To keep under observation all enemy bases. It must not be possible for any enemy party to move out of their base without the knowledge of our local intelligence branch. No. 1 is the concern of every Volunteer and even of every citizen. Conversations of every representative in clubs, in their homes, their movements, etc. will indicate enemy intention and will be reported to the immediate superior officer . . .
No. 2 is of more direct importance and consequence to the individual Volunteer. In this respect every Volunteer must always be on the alert. Every stranger in a locality must immediately be reported to the officer in charge of the area, and if necessary, held in custody until instructions have been obtained. Look out for English accents. The index numbers on motor cars should be noted and compared with lists taken from adjoining districts. In this regard, the numbers of motor cars of Division Commissioners, County Inspectors, District Inspectors and officers commanding troops, should be known to all Volunteers, who will consequently be able to recognize these vehicles directly when they are seen. A Crossley tender conveying a murder gang passes your road, later on you hear of some Irish citizen being brutally murdered. If you have taken the number of that tender you may be able to deal with it the next time you see it.
Get photos of local enemy forces . . .
Post offices: Special attention must be paid to these. The staff of each office or sub-office in your area must be carefully reviewed and those willing to assist in the intelligence department carefully selected and kept in constant touch with. Even the smallest office must not be overlooked, and there are scraps of information about the enemy to be picked up even in these, and it is in the assemblage of these scraps that results will be obtained. This Branch of the Service must be worked with ceaseless energy, care and discretion. A reliable person or persons in each PO should constantly be on the look-out for letters addressed to

firms in England or Dublin—that is any address or firm with which people generally do not deal . . . Telephone and telegram messages . . . All messages sent by enemy police, soldiers, or agents, should be copied and recorded. . . .

The register number of every motorcar and lorry in your area should be noted and a record kept. The names and ranks of all officers (enemy) in your area should be known to you, as well as their residences, personal appearance and general habits. Changes in personnel of enemy organizations should be notified to the Brigade Director of Information and names of successors forwarded . . . If the Intelligence service is to be of benefit to you and to the entire organization, no detail can be neglected, nothing which observation can command must be unknown to you. . . .

(Signed) Brigade Intelligence Officer[18]

In addition to the above, all company captains appointed four men to report directly to the battalion intelligence officer. This meant that the 16 companies in the city between them contributed 64 men to intelligence-gathering. It meant you had 74 IRA men more or less fully engaged in what might be called espionage, plus the activities of the intelligence officers of battalions outside the city. By contrast, the British Army's 6th Division and 17th Light Infantry Brigade's combined intelligence staffs totalled five officers, three clerks and one photographer, and their command included most of Munster, though RIC intelligence work also led to several important arrests both in 1920 and 21.[19]

There was also what O'Donoghue called the 'other branch of intelligence', the civilians, a 'wide variety of men and women, individually selected, who were engaged in duties or employed in positions where they could acquire valuable information about the enemy'. This meant you had a vast network of informants supplying information and men processing it. This often led to the situation, as one Post Office employee who ran messages for the IRA put it, where 'you worked for one government and were paid by another'.[20]

It is difficult to establish how much of the information, apart from that gathered by the brigade squad itself, was channelled back to O'Hegarty and O'Donoghue. But the BMH witness statements suggest that most of it was. This implies that while there were maverick groups from the different battalions carrying out killings and random shootings within the city IRA,[21] the vast majority of such killings were ordered by the brigade command. The downside of all this is that such an extensive network is also a breeding ground for paranoia and suspicion. The mere act of visiting a barracks or a police station or having contact with the police or military meant you could be immediately labelled a spy.

In February 1921 as the city IRA came under increasing pressure, Seán O'Hegarty left for the hills of mid-Cork to run the brigade column. O'Donoghue was now effectively in charge in the city. This change, whether coincidental or not, led to a sudden increase in the targeting of civilians suspected of spying in the city. Up until then only a handful of suspects were quietly abducted, interrogated and shot; now suspected 'spies' were being mown down in the street. Of course shooting people in cold blood was much easier to do and had, from the IRA's perspective, the added advantage of terrorising the population into silence. Public shootings of suspects reached a peak, with seven civilians killed in the city in February, three in March, four in April, five in May, and thereafter a steady trickle all the way to the Truce. There were many more attempted killings. From early February 1921 it was open season on alleged suspects in Cork.

By 1921 Cork city had become a web of intrigue. All strangers instantly became suspects and, as we'll see, though most British agents arrived in Cork from elsewhere, the vast majority of the suspects shot were home-grown. Cork had truly become a city of spies.

Chapter 12

LOVE IN A CITY OF INTRIGUE

Snatches of information from maids and porters and wastepaper baskets, times of comings and goings, places with lights on after curfew; all manner of whispers and overhearings turned themselves into dossiers and reports.[1]

Sometime in mid-1919 a tall striking-looking woman in a state of obvious distress was seen at the altar in Holy Trinity church at Fr Mathew Quay in Cork. She had a little boy beside her in a go-car. When the old Capuchin brother tending the altar saw how tearful the woman was, he asked what was troubling her. She said she had lost her child and had despaired of ever getting him back. The Brother suggested that she call to the friary where he would find one of the priests to console her. The priest she met at the friary was Father Dominic, a well-known Capuchin priest and fiery republican and brother of Joe O'Connor, quartermaster of the Cork No. 1 Brigade. The story the lady told Fr Dominic is one that has been described in detail elsewhere.[2] However, it is necessary to repeat it here because of its relevance to the subject of this book.

Her name, she said, was Josephine Marchment Brown. Originally Josephine McCoy, she was the daughter of a head constable of the RIC who had been stationed in Cork. In 1913 she had married a Welshman, Coleridge Marchment Brown, who became a soldier in the British Army and was killed on the Western Front in 1916. They had two sons: Reggie, who was born in 1913, and Gerald, born a few years later. She returned to Cork soon after her husband was killed, bringing her younger son with her and leaving Reggie in the care of his paternal grandparents in Wales. As her loyalist credentials appeared to be beyond reproach, she got a job with the British Army in Victoria Barracks, acting as a stenographer and secretary to a Captain Woods who was on General Strickland's staff.

Her problems began in 1917 when she sent for her elder son and her husband's parents refused to give him up. There followed a prolonged custody battle over the child, whom the Browns apparently wished to be raised as a Protestant, a battle which Josephine lost. Reggie was now being raised in south Wales while a broken-hearted Josephine was back in Cork. The Brown family claimed that conditions in Ireland were too unsettled for raising a child and that the young widow might not be able to bring him up properly. The judge in London agreed with them.[3]

On hearing her story, Fr Dominic got in touch with Florrie O'Donoghue, who immediately saw his opportunity to place a spy high in the British Army organisation in Cork. Through Fr Dominic he negotiated with Josephine Brown that if she would agree to pass on information on British Army movements to the IRA, he would do what he could to return the child to her. She was easily persuaded for, quite apart from the predicament she found herself in, she had no great love for her employers in the British Army, finding them aloof, arrogant and disdainful of their Irish staff.

When O'Donoghue put his proposal to Seán O'Hegarty, it was dismissed as fanciful. O'Donoghue had to go to Michael Collins, who gave the operation the go-ahead and helped provide the logistics for an IRA team to visit Wales and spring the boy. O'Donoghue himself and two others went to Cardiff and, after a variety of setbacks, they kidnapped Reggie in late November 1920 and brought him back to Cork. After a brief reunion with his mother, he was kept in Youghal with Josephine's sister and at a convent in mid-Cork for the duration of the conflict.

Josephine Marchment Brown took the codename 'G', after her younger son, who was with her when she went into Holy Trinity church. She supplied the Cork No. 1 Brigade with much useful information from the British 6th Division HQ in Victoria Barracks.[4] According to O'Donoghue, there were many cases in which orders issued by General Strickland reached his brigade commanders only a day before they were in IRA hands.

The upshot of the story was that Josephine and Florrie O'Donoghue began a relationship and were married in April 1921. The kind of life they lived in the six months up to the Truce has been recorded by Seán O'Callaghan in his book, *Execution*.[5] 'It was a period of the utmost strain for both, and Florrie and other IRA senior officers often evaded arrest by staying in her house, which was above suspicion. Details of Captain Kelley's [*sic*] spies and informers reached the IRA almost as soon as they reached Divisional Intelligence. Raids proved fruitless, many valuable IRA lives were saved, and spies were ruthlessly eliminated as a result of information supplied by Josephine. . . .'

The 'period of strain' appears to refer in particular to the month of November 1920 while Florrie was away in Wales organising the abduction of Reggie Brown. Three British Army officers were taken from a train in Waterfall a few miles south of the city and executed by the IRA. Two other

officers had disappeared some weeks earlier in north Cork and an intelligence
officer had been found shot dead near Ballincollig.

O'Donoghue was a highly intelligent man and was the first serious
historian of the conflict in Cork. His histories of the period, biographies of
Liam Lynch[6] and Tomás MacCurtain,[7] are well written, detailed and fair-
minded. There are, however, significant gaps in his work. He more or less
ignores events in the city after the death of MacCurtain in March 1920 and
neglects to give any indication of the extent of the killing of alleged spies in
the city, which he must have known about, given his pivotal role in the
intelligence system. The execution of 'spies and informers', perhaps
understandably, rarely merits more than a passing comment in his published
works. This is a significant omission. Seán O'Hegarty has often been given the
credit, if that is the word, by O'Donoghue for the ruthlessness of the IRA's
campaign in his brigade area. However, the elimination of 'spies' in the city
after January 1921, when most of the brigade staff decamped to the
countryside, occurred during the period when O'Donoghue was in charge.

On other matters O'Donoghue could be frank, especially in his
unpublished papers, which are a treasure trove for historians of the period.
He has left rare insights on the character of the leaders of the movement but
could be very cutting in a subtle way: 'Where he [Terence MacSwiney] differed
from Tomás was that he did not have MacCurtain's shrewdness, an instinctive
knowledge of countrymen: neither had he O'Hegarty's lashing tongue and
rapier-like intelligence. He was a gentle soul and it was part of our tragedy
that he had to be a soldier. He never looked well in uniform.'[8] Of Richard
Mulcahy he states: 'What remains clearest in my mind is that I was shocked by
Mulcahy's deliberate, cold-blooded blasphemy. I attributed it to a weakness of
character, a desire to appear tough and ruthless.'[9] This is a bit rich coming
from one whose own commander and close friend Seán O'Hegarty was
known to have had one of the most vicious tongues in the entire movement.

In contrast to many IRA men, O'Donoghue was fair in his judgment of the
British: 'Except occasionally, in the case of some particularly reprehensible
outrage by Auxiliaries or Black and Tans, I never felt a burning hatred for
them. I often wondered what that violent hatred in our men sprang from and
questioned if there was not some cold unnatural streak in myself. . . . The
more my intelligence work enabled me to read their minds, the more familiar
I became with their responsibilities, problems and difficulties, the more the
possibility of violent hatred for them as individuals vanished.'[10]

This respect for soldiers and indeed for the British is repeated throughout
his work. Even his arch-enemy Captain Kelly is described as 'a good
intelligence officer', though he is not forgiven for refusing to return a
document of Terence MacSwiney's after the Truce. 'This was a petty meanness
that I have never been able to forgive.'[11]

But all this overlooks his other role in Cork. For Florrie O'Donoghue was more than just an intelligence officer for the Cork brigade. He was also 'Centre' or head of the IRB in Cork. The Irish Republican Brotherhood, that secret society that had been in operation since Fenian times, was by 1920 largely under the control of Michael Collins. This was a small cadre of men dedicated to physical violence as a means of forcing political change. Its secret nature was problematic for many more moderate republicans. Both Tomás MacCurtain[12] and Terence MacSwiney resigned their membership, while de Valera did the same because he felt that belonging to a secret society was not in keeping with the open political activism he believed Sinn Féin should be involved in.[13] It was also considered a sin for Catholics to become members of a secret society.

A branch had been set up in Cork as early as 1906 with Seán O'Hegarty as Centre. By 1920 Florrie O'Donoghue had taken over when O'Hegarty became brigade commander.[14] This made him, in effect, Michael Collins's man in Cork and he appears to have been in almost daily contact with Collins. Indeed from the spring of 1920 he was under instructions from Collins to take no overt part in IRA operations, and after an attack on Blarney RIC Barracks early in 1920 remained aloof from offensive operations.[15]

In order to understand some of the paranoia and suspicion that, along with well-grounded fears of British reprisals, informed the planning and operation of the intelligence squad and its attendant hitmen, we need to see O'Hegarty and O'Donoghue as coming from the essentially secretive background of the IRB. Most of the original 'active squad' in the city, activists such as O'Donoghue, O'Hegarty, Mick Murphy and Roibeárd Lankford were members of the IRB. This was a group comprising the most diehard IRA men in Cork who saw themselves as an elite, militarists who used violence as their principal *modus operandi* and who were deeply suspicious of what they considered to be the pussy-footing and compromising poses of Sinn Féin as a political party. O'Donoghue, O'Hegarty and Joe O'Connor were quite proud of the fact that they were the only IRA leaders in Cork who did not become members of Sinn Féin. Like their equivalent in the British military establishment, the IRB had no time for the 'frocks'. Violent action, not political manoeuvrings, was their game.

And as befits a clandestine operation, they were past masters in the art of putting together structures that of their nature depended on secrecy for their effectiveness. Thus various units and companies within the Volunteers operated on a need-to-know basis. It is evident from the BMH witness submissions that while the city IRA was centrally controlled, those on the periphery, the ordinary Volunteer on the street so to speak, was essentially in the dark as to the reasons for his orders. Since the sources of intelligence were secret and the transmission of information was secret, the reasons for the decision to execute so and so were also secret. As far as the IRA was concerned, this was literally blind justice. Those doing the killing were often told a story that was quite at odds with the actual background for such executions. This was necessary, for if someone was caught after a shooting he would not be in a position to give away the reasons behind it. He had been simply told to shoot a 'spy'. What the spy had done to deserve this fate was not the concern of the gunman. It is important to remember that people like Corry and many of those who left witness statements to the BMH were mere cogs in a wheel. It meant that death was dealt out at a distance. You could give a hit squad of one or two individuals orders to shoot somebody and the killing might not occur until weeks, months, or in some cases even years afterwards. As we'll see, orders might be acted at such a remove that people under a death sentence could be going around for years without knowing it. Meanwhile some local gunman with a revolver in his pocket was just waiting for his opportunity. This was a killing *system*, death by remote control. How justified it was in military, if not in moral terms, depended on the quality of information it was based on in the first place.

Chapter 13 ～

WHO WERE THE SPIES?

The large number of civilians shot by the Cork city IRA in 1920/21 poses significant problems for the historian. On the face of it, the high proportion of ex-soldiers among the victims might suggest that ex-soldiers were targeted for no better reason than that they were ex-soldiers and therefore made easy targets. Jane Leonard has ascribed the killing of ex-servicemen to the withdrawal of British troops to barracks in the spring of 1921, thus making more legitimate targets harder to kill.[1] It was also much more difficult to assassinate RIC men than it had been for much of 1920. According to this thesis, RIC men were initially shot because the IRA needed a convenient enemy and isolated policemen made easy targets. Then when RIC men, because they had effectively withdrawn to urban barracks, were harder to kill, it became the turn of ex-servicemen. These were an even easier prey for IRA violence and the large numbers of them shot can also be ascribed to the IRA's need for retaliation for the execution of its own members by the British. The statistics of violence certainly appear to support this thesis, with RIC men targeted largely in 1920 and ex-servicemen in 1921.

This thesis, while it may be true in some cases, is too simplistic to account for all or even for many of those killed. There can be little doubt that revenge was a major motive in some cases and that many of those suspected of spying were shot out of suspicion and little else. It is also true that the reasons for the shooting of any particular individual has been lost with the passage of time and the need for secrecy that covered all IRA activities. On the other hand, it is true that statistically those groups shot by the IRA as spies do not correlate with the groups who gave the most information—women, clergymen, shopkeepers, IRA men and their families being the main informers, while ex-servicemen and Protestants were the main victims.[2] However, the only way to see if the IRA was targeting ex-servicemen for no other reason than that they were ex-servicemen, is to look at individual cases.

The term 'spies and informers' is also too broad to be used as a general term. Certainly men (or women) sent in by Dublin Castle or British Military Intelligence could and should be described as spies. Similarly those members of the IRA or their families who volunteered information on their colleagues should be called informers. But should a loyalist such as Mrs Lindsay, who happened to notice IRA men preparing for an ambush and reported it to save lives (after informing the local priest to convey the message to the IRA and thus save lives on both sides)[3] also be called a spy or informer, even though she was only being true to her own convictions? For that matter, should her chauffeur James Clarke be considered a spy even though he never informed on anybody? Should everybody who visited a barrack or who happened to be friendly to British forces be considered a spy? If so, a significant sector of the population of Cork city and the better-off suburbs and harbour towns could conceivably be considered to have been spies.

As we have seen, there were 40 civilians shot by the IRA in the city and its environs during the War of Independence whose names can be easily identified. Of these, 20 were abducted, shot and their bodies buried. Most of the rest were ex-soldiers. Looking at the individual cases, the victims can be subdivided into the following: British undercover agents, IRA men who turned informer, old enemies of the IRA believed to have passed on information on IRA activities, paid informers, friends of RIC men and military personnel, individuals taken as hostages and those loyal to Britain. There is obviously some overlap between some of these groups.

We will first look at British undercover agents. This is the most obscure group and consisted of individuals sent in by the various secret service agencies on the British side to infiltrate the IRA or at least get information on its activities. We have already seen three of these in the case of Quinlisk and 'Saunders' and his handler Dan Shields. These agents were usually out-of-town operatives. Two other likely cases were Michael O'Brien[4] and James Gordon. Gordon who, as we've seen, was probably the first to be killed out of Sing Sing, was an ex-member of the RIC from County Leitrim who had joined the army in 1914 and was wounded during the war.

Some had narrow escapes. A well-known sportsman in Cork at the time worked as an official in the Cork GAA office. However, he was also reporting to Dublin Castle on anything he heard in GAA circles concerning the activities of republicans. (Membership of the GAA and Sinn Féin and indeed the IRA often overlapped.) His practice was to send reports of his spying activities to Dublin by post and his GAA activities to GAA headquarters in Thurles. One day he mixed up his envelopes, sending his GAA reports to Dublin Castle and his spying reports to GAA headquarters. The Thurles men, who were in the IRA, rushed to Cork, made contact with the local brigade and cornered him in the South Chapel. He would have been shot but for the intercession of the parish priest, who negotiated with the IRA. He was finally let go on condition that he leave Cork immediately. This he did, departing for Belfast on the first available train and going from there to South Africa.[5] He was never seen again in Cork.

We can get some insight into how these men were recruited from the case of Rennie and Gormley. Rennie was an undercover agent sent from Dublin to Cork and captured by the IRA after the Truce while posing as a representative of an English firm of motor car manufacturers.[6] While there is some evidence that he was in fact originally a native of Cork city,[7] Rennie claimed he first came to Ireland in 1917 in the British Army. Being demobilised early in 1920, he joined the RIC in October of that year. After two weeks in the RIC he was given a job in the secret service, his boss being an agent called Nicholls and his headquarters being the Sailors and Soldiers club in College Street in Dublin. He left for Cork after the Truce, and while he claimed he was not actually spying during that period, he was in a position to resume his spying activities in the event of the Truce breaking down. Richard Mulcahy wrote: 'He was, I feel certain, connected with the robber gang. The attached wire will show that he was recalled from Wales by Gormley, the secretary of the Sailors and Soldiers Club, for some job. This was the normal way of getting the crowd together for such jobs.' The wire, which was intercepted by the IRA, read 'Boys enquiring for you here—Gormley.'[8]

Rennie was held for many weeks in the latter half of 1921, being eventually handed over to the RIC at the height of the Treaty negotiations in November 1921. He may even have been recruited for an assassination job. He owes his survival to the fact that Mulcahy, Brugha and Collins were aware of his existence and the fact that he was captured during the sensitive period of the Treaty negotiations. Had it been earlier or later, he would no doubt have been shot.

The case also suggests that the Sailors and Soldiers club in Dublin may have been a centre for the organisation of clandestine secret service spying operations. As we'll see, there is a suggestion that soldiers' and sailors' homes in Cork were similarly used, at least for a period. Ex-servicemen's associations in Britain were regularly the targets for the secret services wishing to infiltrate left-wing organisations in search of Bolshevik sedition.[9] It was, at the very least, a logical place for the military authorities to recruit agents.

The second group was IRA men turned informers. This is the most detested of all the classes of informants from the IRA's own standpoint. There were a number of well-known examples in the city, though they are not listed in Table 3 because they were not actually killed. Probably the best known was Daniel McDonnell, better known as 'Monkey Mac'. McDonnell had been in the RAF during the Great War and thereafter worked as a barber in Patrick Street.[10] He had apparently joined the Volunteers in 1918 or 1919 and was immediately suspected of passing information on to the military. He was tarred and feathered in 1919 by the IRA and deported from the country.[11] However, the following year McDonnell was back in Cork and living on his nerves. (He was ironically also to be on the receiving end of Black and Tan 'justice' when his barber's shop went up in flames as part of the burning of Cork city centre on the night of 11 December 1920.)[12] There is little doubt but that McDonnell was a dangerous fellow. 'Monkey was extremely bitter against George Sisk. This had got so bad that I had to send George to Cardiff or Swansea where he stayed for several months until the Truce came.'[13]

On the night of 21 February 1921, McDonnell was returning to his home in Evergreen Road after work when he was shot by four IRA men led by Mick Murphy. Though he received seven wounds, they were not fatal—the bullets used were damp—and he survived. An hour or two later, while he was being treated in the South Infirmary, the military arrived and moved him immediately to the Military Hospital, where he made a complete recovery.[14]

From then to the Truce McDonnell remained in Victoria Barracks where he was routinely used by the army to identify IRA prisoners and sometimes was believed to go out on raiding parties. When Mick Murphy was brought before him in June 1921, however, he pretended not to recognise him.[15] He was spirited out of Cork after the Truce and made his way to England. An IRA execution party sent over to track him down in April 1922 found that he had been jailed for seven years for theft. The jail sentence saved his life. McDonnell appears to have been a ne'er-do-well and petty thief; he was the kind of fellow 'who would steal coats at a dinner' was how Connie Neenan, who commanded the south city battalion in the lead-up to the Truce, described him. He achieved near-mythical status in Cork and was feared by nationalists and loyalists alike. ''Twas the Monkey recognised me.'[16] He was awarded £2,000 in compensation by the courts for his injuries.[17]

While Monkey Mac is an archetypal Cork character, a completely different kind of ex-soldier was the almost equally well-known and equally detested 'Cruxy' Connors. Patrick Connors, nicknamed 'Cruxy' because he had won the *Croix de Guerre* during World War I, had been a sergeant major in the British Army. In late 1920 while working as a military agent, he joined the 1st Brigade's flying column.[18] He then appears to have gone underground from a British point of view, providing no further information for several months. Whether this is because he liked his new comrades too much or because he tired of the game is unclear. In any event, he was blamed for betraying a large ambush organised by the Cork No. 1 Brigade at Coolavookig outside Macroom, when he is alleged to have fired his Lewis gun into the ground rather than aim it at the military party being ambushed. The ambush was only partly successful and resulted in an inquiry instigated by IRA GHQ which found that there were many organisational reasons for its failure, primarily incompetence on the part of the leadership.[19] Connors then went on the run from the IRA. He was captured by the RIC in possession of a revolver and severely beaten. The RIC was initially reluctant to believe his story that he had been a military spy. However, after they consulted with the military authorities on their new captive, he was soon back with the British Army and resident in Victoria Barracks. He is alleged to have reappeared as part of a British Army raiding party at Ballycannon, near Clogheen outside Cork, at the end of March, where six Volunteers were shot after giving themselves up. Connors was apparently recognised but again took cover in the army barracks, where an attempt was made to poison him. He and his family were given passage to America after the Truce. In April 1922 the Cork IRA managed to track him down to an address in New York and Seán O'Hegarty sent an assassination party to shoot him.[20] Connors was walking down Central Park West when a man climbed over the park wall and fired a revolver at him.[21] Though badly wounded, he survived the attack, thanks to prompt intervention in a New York hospital. On returning to Cork the IRA men claimed they had killed Connors. The story went into local lore as one of the legends of the revolution. Connors, however, appears to have lived for many years afterwards in America, thanks to the skill of a capable surgeon.

Two others who fit the category of IRA men who gave evidence on the city battalions were James Herlihy and Din Din Riordan. Herlihy, a member of the 2nd Battalion, was sent to Victoria Barracks to get a permit for a gun. Soon afterwards the British Army raided his unit, arresting Connie Neenan among others. The blame fell on Herlihy; he apparently confessed to passing on details to the military but could give no reason for doing so other than that he felt like doing so.[22] He falls into the category recognised by British military intelligence of those who gave information for no better reason than they felt like it. He was shot by the IRA and buried in the bogs at Farmer's Cross, a few miles south of the city.

Din Din Riordan, also apparently an ex-soldier and IRA gunman from Kerry, came under suspicion of passing on information to the Black and Tans which set in train the notorious Broad Lane killings of November 1920.[23] Riordan was taken to the viaduct on the Bandon road by a group that included Frank Busteed, the Gray brothers and Dick Murphy, brother of Mick. There a confession was extracted from him and he was shot and his body buried.[24]

Peter Hart has shown that inside information given by IRA men themselves was one of the most important sources for the British, yet these are the only recorded examples of city-based IRA men getting shot for such betrayals. Florrie O'Donoghue claimed that Connors was the only known traitor within the ranks of the Cork city IRA, though clearly there were others. Pat Margetts, a soldier in Victoria Barracks who acted as a spy for the IRA, claimed he often warned Seán O'Hegarty that there were informers within his ranks. O'Hegarty did not heed the warnings, nor did he appear to want to, being deeply suspicious of Margetts because he was a soldier.[25] O'Hegarty and O'Donoghue appear to have been blind to the possibility that IRA men could have been talking to the other side. This seems extraordinary in view of the numbers of spies the IRA itself ran both in the military and the RIC. The finger of blame appears to have been always pointed outwards. Yet those who died at Broad Lane, Clogheen, Nadd and Mourneabbey were all betrayed by inside informers. There is certainly a case to be made that the IRA ignored leakages from within its own ranks in favour of suspicion of other groups such as ex-soldiers, though at least some of the ex-soldiers shot were probably acting as spies of one kind or another.

Another group of IRA targets were what could be described as old enemies of that organisation. There had long been rivalry between the Volunteers and gangs of unemployed ex-servicemen in Cork city, which often spilled over into brawling and street fighting.[26] While this can be put down to the inevitable clash between 'British' Ireland and republican Ireland, it was also fuelled by unemployment and resentment on both sides. Some ex-servicemen may have taken to spying for the military and the RIC to get their own back on the Volunteers, or they may simply have been convenient enemies.

A good example of this was the case of Michael Walsh. Walsh, aged 43, was an ex-soldier from Blarney Street who had fought in the Boer War.[27] Known as 'Mickeroo', he had been a foreman in Ford's motor works where many IRA men were employed, but he had to leave his job owing to IRA intimidation. Walsh was caught in August 1920 in Cork Union Workhouse, where O'Hegarty had worked as a store manager. He was in the company of a Mrs Marshall, 'a woman of easy virtue' who was passing on information to the military. Both were sentenced to death but were rescued during an army raid. Walsh fled to England but foolishly returned at the end of 1920.[28]

Frank O'Connor's short story 'Jumbo's Wife' is said to be based on that of Walsh. The essence of the story is that Jumbo's wife, who cannot read or write, asks an IRA man to decipher a letter her husband received in the post. The letter is a money order for payment by the military authorities for Jumbo's spying activities. While one should be wary of using fiction as a reference, this story is quite well known on Cork's north side and has also been verified by other sources.[29] Certainly the intelligence officers of the city brigade were constantly on the look-out for Walsh, with the intention of shooting him. It was alleged that he had a habit of checking pubs on the north side for known IRA activists and alerting the military.

In January 1921 he was lucky to escape with his life when an IRA hit squad fired 14 bullets into his house. On 14 February he was in hospital in the Cork Workhouse suffering from dropsy when he was dragged out of bed in his pyjamas and slippers by a group of senior IRA figures, including Tom Crofts, Mick Murphy and members of the ASU who shot him dead on the side of the road. The plaque tied to his pyjamas read: 'Caught at last. Spies and Informers Beware. IRA.' He had told a friend he had had a presentment he would not come out of the workhouse alive.[30]

Was Walsh guilty of spying? His sister at the inquiry into his killing stated: 'Some time ago the deceased was arrested after curfew by the military and taken to the Bridewell. In his pocket were found three Sinn Féin summonses.' Arresting informers, especially after curfew, was a standard procedure used by military intelligence to get to talk to their men.[31] The fact that Walsh was arrested in this manner is itself suggestive that he may have been an informer. But the case is by no means proven.

Another old enemy of the IRA was William Mohally. Mohally had been a recruiting sergeant during the Great War and had long been known to hold anti-Sinn Féin views. He was employed as a night watchman at a premises in King Street (now MacCurtain Street). When on 20 February an attempt to shoot him on the Lower Road failed, he too was followed into hospital, this time the South Infirmary. With the help of friendly staff, the ward was sealed off and the unconscious Mohally placed on a stretcher and carried outside the hospital gate. 'One of them bent down over him, placed a revolver in his mouth and fired. An interval of a second or two elapsed before any remark was made. Then one of the assailants said, "Give him another", then they walked away and Mohally was dead.'[32] In reply to a House of Commons question, Chief Secretary for Ireland Sir Hamar Greenwood stated: 'There appears to be no doubt that he [Mohally] was cruelly done to death because of his friendly association with the police and military authorities.'[33]

The IRA is reckoned to have killed 82 ex-soldiers prior to the Truce,[34] 28 in Cork city alone and at least another dozen afterwards. Some of these were spies; many were probably not. All were regarded by the IRA as ruffians. Later they were afforded the opportunity to get their own revenge when they joined the new Free State Army in huge numbers. By then it was a case of the empire striking back.

PART III

Chapter 14

THE MYTH OF THE
ANTI-SINN FÉIN LEAGUE

The killing of loyalists by the Cork IRA between 1920 and 1923 is one of the most contentious issues of the period. Only in recent years has it been debated to any significant extent in Ireland and it is still a very divisive subject. Broadly speaking, it can be divided into two parts: the killing of loyalists in Cork city and west Cork during the War of Independence and the killing of Protestants in west Cork in 1922 and during the Civil War.

During the Anglo-Irish conflict a small number of Protestants were executed because they were believed, either rightly or wrongly, to have given information, while others were taken as hostages, particularly in west Cork in the months immediately preceding the Truce.[1] However, the most notorious massacre occurred after the Anglo-Irish war was over. This was the murder of 14 Protestants, mostly in the Dunmanway area. A common misconception of the west Cork killings is that these occurred during the Civil War. In fact, they were carried out in April 1922, some two months before the Civil War began. So these were murders carried out in peacetime, not just after the Truce but after the Treaty as well. In that narrow academic sense they were not part of either conflict. In the broader sense, however, they were.

We need to look briefly at the Bandon massacre, as it is sometimes called, in order to give a context to the earlier killings of Protestants, which will be the subject of much of the rest of this book. And also because the killings of 1922 had their origin in the period we are looking at here, the first few months of 1921. On the night of 26 April 1922, a member of an IRA group raiding a house belonging to a Protestant family called Hornibrook, who lived in Ballygroman, Kilumney, outside Cork, was shot dead by a member of the household, an ex-British Army officer, Captain Herbert Woods.[2] The Hornibrooks were loyalists. The next day Thomas Hornibrook, his son Sam and Herbert Woods were taken and executed. Their bodies were never recovered. Over the next few nights some 11 other Protestants of all ages and various occupations, mostly in the Enniskeane, Ballineen and Dunmanway areas, were dragged from their beds and murdered. The Protestant population of west Cork, convinced that a major pogrom was on the way, fled the area in large numbers. Were it not for the immediate intervention of Seán Buckley, the local IRA intelligence officer who stepped in to prevent further bloodshed, the massacre might have been greater still, something that earned him the gratitude and support of many west Cork Protestants when he later stood for the Dáil. The killings, now usually described as having not been officially sanctioned by the IRA but rather the actions of maverick elements within the republican movement, were condemned locally and nationally afterwards by both sides of the Treaty divide.[3] Though the killings did not continue beyond the week in question, no censure was taken against the perpetrators.[4]

The net result was widespread terror on the part of west Cork Protestants, trainloads of refugees passing through Cork city and 'for two weeks there wasn't standing room on any of the boats or mail trains leaving Cork for England'.[5] The massacre received extensive coverage in the British press.[6] British officials expressed grave concern and destroyers were sent to patrol the coast of west Cork to provide what assistance they could.

The reason we are interested in it in the context of this book is that it illustrates something at the very heart of this and indeed similar conflicts. This is the concept of cycles of escalating terror born out of mutual revenge. This series of actions probably had its origin over a year earlier, in January 1921. On the 22nd of that month what appeared to be a platoon of British soldiers made a visit to the farm of Tom Bradfield outside Enniskeane in the Bandon valley.[7] Bradfield, a Methodist who was in the middle of his day's work, asked them inside and they were given tea with the family. So satisfied were the Bradfields that they were dealing with soldiers that Tom Bradfield said that if he had information of an intended ambush, he would pass it on. The 'British soldiers' were in fact a group of IRA men in disguise, led by Tom Barry, who could affect a very passable English accent.[8] That night they returned and shot Bradfield in the back of the head in an execution-style killing, leaving a placard around his neck stating he was killed 'for intending to inform on the movement of Republican troops'. Two branches of the extended Bradfield family were again targeted in the massacre of 1922 and a cousin, John Bradfield,[9] was shot dead.

A few days after the killing of Tom Bradfield, a local farmer, Dan Leary, was caught and nearly flogged to death by masked and armed men,[10] almost certainly either RIC men in disguise[11] or British intelligence men in mufti. Ironically, when they were finished with him, they brought him home. A week later two brothers called Coffey, aged 19 and 22, who were neighbours of Bradfield and members of the local IRA, were shot dead near to where Bradfield had been killed. Their killers appeared to have been civilians since they too were dressed as farmers.[12] Again the killers were members of undercover British forces.

This story illustrates a phenomenon that was typical of the conflict and was replicated many times throughout Cork during the period: the cycle of revenge killings. Typically a civilian or combatant on one side is killed by the other, who then sets out to revenge the first killing by either seeking informers as scapegoats or, in the case of many British killings, simply shooting dead some unfortunate who happened to be in the wrong place at the wrong time. The killing of Tom Bradfield almost certainly led to the torture of Dan Leary and the shooting of the Coffeys. It also probably set in train, if not the exact sequence of events that led to the Bandon massacre over a year later, at least the atmosphere in which it was carried out.

A related example of this—and one that is of particular relevance to our narrative—is the complex series of events that led to the execution of three junior British officers taken off a train in Waterfall in November 1920. This can be traced back to the previous summer in west Cork when, acting on information gathered by the RIC, Tom Hales and Pat Harte, commanding officer and quartermaster of the 3rd Brigade IRA, were captured by the Essex Regiment.[13] They were savagely tortured by British Army intelligence officers both in Bandon Barracks and later in Cork, having their nails pulled out with pliers and their teeth broken. Harte had a nervous breakdown as a result and died some years later in an asylum. In his report on his 'interrogation', which found its way to Collins[14] and was published in *The Irish Bulletin*[15] (this was something of a propaganda coup for Sinn Féin, as well as being a significant public embarrassment for the military. The army and the RIC were furious at the leak).[16] Hales mentions a Lieut Green as one of his tormentors along with the notorious Captain Kelly and Lieuts Koe and Richardson, all members of the intelligence department attached to the 6th Division in Cork. These four were placed right at the top of the IRA's most wanted list.

Richardson, a flight lieutenant in the RAF who was carrying out intelligence work for the army, was subsequently shot by the west Cork IRA in Newcestown on 9 October 1920.[17] A month later, in November 1920, Con Conroy, an IRA spy who worked in Victoria Barracks, learned that a Lieut Green was leaving Cork Barracks for Bere Island; the word was passed out to Bob Lankford, who passed it on to Brigade HQ.[18] Lieut N. H. W. Green, along with his fellow Education Corps officers, Lieut Chambers and Lieut Watts of the Royal Engineers, were taken off a train in Waterfall by a number of the city men and shot and their bodies buried. None of the three appears to have been an intelligence officer. The two Education Corps officers were on their way to inspect army schools in west Cork, while Watts had been in Cork only for a short time and had been employed as an electrician in the army.[19] All were in mufti. Green was armed; the others were not. The British Army, at a loss to explain why the three men had been singled out while at least two other officers on the train were ignored, suggested that Chambers might have been targeted because he had been at the scene of the arrest of a Fr O'Donnell in

Killarney in 1919, while both Green and Chambers had witnessed the shooting of two RIC men at Ballybrack in County Kerry. No explanation could be found for the shooting of Watts.[20]

Either way, the IRA appear to have got the wrong Green. A Lieut Good, who was travelling with Chambers and Green on the day of their abduction, stated at the inquest: 'As a friend of Capt [sic] Green, I know that he had nothing to do with the arrest of Tom Hales. He had taken no part in the round-up of Sinn Féiners.'[21] Good's concern with the capture of Tom Hales is understandable, since the *Irish Bulletin* article had been published a month earlier and publicly named the officers involved in the Hales episode. However, the explanations put forward by the military as possible reasons for the execution of the three men are speculative. It is far more likely that the IRA assumed that Lieut N. H. W. Green (who was acting captain by this time) was the man they were looking for in connection with the Hales case. Letters between Michael Collins and Florrie O'Donoghue suggest a long-term obsession with getting revenge on Hales's torturers. That N. H. W. Green may not have been the intelligence officer Green has never been admitted by the IRA or indeed accepted since.

British attention then fell on a local IRA man, Walter Leo Murphy, who was blamed for the killings. In June 1921 Murphy was finally tracked down by members of the Manchester Regiment who, at the end of June, after picking up 'four officers in Cork', shot him dead as he emerged from Donovan's pub in Waterfall. The 'four officers' were intelligence men, probably policemen brought along to identify Murphy. Also captured was Charlie Daly, a senior officer in the 2nd Battalion of the city IRA. The next day he was handed over to members of the Hampshire Regiment, one of whose officers he had shot. They too got their revenge. 'Daly attempted to escape from his escort proceeding from Victoria Barracks to Cork Gaol and was shot dead.'[22]

But the violence did not end there. Less than a week after Murphy and Daly were killed, on 4 July the IRA surrounded a group of drummer boys, members of the Manchester Regiment who were playing football at the army soccer pitch at nearby Ballincollig Barracks. They abducted three boys, Matthew Carson, John Cooper and Arthur Chapman, who were aged 18, 16 and 17, and shot them in a lane near Ovens and buried the bodies under a hedge. It was, in the public eye at least, a new low in the history of the conflict, and fed into British anti-IRA propaganda.[23]

This is a classic example of the kind of cycle of escalating violence that went on, with both sides acting out of revenge on the basis of dubious information. As regards the killing of the three officers, the evidence is that it was carried out by members of the city battalions. Murphy may have been involved or he may not.[24] What is important is that because he was a local, his was the name the British had, just as Green was one of the names the IRA had. You were shot because the other side had your name, whether you were guilty or not. The three drummer boys were simply soft targets.

Back in west Cork the killing of Tom Bradfield and its aftermath led to something else: the IRA, knowing that Leary and the Coffeys had been assaulted by what appeared to be farmers, were convinced they had been attacked by a vigilante band of local loyalists out to exact revenge for Bradfield's killing. The Coffeys' killers were in all probability acting out of revenge for Bradfield's murder, but they were not a vigilante band of loyalists. The Coffey brothers were killed by a group of undercover RIC men and army officers disguised as farmers, who dressed in civvies and operated out of Bandon RIC Barracks.[25]

The important point is that the killings were *believed* to have been carried out by local Protestants and so the Protestants of west Cork came to take the blame. These loyalists were said to belong to some kind of Protestant Action Group,[26] also known as the Anti-Sinn Féin Society or League and the Loyalist Action Group. This shadowy organisation was said to be affiliated to the County Anti-Sinn Féin Society, the Unionist Anti-Partition League and to the Grand Orange Lodge of Ireland.[27] Though some west Cork loyalist farmers did pass on information on the IRA and suffered the consequences, there is no evidence for the existence of these leagues. But it is what is believed in such situations that is important. When, the following year, the 14 Protestants were murdered, they too were deemed to have been members of this Anti-Sinn Féin Society or League.

As a result, the myth of the Anti-Sinn Féin League grew up over the years in the writings both of IRA men themselves and some historians. We have already seen it in the context of the city in this book. It went under the various names listed above: the Loyalist Action Group, the Protestant Action Group, the County Anti-Sinn Féin Society, the Unionist Anti-Partition League, all names suggesting a county-wide, if not a country-wide, counter-revolutionary conspiracy organised by southern loyalists to combat Sinn Féin. According to this conspiracy theory, it was deemed to have its roots in Freemasonry.

Yet not a single one of 700 or so Cork Protestant applicants to the Irish Grants Commission[28] admitted to being a member of any such organisation or even mentioned it, even though it would have significantly helped their case for compensation. Many of these applicants, having been driven from Ireland as a result of the revolution and in a small number of cases for having helped the British forces against the IRA, were by then living in England and so would have no reason not to claim such a membership. A number of them, some 15 Protestants from Cork as a whole, who freely admitted having given information to British forces for a variety of reasons, never claimed membership of any sort of Anti-Sinn Féin League or its equivalent.[29]

A typical supposed member of this version of the Anti-Sinn Féin League was Sir Henry Forde, a large landowner near Bandon. Forde's case is worth looking at in some detail because it is one of the few instances where both sides of the story can be seen. Forde, who was expelled from Ireland, wanted to return a year later to visit his sister who was ill and he contacted Arthur Griffith on the matter.

There is no question that Forde was a loyalist; indeed he had been a member of the Orange Lodge of Bandon in the early years of the century. Forde's problems began in the spring of 1921. 'In March 1921 Comdt Barry gave me orders to draw up a form ordering Henry Forde to clear out of the country within 36 hours. Forde was suspected to be a very dangerous man, very often in link with the RIC. He was also a member of the Orange Hall in Bandon.'[30] Forde is described as 'very Loyal. It is believed he was a member of the Anti-Sinn Féin gang, which is undoubtedly an offshoot of the Orange Society of which he is a member. I think he is better out of the country for the country's good.'[31]

Forde himself paints a very different picture. After explaining how he had been driven out, he goes on to say: 'I never interfered with the movements of Sinn Féiners [though] my principals were Loyal. About March 30, 1921 I got a notice through the post, signed IRA, ordering me out of the country within 36 hours and failing to comply I would be shot at sight. It seemed to be like a joke.' Forde consulted Denis Buckley, a local builder and brother of Seán Buckley, who advised him to go while at the same time saying 'he would do what he could for me on the matter. I left on the same day and am out of home since.' On the matter of passing on information on IRA activities, Forde states: 'I candidly say I am not guilty of what I am accused of. I have always been on the best of terms with my Roman Catholic friends.'[32] He goes on to say that he wished to return to Bandon to visit his sister who was ill. In the spring of 1922 it was certainly not safe for known loyalists and alleged 'spies' to return to Bandon and he did not do so. His farm was then distributed among its former tenants and is one of 11 'spy farms' in west Cork dealt with by the Provisional government in the post-conflict period.[33]

Was Forde a 'spy' and a member of the so-called Anti-Sinn Féin League? Unlikely, yet the term persisted as evidence that there were hundreds of loyalist bogeymen who were only too ready to betray the republic and that they had formed themselves into a counter-revolutionary organisation. This might be regarded as some kind of sectarian hysteria brought about by paranoia and the deprivation suffered by men 'on the run', were it not for a number of other events that took place in the area during the conflict. For there were other things that happened in the Dunmanway area in late 1920 and early 1921 that poisoned the atmosphere for Protestants. These were also of a sectarian nature.

On 15 December 1920, a few days after the burning of Cork city, the Auxiliary unit responsible for the arson attack, K Company of the ADRIC, was expelled from Cork city by General Strickland, Commander of the British

Army in the south. They then found themselves in barracks in the draughty, damp and deserted workhouse in Dunmanway. κ Coy, selected from other Auxiliary units for its particular brand of ruthlessness, contained a significant number of Belfast Orangemen among its ranks and was of its nature sectarian.[34] On the night of the burning of Cork, a Roman Catholic priest in Patrick Street was lucky to escape with his life when forced to his knees with an Auxiliary revolver to his head. In Dunmanway a few days later, the parish priest, Canon Magnier, was not so lucky. Stopped by a patrol of κ Coy, in the company of an IRA Volunteer Tadhg Crowley, who was also murdered, he was shot through the head and his body flung into a ditch. A 'column of Black Irish from Ulster', as one British Army officer put it, pulled down the Maid of Erin statue in Bandon and burnt down the hotel in which they had stayed.[35] On 24 January undercover Auxiliaries with northern accents broke into the De La Salle community in Dunmanway and shot and wounded a Brother of the order.[36] A young Auxiliary, known only as 'Charlie', writing to his mother, described the behaviour of κ Coy in Cork and Dunmanway:

> In all my life and in all the tales of fiction I have read I have never experienced such orgies of murder, arson and looting as I have witnessed during the past 16 days with the RIC Auxiliaries. It baffles description and we are supposed to be officers and gentlemen. There are quite a number of decent fellows and likewise a lot of ruffians.
>
> On our arrival here from Cork one of our heroes held up a car with a priest and a civilian in it and shot them both through the head without cause or provocation. We were very kindly received by the people but the consequences of this cold blooded murder is that no one will now come within a mile of us and all the shops are closed . . . the poor old priest was 65 and everybody's friend.[37]

The treatment meted out by κ Coy in the area was to be remembered for generations, though it pales into insignificance when compared to the almost entirely forgotten killings of April 1922. So perhaps the claim that the Anti-Sinn Féin League was in some way connected with the Grand Orange Lodge of Ireland did have at least some, admittedly skewed, basis in reality. The behaviour of κ Coy when billeted in Dunmanway was so outrageous that it was disbanded and replaced in the spring of 1921 by O Coy. It was then that the Protestants of the area made the mistake that would see the IRA turn on them with such vicious intent a year later.

Some recent accounts[38] of the killings have attempted to suggest that, in the case of the west Cork Protestants murdered in April 1922, they were all deemed to have been informers, the 'evidence' against them being a diary of an Auxiliary intelligence officer found in Dunmanway workhouse after O Coy departed in February 1922.[39] The diary does contain the names of four informers: a Protestant, a Catholic and two IRA men. The main problem with this argument is that none of those listed as informers in the diary was ever targeted. Also the information in it was largely out of date by 1921 and reflects what was known by the RIC before the arrival of the Auxiliaries in December 1920. To take one example: while there is significant local knowledge in the details contained in the diary—of the kind that could have been obtained from the informers listed—there is no mention of anybody called Tom Barry as a member of the IRA, let alone as leader of the west Cork column. Many other senior figures of the west Cork IRA are also notable by their absence. The rationale is that those killed in 1922 were listed in the diary as 'helpful citizens'. Yet surely if the diary was the reason these people were killed, it would have made more sense to kill those actually listed as 'informants'. Furthermore, the so-called list of helpful citizens, if it exists, has never been placed in the public domain.[40]

According to this self-serving thesis, the Protestants of Ballineen and Enniskeane were supposed to have organised a Loyalist Civil Wing in a rally held in Murragh churchyard near Enniskeane 'on a dark night during curfew'.[41] Something like this probably did happen as a result of motions introduced as part of Martial Law around Christmas 1920[42] for the recruitment of 'Civil Guards' to patrol known 'hotspots'. It may even have been led by Rev. Ralph Harbord, the so-called 'principal victim' of the pogrom, though it is far more likely to have been led by Auxiliaries resident in the area. (There is no evidence to implicate Harbord in this, other than the fact that he was subsequently shot.)[43]

The British government, upon the implementation of Martial Law, proposed in late 1920 to set up vigilante groups to patrol towns and villages during curfew hours. Attempts were made in several places to put such structures into operation. These were to include loyalists[44] and, when loyalists were reluctant to take part out of fear, any other available male members of the population as could be conscripted were forced on patrol. 'Young men, four at the time, [were cashiered] to cover a 24 hour period and give notice of any outrage.'[45] The Dunmanway Auxiliaries were particularly assiduous at implementing these proposals and there are a number of reports of their operation in the Bandon valley, in which it has to be said IRA men themselves were happy enough to participate since it meant they were effectively above suspicion.[46] However, they were not so happy when Protestants took part: 'J. Kingston, Drimoleague, head of the Civil Guard appointed by o/c troops received a threatening letter stating death if he does not cease patrolling.'[47]

What the Bandon valley Protestants (and some Catholics) were really 'guilty' of was of having friendly relations with the later detachment of Auxiliaries. For when the notorious K Company was replaced by O Company under Colonel de Haviland in March 1921, the latter went to considerable lengths to improve relations with the locals over the next year. De Haviland's wife held soirées to which the local better-off wives were invited.[48] It was not without reason that the women of west Cork were said to have learned about rouge and lipstick from the wives of Black and Tans. 'Seventy years later that was still remembered. Grandma said that the Black and Tan womenfolk had introduced west Cork to rouge, powder, lipstick and bobbed hair. ("Don't go looking like a Black and Tan's wife" the nuns would say to girls who wore make-up.)'[49] But loyalists were never forgiven for this fraternising, though revenge was meted out only to Protestants, not Catholics.[50]

The result of the civil guard proposal and of General Strickland's very public espousal of these 'Vigilance Committees' in an interview carried in several newspapers in January 1921 was to greatly increase the level of suspicion against Protestants in republican minds.[51] The use of the term Anti-Sinn Féin League and other similar terms to denote a supposed loyalist counter-revolutionary movement has its origin in this period. However, the term itself originated earlier and from a somewhat different, though not entirely unexpected, source.

Chapter 15 ∼

THE REAL ANTI-SINN FÉIN LEAGUE

If any members of His Majesty's Forces or any loyalists in your district are interfered with or harmed in any manner, you in addition to other members of your tribe will pay as severe a penalty as the Anti-Sinn Féin League may authorize. Take this as a formal warning, if you value your life. Your movements will be and are closely watched. The Iron Hand of the Anti-Sinn Féin League can be very destructive and never fails its duty.
THE HEADQUARTERS OF THE ANTI-SINN FÉIN LEAGUE, DUBLIN[1]

The term 'Anti-Sinn Féin League' (or Society) is mentioned several times in the actual historical record and most references to it occur around the same time and probably have the same origin. Many of them refer to Cork, in particular Cork city, and the time is the last three months of 1920. The RIC County Inspector's Report of November 1920 refers to the violence in the city coming from three sources:[2] 'Crimes', according to the report 'are attributable to Sinn Féin, which comprises the IRB and the IRA, and the Anti-Sinn Féin Society. . . . During the last month there is such a feeling of revulsion and abhorrence at the atrocities committed by Sinn Féin that a new organisation known as the Anti-Sinn Féin League has sprung into existence. This organisation is also secret and its personnel are unknown to the police.'

So far so good, but the CI gives the game away with his next sentence. 'It is believed that many of the recent burnings in Cork are attributable to it.' Now anybody with even the slightest knowledge of the arson campaigns waged in Cork in the final months of 1920 knows that it was the Black and Tans/Auxiliaries who carried out most, if not all, of them. The other source often quoted by historians is a mention of the Anti-Sinn Féin League in the diaries of Mark Sturges. Sturges, the assistant Under-Secretary of the Dublin Castle administration, kept a diary for the entire period, a droll and somewhat cynical account of the operation of Dublin Castle, which has recently been published.[3] On 14 December 1920, a few days after the burning of Cork city,

Sturges wrote: 'Later we saw Major Holmes, D.C. Cork, who says that the Saturday fires were almost certainly started not by any organised body but by single individuals who got together casually, as it were, for mischief; an odd subaltern perhaps, a policeman, an odd Auxiliary, doubtless some civilians and, after the start, many real hooligans out for loot. The Anti-Sinn Féin League he told me, does exist and is not a myth to cover The Armed Forces of the Crown.'

It is of course possible, as some have done, to take that statement at face value. However, in the context of the time it was written, Peter Hart's assertion that Holmes was just trying to excuse his own men from culpability for the burning of Cork is almost certainly correct, just as the county inspector of the RIC had been trying to do something similar a month earlier.[4] Cork was burned by 'The Armed forces of the Crown', more specifically by K Company of the ADRIC, incensed after the ambush at Dillon's Cross. Furthermore, all the evidence suggests that the Anti-Sinn Féin League, in its Cork city manifestation, was used as a cover for the excesses of the Black and Tans and Auxiliaries themselves. But it was also used as a term for undercover British forces, the so-called 'murder gang' who pulled out and shot individuals suspected of IRA activities and also innocent civilians throughout the period.[5]

The most detailed recent work that deals specifically with the executions carried out by the Cork No. 1 Brigade in Cork city is *Informers, Intelligence and the Anti-Sinn Féin Society, The Anglo-Irish Conflict in Cork City 1920–1921* by John Miller Borgonovo.[6] This is a well-researched and comprehensive study of many of the killings of various alleged informers carried out in the city during the War of Independence. Borgonovo claims that the evidence suggests there may have been a counter-revolutionary organisation of Protestant loyalists operating in Cork city. This subject needs to be looked at in some detail because it lies at the core of much of the rest of this book.

The core of Borgonovo's thesis is that there existed in Cork city an organisation of Protestant businessmen set up as a counter-terror group to report on IRA activity. This, he suggests, may have been called the Anti-Sinn Féin League, and in a situation similar to that pertaining in west Cork, where initiatives emanating from the British military side were conflated into a conspiracy supposedly concocted by Irish Protestant loyalists, creates a unified theory to explain why Protestants were killed in the city during the conflict.[7] The theory holds that the half-dozen or so Protestants killed in Cork city were all members of such a group and that the unfortunate George Tilson was also one.

This may of course have been the case. The accounts left by many IRA men, if taken at face value, support such a thesis. 'So and so was killed because he was a member of the Anti-Sinn Féin League', or variations thereof, is a catch cry that is repeated many times by survivors in the Bureau of Military History witness statements. But does it stand up to close scrutiny? Well, Florrie

O'Donoghue, who knew most about the period and had insights that the majority of his men did not share, never mentions an Anti-Sinn Féin League. He does, however, state that some loyalists in Cork city were helping British Intelligence:

> It is true of course, that in Cork as elsewhere, there was a considerable Unionist minority and a considerable 'garrison clique' which through sentiment and self-interest was loyal to the Crown. Some members of this section of the community carried their loyalty to the point of forming a civilian branch of British Intelligence, but they were so out of touch with the popular movement that their value to the enemy was slight. Those who showed signs of becoming dangerous were quickly eliminated.[8]

This, on the face of it, reads more or less the same as the Anti-Sinn Féin League scenario. However, as we'll see, a different and more convincing interpretation can be made from these lines.

Broadly speaking, John Borgonovo's thesis is that there was a Protestant civilian spy ring, going back to the Admiralty in Queenstown during World War I, which gathered information for the British government. This then re-emerged in the latter part of 1920 in the form of threatening letters to the press and posters pasted up around Cork purporting to come from the ASFL. Then in November 1920 and February 1921 the IRA 'struck back', killing four prominent Cork Protestants and driving a fifth, George Tilson, to suicide. For good measure another was killed on the eve of the Truce and several Protestant businessmen were forced out of Cork in the spring of 1921. This, so the theory goes, finished off the ASFL for good.

What are we to make of this perfectly plausible theory? It more or less agrees with many of the statements left by surviving IRA men, which cannot be discounted just because they all come from the same side. On the other hand, apart from the CI's report and the Mark Sturges comment above, there is no evidence either in British intelligence reports or from the claims of the Irish Grants Committee applicants that such a civilian organisation ever existed. Surely if there was such a grouping it would have deserved mention in the intelligence report of the Record of the Rebellion in Ireland, and if not in that, then in Winter's report as head of intelligence at Dublin Castle.[9] Yet neither mentions it, claiming on the other hand that, with the exception of a number of west Cork farmers, the Protestant community was virtually worthless as a source of information. 'A few but not many, were brave enough to assist Crown Forces with information.'[10] Then there is the situation where nearly 4,000 loyalists could have applied for compensation for their sufferings at the hands of republicans, yet did not mention it either.

How are we to reconcile a situation where several Cork city IRA men claim they shot Protestants because they belonged to an Anti-Sinn Féin League, when there is no suggestion from the Protestant community that such an organisation ever existed? The evidence has to be dissected and studied in detail and done on a case-by-case basis.

Take, for instance, the Admiralty intelligence operation apparently carried out from Queenstown. The intelligence-gathering operation at the Admiralty is relatively well known; it was run in Ireland by W. V. Harrel, a former assistant commissioner of the DMP. This bypassed the admiral commanding at Queenstown and reported through the governor of the Bank of Ireland to Captain Reginald 'Blinker' Hall of the British Secret Service.[11] Hall, nicknamed because of his persistent habit of blinking, was obsessed by the threat of a German invasion. This surveillance system did exist, but during World War I, not during the War of Independence. After the 'German plot' of 1918, Hall was disgraced and his views never taken seriously after that. None of the individuals mentioned as Hall's agents was ever subsequently targeted by the IRA.[12]

Moreover, intelligence-gathering by the Admiralty has one other basis in reality. It was standard practice for the Royal Navy to gather shipping intelligence to keep track of what was coming and going from the ports, as well as carrying out regular coastal-watching duties. The Admiralty in Queenstown would always have been engaged in this activity and was probably keeping an eye out for 'sedition' in the process, in other words, routine military and naval intelligence. But this is a far cry from a Protestant Anti-Sinn Féin League fighting back against the IRA.

The next plank of the theory does, however, have the ASFL fighting back against the IRA. This comprises a series of letters to the press and threats posted up around Cork in 1920. The first such reference occurred in April, shortly after the murder of Tomás MacCurtain.

> The theory is gradually gaining ground . . . that Mr MacCurtain, the Lord Mayor, fell victim to a new secret Anti Sinn Féin Society, modeled and run upon the exact lines of the famous Ku-Klux-Klan. . . . In the opinion of men best fitted to judge, the murder of MacCurtain may be followed by a sort of ugly triangular duel between the forces of the Crown, Sinn Féin and private bands of avengers.[13]

This, of course, was prophetic, though not quite in the way intended by the writer. Was MacCurtain shot by a 'private band of avengers'? All the evidence suggests that he was shot by the RIC. In July a schoolteacher in Timoleague called Murphy was dragged from his home, interrogated, beaten and threatened by a group of disguised men who claimed they were members of the 'Anti-Sinn Féin organisation'.[14] This is eerily similar to the treatment meted out not too far away to Dan Leary some six months later and was almost certainly carried out by undercover security operatives.

Notices purporting to come from Anti-Sinn Féin societies appeared in areas as far apart as Tipperary, Kerry,[15] Antrim[16] and Wexford,[17] invariably in connection with 'the murder or injury' to any local member of the Royal Irish Constabulary or Auxiliary forces.[18] 'We have declared war. The military has been too lenient. This is our fourth day in Ireland, so get ready. Which is it? We work mysteriously but deliberately.'[19] Many of these Anti-Sinn Féin statements originated in the *Weekly Summary*, the newspaper of the RIC. One can draw one's own conclusions.

Cork, moreover, was to get the brunt of the attention of this 'league':

At a specially convened meeting of the All-Ireland Anti-Sinn Féin Society held in Cork in 11th day of October 1920, we, the supreme Council of the Cork circle, have reluctantly decided that, if in future any member of His Majesty's Forces be murdered, two members of the Sinn Féin Party in the county of Cork will be killed. This will apply equally to laity and clergymen of all denominations. In the event of a member of His Majesty's forces being wounded, or an attempt made to wound him, one member of the Sinn Féin Party will be killed, or if a member of the Sinn Féin Party is not available, two sympathizers will be killed.[20]

Given what we have already seen about the behaviour of K Coy of the Auxiliaries who began to arrive in Cork around this time, this statement should come as no surprise to us. Similar notices signed by the Anti-Sinn Féin Society appeared four weeks later when the IRA kidnapped and executed the three British officers at Waterfall.[21]

If it is true that these are in fact documents originating from a loyalist civilian organisation, then the IRA would have been quite right in its assessment of the situation and the killing of members of this organisation would be a logical extension of this. Let's look at the language of the notice posted in the Cork newspapers of 13 October 1920. Would a Protestant civilian organisation loyal to the Crown and set up to fight the IRA advocate the killing of laity and clergymen of all denominations? Would it advocate tit-for-tat killings in the event of policemen or British soldiers being attacked? Considering that what middle-class Protestants, as well as Catholics, wanted more than anything else was peace and stability and an end to the fighting, then this looks like a dubious way of achieving it.

On the other hand, the language is precisely the same as that used by the Auxiliaries and the Black and Tans in their threats of retaliation and reprisal which appeared almost daily in the newspapers in the last months of 1920. The obsession is with 'members of His Majesty's forces' and with reprisals in the event of one of their members being killed or wounded. This document almost certainly originated from a British source with its ignorance of the situation in Ireland, as demonstrated by the naming of the 'Sinn Féin Party' as the enemy.

Most people living in Ireland in late 1920, loyalists included, would have been able to distinguish between the 'Sinn Féin Party' and the IRA. In most documents that I have read that had been written by Irish Protestants, the IRA is usually referred to as such, and Sinn Féin as 'Mr de Valera's party'. People outside of Ulster could distinguish between the politics of Sinn Féin and the methods of the IRA. Cork city had seen three Sinn Féin lord mayors in a row. They were well regarded by both Protestants and Catholics. This document could not have been written by native Corkmen of any denomination. The statement 'this is our fourth day in Ireland' says it all.

Furthermore, it is implicit in the letters and notices that this All Ireland Anti-Sinn Féin Society would implement its own threats of reprisal. There was no group of Protestants, outside of the UDA in Ulster, with the wherewithal to even contemplate such a course of action. There has never been any suggestion of the existence of a branch of the UDA in Cork operating under any name. Undercover army and RIC death squads, on the other hand, were carrying out such reprisals almost on a daily basis.

The document is also interesting from another point of view. The use of the term 'supreme Council of the Cork circle' is the language of secret societies. Seán O'Hegarty and Florrie O'Donoghue were the core members of the IRB in Cork. This Anti-Sinn Féin League was going to some pains to paint itself as the equivalent of the IRB, well known to the RIC as the most militant wing of the republican movement, though not so well known to the general public. It is also the language of Freemasonry. While O'Donoghue never makes a reference to the term Anti-Sinn Féin League in all his copious writings, he does refer to the existence of a 'Freemason Intelligence Organisation',[22] probably the 'branch of British Intelligence' referred to above. As we'll see, while this term has some basis in fact, it is not the same as the Anti-Sinn Féin League.

It is almost certain that these documents and statements originated from sections of the RIC or the Black and Tans/Auxiliaries or from undercover military hit squads. What is interesting to note is that, from mid-December 1920 when General Strickland expelled the Auxiliaries from Cork city as a result of the burning of the city centre, these notices and threats ceased to appear either in the streets or in the press in Cork.

Borgonovo makes much of General Strickland's inflated claims of getting help from the community to combat the IRA in his vigilante statement of January 1921. He is right in one thing: many in the Cork loyalist community, both working class and upper class, would probably like to have given information if they had it, and, as we'll see, a few did. But the vast majority were too terrified to do so. The feeling of Cork city loyalists towards the hamfisted handling of the 'Irish Question' in general and the attempts by General Strickland to recruit spies and curfew patrols from among their ranks can be seen from the account of Olga Pyne Clarke, whose own family were well-connected Cork Protestants.

> Shortly after this scandal [the burning of Cork city] . . . He [Strickland] stamped into my father's office and in his extremely rude, brusque manner said 'Look here, Clarke, you are trusted by both sides: it's your duty to give me information.' Father, looking him in the eye, calmly said 'I will not inform against my own countrymen: it is your duty to control the rabble your Government has let loose on Ireland. Good morning.' Going purple in the face, the General stormed out, crossed the Mall to Grandfather's office, and received the same reply.[23]

This view is also reflected in letters to the newspapers from loyalists in the weeks after Strickland's ill-conceived 'plan'. 'Sir . . . What exactly does the Military Governor suggest that Loyal citizens do? They cannot give information because they have none. They cannot fight either for or against the King for they have no arms.'[24] The letter goes on in a similar vein, saying effectively that the 'Republican Army' was running the country and that loyalists were in no position to do anything about it. Another letter to General Strickland from an anonymous loyalist also reveals the impracticality of Strickland's appeal and the fear under which loyalists lived. 'If a public meeting was called and denounced the murder of the police and military, why, sir, our lives would not be worth a week's purchase.'[25]

Strickland was to get his own back on Cork loyalists for their reluctance to supply him with information on IRA activities. In one of his press releases at the end of 1920, after finally conceding that the burning of Cork was carried out by 'two or three Black and Tans' with the help of 'the small ruffian element which any big city hides in its bosom', he repeats the claim: 'There is evidence too that an Anti-Sinn Féin society exists in Cork. It is composed of extreme loyalists . . . who have similar designs against the Sinn Féin gunmen of similar character to the designs of the Sinn Féin ambushers against the Black and Tans.'[26] There was an element of truth in this—these killers did exist—but they were a lot closer to Strickland than he was prepared to admit. To suggest that a whole section of Cork society was prepared to go out and shoot IRA men was disingenuous to say the least. But it set in train a series of events that were to have the direst consequences for Cork Protestants over the next three years.[27]

The other problem with the claim that Cork city Protestants were running some sort of Anti-Sinn Féin League is the lack of any reference to it in the British intelligence report cited earlier. As we have seen, the report states specifically that, with the exception of Ulster and some farmers in the Bandon valley, 'loyalists' were virtually worthless as sources of information. If Protestant farmers in the Bandon valley and along the border counties were cited as having given information, then why is there no mention of an organisation in Cork city doing the same?

The 'Anti-Sinn Féin League' as it was constituted in reality was a cover name for British undercover death squads, who carried out assassinations and arson attacks usually under the cover of darkness. DC Holmes knew well what he was talking about when he told Mark Sturges there were civilian killers on the loose. They were almost certainly operating with his blessing. It is difficult to ascertain whether these were army men or policemen or a combination of both, for they were technically civilians. They were the 'third force' unleashed on the country along with new divisions of the RIC. Their aim was to 'outmurder' Sinn Féin. As the army intelligence report put it, 'Probably the most effective organisation was one consisting of ex-officers who worked in plain clothes in the street.'[28] While some were English, many of these ex-officers were probably of Irish loyalist stock. As we'll see in Part VIII, along with the army and police killers these were the real Anti-Sinn Féin League.

If anybody has doubts as to who constituted the actual Anti-Sinn Féin League, they need look no further than the House of Commons debates that dealt with the issue. These make it clear that the Anti-Sinn Féin League was a cover name for British undercover agents of various types. 'This society boasts of being engaged in an active murder campaign . . . [are there] any relations between the Intelligence Service in Ireland and this society and whether any steps have been taken to suppress this organisation?' asked Lieut Commander Kenworthy in the House of Commons on 25 November 1920. The answer of course is that they were one and the same, though Dublin Castle and the military kept on denying it.[29]

John Borgonovo has an excellent chapter on the operation of these hit squads and has found evidence that, of the 19 IRA Volunteers killed by British forces in the city, ten of the killings involved military officers in disguise.[30] A significant number of innocent civilians were also killed by these undercover assassination squads. For instance, in a city hotel a barman called Michael Leahy, who just happened to share his name with the 4th Battalion IRA commander, was marched upstairs by a 'civilian' intruder one evening in June 1921. The intruder asked him his name. When he replied, the man calmly shot him through the head and strolled out the front door, instructing a passer-by as he did so to call an ambulance, because 'somebody had just been shot in the house'.[31] There were many instances of this kind of killing by disguised British forces in Cork city during late 1920 and early 1921.

The ruse of dressing up as civilians was also consistently used by regular army raiding parties. As early as the spring of 1920 a detachment of intelligence personnel raided a house in which Liam Lynch had stayed near Fermoy and burnt it down. They were dressed as civilians and clergymen.[32] A girl in County Clare had her head shorn by a group of 'civilians' calling themselves members of the Anti-Sinn Féin League in April 1921 in a direct imitation of IRA intimidation techniques. She said she was sure they were police.[33] Such squads operated with impunity, particularly in Dublin and Cork. The so-called Anti-Sinn Féin League appears to have been run along similar lines to the Cairo gang in Dublin: officers and ex-officers in mufti, perhaps attached to barracks, though more likely not.[34]

However, some loyalists did pass on information. Strickland may have been more successful in appealing to some loyal citizens. As O'Donoghue noted:

> With one exception, civilian spies constituted no real danger to the IRA but this exception nearly cost the Brigade dearly. He was a retired army officer and one day he sent a message by hand 'in clear' to Captain Kelly, giving accurate information of the movements of the Brigade staff officers to their billets outside the city. The message fell into the hands of the Brigade Intelligence organization and that night the writer of it was executed.[35]

Though he was not executed on the night the message was intercepted, this almost certainly refers to the killing of Major George O'Connor, a retired British Army officer who lived at Rochestown on the south side of the city, near where the brigade had one of its headquarters.

O'Connor was dragged out of bed and shot on the eve of the Truce in July 1921. However, this was not the first attempt on his life. The IRA had previously tried to kill him in early February, but instead it was his wife who was badly injured.[36] O'Connor, an elderly JP and noted antiquarian and historian who had fought in the Boer War, was a prominent member of the Southern Unionist Party and was described at the military inquiry into his death as 'definitely a loyalist'.[37] The retired British Army major was still active as a magistrate in court sittings in Douglas[38] in defiance of IRA threats. He was the principal signatory of the Dominion Home Rule document of August 1920.[39] He probably reverted to type when he recognised Seán O'Hegarty (whom he would have known from appearances before the Cork courts)[40] and other IRA men, including Florrie O'Donoghue, travelling along a road to their headquarters on the south side of the city in the winter of 1920.[41] The military mounted a trap for them on the following nights, but the IRA men had been warned.[42]

O'Donoghue claims that O'Connor was one of only two spies for whom documentary proof of their activities was available (his letter had been smuggled out from Victoria Barracks by Josephine Marchment Brown, copied and put back by the time the military authorities realised it).[43] O'Connor may well have been one of the main reasons for the vitriol with which O'Donoghue subsequently referred to the 'loyalist garrison' of Cork. For it is from this time onwards that O'Donoghue began to bombard GHQ with warnings of the dangers of 'loyalist' betrayal. 'Members of England's faithful garrison of civilians—by far more particularly dangerous—not merely hostile, they were anti-Irish and regarded themselves as honoured in any service they could do for England.'[44]

O'Hegarty and O'Donoghue were badly rattled by the discovery of the information O'Connor sent in. But for the letter being intercepted, the entire staff of the brigade would have been either killed or captured. It was to determine their attitude towards loyalists for the rest of the campaign and afterwards. The other way to look at it of course is that O'Connor was merely helping the British Army, which was, after all, his own army.

O'Connor's identity as the writer of the letter is reinforced by the manner in which he was eventually put to death. On the eve of the Truce, five months after his wife was shot, seven members of the 9th Battalion based at Passage West[45] arrived at his house in Hop Island, took him outside in his pyjamas and shot him dead at the side of the Rochestown Road.[46] Though many scores were settled in the last 24 hours before the Truce, O'Connor was the only one so publicly executed.

Chapter 16 ～

THE NOVEMBER ABDUCTIONS

From the list of killings in Table 3 it will be immediately apparent that a cluster of disappearances occurred in late November and early December 1920 when in the space of two weeks four men were abducted from Cork city, never to be seen again. This rate of killing was only surpassed in February 1921 when seven more were shot dead in the city. As we have seen in the case of Monkey Mac, there were also non-fatal shootings in February 1921. Almost all the Protestants killed in Cork city during the War of Independence were killed during these two periods.

The first abduction occurred on 24 November when an ex-soldier, Tom Downing, a leading figure in the Federation of Demobilised Sailors and Soldiers, was kidnapped on his way to a meeting of the federation. He too was never seen again, though Florrie O'Donoghue reported to the IRA's adjutant-general: 'This man was convicted and shot as a spy at Cork on 28 November 1920.'[1]

On 29 November, two Protestants, James Blemens and his son Frederick, were both abducted from their home on the Blackrock Road and 'taken to an unknown destination'. The affair 'caused quite a sensation', according to the *Cork Constitution*. In the *Cork Examiner*'s account:

Sometime after 7 o'clock on Monday evening Mr James Blemmens [*sic*] Instructor in Horticulture and Beekeeping under the Department of Agriculture and Technical Instruction for Ireland was removed from his home on Blackrock Road and taken to an unknown destination. It was stated that his son, Mr. Frederick Blemmins [*sic*] had been missing since some time in the afternoon. A number of armed men took part in the removal and a motor car was drawn up some distance from the house. In this the man was placed and removed under armed guard. No explanation for the occurrence was forthcoming. Mr Blemmins was popular with many citizens as well as residents in various parts of the county.[2]

'Mr Blemens was well known as an efficient and popular instructor and the affair has caused quite a sensation.'[3]

Neither James nor Fred Blemens was ever seen again, though Seán O'Hegarty reported a year later as part of an inquiry put in place by Richard Mulcahy: 'These men were both executed as spies after trial and conviction here at Cork . . . the date of execution was December 2.'[4]

On 9 December another ex-soldier, a 22-year-old working-class Protestant called George Horgan, was abducted from his home in High Street.[5] He was executed on the same day for 'espionage'[6] and his body buried at Lakelands, Blackrock, a farm described as a 'Sinn Féin Prison' by the RIC.[7] After the Civil War his remains are believed to have been returned to his family. Downing was shot and buried in Knockraha. The Blemenses may have been killed there too.

Interestingly, British reactions to the abductions varied. In the case of Downing and George Horgan, the Black and Tans went into threatening mode, putting up notices around the streets and in the newspapers, some of them purporting to come from the Anti-Sinn Féin League and threatening dire consequences if Downing and Horgan were not released, even forcing the *Examiner* staff to print one of the notices at the point of a gun.

As we have seen, the ex-servicemen's associations may have been used by British Intelligence as centres for gathering information.[8] Was the Cork ex-servicemen's club being similarly used? We have no evidence of it, though we have already seen the coded messages between Gormley and Rennie from the Dublin branch of the Soldiers and Sailors Club.[9]

Seán Healy of the city IRA, who spent part of the conflict in the east Cork area, left another version of Downing's capture:[10]

> One of these men [spies] was employed as a Post Office clerk where he was in a position to obtain important information for the enemy. Seán Culhane, J. J. O'Connell and I got instructions to put a stop to his activities. When he was picked up, walking along King Street one evening, we arrested him and conveyed him to 'an unknown destination' [in Knockraha] from which he never returned. Several others were dealt with similarly. Other spies were liquidated in the public streets.[11]

Sinn Féin TD Liam de Roiste had his own view as to why Downing was kidnapped: 'I do not know exactly who Mr. Downey [*sic*] is, but he is probably a man that common reports say is in some way attached to the detective force, and the presumption is that he has been captured by some of the Volunteers.'[12] It may well be his work that condemned Downing or that he was a police spy. For Downing was not a Post Office employee. Rather, he worked as a civilian telegraphonist in the Royal Engineers at Victoria Barracks.[13] Civilians employed with the RE were widely assumed by the IRA to have been bearers of information to such an extent that they were often afraid to leave the barracks after work. This even reached the stage where they got the director of intelligence in Victoria Barracks to sign a declaration that they were *not* spies. There is no evidence that they were. Even so, they still suffered significant intimidation.[14] They were also suspected by the British side of carrying information out of the barracks to the IRA. As piggy-in-the-middle they could not win either way.[15]

Downing is one of the very few direct references to specific individuals being taken to Knockraha, but it confirms that it was the routine place for the brigade's disposal of 'spies and informers'. This was also the time when Seán Culhane captured the two RIC men, Ryan and Carroll, and recalled later that Corry's unit 'had several prisoners in it [the mausoleum] and they used to shoot them at night.'[16]

Was Downing a British agent or merely a civilian clerk who worked for the military? One suggestion is that he might have been trying to work as a double agent. Major Percival, who ran the intelligence operation of the British Army in west Cork, remembered 'on one occasion, the secretary of the Demobilised Soldiers and Sailors Federation asked for an interview with me.' On being admitted he offered to help us. We had several interviews until I discovered one day that he also held the position of a Battalion commandant in the IRA and that his visits were designed to gain first-hand information of the interior of our Barracks.'[17]

Percival is wrong in asserting that Downing (if it was Downing) was an IRA commander. There was, however, a Daniel Downing, a senior member of the Cork city IRA. However, the disappearance of Downing may also relate to the kidnapping of the three British officers at Waterfall which had taken place two weeks earlier. The official British Army report on the disappearance of the three suggests that the leakage of information on their movements most likely came from the garrison adjutant's office where the men collected their expenses before leaving and where one civilian was employed,[18] or else from the RE office where six civilians, including Downing, worked. The army was right; the leak did come from the garrison adjutant's office, for the civilian who worked there was Con Conroy who brought the information out to Roibeárd Lankford. Did Downing know something about Conroy? Or, as a telegraphonist, was he a potential threat to Josephine Marchment Brown? Did she uncover him as a spy?

Was Downing asking awkward questions about the three officers in the weeks after their disappearance? Lieut Watts was a Royal Engineer and would probably have been known to Downing.[19] Or was he shipped to the IRA by British military intelligence as a double agent? Was he shot because he knew something about the abductions and the IRA was afraid he might report back what he knew to the British? Whatever the reason, he ended up in the bogs of Knockraha.

What is also interesting is that Downing's abduction occurred less than two weeks after the IRA had uncovered a girl who *was* acting as a British agent in the General Post Office.[20] May Kennedy, the daughter of a particularly notorious Mallow RIC man, was moved to the countryside and after a few days brought back to Cork docks and deported. However, there is nothing to connect her to Downing.

Horgan's is a more clear-cut case. Horgan's mother, the widow of an RIC man, lived at 62 High Street, next door to three houses, Nos 60, 61 and 61a which were commandeered by the RIC and where over a dozen policemen lived, some of them almost certainly plain clothes officers. There is even a connection with the YMCA, for Horgan had been a member of the city YMCA during World War I, though his membership had lapsed by 1920. (This is not unusual; most Protestant boys in the city had been members at one time or another.) What is unusual about Horgan is that he is listed among those members who were killed during the war, suggesting that he was missing for some considerable time and had been either a prisoner of war or severely injured.[21] In any case, he disappeared when he was taken away from his house by armed men on 9 December 1920. He was shot and his body buried near Blackrock.

All this, and the Black and Tans' threats of reprisals, suggests that Horgan was at least connected to the police.[22] Horgan had also been a member of the Royal Army Service Corps (RASC) during the war. Two other men, William Sullivan and Finbarr O'Sullivan, who lived in the same area and who were later shot as alleged spies, had also been members of the RASC.

It is interesting to note that Downing and Horgan, along with Det. Sgt Ryan, Constable Carroll, and Warder Griffin from Cork Jail, who were captured around this time and released on the promise that they would help the IRA, were the only abductions to merit such reprisal threats. The Blemenses, on the other hand, got no attention at all from the police. This suggests that, to the police at least, they were not as important as the others, though they were abducted in the week between Downing and Horgan. Though their abduction received much more press coverage, there were no threats by the military or the police to secure their release. The RIC county inspector in his December report merely noted: 'They were suspected [by the IRA] of giving information to Crown forces, hence the outrage.'[23] This should not be construed as evidence of guilt. A similar tone of resignation is to be found in the County Inspector's monthly reports for many of the IRA's killing of civilians.

This is all that is available in the public record for the November abductions. Martin Corry stated that young Parsons had been taken at this time. Yet there is nobody called Parsons among them.

Chapter 17 ⤳

YET ANOTHER SPY CIRCLE

M ick Murphy was the commandant of the 2nd Battalion of the Cork No. 1 Brigade. A member of the IRB and a well-known hurler, he was a square-shouldered, powerfully built man with a reputation for fearlessness and daring. He was also a voluble character and left several colourful accounts of his activities in the War of Independence and Civil War. As commander of the battalion in which many of these killings took place, his version of events, which he gave both to Ernie O'Malley and to the Bureau of Military History, are of some importance. Several of his men also gave accounts to the bureau. It is Murphy's account of the killing of Parsons and the Blemenses that is of interest here. His account to the bureau is entitled, 'The Shooting of Blemens and Parsons':[1]

> Sometime during the month of November 1920, word was brought to me that a youth named Parsons was seen very often in the vicinity of my house (where I very rarely slept). I put a Volunteer watch on Parsons and came to the conclusion that he was acting as a spy for the enemy. I reported the matter to Seán Hegarty, the Brigade O/C, who told me to pick up Parsons for questioning. This was done and I personally interrogated Parsons.
>
> After a considerable amount of questioning on my part, Parsons admitted he was a spy. He told us he was a member of the junior section of the Young Men's Christian Association (a Protestant organization) in Cork and that in this organization there were two sections, a senior and a junior, whose purpose was to report on any IRA or Sinn Féin activity that came to their notice. Parsons gave me the name of those most prominent in the YMCA spy sections and these I duly reported to the Brigade O/C.

This is broadly in agreement with Corry's version of events. It is now, however, that it appears to take on an even greater significance. 'Parsons also told me that it was he who had notified District Inspector Swanzy of the RIC that Tomás MacCurtain had returned to his [MacCurtain's] on the night of 19th March 1920. (This was the night MacCurtain was assassinated.) Having reported all these facts to the Brigade o/c, he ordered that Parsons be shot. This was done.'

Murphy then goes on to link these events with the killing of the Blemenses. 'On 1/12/20 the house of a man named Blemens was raided on my directions and Blemens and his son were taken away. They were both shot. These two were members of the senior spy section of the YMCA. Their names were given to me by Parsons. We also had information about them from letters captured in raids on postmen for mails.'

He also links the other Protestants killed in the city with this YMCA 'spy circle': '10 February 1921, Riley [sic] living in Douglas was shot in his home at night. This man was a senior member of the senior secret service of the YMCA. He was manager of the large grocery premises of Woodford Bourne of Patrick Street, Cork. With Riley that night was a retired British army officer named Major O'Connor. He too was shot and killed ... on 16 February 1921 Charles Beale, a YMCA senior secret service agent, was shot and killed.'

There are minor factual errors in Murphy's account: for instance, it was Beale not Reilly who was the manager in Woodford Bourne and Reilly was not shot in his home at night. The account appears to hold together as a unified theory to explain the killing of Protestants in the city during the conflict: they were all described as members of a secret 'spy' society, not this time called the Anti-Sinn Féin League but one operating out of the YMCA. This effectively is the basis for John Borgonovo's conclusions.

What jumps out immediately is the suggestion that there was a link between Parsons and the other members of this 'spy society' and the killing of Tomás MacCurtain. If this were true, it would go a long way to explain the ruthlessness of the IRA campaign against these men. Corry, however, does not mention anything about Tomás MacCurtain in either of his accounts of the killing of Parsons, though he does link the trial and execution of Constable Williams with MacCurtain's murder.[2] This is surprising since Corry was virtually reared next door to MacCurtain's family in Mourneabbey and MacCurtain was one of his biggest influences. Similarly, Florrie O'Donoghue, in his biography of MacCurtain, does not mention any youngsters as having been watching his house on the night in question, nor does he mention it in any of his many analyses of the assassination of MacCurtain.[3]

Murphy had given a similar account of the killing of Parsons to Ernie O'Malley some years earlier. This is worth quoting in full because it is more explicit, as one would expect when Murphy was talking to someone from his own side. Again, he links all the killings.

> Parsons was a fifteen-year-old, the son of an Englishman. He was captured by Tadhg O'Sullivan who saw him touting around. This young lad Parsons admitted quite freely that he was watching my house and that he was employed by the police. Furthermore he said he had been tracking

Tomás MacCurtain before Tomás was murdered. Swanzy the DI had made use of him. Then he tracked Tomas MacCurtain to his house and went over to King Street RIC barracks and there he told Swanzy that MacCurtain was at home. And what did you get for this I asked him? A glass of port, he said. There was a Junior and Senior Secret Service in the YMCA and they had meetings in Marlborough Street. I wanted to have them shot the next time they'd meet, but Seán O'Hegarty said 'that's not the way'. Then we killed them one by one. Parsons was shot, he was the most open spoken young fellow that I ever met in my life. He gave us their names and he told us their meeting place, the YMCA. He also told us that they used to meet in a house in Roxborough Road and that a Mrs Brown lived next door. It was Blemens house they met in, a father and a son and a daughter lived there.

Mrs. Brown was in touch with Florrie O'Donoghue and she told Florrie about him. We got in the back and we saw them and we heard them and they were shot one by one and in groups. Blemens and his two sons were shot one night. The Blemens [*sic*] didn't give anything away. One of them said I don't know anything but the old man might know something, they didn't think they would be shot. We shot the sons one by one and then we shot Blemens who was dead drunk . . . Perhaps it was patriotism on their part that made them do it. We buried the bodies in Carroll's Bogs. Every spy who was shot in Cork was buried so that nothing was known about them, they just disappeared.[4]

Though the account again contains some factual errors, for instance only one of Blemens's sons was killed and they lived on the Blackrock Road, not the nearby Roxboro Road, many of the details appear convincing. It also seems to confirm that James and Fred Blemens were killed near Knockraha— Carroll's Bogs are on the eastern end of the Rea, off the road between Watergrasshill and Liamlara. And it confirms that Parsons was a 15-year-old. Neither account, however, mentions any other boys being picked up and executed on foot of Parsons' confession.

The main difference between the two versions is the mention of a Mrs Brown, who lived next door, as one of the sources of the information on Blemens and that Florrie O'Donoghue was party to the operation. A quick check of Guy's Postal Directory for Cork[5] and the O'Donoghue Papers confirmed that this was none other than Josephine Marchment Brown, Florrie O'Donoghue's spy in Victoria Barracks and later his wife. James and Fred Blemens lived in No. 1 Braemor, Old Blackrock Road. Mrs Brown lived in No. 2 Roxboro Terrace, two doors away. Clearly, Mrs Brown could have come across evidence in Victoria Barracks that the Blemenses were British agents, alerted the IRA through Florrie O'Donoghue, who would then have arranged the abduction. Murphy again goes on to mention Major O'Connor and 'the manager of Woodford Bourne' as other members of the group.

There is another anomaly between the two accounts: to the BMH, Murphy claimed it took a considerable amount of questioning to extract a confession from Parsons. This would tally with Corry's description of the torturing of the youngster by attempting to hang him. However, to Ernie O'Malley, Murphy stated that Parsons 'was one of the most open-spoken young fellows I ever met in my life. He admitted quite freely that he had been watching my house and that he had been employed by the police.'

There is a clear contradiction here: if he 'admitted quite freely' that he had been watching Murphy's house and was 'one of the most open-spoken young fellows I ever met in my life', then why did it take the threat of hanging to extract information from him? Why does Corry not mention the MacCurtain connection? Why is there no mention of the kidnapping of a teenager during November 1920 in either of the newspapers of the day or in the RIC reports? If Tom Downing and George Horgan were working for the police and their disappearance caused outrage among the Black and Tans and Auxiliaries, then why did young Parsons not receive similar attention if, as Mick Murphy states, he too was working for the police? Surely the disappearance of a teenager would merit some public comment.

And there is another contradiction in the timing of Parsons' alleged abduction. Corry stated that Parsons was brought to him by 'the city flying column' under the command of Peter Donovan, while Murphy states he was caught by Tadhg O'Sullivan, who was killed by the RIC at the end of April 1921. This suggests that if Peter Donovan led the group that captured Parsons, then it is likely to have been after 20 April. If Tadhg O'Sullivan captured him, it was before that date. We know from the confession of 'Saunders' that Tadhg O'Sullivan, a Kerryman and one of the most active IRA men in the city, was high on the RIC's wanted list before being finally tracked down to a house in Douglas Street and assassinated by undercover RIC men.

It is difficult to explain away these contradictions, particularly as Murphy's account is partly backed up by others from the 2nd Battalion, even if their information in some instances appears to be second hand.[6] Like Florrie O'Donoghue, the last two men, Jerry Keating and Patrick Collins, claim the Freemasons were behind the operation of this 'spy ring'. Keating and Collins also refer to the 'Anti-Sinn Féin League'. Clearly the accepted view among Murphy's men was that there was a 'spy circle' in operation in the YMCA, whatever it called itself. This was their version of the Anti-Sinn Féin League; claims of Masonic involvement were also made. It was a neat conspiracy theory, but was it all true? The only way to get to the bottom of it would be to confirm Parsons' death from a source other than the recollections of Old IRA men. And that was not going to be easy.

PART IV

| THE CORK YMCA

England is training thousands of imperial soldiers by means of her organization the Baden Powell Scouts. This organization takes the Irish child at an impressionable age and passes him from one standard to another of military training until he has reached military age. He is pledged to be loyal to the British throne and to his scout masters and may be used by those who control the organization for counter-revolutionary activities. The grave danger to Ireland of allowing this embryo English army the right to train in our midst is so obvious that it hardly needs emphasis.[1]

The first and most obvious place to go looking for answers was the YMCA itself. And the YMCA, like many such organisations, helpfully provided a regular account of its activities in the Cork newspapers, more specifically in the loyalist-leaning *Cork Constitution*. Yet in reading through the 'YMCA Notes', there is nothing to suggest anything untoward happening, certainly nothing to suggest that five or six of its members may have disappeared off the streets of Cork, never to be seen again. The first AGM of the association to be held after the Truce and therefore the first that would be expected to reflect anything that happened during the previous 12 months was held on 21 October 1921. Surely, if boys vanished or their families were forced out of Cork as a result, they would be remembered in the prayers of the assembly, or at the very least some veiled reference to such events would have been recorded.

Yet there is no such reference. The meeting began with prayers and a reading from Scripture.[2] The assembly concerned itself with devotional issues and with discussions on the missionary activities of the organisation in such far-flung outposts as Serbia, Palestine, Burma, Egypt and the West Indies. The only reference to local matters was a brief discussion on the financial situation of the Cork branch and satisfaction that 58 new members had been found for the year, along with 30 new subscribers. The meeting expressed its gratitude to a Mr J. H. Julian and his wife for all the work they had done for the association over the years and who were about to leave Cork to take up residence in Liverpool. The rest of the meeting consisted of the usual platitudes associated with such events. Indeed, it gives an interesting insight into devout Protestantism as it was practised in Cork in the early part of the twentieth century.

There is nothing to suggest that anything traumatic had been inflicted on the association's membership during the year. All the officers who had been present in 1920 were there again in 1921. The only vague reference to the conflict that so recently had raged all round the YMCA headquarters in Marlborough Street was a prayer that 'in these perilous times and serious days' the membership 'wanted divine strength, and if they looked to the Lord Jesus Christ, he would see them through'—a comment that could be made at any evangelical meeting anywhere in the world at almost any time.

So there was either a spectacular cover-up going on, or else very little had happened to the YMCA at that stage. Surely if there was a big conspiracy operating out of the Cork city branch and people had disappeared or been shot, there might at least be indirect evidence of it in the YMCA's own internal records. Luckily, those records are still extant and on several occasions the director of the Cork YMCA kindly allowed me to rummage through his trunkful of old registers and other documents.

What I found was that there were indeed junior and senior sections, but this merely referred to the membership. The boys were the junior members and the officers the senior members. At least the IRA had got the junior and senior bit right. But this was the way the association had been structured; there was nothing to suggest these were junior and senior 'spy' sections.

The Cork YMCA in 1920 and 1921 was run by members of the Cork Protestant middle class, mostly from the families of business people and professionals in the city. The leading figures were Methodists, Baptists, Presbyterians and Quakers, though there was also a significant Church of Ireland membership—and the occasional Roman Catholic. The chairman was Alfred Beale of the well-known Cork Quaker business family. The Beales, originally a family of shipbuilders and engineers, were well known for their philanthropic activities.[3] Abraham Beale, an uncle of Alfred Beale, was secretary of the Cork Society of Friends Relief Committee during the Great Famine and died of typhus fever in 1847 as a result of his work with the destitute.[4] The general thrust of the YMCA's activities, as one would expect, was what could be called 'good works', evangelical Christianity, raising money for missionary activities and running camps and activity centres for the Protestant youth of Cork.[5]

One of the more interesting things about the city YMCA was the number of what might be called 'liberal' Protestants among its membership. Liberal Protestants such as Henry Dale and John Leslie were still members as late as 1920/21. One of its leading members was Thomas Farrington, professor of chemistry at UCC. Farrington, a Baptist, had been a Protestant Home Ruler and a member of William O'Brien's All For Ireland League in the early years of the century before running as a moderate Unionist in the 1918 election.[6]

Another prominent member was Benjamin Haughton. Haughton, a Quaker and a well-known city businessman, was noted for his efforts to secure peace and for fundraising activities on behalf of the White Cross, set up as a relief organisation to help alleviate distress in Ireland. He was later to be made a senator in the Free State Seanad.

The only place where the YMCA seemed to interact with the conflict was a meeting held between Sinn Féin TDs Liam de Roiste and Barry Egan and Cork business people in March 1921. De Roiste left an account of this meeting, held under the auspices of the Quaker-led American Relief Delegation. The meeting, held at Haughton's home, consisted mostly of Cork businessmen, but it also included Henry A. Harris, the general secretary of the YMCA.[7] Its purpose was to try to establish backroom links between Dominion Home Rulers—as city loyalists had now become—and Sinn Féin, with a view to finding a resolution to the conflict. Haughton had a long history of such work, having been part of a delegation that visited Lloyd George with peace in mind as early as August 1920.

'I have been in strange company this afternoon, for me very strange company. Haughton, the head of the Cork Timber and Iron Company . . . He is a Quaker, hence an advocate of peace.' De Roiste goes on to list the 'strange company' he found himself in: Haughton, George Crosbie of the *Cork Examiner*, Privy Counciller Sir Stanley Harrington, Sinn Féin Deputy Lord Mayor Barry Egan, Frank Daly of the Harbour Board, Frank Barrett of the Provincial Bank, Claude Mercier, also a member of the Cork Harbour Commissioners, described as a 'non-Catholic', and Harris, who seems to have acted as secretary to the meeting.

The meeting appears to have been successful. 'The views of Haughton are simple enough: he was a Unionist—his son was in the British Army during the war. He now says he is in favour of Dominion Home Rule: the only link to be to the Crown—the Irish people to accept King George as King of Ireland . . . Here's a thought: non-Catholic "Unionists" like Beamish and Haughton are far sturdier men than a Catholic unionist or Home Ruler like Harrington.'[8]

In fact, this meeting has some historical significance since it represents the start of the ultimately fruitful attempts by the southern Unionist faction to talk to Sinn Féin and bring about a resolution between the latter's position and that of the British government. Lloyd George later expressed his thanks for this intervention. 'We had a good deal of pressure from Unionists in the South of Ireland when the rebellion was progressing. In fact, the first deputation I received on the subject . . . was from Unionists in Cork and Dublin on behalf of the unionists of the South of Ireland. They pressed us into negotiation and suggested Dominion Home Rule as a method of settling the dispute.'[9]

The other place where the Cork city YMCA appears to cross paths with the conflict raging around it was a special multi-denominational prayer meeting held at the Marlborough Street building on St Patrick's Day 1921 attended by all the leading Protestant groups, where 'many earnest prayers for the healing of Ireland's wounds and sorrows' were said.[10]

The tolerant, liberal stance of many members of the Cork city YMCA may not be reflected in YMCA branches in the county, though this is difficult to prove. These appear to have been dominated more by ascendancy figures. For instance, the Bandon and Queenstown branches were under the presidency of Lords Bandon and Barrymore respectively, leading unionist figures in the south, while other branches were controlled by Church of Ireland ministers. There were also YMCA branches in Kinsale, Mallow, Midleton, Skibbereen and Youghal. These appear to have been independent of each other.[11]

But the IRA was right in one thing. There had been, as might be expected, close links between the Cork YMCA and the British military, especially during World War I.[12] Like many similar organisations, the Cork YMCA had sent a substantial number of its members to the trenches. Some 59 Cork members are listed as having volunteered, of whom 19 died. This close relationship extended to the organisation running canteens and shops in the principal army barracks throughout Munster.[13] During the war over 30,000 travelling soldiers and sailors were accommodated at the organisation's hostel in King Street. In Britain the YMCA was effectively seen as an auxiliary corps of the British Army during World War I, its members even receiving World War I service medals for providing support to 'the troops' during the war.[14] However, by the 1920/21 annual report all references to military activity had ceased, except for one event: in October 1920 the Cork YMCA received an award for its contribution to the war effort.

'Public investiture of the Order of the Red Triangle for voluntary work carried out during the War to support the military . . .' was conferred on the Cork YMCA. 'Brigadier General Higgison, Commander of the Cork Garrison carried out the investiture.'[15] There is a list of the activities of the Cork YMCA during the Great War in the *Cork Constitution* of 3 May 1921,[16] when Harris left Cork to take up the running of East Bristol YMCA. Was it this kind of pro-British activity that had drawn the attention of the IRA to the YMCA in Cork in the first place and that also led to the burning down of the Bandon YMCA building on 30 June 1921?[17]

However, there is little hint of anything specific that might constitute a threat to the IRA; certainly no evidence of anything that suggested spying activities. Going through the records of the YMCA from 1915 to 1924, it appears to have been nothing more than a run-of-the-mill Christian youth club, albeit one linked to the army. The kind of activities the YMCA was involved in can be seen from the annual report of the previous year. 'The Junior Department and Boys' Brigade under the presidency of Mr. James Burchill, looks after this department and all are to be congratulated. . . . The Bible classes were well attended. This was always a leading feature and we are pleased to see the Junior Section supporting it so well. Physical drill, gymnastic classes, occasional school evenings were other items in the winter months. Camp in summertime was open in Crosshaven where helpful happy days were spent. A special word of thanks to the ladies who happily supplied teas for the lads and homemade dainties. Also our H. A. Harris, Divisional Secretary, for his efforts in a successful membership campaign.'[18]

Not exactly the behaviour of a secret service agency, or even a cover-up for a secret service agency. Anybody who has had any experience of organising the lives and recreation of youngsters will know more or less what was going on. Yet the conflict did impinge on the YMCA. The annual minutes of the Irish executive for December 1920 stated:

> . . . in the main we have been exempt from any interference, but one or two regrettable incidents during the year indicate the dangerous environment by which we are surrounded. In July last an attempt was made to set fire to our Divisional stores in Cork. Fortunately, the fire was checked at an early stage. Damage however was done to the extent of about £800 and most regrettable of all, Mrs Ward, our caretaker's wife, died as a result of the shock and fright. About the end of October our Divisional motor was also seized at Bantry . . . That we have suffered so little comparatively, considering the terrible state of the country, is to all of us a matter of deep thankfulness to God.[19]

No mention of any disappearances or deaths other than that of Mrs Ward. But the big question was: was there anybody called Parsons on the membership or subscription lists?

The answer is yes. The annual reports of 1919/20 and 1920/21 contain the names J. and S. Parsons as membership subscribers. J. Parsons, however, was no longer a member from June 1920, while S. Parsons was still on the membership list in 1921/22, suggesting that he could not have been the boy killed by the IRA.

So was J. Parsons the boy killed by the IRA? If so, he was no longer officially a member during the period when he was supposed to have been killed. The matter is further complicated by the presence of an adult, one James S. Parsons, listed as having attended the annual burser's meeting on 30 September 1921,[20] though his name does not appear in the membership or subscription lists for either section and he was not a member of the committees of the organisation in any of the years looked at. The most obvious conclusion is that James S. Parsons was the father of J. and S. Parsons. However, there is nobody called James Parsons recorded as living in Cork city at the time.[21]

The most striking thing about reading through the General Committee Year Book[22] is how little the YMCA seemed to be affected by the conflict going on around it. Surely if one of its members had been secretly abducted and executed in November 1920, that would have been reflected in the minutes of the general committee meetings of that or the next month? If it happened, then nobody took the trouble of referring to it or recording it. If half a dozen members had subsequently disappeared, surely there would have been at least some veiled references to it during the spring of 1921? Again nothing.

Was the YMCA an organisation seething with loyalist and indeed 'anti-Irish' activity such as one might find in Belfast, at least as defined by the IRA? Well, an offer made by the Gaelic League in the spring of 1922 to teach Irish to the boys was gracefully accepted and 30 members were given instruction. So while there had been strong institutional support for Britain during the Great War, there was nothing to suggest that similar support was being proffered in the war against the IRA. The absence of references to military activity from the summer of 1919 onwards suggests that the YMCA was in touch with the changes afoot in Ireland and, along with many Protestants in Southern Ireland, was prepared to make its peace with the nationalist revolution. This is reflective of the general *rapprochement* in relationships between Southern loyalists and moderate nationalists in the period after World War 1.[23] So the city YMCA appears at least on the face of it to have been no hotbed of radical loyalism; there isn't a hint of counter-revolutionary tendencies anywhere in the YMCA records. This was an organisation keeping its collective head, if not in the sand, at least keeping it down. This was no Anti-Sinn Féin League.

One way in which the YMCA might, if only inadvertently, have facilitated some form of spying activity was by renting out rooms to various other organisations and groups that might well have used it for undercover activities. It is very possible that it may have rented rooms for meetings to some of the groups involved in the war against the IRA. When in September 1921 a Sergeant O'Sullivan of the War Pensions office was looking for a room where he and another ex-soldier could train for a boxing match, he was turned down 'with regret', suggesting that the YMCA may have had its fingers burnt on the matter of renting out its rooms.[24]

Another place of possible conflict was the soldiers and sailors hostel run by the YMCA on Railway Street. As we have seen, soldiers' homes may well have been used both as a place for agents to stay and possibly also as recruiting grounds for informants. While there is no direct evidence that the YMCA hostel on Railway Street—housed on property owned by the Beales—was used for this purpose, it would be naïve to think it was not.

There were some rumblings of unease, however: while things appeared to go on pretty much as normal all thorough 1920 and for the first four months of 1921, suggestions that everything was not quite as it seemed began to be made in May 1921, when the summer camp planned for Crosshaven was cancelled after the St Luke's Boy Scouts hall in Riverstown was raided and 'robbed of its entire contents'. Then the Ladies Committee's American Tea, a fundraising event, was cancelled owing to the 'extremely distressed state of the country'. 'The Secretary explained that since the last meeting (13 June), circumstances had arisen which he thought made it unadvisable to proceed with the American Tea.'[25] Something had happened in early May and also between 13 and 17 June that gave at least some reason for concern.

There is one ominous statement in the YMCA records for the year 1921. This is a reference to the fact that 'several of our younger members have recently gone abroad; we have given them letters of introduction to YMCA branches in the various cities in which they have settled.'[26] This is an odd statement, given that youngsters are unlikely to depart without their families. But even taken at face value, it suggests that young men or boys had to depart Cork in a hurry, at some time between the raid on the Boy Scout hut in May and the end of 1921 when the report was written.

Was this connected to the discovery in the downstairs toilet of the YMCA (which was used by the public) of 'a piece of paper . . . purporting to come from CO IRA, Cork District, containing a threat'?[27] There is no hint as to what the threat actually was. But it came from the IRA. It is reasonable to conclude that the YMCA had cancelled its activities and the boys had had to leave Cork in response to an IRA threat. The threat was 'fully discussed' at the general committee meeting of 22 June, but it was decided to carry on as usual. The only decision coming out of the meeting was that the public was no longer to be allowed access to the toilet. The note was placed in a safe. There is no suggestion that it was even passed on to the military or police. Everything seemed to be back to normal by the next meeting of the committee on 9 September.

This note is surely significant. The timing is the period leading up to the Truce. Was it perhaps in connection with the Parsons boy or one of the others whom Corry claimed had been shot on foot of evidence extracted from Parsons? If so, then Parsons was captured and executed not in November 1920, but in May or June 1921. But if that is the case, then who were the others whom Corry stated had been executed on foot of information extracted from him and when were they killed?

And there are other problems arising out of the YMCA's records. There is no trace of anybody called Blemens or any variations of that name in any of the yearly lists of members of the organisation. If Mick Murphy is right and Parsons' information led to James Blemens being arrested as the head of the 'spy ring' operating out of the YMCA, then surely either he or some other member of his family would have been members at some stage. Yet, plausible and all as Murphy's account seems, this is not the case. No member of the Blemens family ever seems to have taken part in YMCA activities.

Nor are there any connections between the YMCA and any of the other Protestants killed in Cork during the War of Independence. Despite the claims of Mick Murphy and his men, neither Major O'Connor, Alfred Reilly nor James Beal are listed anywhere in YMCA records either as members or as subscribers.[28] A trawl through the records of the YMCA and the Cork newspapers failed to reveal any evidence of the disappearance of YMCA youngsters either in 1920 or 1921. The only concrete connection between the YMCA records and those publicly shot by the IRA is the fact that George Horgan had once been a member. Yet Horgan was the only Protestant whom the IRA survivors do *not* connect with the YMCA. The whole thing seemed utterly confusing.

But there was one youth group that also had military trappings—the Boy Scouts. In Cork city the Boy Scouts were organised along parish lines, with each Church of Ireland parish having its own scout troop. In addition, there was a scout troop associated with the Presbyterian church, while Methodist, Quaker and Baptist Boy Scouts were run from the YMCA. They marched in uniform every Sunday morning. Considering that the problems for the YMCA appear to have started around May 1921 with the raid on the Boy Scout hall in Riverstown, it is reasonable to believe there may be a link between the two. The IRA had a long and disreputable history of attacking Boy Scout troops in the South of Ireland and was still doing so as late as 1928.[29] It seemed to come down to one of two things: either the scouts operating out of the YMCA were caught spying on the IRA, or the IRA was simply using them as soft targets to get at the British. But which was it?

| ON THE RUN

One thing that might cast light on the timing of young Parsons' death, seeing that there is no mention of him in the public record, might be the movement of the IRA men involved. This can be put together from the recollections of various survivors. The policy, at least among the leadership of the IRA, was to move key men around the brigade area as they came under pressure from the British. Thus Seán O'Hegarty spent much of the spring of 1921 with the brigade column operating in mid-Cork. The column itself was under the command of Dan 'Sandow' Donovan, probably the most famous of the city IRA men who spent most of the conflict away from the city after being one of the assassination team that shot Divisional Commissioner Smyth in the County Club on the South Mall in the summer of 1920.[1]

By late spring of 1921 the two battalions in the city were coming under increasing pressure, having suffered severe losses of personnel and munitions after the establishment of Martial Law. During the first week of May, Mick Murphy moved to mid-Cork to command the brigade column,[2] while Donovan came back as O/C of the city ASU, with Connie Neenan taking over as commander of the 2nd Battalion.[3] Murphy had only returned to Cork a day when he was arrested by the RIC at Stenson's pub in Douglas Street on 13 June.

If Murphy is correct, there is little doubt that he was a central figure in the capture and interrogation of young Parsons and that Parsons was important in his recollections. This means the abduction of the boy occurred either some time before the first week of May or else after Christmas 1921 when Murphy himself was released from internment, which would of course mean he was killed well after the Truce or even during the Civil War.

Mick Murphy says Tadgh O'Sullivan captured Parsons. O'Sullivan, originally from Kerry, was one of the leading figures in the 2nd Battalion. He was one of the most wanted men in Cork and the police finally caught up with him on Douglas Street on 20 April, where he was shot dead by undercover RIC men. Assuming that Murphy is right, this means that Parsons may have been captured before 20 April, rather than after the Truce.

Yet Martin Corry said it was Peter Donovan who brought Parsons to him.

Donovan was in charge of the city ASU only for a brief period, probably in April,[4] and he was in charge of the 2nd Battalion for a brief period between the death of O'Sullivan and his own capture a few weeks later. Donovan was involved in many operations carried out by the city battalions.[5] Unfortunately, he left no records or accounts of his experiences in the IRA. However, Connie Neenan, who was an IRA leader in the south side of the city during this crucial six-month period, did leave a record.

Neenan, a popular figure in republican and GAA circles, remained in the IRA and went to America after the Civil War and was involved in ticket smuggling for the Irish Sweepstake.[6] He returned to Cork a wealthy man and set up a number of businesses. In later years he played a major role in the development of St Finbarr's GAA club. He gave many accounts of his experiences, including one to Ernie O'Malley. He was captured by the military in August 1920, an account already described in the context of the killing of James Herlihy, but he was released in England in March 1921. After evading the detectives put on his trail, he returned to Cork a few days later accompanied by Tadhg O'Sullivan whom he implies had also been in England over the winter. This narrows down Murphy's account of the capture of Parsons to some time between mid-February and 20 April 1921.

Neenan also mentions the YMCA killings, confirming the allegation that boys from the YMCA had been trailing IRA men and that one boy had confessed to having watched Tomás MacCurtain's house on the night he was shot—though he does not name him as Parsons.

> We did not know then that the British had organized the youngsters of the YMCA to trail our men. They were mostly from good families. It was only then, 15 months after the murder of Tomas MacCurtain, that we learned that a kid of fifteen had tracked him home that night. Both kids confessed to their trackings and they were killed. We thought that that was the end of the YMCA organization, such as it was, and it was just before the Truce.[7]

Further on, Neenan mentions another teenager caught near Douglas in June 1921. 'This was a young kid, a nondescript type, and we shot him.'The kids, it seems, were from 'good families'; at least three were killed. The plot was uncovered some 15 months after MacCurtain's assassination, which occurred on 20 March 1920. This suggests the boys were captured just before the Truce—15 months after the killing of MacCurtain. While the dates are at odds with the other accounts, this is a third relatively detailed account of the abduction of YMCA youngsters, who were likely to have been 14-, 15- and 16-year-olds on the basis of Neenan's information.

But there were still major question marks apart from the dates. Who was Parsons? Was he the J. Parsons named in the YMCA records of 1919/20? Why is there no record of his disappearance in the YMCA, or no letters from his family trying to track down his whereabouts? Why was the RIC quiet on the matter if indeed they knew about it? Who were the other boys? Were they killed just before the Truce—or just after the Truce as Corry stated? And why is there nothing in British records about them, though the vast majority of IRA 'outrages' were catalogued in military inquiries?[8] British records are weak on the matter of the 'disappeared'. As we've seen, the list published in the press in August 1921 is not complete and reflects only what is in the RIC's records: there were many others who disappeared who are not listed.

On the other hand, the kidnapping of a 15-year-old, even if he were a spy, which the British could deny in any case, would have had considerable propaganda value. A trawl through the papers of Major Charles J. Foulkes, best known for developing the use of poison gas on the Western Front and who was put in charge of propaganda (with also a significant input into intelligence) in the 6th divisional area, yielded nothing.[9]

Foulkes, despite being very busy in his efforts to 'dig the dirt' on the IRA— he describes the killing of off-duty soldiers, the stripping and tarring and feathering of women, the use of dum-dum bullets—never mentions the killing of 15-year-olds.

Likewise, exhaustive searches of the two Cork daily newspapers and the county inspector of the RIC's monthly reports found no evidence of the kidnapping of 15-year-olds, though most of the abductions in the August 1921 list are noted.

There was, however, one report of the kidnapping of a teenager in Cork and to my knowledge, it is the only one filed in a newspaper. It is found in an unlikely source, the London *Times* of 18 May 1921. It is part of the 'City of Spies' article referred to earlier.[10]

> And there were incidents of another sort. There was a calm spring evening when I made my way out to Blackrock and walked back along the river road. Near to the city, at an open ground where children play, high commotion prevailed. Mothers, fathers, children and strangers were all jabbering together in a crowd, pointing in the direction of the town. Somebody's child, it appeared, had been kidnapped by a mysterious individual in a motor car.

This is an eyewitness account of the abduction of a youngster, the only one we have. Peter Hart also quotes this section of the article and goes on to speculate:[11] 'Which side was the mysterious individual on, if any? What was his motive? The area was a favourite hunting ground for the IRA, who abducted and executed several young teenagers about this time but we shall never know for sure what happened.'

To my knowledge, Peter Hart's comments and that little section from the *Times* are the only published hints that youngsters were abducted in Cork at this time.[12] What's more, they place the events exactly in the time frame we're talking about: the late spring and early summer of 1921.

Clearly, 'somebody's child', whoever he or she was, was abducted on the Blackrock side of the city some time in early to mid-May 1921. Indeed, there is still a little area of parkland at the city end of the Blackrock Road and a larger area of waste ground to the north of the Old Blackrock Road.[13] This is the area where the Blemenses lived. The only problem with linking the two is that Blemens and his son were some four months dead at this stage. So the boy abducted on the Blackrock Road in April or May could not have been the source of the information that led to the deaths of James and Fred Blemens.

However, 'somebody's child' was abducted on the Blackrock Road in broad daylight on a fine spring day. This suggests that it was an IRA job. Owing to the curfew, the IRA avoided operations after dark. The 'mysterious individual in a motor car', moreover, suggests similarities between this abduction and that of the Blemenses some four months earlier. The motor car took off in 'the direction of the town', which could have meant towards the city or towards Blackrock. In another twist to the story, when the copies of the *Times* containing the 'offending' article arrived in Cork, they were taken from the railway station by the IRA and dumped in the river.[14]

There are many possible interpretations of the story. But before we deal with the kidnapping of teenagers, we must first go back in time and look in more detail at the capture and execution of James and Fred Blemens at the end of November 1920.

Chapter 20 ~

THE DEATHS OF JAMES AND FRED BLEMENS

James Blemens was 56 years of age, a horticulture instructor and a man described by the *Cork Constitution* as being 'well known as an efficient and popular instructor'.[1] His son Fred was 31 and a shop assistant. Blemens Snr was described by the *Cork Examiner* as being 'popular with many citizens as well as residents in various parts of the country'.[2] As an instructor in the Department of Agriculture and Technical Instruction, he was a product of Horace Plunkett's vision of knowledge and education advancing the lives of the less well-off in rural areas.

James Blemens appears to have been a Dublin Protestant who had moved to Cork some time between 1901 and 1907. In 1909 he was living at No. 2 Braemar on the Old Blackrock Road, a few hundred yards from the South Infirmary Hospital in what was then the edge of the city.[3] His wife Elizabeth, also a Dublin woman, died in 1918. They had six children still living in 1911, two others having died in childhood.[4]

In 1920 only two of the family were still living with their father at Braemar: Fred, who was now the owner of the house, and James Jnr, who was 27, both of whom worked as shop clerks in the city. (Mick Murphy says a girl was also living there. This may have been a servant.) While Blemens may have been a loyalist, he does not appear to have been of the 'staunch' variety. Neither of his sons, for instance, volunteered to fight in the war, let alone join the Ulster regiments, as did some young southern Protestants, though both were eligible.[5] You get the impression that these were quiet people, living in Cork, keeping their heads down, minding their own business.

So why were they killed? Were they spies, guilty of espionage, as Seán O'Hegarty reported to IRA headquarters? Were they guilty of setting up a 'spy circle' in the YMCA, as Mick Murphy claimed? Were they part of the 'Freemason spy ring' that Florrie O'Donoghue claimed operated in Cork? As we have seen, there is no evidence that any member of the Blemens family had ever had any connection with the Cork YMCA. Nor indeed were they Freemasons.[6]

Then there is the matter of what they divulged, or rather did not divulge, under interrogation. Though Blemens was allegedly 'dead drunk', he 'didn't give anything away'. 'One of them said: "I don't know anything, but the old man might know something."'[7] This suggests two things. The IRA plied Blemens with alcohol, probably to make him talk. Yet Blemens told them nothing. Then Mick Murphy says something that may be significant: 'They didn't think they'd be shot.' One of the common themes running through the inquiries into killings of civilians accused of being spies is the number of times the victims had some premonition they were going to be killed. Michael Walsh knew when he went into the Cork Workhouse that he would not come out alive.[8] Two young men shot in north Cork 'knew the Sinn Féiners' were going to get them.[9] George Tilson spoke of the 'overwhelming danger'.

Yet the Blemenses 'didn't think they'd be shot'. This was ten days after the Bloody Sunday killings in Dublin, a few days after Tom Downing vanished into thin air and a few weeks after the IRA abducted and executed three British officers at Waterfall. Blemens was an intelligent man. If he had been gathering information for the British, as he might well have been as a horticulture instructor travelling around the county, then he would have known what was in store for him from the IRA. Blemens, however, did not appear that concerned. If nothing else, he might have confessed in an effort to save his own skin. Yet he didn't. 'I don't know anything but the old man might know something,' Fred Blemens said. The old man, though (apparently) drunk, didn't say anything either. The chances are that he didn't know anything, or at least he did not know the answers to the questions the IRA men were asking him.

Mick Murphy is adamant in his account to Ernie O'Malley that Blemens and his *two* sons were shot that night.[10] Yet we know that only one of Blemens's sons was killed with him. So who was the other man? It could have been Tom Downing; yet Downing could hardly have been mistaken for a son of Blemens—and the evidence from the north side of the city is that he was captured alone and taken to Knockraha.

However, the fact remains that the Cork city IRA did not, at least at that stage, go around killing Protestants just for the sake of it. Proportionally speaking, no more Protestants than Catholics were killed in the city during the War of Independence. The IRA did not like Protestants, but at least during the Anglo-Irish conflict itself they did not target them in the city merely for sectarian reasons. So the Blemenses are unlikely to have been killed simply because they were Protestants; they must have been picked up and killed for some specific reason perhaps with espionage overtones. But what was it?

According to Mick Murphy,[11] the information that led to the abduction of the Blemenses originated from Josephine Marchment Brown who lived two doors away and was passed on through Florrie O'Donoghue.[12] Did Josephine have evidence garnered from Victoria Barracks that they were spies? Or did she suspect them simply because they were neighbours and she was under stress at the time?[13] Because Florrie O'Donoghue never once mentions the Blemenses nor makes even a veiled reference to them in his papers, we cannot say for sure. No evidence of what she brought out to incriminate them has survived, though reams of other material has.

One logical conclusion is that she was under such a strain during that November that she became frightened of her Protestant neighbours and turned them in in case they *might* inform on her. For there is another amazing coincidence: Reggie Brown, Josephine's son, was abducted from his grandparents' house in Wales by Florrie O'Donoghue two days after the disappearance of the Blemenses. It is hard to believe there is not some connection between the two.[14] It is clear that while Florrie O'Donoghue was in Wales at the time, it was he who had given instructions for their abduction. Newspaper reports state that the boy's mother was known to live in Blackrock in Cork. They even carry notices looking for any information that might lead to the recovery of the boy. A reward is mooted in one report on the kidnapping in early January.[15]

There may have been another reason for her paranoia. There was gossip in the area. In the weeks after Reggie Brown was returned to Cork, his grandmother in Barry, Mrs Perry, received anonymous letters stating that the little boy was in Cork with his mother.[16] O'Donoghue's correspondence suggests that this was a Miss Murphy who lived at No. 3 Roxboro Terrace.[17]

And there is yet another possibility. According to Frank Busteed, the house at Roxboro Terrace was used as a 'safe house' by IRA men on the run.[18] Perhaps the Blemenses were removed because they were believed to be a security risk. There was much reporting on the abduction of Reggie Brown; what would today be called media speculation rambled on in both the Irish and the English press until January. This would attract attention right to the heart of IRA activities in Cork. According to Busteed, the house was 'above suspicion'.[19] Was it above suspicion because the only people who might suspect it were dead? One way or another, James and Frederick Blemens vanished off the face of the earth, never to be seen again.

Nor does it say much for the investigational abilities of the RIC, Scotland Yard or the military that they do not appear to have connected the disappearance of the Blemenses with the disappearance two days later of Reggie Brown. All the RIC County Inspector's Report has to say of the Blemens case was the usual 'that they were suspected of giving information to the Crown forces, hence the outrage'.[20] These are all plausible reasons for the killing of the Blemenses and they might also explain why Mick Murphy would want to link them to the YMCA. By claiming that young Parsons had given information that led to the Blemenses and that it was they who had organised the 'spy circle' in the YMCA, he gets away from the possibility that the Blemenses might have been executed simply out of convenience. Yet if the

Blemenses were killed because they might be a security risk, then why was the other son, James Jnr, not killed too?[21]

Apart from their matter of fact brutality, these deaths do not lend themselves to easy analysis. James and Fred Blemens may have been killed for any one or a combination of these reasons. While all would appear to be plausible, the key to their deaths must lie with Josephine Brown and Florrie O'Donoghue, for it was they who informed Mick Murphy about them. In the meantime, if James Blemens could not have been the organiser of the supposed 'spy circle' operating in the YMCA, as purported by at least some of the IRA men, then who was, assuming that such a spy ring actually existed?

Chapter 21 ~

| DEATH OF AN ORGANIST

Two months were to pass before the next killing of a Cork city Protestant. His name was Alfred C. Reilly, and he was the managing director of Thompson's Bakery in King Street, one of Cork's best-known businesses. He was shot dead on 9 February 1921. Reilly is variously described in the accounts of IRA men as a member of the Anti-Sinn Féin League[1] or as a senior member of the YMCA spy circle.[2] Others go one better and state that he was part of the Freemason spy organisation operating out of the YMCA.[3] Yet Reilly was not a Freemason,[4] or a member of the YMCA.[5]

Reilly's is one of the most puzzling of all the killings carried out during the conflict for he was a very unlikely target. He had married into the Thompson family and ran the family company, F. H. Thompson Ltd, the city's largest bakery and confectionery business. A Methodist himself, he was the son of a Methodist minister and a man known for his philanthropic and cultural largesse.[6] He was a well-respected figure, a former Justice of the Peace and a member of a number of cultural and commercial organisations in the city. He had Dominion Home Rule sympathies and was involved with several charities. He was 58 years of age with an MA from the University of London and had been organist at the Wesleyan chapel on Military Hill for 38 years.[7] On the evening of 9 February 1921 he was found dead on the road outside his home at the Hill, Douglas. He had been shot four times: in the chest, the abdomen, in the left arm and on the right side of his face. Death appears to have been instant.[8] Sinn Féin TD Liam de Roiste recorded in his diary: 'In one case of a Mr. Reilly, managing director of a large bakery place, there seems to me a grave doubt as to who shot the man and the motive for it.'[9]

The outpouring of condolences from a wide variety of organisations on his death is evidence of the high regard in which Alfred Reilly was held in Cork.[10] 'The death of the deceased will always remain a mystery.'[11] He was described as 'an excellent employer of labour, popular with his employees, and ever ready to put his hand deep in his pocket to contribute to local charities'.[12] 'The crime was surrounded by mystery which they [the people of Cork] could not fathom.'[13]

Officiating at his funeral, Rev. James Alley, the Methodist minister for

Cork, stated that, far from being a loyalist of extreme opinion, everybody 'knew how liberal the deceased was in his views. Three years ago he signed a document in favour of a broad nationalist settlement of the troubles of the land and the two local newspapers the other day bore testimony to his efforts in connection with the release of the late Lord Mayor.'[14] This was a reference to a petition Reilly organised among members of the Methodist community and forwarded to the British government in an effort to secure the release of Terence MacSwiney.[15] On the day of his death his wife told a reporter that she did not think her husband had an enemy in the world.[16]

Reilly was well thought of by nationalists and marched in the funeral cortège of both Tomás MacCurtain and Terence MacSwiney[17] and was a leading member of the Cork Literary and Scientific Society. In fact the day before he was killed, he was at a meeting of that society along with Sinn Féin Alderman Stockley, professor of English at UCC, who himself some months earlier was lucky to escape a Black and Tan bullet as he walked home along the Western Road.[18] To judge by the comment of Liam de Roiste and the fact that Deputy Lord Mayor Barry Egan attended his funeral,[19] Sinn Féin politicians appear to have been as puzzled as anybody else as to the reasons for his murder. Even in a community accustomed as it was to daily violence, there was what amounted to a public outcry at his killing.

For these reasons, the death of Reilly has always seemed puzzling to historians. 'A man of blameless integrity. It was not simply that he would not do what was mean or shabby—he could not even stoop to anything dishonourable.'[20] It seems strange that a man like that would have betrayed what he himself believed in, effective national sovereignty for Ireland. His relationship with local IRA men in Douglas—they had offered to guard his orchard the previous autumn—seems to have been good. Some have even claimed that Reilly was killed by the Black and Tans.[21] Another theory was that the killing arose out of personal animosity owing to his position as a major employer, revenge for some slight, real or imagined. In many ways it would have made more sense if the killing of Reilly *had* been carried out by the Black and Tans.

However, there is no question as to who his killers were: Mick Murphy, Connie Neenan, Frank Busteed and others all claim it was the IRA that killed him. The placard found on his body claimed he was a convicted spy and was signed by the IRA, though he had received no death threats. The manner of his death is described by William 'Sailor' Barry, one of the men who carried it out:

As a result of information received by our Brigade Intelligence Service it became known that an organization run by the Free Masons and the YMCA had been formed in Cork to spy on the movements of IRA men in the city and to report on this to the British Authorities. One of the prominent men in this organization was named Riley [*sic*] who was

manager of Thompson's Bakery and lived in Rochestown, Co. Cork. This
man was reported to be the paymaster for the spies.

Early in February 1921 I received instructions from the Brigade to take
into custody Riley and have him executed. On the evening of 10 February
1921, as he was returning from work in King St in his pony and trap, four
of us, armed with revolvers, got into the trap and drove him to his home
in Rochestown. We shot him outside the gate and affixed a card to the
body with the words 'Spies and Informers, Beware' written on it.[22]

Yet, as we've seen, Reilly was neither a Mason nor a member of the Cork
YMCA. The military inquiry into his death suggested that he was killed because
he had been a Justice of the Peace. According to his wife, 'Mr. Reilly was a JP
for the County of Cork but has taken no active part in police court work for
about the last six years. I am sure that my husband took no part in any
political organisation.'[23] The killing, at least as far as the family was
concerned, appeared to have been without motive.

So why was Reilly killed? Was he, as William 'Sailor' Barry stated, the
'paymaster' of the Freemason/YMCA spy ring? Considering that he was a
member of neither organisation that seems unlikely.[24]

Another possibility is that he was mistaken for Major O'Connor. They
were near neighbours.[25] As we have seen, an attempt on Major O'Connor's
life had been made a few nights previously.[26] Both men would have been
known to each other;[27] both were JPs; they looked alike, being in their late
fifties, with full heads of grey hair and moustaches. Perhaps the IRA, intending
to shoot O'Connor, shot Alfred Reilly instead. However, Barry's description
suggests that this was not the case. His account fits precisely the conspiracy
theory held by the members of the 2nd Battalion. It is likely that the reasons
he puts forward for the killing are the reasons he was given. He knew where
to find Reilly: at the bakery. The balance of the evidence suggests that Alfred
Reilly was deliberately killed.

Alfred Reilly and Major O'Connor had both served in the Douglas courts
as JPs over the previous 25 years, but with one crucial difference: Major
O'Connor was still serving as a magistrate[28] while Reilly had ceased playing
an active role in the Cork courts some six years previously.[29] Not only that,
but he had been fined for refusing to carry out jury duty from the start of 1920
when republicans were beginning to face the courts on various charges.[30]

It is possible that Reilly was shot because he may have been with O'Connor
on the night of the first attempted assassination—Mick Murphy states that
Reilly was with O'Connor on the night *he* was killed[31]—or because he was
believed to be in some way connected to the letter that was intercepted at
Victoria Barracks. His shooting would have sent a message out to all other JPs
and court officials that any attempt to identify IRA men would have the direst
consequences. Was this part of Florrie O'Donoghue's dictum that 'any

organisation that will get the population to keep their mouths shut will certainly have done considerable work for the Army'?[32]

This may also have been the reason why, a week after Reilly's shooting, George Tilson received the threatening note that led to his suicide on the London train as it pulled into Paddington.[33] Old IRA men were more than happy to claim Tilson as one of the Anti-Sinn Féin League, though I have seen no specific reference to what he was supposed to have done or who targeted him either among the BMH submissions or in the interviews with Ernie O'Malley.

It is very likely that the note received by Tilson was intended for his brother who was also a JP and who had just moved out of the Tilson family home. Reggie Tilson, like Alfred Reilly, was a Protestant Home Ruler. He was the owner of a soft drinks manufacturing company, Cade and Co., and had been High Sheriff (Deputy Lord Mayor) from 1913 to 1916. He was well thought of, to judge by histories of the lord mayorship.[34] In fact, Connie Neenan states that George Tilson worked for Cade's, suggesting that the threatening note may well have been received by the wrong brother. R. H. Tilson also attended Reilly's funeral[35] and, like Reilly, refused to carry out jury duties in cases against republicans.[36]

We don't know how many JPs received similar threats around this time though some did, and as we'll see, so did some Cork solicitors.[37] In any case, no other magistrates or court officials, aside from O'Connor, were killed by the IRA in Cork city during the War of Independence. Furthermore, O'Connor is on the IRA GHQ's list of British spies, while Reilly and Tilson are not.[38] It is still possible to believe that Reilly, O'Connor and Tilson were part of some sort of spy ring, but there is no evidence to support it other than the fact that they died violently. In contrast to many alleged 'spy' families, both Tilson and Reilly's families were not forced to leave Cork, and Reggie Tilson was to remain a respected peace commissioner until the 1930s.[39]

There was one other Protestant killed in Cork city in February 1921, however. His is a name we have come across before. He was James Charles Beal and his name *is* on the IRA GHQ list of spies.[40] There is little to connect him with the Tilsons or with O'Connor or Reilly, except that he was killed a week after Reilly and two days before Tilson received his death notice. He was, however, intimately connected to the Blemens family and, like the Blemenses, was an outsider and not part of the Cork establishment. Apart from Major O'Connor, he was the last Protestant to be publicly assassinated in or near Cork city during the Anglo-Irish conflict. But it is to Beal that we have to look for at least part of the reason why James and Fred Blemens were abducted and killed some two months earlier.

Chapter 22 ~

A SORROWER WRITES

On the morning of 14 February 1921, Philip Dennehy noticed the body of a man lying in a field at the family farm at Dennehy's Cross on the western outskirts of Cork city. The body was facing upwards. The man had been shot once in the face and twice in the abdomen. Oddly, there were no exit wounds. There was a piece of cardboard attached to the body printed in ink in rough capital letters 'Convicted spy. This is the penalty for all those who associate with the Aux. Cadets, the Black and Tans and the RIC.' It was signed 'The IRA, p.s. Beware.'[1]

The man's name was James Beal. He lived at 7 Laurelhurst, College Road, just beside University College Cork. He was an accountant by trade and manager of the wine department of Woodford Bourne, an upmarket grocery outlet on Patrick Street.[2] Beal, an Englishman who had lived in Cork for around 11 years, had left his place of work at 7 pm on the previous evening to go home. His importance to this narrative was that he was married to Sarah Blemens and so was the son-in-law of James Blemens and worked with James Blemens Jnr in Woodford Bourne.[3] So, in effect, he was the third member of the Blemens family to die in the conflict.

As in the case of Alfred Reilly, Beal is often cited as a leading member of the Anti-Sinn Féin League, as the 'paymaster' of the spy circle of the ASFL and as a YMCA secret service agent.[4] In one account he is said to have had £1,000 on him for the payment of spies under his control,[5] though this was probably a fabrication since the men who shot him do not seem to have remembered it. 'We found in his possession papers giving valuable information relating to the spy organisation with which he was connected.'[6] 'As a result of disclosures which came to light in the papers found on Beale [sic], members of his organisation were picked up by other IRA companies in the city and suitably dealt with. This had a discouraging effect on the Anti-Sinn Féin League which faded out, thus removing a serious threat to the Cork IRA.'[7]

Some papers *do* seem to have been found on Beal; his brother-in-law stated at the military inquiry into his death that a small Treasury notebook that he usually carried in his pocket was missing.[8] This later narrowly avoided discovery in a British Army raid:

Mick Buckley was arrested when the Battalion dump at Vernonmount was raided by the military. On the occasion of that particular raid Buckley had brought the papers taken from Beale [*sic*] (the spy who was shot by us) to Vernonmount for Mick Murphy, the Battalion o/c. When Buckley was in gaol in Cork his sister went to see him and asked about Beale's papers. He said they were hidden under an old bucket out in the field at Vernonmount. Sure enough, the papers were found by us just where Buckley said they were. If they had been discovered by the military in a raid he would have been tied up with the shooting of Beale and would most certainly have been executed by the British.[9]

All this suggests is that here at last among the Protestants shot in Cork we have firm evidence of a British agent running a team of informers in Cork city, which of course would also go some way to explaining the disappearance of James and Fred Blemens some months earlier.

Furthermore, all the IRA men connected with the killing refer to Beal as either 'Charles Beale'[10] or 'Harrison Beale'.[11] As we have seen, there was a Charles E. Beale among the senior officers of the YMCA; he was a partner in the firm of Harris and Beale and a member of Cork Chamber of Commerce. He was at least an acquaintance of Alfred Reilly and had been at his funeral. Is this the connection we have been looking for? Had the IRA finally found the real paymaster of the 'spy ring' operating out of the YMCA and that members of the organisation were subsequently picked up and 'suitably dealt with' and that this finished whatever loyalist spying organisation was operating in Cork? The scenario looks plausible, but it is almost certainly incorrect.

There are two problems with the theory: Charles E. Beale lived to a ripe old age and was never targeted during the conflict.[12] The Beales were still involved with the Cork YMCA well into the 1930s.[13] James Beal had no connection with the YMCA though he was a Freemason. The second problem is that Beal was the last Protestant, apart from Major O'Connor, to be publicly shot dead in Cork city prior to the Truce. If the papers found on Beal contained a list of spies of the Anti-Sinn Féin League, then who were they? There appear to have been no Protestants killed in Cork city during the War of Independence after Beal's death, apart from Major O'Connor and, as we've seen, the first attempt on O'Connor's life was made two weeks before Beal's death. Certainly five civilians were shot as spies in the month after Beal's killing, but these were mostly ex-soldiers.

And what are we to make of the list of 'spies' supposedly found on Beal? Well, there is an answer to this question and it manifested itself in one of the more extreme examples of the paranoia and suspicion of the IRA at the time. This is the collection by the IRA, which began at the time, of the names and addresses of all the Freemasons in the Munster region. There are several of these lists among the papers of Florrie O'Donoghue[14]—the collecting continued until well after the Truce—detailing the names and addresses of up to 200 Masons from Cork and Kerry, and there are many letters concerning the menace of Freemasonry in the papers of IRA survivors.[15] O'Donoghue refers to the 'Freemason Intelligence Organisation',[16] 'Members of England's garrison of civilians—by far more particularly dangerous—not merely hostile, they were anti-Irish and regarded themselves as honoured in any service they could do for England. They were in the main intelligent observers with wide business and social contacts and the Masonic cement kept them well integrated.'[17]

One of the lists of Freemasons in O'Donoghue's papers stands out from the others in that it is described as a 'captured document' and is to be found in a cache of British military papers captured from various sources between January and June 1921.[18] This is a typed list of 181 Freemasons, mostly from the city, in alphabetical order and meticulously compiled. Is this alphabetical list the contents of Beal's treasury notebook, which was probably an address book? There are no records of any other sources of 'captured' Freemason membership lists during this period and Beal was a Freemason. At first glance it certainly looks as if it might be the list that was found on Beal.

In May 1921 the 1st Division leadership—effectively O'Donoghue and Liam Lynch—wrote to GHQ that 'we shoot one loyalist' for each prisoner shot by the British, with 'Prominent Freemason Officers to be the first to suffer.'[19] For their part, Collins and Mulcahy at GHQ, mindful no doubt of the adverse publicity being generated as a result of the killing of Mrs Lindsay[20] and others, tried to put a brake on this rush to attack loyalists. 'I want you to hold your hand on this matter',[21] Mulcahy replied. O'Donoghue replied again in early June applying further pressure for the go-ahead for the killing of loyalists,[22] the implication again being that Freemasons were to be the first in the firing line. Again, GHQ was adamant: 'No persons shall be regarded as enemies of Ireland, whether they be described locally as Unionist, Orangemen, etc. unless they are actively anti-Irish in their actions.'[23] The collecting of membership lists of Masonic lodges was to continue after the Treaty and they were to be the first to be shot should hostilities with Britain break out again.[24]

From the above accounts and the statements of O'Donoghue and others, the impression is given that members of the Anti-Sinn Féin League in Cork were all Freemasons bound by the 'Masonic cement'. However, a trawl through the membership lists of the Cork city lodges for the early part of the twentieth century failed to find either of the Blemenses, Major O'Connor or Alfred Reilly, or indeed anybody called Parsons.[25] Nor are any of them named in the lists of Munster Freemasons gathered by the IRA. Of the Protestants publicly shot in Cork during the War of Independence, only Beal was a Mason. On the basis of this evidence, the 'Masonic cement' could have been binding only one man.

It is my belief that it was the treasury notebook found on Beal that first led to the obsession with Freemasonry that was to characterise much of the Cork brigades' correspondence for the remainder of the conflict. It is in the period immediately after the shooting of Beal that the intelligence officers of the Cork brigades begin to report on the 'Masonic peril'. In the extensive memo sent by Florrie O'Donoghue to all intelligence officers in late 1920,[26] detailing the kinds of institutions to be watched, there is no mention of Protestants, loyalists, Freemasons or the YMCA—and this was written after the killing of the Blemenses and George Horgan. Clearly, the IRA had no information on the supposed 'Masonic menace' at that stage.

The card attached to Beal's body and found by the *Cork Examiner* reporter read: 'Convicted spy. The penalty for all who associate with the Aux. Cadets, the Black and Tans, and the RIC. IRA. PS Beware.'[27] Yet his brother-in-law, the younger James Blemens, stated: 'I do not know of anyone having enmity with my brother-in-law. I know of no possible reason why anyone should do him violence. So far as I know, he did not associate with any members of the Police Force or with the Auxiliary Police.'[28] As we shall see, James Blemens is correct in this, but merely on a technicality. 'When I heard he was missing I was afraid for him because my father and brother disappeared on 29 November 1920 and I have never had any idea since how or where they went or what has become of them.' This in itself is an interesting statement and gives an insight into the minds of the Blemens family in the months after the disappearance.

The most obvious possible reason for his killing is that Beal was asking awkward questions about the disappearance of his father-in-law and brother-in-law. He might have been snooping around, visiting police and military barracks, a form of behaviour that would have immediately brought him to the attention of the intelligence operatives of the IRA. Perhaps Beal was one of those who were 'eliminated before he got too close', to use O'Donoghue's phrase. Yet James Blemens's evidence seems to suggest that this was not the case: 'I do not know of his making any enquiries personally into the disappearance of my father and brother.'[29]

The surviving members of the Blemens family went to some lengths to establish what had happened to their father and brother. There are a number of letters from the family and one from Rev. Babington, the Dean of Cork, in the Michael Collins papers,[30] pleading for any information on the missing men. There is another letter in the *Morning Post*, which was also carried by the *Cork Constitution* of 3 August 1921.[31]

A SORROWER WRITES IN THE MORNING POST

I should like some Member of Parliament to ask for the release of our kidnapped loyalists or to have some statement as to whether they are alive and well and why none of us can hear a word from them. Has England forgotten her loyalty? Is she callous to the fate of those whose only fault was loyalty to her King? Some of the kidnapped are eight months away and one man, who was taken with his son, had his son-in-law cruelly murdered a few weeks after—three out of one family. Surely, their cry must touch all hearts. The silence is too dreadful.

A Sorrower

This letter came from Matilda Blemens, Blemens's younger daughter. However, the last twist in the tale is given in an even more harrowing letter from Matilda and James Blemens Jnr to Michael Collins, dated 21 December 1921:

> Mrs Beal died yesterday, December 20th. She was the widow of Mr. James C. Beal, who was shot last February near Cork and daughter of Mr. James Blemens who with his son Frederick was kidnapped from his home on November 29th 1920 and not heard from since. Matilda and James Blemens in their great grief implore information about their father and brother, our home is desolate and our hearts are breaking. Can you help us?[32]

Sarah Beal née Blemens died aged 34 on 20 December 1921, a year after her father and brother disappeared and ten months after her husband was shot dead.[33] We don't know the precise medical reason why she died. What we *can* say is that she certainly died of a broken heart. She couldn't face another Christmas. She is the final victim of the terrible saga that befell the Blemens family of Cork.

Chapter 23

SOME UNDERCOVER CONNECTIONS

S o why were Beal and the Blemenses killed? Were they British agents? Were they innocent victims of some sort of paranoid madness that saw a spy in every Protestant and a Freemason in every spy? Were they part of a witch-hunt against prominent city professionals and loyalist business people that began at this time?[1] James Blemens Jnr appears to have been at a loss as to why his father and brother had vanished and why his brother-in-law had been shot dead. Matilda Blemens states that their only fault was loyalty to their king. The question is: did 'loyalty to the King' go so far as to act as spies for the king? Certainly, the IRA must have believed this to have been the case or else the men might not have been killed. But from what we can establish from census records and other records, the Blemens family do not appear to have been fanatical loyalists.

As we have seen, one plausible theory is that they were killed because they lived near the 'safe house in a quiet street' where Josephine Marchment Brown lived; that they were got rid of simply because they posed a potential threat to the core of IRA operations; and that Beal was subsequently shot to prevent awkward questions. Yet the other members of the Blemens family were not harmed, though they did leave the house at Braemar[2] and moved in with Sarah Beal on College Road.

It should be apparent by now that many of the reasons put forward by IRA survivors for the killing of various 'spies and informers' do not stand up to close analysis. The only ones who knew exactly why people were killed were senior brigade officers and they invariably stayed quiet about it.

Could it be that there was a 'Freemason spy ring' in operation in the city and that Beal was the only one shot? Were there other Freemasons whose names were found on Beal who, instead of being killed, were driven out of Cork? Colonel Higginson, commanding the 17th Infantry Brigade in Cork, noted on 7 March, some three weeks after Beal was killed: 'The question of ejectment by means of threats of Loyalist farmers and businessmen in the 17th

Brigade area has now become so serious in extent that some means of combating it is immediately required.'[3] It is clear from Higginson's letter that what he had in mind was the expulsion of loyalist farmers, mostly in the Bandon valley. The Sweetnams, Connells, Shannons, Stanleys, Goods, Dalys and Harolds were severely intimidated at around this time, as indeed were the Bradfields and Thomas Hornibrook. Farmhouses were torched and cattle driven off; intimidating raids were carried out on an almost weekly basis.[4] Something similar, however, appears to have been happening in Cork city, but on a smaller scale. 'This policy is now being extended to the towns. Information has recently been received that certain firms in the city of Cork have received secret orders to quit.'[5]

The RIC county inspector in his report for April stated that 'some loyalists have left the county in receipt of receiving notice from the IRA'.[6] He does not, however, specify from what part of the county they left. Higginson goes on to suggest that such individuals be compensated through the courts for suffering malicious damage. This indeed appears to have been the route taken and many of the farmers named above did indeed subsequently receive compensation.[7] This appears, however, to have been mostly confined to west Cork. While large compensation cases were brought by city companies against the government for the excesses of Crown Forces during the burning of Cork and other wanton damage caused by British forces, and for the burning of houses by the IRA in May 1921, there appear to be none for the forced expulsion of businesses out of Cork at this time.[8] Yet some Cork city business people apart from George Tilson were expelled. Liam de Roiste wrote on 19 February, the week after Beal was shot: 'There is a rumour that three prominent business men have been ordered by the IRA to leave Cork. The rumour has been around for a few days but I have not heard whether it has a basis in fact or not.'[9] It did indeed have a basis in fact. George Tilson was a case in point; his demise was more than a rumour, but who were the others?

There is no shortage of candidates for the loyalists driven out of the city in the spring and early summer of 1921. James T. Mulligan, who owned a gunshop in King Street, had to leave on no fewer than four occasions in 1921 and 22—'for reasons of personal safety'.[10] Thomas Stewart, a resident of Gardiner's Hill and a Freemason, was forced out of his employment (with Murray's, a Belfast firm) in February as a result of the Belfast boycott.[11] Another businessman, Richard Baker, was forced to live 'some fifteen miles away from my home',[12] while auctioneer William Wood had to leave Ireland for six weeks from April after being briefly kidnapped and having a gun cocked in his ear by the IRA.[13] Thomas Shepperd, principal assistant in the office of the Crown and Peace, was ordered out in April 'under penalty of death'.[14]

And there are many other less dramatic examples. Businesses such as Dobbin/Ogilvie and Byford and Co. were blacklisted in the spring of 1921 as a result of the Ulster boycott.[15] People with Ulster associations were particularly at risk in this context. 'Tobacco manufactured by Messers Gallagher and Messers Murray . . . has been virtually driven off the market.'[16] The elderly Rev. T. C. Day was forced out of Ireland for entertaining 'Tommies' at his house and for putting up members of the coastguard after their station was burnt out.[17]

But the real reason for Beal's death did not emerge until some four months later and it is extremely doubtful that any notice was taken of it even then. It is also likely that the only people within the IRA who knew it intimately were the senior brigade staff such as O'Donoghue and O'Hegarty. What's more, it probably had little to do with Beal's membership of the Freemasons, though that did not prevent the IRA from assuming that it did.

At the hearing of the criminal injury case on the shooting of Beal at the Cork Quarter Sessions of June 1921, Sarah Beal stated that a fortnight before his death, 'some men called to her home and asked for her husband, but he was not at home at the time. She asked the men if she could do anything for them. They did not answer her straight. She thought they might be looking for an appointment in the shop. They muttered something and went away. They would not be the sort of men her husband would mix with,' Sarah Beal said. 'They wore mackintoshes.'[18] While there is no proof that these were IRA men, there is more than a reasonable chance that they were, for this was the first week of February, the week when the onslaught on civilian 'spies' began in earnest. It was probably an IRA hit squad in search of Beal.

But it is when searching for a possible motive for the killing of her husband, and by extension the abduction of her father and brother, that Sarah Beal inadvertently suggests the most likely reason why they may have been killed. For she states that 'she had two officers of the military police lodging in her house on the College Road some time ago. One of these officers was wounded outside the Palace Theatre and afterwards left Cork, but her husband continued to correspond with him.' According to the lists smuggled out of Victoria Barracks by Josephine Marchment Brown, it appeared to be standard practice for many British officers to live in civilian quarters.[19] According to the IRA's own list of British casualties, there was only one officer wounded in the streets of Cork during the winter of 1920/21 who could fit the description of the man wounded outside the Palace Theatre. This was Lieut G. E. Green of the RASC, who was wounded, ironically, in a fracas with a group of drunken Auxiliaries not far from the theatre at the corner of King Street and Bridge Street on the night of the burning of Cork city, 11 December 1920. Green, believing he was about to be attacked, pulled out a revolver and accidentally shot himself in the thigh. He was not a member of the military police, though presumably that was what he told the Beals. But there is evidence to suggest that he was an intelligence officer and one of Captain Kelly's men.

But he was more than that, for Green is a very likely candidate to have been the Lieut Green who had been present at the torture of Tom Hales and Pat Harte and was one of the intelligence officers the IRA had been seeking ever since the Hales interrogation of the previous summer. Another of Hales's torturers, Flight Lieut Richardson of the RAF, had been shot dead in Newcestown on 9 October. The others, Captain Kelly and Lieut Koe, were never caught, while the Lieut Green shot at Waterfall was the wrong man. What this suggests is that Beal, and by extension the Blemenses, may have been shot because of their association with British intelligence officers, one of whom was Green.

George Edward Green is something of a shadowy figure. Like all the intelligence officers employed in the conflict, his movements are difficult to trace. On the face of it, he appears merely to have been a transport officer. After spending two years in the trenches in France, he was ordered to rejoin the RASC in July 1919 for service in Ireland. After some months training in Aldershot[20] he arrived at British Army Headquarters in Parkgate Street in Dublin in the autumn of 1919.[21] On 10 February 1920 he was transferred to Cork to replace an officer who was being repatriated. He then spent a short period in Belfast before returning to Cork on 12 May, where he was nominally assigned to the transport section of the RASC in Victoria Barracks. So was he simply an officer in charge of transport or had he some more secretive role?

The only clue comes from what happened to his army service record subsequently. The file was 'weeded' in 1954 and a large quantity of documentation destroyed by the military censor. This led to the very curious situation where we can learn that he had several operations for piles when stationed in Dublin, while at the same time having no idea what he was actually doing in either posting. Maybe he was doing nothing other than organising transport. However, there is one interesting comment on the Protection Certificate issued on his resignation: 'Checked on 16/6/21 that George Edward Green was the officer serving with 53 Co Cork [sic] on 8th June 1920—per officer's own statement in A.F., E.F.9 (Medal Roll).'[22]

This suggests that George E. Green was recommended for a decoration for his services or produced documentation for a medal citation for someone else relating to an event that occurred on 8 June 1920. There was only one significant 'success' against the IRA in Cork on that date. This was the midnight raid on a house in Ballineen in west Cork in which a number of IRA activists were captured.[23] For apparently captured that night were two men whom the British Army had been seeking for a long time: Jim Crowley, a senior guerrilla leader in the area, and his brother John. Unfortunately from the army's point of view, they were the wrong Crowleys; the James Crowley captured was not the man they had been looking for, but was rather a minor figure in the IRA. However, the two men got such a beating from army intelligence personnel that one or other of them leaked some information on

IRA activities. Shortly after they were released, John Crowley disappeared, never to be seen again—executed by the IRA as a 'spy' and his body buried.[24]

This is important from a number of points of view. It links Green to intelligence operations and to the mishandling of prisoners. It also suggests he was operating in West Cork at around the time of Hales's and Harte's torture a few weeks later. As we have seen, most of the intelligence work and indeed the majority of medal citations were handed out to members of the RASC, MGC, RGA and so on. Green had served in both the RASC and the MGC. This was also the time of year when medal citations were forwarded. George Horgan, and William Sullivan and Finbarr O'Sullivan, both of whom were killed at around the same time as Beal, all had connections with the RASC.

This may of course be mere coincidence, but the pattern is clear enough. The three ex-soldiers shot as spies in the south-east corner of the city during the winter and spring of 1920/21 were either members of, or had connections with, the RASC. Green, an officer with the RASC, was staying with the Beals. The clear implication of all this is that Beal and the Blemenses were shot because the IRA believed they may have had a connection with Green, who was in all likelihood running agents in the city. They may have been guilty of spying themselves or they may not. (It is interesting to note that Fergus Molloy,[25] who was shot as a spy in Dublin in March 1920, was also a member of the RASC while Green was still stationed there. There is little doubt that Molloy was reporting to military intelligence because he was still a member of the military.)[26]

What's more, the IRA were well aware of Green's shooting and reported it immediately to GHQ so that Green appears on the IRA's casualty list for December 1920 as if he had been shot by the IRA themselves.[27] This is despite the fact that the fracas on King Street was over in a matter of minutes and Green was removed immediately to the military hospital. He also went on a month's leave as a result of the shooting, which would account for James Beal having written to him, and he did not return to Cork. The inclusion of Green's name with his correct initials and regiment in the IRA's December list of Crown casualties suggests that the IRA was very interested in Green and what had happened to him. It also suggests that his movements were being monitored and that when he pulled out his revolver upon being stopped at King Street, he believed he had good reason to do so. It also suggests a man who was living on his nerves.

The implication of this is that the Beal was either spying for Green or was shot for giving lodgings to British Army intelligence officers. Green was one of the most wanted men on the IRA's lists. Beal continued to correspond with him after he had been moved out of Cork, probably connected to the undercover organisation that called itself the 'Anti-Sinn Féin League'. The correspondence may have been innocent or otherwise. Either way, considering that the IRA intercepted the mails going into and out of Cork, the very act of writing to Green would have been enough to seal Beal's fate. Beal, as his brother-in-law stated, probably truthfully, had no contact with the police force or with the Auxiliary Police. He had plenty of contact with the military, though, and more specifically with that most shadowy of all units, the undercover operatives who in this instance no doubt called themselves 'military police'.

All this suggests that the Blemenses were abducted either as part of the IRA's efforts to track down Green or because of the association between the family and British undercover agents, the real Anti-Sinn Féin League.[28]

What is very interesting is that Florrie and Josephine O'Donoghue always maintained subsequently that the three officers killed at Waterfall were intelligence officers, while to the British this was merely the cold-blooded murder of two education officers and a member of the Royal Engineers, who were seen as non-combatants.[29] Roibeárd Lankford claimed it was Con Conroy who passed on the information, which is what the British military suspected. Yet Josephine claimed it was *she* who brought the information out of Victoria Barracks. They cannot both be right. All we can say is that members of the city battalions were involved in killing the men at Waterfall.

I believe Josephine claimed the Waterfall three because it suited the IRA to claim they were IOs. To admit that they were still chasing Green some two months after the others had been executed would have been tantamount to admitting that the Waterfall three were not whom the IRA said they were. And it would also mean admitting they had failed to get another of Hales's torturers. Florrie O'Donoghue and his wife went to their graves claiming that the officers killed in Waterfall were intelligence officers, though they almost certainly knew otherwise. The torture of Tom Hales, as we have seen, led to the killing of Richardson and the search for his other tormentors, Lieut Green, Captain Kelly and Lieut Koe.[30] However, the execution of Lieuts Chambers, Watts and Green, and the deaths of Beal and James and Fred Blemens—and possibly even of Tom Downing, were also a consequence of the thirst for revenge for the torture of Tom Hales.

John Borgonovo quotes an undated memo from the 6th Division, probably written in the spring of 1921. This deals with the 'transfer to England of loyal inhabitants who for various reasons have incurred the displeasure of the IRA and are therefore unable to reside in their homes'. Most of the people concerned come under the following headings:

a. Those who have given information.
b. Those who have given evidence.
c. Those who on account of their loyalty have already been attacked by the rebels, or are likely to be if they remain in their homes.

At present, Class (a) are re-compensated out of a special intelligence fund and transferred to England.[31]

We have seen how Cruxy Connors, Michael Walsh, Monkey Mac and their families were spirited out of Cork by the military authorities when they came under IRA suspicion. The Blemens family, on the other hand, never left Cork, though it would have been easy for them to do so. Rather, the remaining members of the family left the house at Braemar, which then lay vacant for a year, and moved across the city to live on College Road[32] where James Blemens Jnr lived until his death in 1969. All this suggests that the British authorities, at least, did not consider the Blemenses to have been actual spies.[33]

Even in death the Blemenses had one final indignity inflicted upon them. After their interrogation when they finally reached Carroll's Bogs, in one account somebody noticed that 'the Blemens had a good pair of shoes' and that a good pair of shoes were not going to go to waste. So 'the lads took the shoes off them'.[34] While the two unfortunate men lay in an anonymous grave, their shoes were being worn around the streets of Cork by a pair of IRA gunmen. This of course is a reflection of the poverty of the time, but the fact that it was remembered more than 30 years later shows more than a fair amount of *schadenfreude*.

Some on the republican side did not share the view that they were spies. Richard Mulcahy in the autumn of 1921 was sufficiently appalled by the case when he received the letters from the family that he instigated an investigation into it.[35] In a memo to the O/C 1st Southern Division dated 7 October, Mulcahy picked out the Beal case in particular as being 'rather bad'.[36] The Cork IRA and Seán O'Hegarty delivered its own answer early in 1922 when it stated: 'Those shot during the war [are] not to be inquired into as they are all Spies.'[37]

The balance of evidence suggests that while Beal may have been working for the Crown or at the very least offering lodgings to its officers, James and Fred Blemens were probably innocent. Their son-in-law had made unfortunate connections. The Blemenses were doubly unfortunate to be living in the wrong street with the wrong neighbours. They were victims of an extraordinary conjunction of circumstances. Their's is the tragedy of war.

PART V

Chapter 24 ~

| A TALE OF TWO SPIES

During January and February 1921, the first two months under Martial Law, the British Army and the RIC reported a significant increase in the amount of information being derived from the civilian population. While we have to allow for hyperbole and the tendency to write over-optimistic reports, the start of 1921 seems to have been a period of success for the British Army in Cork city and the surrounding area. The RIC county inspector's report for January stated: 'Hardly a day passes but that information of contemplated ambushes comes to hand . . . Six cases have been reported of parties of armed men (30 to 100) lying in ambush in the city and suburbs . . . in at least three cases the information was found to be correct.'[1] This *is* hyperbole. Parties of up to 100 men never operated in Cork city. Nevertheless, the army and police do appear to have been getting significant information on IRA activities. The history of the British Army's 6th Division in Ireland stated that 'the Proclamation of Martial Law had undoubtedly frightened a large number of civilians and made them more willing to give information to the Crown forces'.[2] The IRA thought so too and on 9 February began its campaign of assassination of civilians in Cork city, killing 27 known victims between that date and the Truce.

In January, British forces raided a number of Cork No. 1 Brigade arms dumps. The most spectacular seizure occurred at Clogheen, where the military came across a 15-year-old girl named Mary Bowles wearing a bulky dress. Under the dress was found a Lewis machine gun, an armoured vest and two loaded pistols. Near by they discovered three rifles, a quantity of ammunition and some revolvers, and they arrested four men. On 20 January, while blowing up two business premises in Washington Street as an 'official reprisal' for the shooting of Detectives Maliff and Ryan, they discovered some more ammunition and Volunteer uniforms. In Carrigrohane, four rifles and a dozen shotguns were captured on the same day. The following day Michael Kenny, who had led the Dillon's Cross ambush, was captured by the RIC after having been given away by a neighbour. On 24 January, again in Clogheen, the military located ten IRA revolvers and a dozen rifles. On 28 January 'a quantity of ammunition' was discovered in a house in Paul Street.

The biggest success, however, occurred on 8 February when an army platoon surrounded an IRA unit at Rahanisky House near Whitechurch, some five miles north of the city.[3] Eleven IRA men were captured, including a senior brigade officer, Seán MacSwiney, brother of the late lord mayor. A week later, at Mourneabbey, the flying column of the Cork No. 2 Brigade, which up to that point had suffered few setbacks, was surrounded by British troops while in position to mount an ambush. Four members of the column were killed in the shoot-out, eight prisoners were taken, two of whom, Patrick Ronayne and Thomas Mulcahy, were subsequently court-martialled and executed.

These successes were notable for their precision: for instance, no other houses were searched on the day Rahanisky House was raided. The detachments of British troops who surrounded the No. 2 Brigade column at Mourneabbey knew exactly what they were doing. Some of the raids, such as the capture of Mary Bowles, may have been fortuitous, but there is little doubt that the Rahanisky raid and the Mourneabbey shoot-out were based on accurate information.[4] Clearly British Army intelligence had a 'mole' close to the centre of IRA activity north of the city.

'Saunders' claimed he and his handler Dan Shields were responsible for providing the information that led to Mourneabbey, though two other men were shot in connection with it. But what about the others? The answer for some of them can be found in the events of the morning of 8 February at Rahanisky House.

At 5 am a detachment of British troops surrounded Rahanisky House owned by a Mrs Bridie McKay. Staying in the house were a dozen or so members of the Cork No. 1 Brigade, including Seán MacSwiney, Michael Baylor, who had taken part in the Dillon's Cross ambush, and Con Conroy, the IRA spy who had fingered the three officers killed at Waterfall.[5] The troops surprised the guard, who escaped uninjured into the darkness after a few shots were fired at him. When an officer knocked at the door, it was opened by Mrs McKay. Nine revolvers, a Mills bomb and a quantity of ammunition were found in the house. The IRA men were arrested along with Mrs McKay and two of her employees, James Carey and Michael Renihan. The IRA men were subsequently court-martialled and jailed for 'conspiring together to levy war against His Majesty the King'.[6]

The hearing, which was held in the Garrison library at Victoria Barracks, was open to the public and was a lively affair. 'There was a large audience in the court, mostly composed of ladies who, apparently, took a great interest in the proceedings.' This was the first time the ladies of Cork had the opportunity to observe an entire column of the IRA in captivity in the one place and, as IRA men were regarded as brave and daring and therefore attractive and intriguing, the ladies filled the court every day during the hearing.[7]

The court was something of a circus, with the IRA men concocting a variety of stories, some colourful, of how they had 'run into each other' in ones and twos on the way home from a dance and had taken refuge at Mrs McKay's because they were afraid to go back to the city after curfew. All the men except Seán MacSwiney claimed they were not members of a proscribed organisation.

The principal matter at issue was whether or not the men were armed—the possession of arms under Martial Law being an offence that could result in the death penalty. All of them, again except for Seán MacSwiney, claimed to be unarmed. As the nine revolvers and the bomb were found in bedclothes and under beds and in one case up a chimney, the army was unable to prove that the guns were in fact the possessions of the men themselves, though it was obvious to everyone in the court that they were. When questioned, each of the accused raised no objections to being tried by the court and, in response to each charge as it was being read out, pleaded not guilty.[8]

Council for Mrs McKay stated that she 'had always been a lady of unimpeachable character who had no connection whatever with any political, seditious or illegal organisation'. Her employees, Carey and Renihan, also claimed in court to be men of good character who were not connected with illegal organisations '. . . who were entitled to be in the house on the night in question . . . where one would expect them to be'. Mrs McKay gave her version of events, of how at around 10 o'clock on the night of 7 February 'two or three men', one of whom she said she was acquainted with, came to her door and told her a story 'which she immediately believed' that they had been at a dance in the neighbourhood and since it was curfew time and they were unable to get back to the city, they asked her if she would allow them to sleep in the house. She did so, getting them mattresses and blankets and allowing them to sleep in the recreation room. She then went to bed and heard no more until the following morning when the military knocked on the door. Mrs McKay expressed amazement that there were more than 'two or three' men in the house and could swear 'that when she left the bedroom there were no firearms there'—though five loaded service revolvers had been found in her own bed by the search party along with a quantity of flat-nosed .45 bullets. 'She had never had a revolver in her life and did not know there were any in the house', was greeted with peals of laughter in the court.[9]

According to her statement, she knew only one of the visitors, Con Conroy, whom the arresting officer also recognised as being the clerk from Victoria Barracks.

Prosecutor to the arresting officer: 'Have you seen that man [Conroy)]before?'
Witness: 'Yes. He is a clerk at the Garrison Adjutant's office.'
Prosecutor: 'Here?'
Witness: 'Yes. Here at Cork Barracks and I had known him as such . . .'

Council for Mrs McKay then read out a statement on her behalf: 'For some time previous to 8th February, she had known Cornelius Conroy and previously there was an understanding that he could be admitted into the house. On the first Saturday of the early Curfew she met him on the Mallow Road and said to him: "Whenever you are on your way, hop in and have a cup of tea with us and if the early Curfew closed in, you could stay the night." [more laughter] About 10 o'clock on the night of February 7th Mr. Conroy and a boy came to the door. When they exchanged salutations he said he was badly caught out because of the Curfew. They were at a dance and stayed longer than expected. Witness said they had very poor accommodation, as they did not live there during the winter. He said anything was better than being caught under Curfew, and they were wearing flowers in their buttonholes. . . . It was perfectly natural that they should be at a dance at the time—just before Shrove.'[10]

The statement went on to describe how, though a few more men arrived, 'there was not a seditious word spoken'. She made tea for them, frying up some bacon, and waited table on them herself. When they had finished, they had a sing-song around the piano. The first tune played was not any 'seditious' song but was rather the 'Marseillaise', which apparently she played herself. Sometime later she 'came downstairs for a hot water jar and the men were there reciting the Rosary'.

'Did you believe at the time that none of those men carried arms?'
'I did, and the funny part of it is, I believe it still.'
'There were no revolvers in your bed?'
'Indeed there weren't. If there were, I would sleep well away from it.' (*Laughter*)
Cross-examined by the prosecutor: 'Conroy is a friend of yours?'
'Well, I suppose you could say an acquaintance.'
'Would you call him a friend?'
'Well, I don't know. I have never found a friend yet in my life, so I can't say if he is a friend.' (*Laughter*)
'You are very unfortunate, Mrs McKay. Let us hope you will find one soon. Will you say he was a casual acquaintance?'
'Well, I suppose so.'
'And you were willing to put up casual acquaintances?'
'Well, I am not willing to do so at all times, but this was an isolated case.'

Two RIC sergeants were then called as character witnesses and both concurred that she was a 'woman of excellent character' who regularly expressed her loyalty to the British Empire and had her house decorated with the flags of the Allies. One of the RIC men remembered seeing the Union Jack on the sofa during the war. Her foreman, James Carey, said he had no knowledge there were armed men in the house, having just heard the knock on the door as he went to bed, followed next morning by the lady of the house opening the door for the military party. As she did so, she said 'Friends, friends, don't shoot', or words to that effect.

Bearing in mind that Con Conroy was one of the most important of the IRA's spies, his evidence is important. Conroy stated he was 26 years of age and had joined the medical corps of the Royal Navy in 1912. He had seen service in Cameroon, East Africa and Russia and had been invalided out in January 1920. He then got a job as a clerk in Victoria Barracks, though he still received his Royal Navy pension. Nobody commented on the incongruity of finding what appeared to be a loyal servant of the Crown conspiring with known IRA men to 'levy war' against that very Crown. Conroy intended to emigrate to America and was to have sailed the previous Sunday, but his departure had been delayed. His passport and boarding ticket were produced in court, the ticket having been provided by his brother, who lived in America.[11]

Conroy had his own reasons for wanting to get out of Cork, for he had already lost his job at the barracks as a result of papers he had smuggled out of Victoria Barracks turning up at the Mary Bowles raid in Clogheen in January.[12] His evidence bore out Mrs McKay's statement that he had a standing invitation to the house. He did say, however, that the story he told of having been at a dance was a 'white lie'. Like the others, he denied any unlawful associations and 'saw nothing of firearms or ammunition that night'. He said the reason for visiting the house was to have a bit of 'racket', i.e. some music and fun. He stated that Mrs McKay and himself had been the piano players for the sing-song. He thought Mrs McKay had gone to bed ten minutes after tea—before the last four men arrived at the house.

The Cork media, however, reserved their most detailed coverage for the evidence of Seán MacSwiney. As a brother of the dead lord mayor and the firebrand Mary, he was bound to attract the most attention. MacSwiney had been living abroad for some years, returning to Ireland only the previous June. Like many of the men caught that night, he was an employee of Ford's, though he had gone on 'sick leave', in other words on the run, in January. His intention now was to save his men from the consequences of being caught with weapons. He accepted that he himself had been armed with a revolver, while claiming that the others were not. He also accepted that he was a member of the Volunteers, while claiming that the others were civilians. It was the reasons he stated for carrying a Colt .45, however, that led the *Cork Examiner* of 25 February to use the headline 'Sensational Evidence by John MacSwiney'.[13] For MacSwiney used the court as an opportunity to publicise something that everyone knew was going on, despite repeated government denials.

'Why do you carry the weapon?'

'For self-defence, because before and after Christmas I had definite information that what were known as the murder gang of the Black and Tans were after me.' Continuing, the witness said he knew they had called at houses and asked for him. He would have used the revolver if attacked. 'You stated you were in danger of your life of a murder gang of Black and Tans. The court doesn't quite understand that. Is there a special section of the Black and Tans?'

'Well, so far as I know, for some time past there has been a special section going around looting and shooting.'

'A special section?'

'Well, I would not say a special section. Whether they have been specially designated for that kind of work, I don't know. What I say is that there were Black and Tans going around for some time past. They had a pretty free hand in the city to do what they liked after curfew hours and they went around looting and shooting, and I have definite information that they called to certain houses asking for me.'

This was the first time the Cork newspapers quoted someone on the activities of the quasi-military assassination squads that had been in operation in the city since the autumn. It caused a sensation, for it put words on what everybody already knew. In the month of December alone four innocent bystanders had been shot dead on the streets of Cork by bands of Auxiliaries, while five IRA men had been killed by night-time hit squads.

MacSwiney went on to say he did not know the owner of the house and had never met her before that night. He said he was the last of the men to go to bed. They had tea, he said, Conroy played the piano and there were songs. MacSwiney, however, noticed something that the others did not. His counsel stated: 'There was a light and fire in the room on the right-hand side. There was a stove in the corner of the room to the left and he thought he saw some of the bacon being cooked there. After supper, Mrs McKay went away and did not come back.' Mrs McKay's absence is the first hint we have of the operation of the only Cork Protestant who freely admitted to being a British secret service agent.[14]

Chapter 25 ~

THROUGH THE EYE OF A NEEDLE

M rs McKay had also gone away earlier that day, and the evidence presented in court by herself and her two employees was every bit as riddled with evasions as was the evidence of the IRA men. For Bridie McKay was an undercover agent working for British military intelligence. In many of the cases described in this book, there are doubts as to the guilt or otherwise of the various individuals shot as spies, the evidence in some cases pointing one way and in other cases the other. There are no such doubts about Mrs McKay. She is one of the 15 Cork loyalists who declared on their Irish Grants Submission that they had given information and the only one to claim that she was an agent.[1]

Bridie McKay was a well-off Cork city scrap metal merchant in her early forties.[2] She also appears to have been something of a black widow. She was born Bride Marie Twyford, the daughter of a Cork merchant.[3] In 1903 she married P. J. Carey, the owner of B. M. Carey and Co., a scrap metal firm operating out of No. 40 Pope's Quay. Two years later Carey died and his widow went on to build up the business, buying up No. 23 in 1906, No. 24 in 1913 and No. 22 in 1914. By the beginning of World War I she owned significant water frontage along Pope's Quay on Cork's north side. If the Carey business boomed during the early years of the century, then it boomed even more during the Great War when the company got a contract from the British government to provide iron and other metals for the military. By 1920 she was paying over £1,500 a year in wages.[4]

In 1913 she married an engineer called Joseph McKay whose own father, John McKay, had set up an extensive agricultural engineering business in John Street, just around the corner from Pope's Quay. Joseph McKay employed 40 people in his business, which manufactured agricultural implements and had considerable connections among the farming community. McKay was a practical man and an innovative engineer. The business was classified as 'Class A' during the war, a business of 'great public importance'—the provision of agricultural machinery being of prime value for food production in a war economy.[5] The business was rated as being worth £10,000 in 1920.

By the standards of the Cork of her time, Bridie McKay was an extremely wealthy woman, the combined value of the two businesses being in the region of £14,000, an enormous sum in 1921. The McKays lived initially in Waterfall on the south side of the city, moving to Rahanisky House soon after they were married. Later they moved between Mrs McKay's own house in Pope's Quay and Whitechurch, spending the summers at Rahanisky House and the winters at Pope's Quay.

She had been employed as an agent by the British military for some two years prior to 1921.[6] She may or may not have been responsible for some of the other setbacks suffered by the IRA in the north side of the city and the surrounding countryside in the winter of 1920/21. Given that the combined McKay/Carey enterprises on the north city quays were significant employers and that the sourcing of scrap and the selling and repair of agricultural machinery would have taken her and her employees on regular trips into the countryside, she was well placed for the gathering of information. In the economy of early twentieth-century Ireland it was a very suitable business for a British agent to be in, with contacts at all levels of society.

But it was her contact with Con Conroy which is central to the episode at Rahanisky House. For according to her Irish Grants application claim,[7] she went to Victoria Barracks on the day *before* the raid to inform the military that a detachment of IRA men was staying at her house. This of course contradicts what she said in her evidence when it looked as though she was as surprised as anyone else that the IRA men had just turned up at the house on the night before the raid. The British Army stated that she reported that 'a small gang of rebels were billeted at her house' at 8 pm.[8] So Seán MacSwiney was right: she left right after feeding the men.

There are many reasons for thinking that the raid was cleverly orchestrated. For one thing there was no bloodshed. The obvious reason for this was the risk that a valuable agent would be shot. The other reason is that she evidently persuaded the IRA men, either before they went to bed or just as the raiding party arrived, to hide their weapons. In fact, one of the raiding party chided Seán MacSwiney for failing to put up a fight, saying they would have a good chance of winning in a shoot-out, even though they were outnumbered two to one.

Mrs McKay stated that 'a number of soldiers of the Intelligence Department visited our dwelling house . . .'[9] This suggests she was well acquainted with the Intelligence Department and that the officer in command of the raiding party was a British Army intelligence officer and some of his men were too.

So what could have led to the unlikely conjunction of events that led to two major spies from either side knowing each other? It appearss that the military had their suspicions about Mrs McKay and believed she might be a double agent.[10] To prevent her warning the IRA, they told her the raid would take place at 10 am the following morning. Then they surprised her by raiding at 4.45 am. They did this, they later claimed, because though 'she had been employed as an agent for two years [she] was considered not unlikely to supply information to both sides'. Clearly Mrs McKay was an intriguing lady.

Conroy gives his address as John Street, a few doors from the McKay business. The British military were aware of Conroy's activities as a result of the Mary Bowles raid in January. Was there a sexual relationship going on between Conroy and Mrs McKay? Conroy appears to have been something of a debonair character and a natty dresser. He was later described by his friend Seán Moylan as being 'big and athletic. His general air of soldierly neatness and his spotless white shirt impressed me who was sartorially in very bad shape.'[11] The atmosphere in the court suggests that the attendance suspected there was some sort of impropriety going on. Conroy had been in the Royal Navy and was well travelled. Was the whole thing some sort of honey trap? It appears that the military were well aware of Conroy's dual role in the barracks and in the IRA and they distrusted Mrs McKay. Perhaps Mrs McKay decided that, seeing as Conroy was about to leave Cork anyway, she would make an attempt to keep him in Ireland, even if he were to be in prison for a while. Subsequent events suggest that some sort of liaison may well have been going on.

There is little doubt that the IRA men were there at Mrs McKay's behest, not because they had commandeered the house. Mrs McKay opened up the house for them, taking her two employees with her. Then she got the IRA men to hide their weapons in her own bed for 'safekeeping'. It would not have been too difficult to get the IRA men to accede to this—the threat of the death penalty would have been reason enough for them to try to hide their weapons as the raiding party entered the house.

Conroy and the other IRA men were sentenced to 15 years' imprisonment. Mrs McKay, Carey and Renihan were court-martialled for their own protection, though they were then acquitted. The fact that the weapons were technically not found on the men and that there was no shoot-out and no Crown casualties meant they avoided the death penalty. The presence of Mrs McKay in the house, ironically, may have saved their lives.

Mrs McKay also claimed in her IGC application that she had been responsible for the Mourneabbey round-up some weeks later. However, she was in prison at the time, so this is likely to be an exaggeration.[12] On several occasions in her compensation claim she mentions that it was the information on the Mourneabbey ambush and not Rahanisky House that led to her being suspected by the IRA of being a spy. It appears she thought she had got away scot-free with the Rahanisky House affair.

'We were court-martialled for our own protection with the further result that the ambush of the military train at Morden Abbey [sic] a little later was forestalled and the raiders caught.'[13] We have already seen 'Saunders'' confession of his part in the Mourneabbey affair. Both, of course, may have made a contribution to it.

On her release from prison after the trial, Mrs McKay was the recipient of a series of threatening letters informing her that she would be shot. Carey appears to have been similarly threatened. She left Cork on 12 March accompanied by Carey, also known as James Carey White. They moved from place to place around England, living in hiding in fear of their lives. Eventually, Carey came back to Cork in August 1921 to find that her other employee, Renihan, had sold off most of the stock from her premises in her absence. Renihan, little more than a petty thief, was charged with robbery, but the charges were dropped and Renihan escaped to Canada and was not seen in Cork again.

Mrs McKay was right to have been paranoid during her period in hiding in England. Not only were the Cork IRA after her, but in December 1921, at a meeting between the IRB and the officers of the London branch of the IRA, a decision was taken to carry out the execution of three people living in Britain: Captain Bowen Colthurst who shot Francis Sheehy Skeffington during the 1916 Rising, Sir Henry Wilson and 'a woman who had betrayed people in Cork and who had been traced'.[14] So Mrs McKay was in good company and was on the highest IRA wanted list. The big irony is that, for whatever reason, the IRA did not get around to shooting her, even though they knew where she was staying.

Meanwhile Joseph McKay, an innocent party to all this, continued to manufacture and sell his agricultural machinery as best he could from the John Street premises. Soon, however, he too was subject to a campaign of intimidation and a boycott was placed on his business, with the result that his customers were too terrified to buy anything from him. By the summer of 1922 things had got so serious that the Lord Mayor Barry Egan had to plead with the IRA on McKay's behalf and he escaped to England. He returned later in the year when he was declared bankrupt. On 23 February 1923 he died of a heart attack at the age of 48. Former Sergeant Warren of the RIC, who was friendly with McKay, wrote in 1929:[15] 'After Mrs McKay was driven out of the country, Mr McKay lived a life of fear and terror. His nerves seem to have been completely broken. Eventually, he died suddenly during her absence. I often tried to console him but failed. I had great sympathy with him to the end.' Sergeant Warren does not say he had sympathy with Mrs McKay.

For her part, Mrs McKay seems to have lived a peripatetic life between 1921 and 1923, coming back to Cork on several occasions, only to be driven out again by threats. Clearly she was a tough lady. She eventually returned for the funeral of her husband in February 1923, by which time the political situation was sufficiently stable for her to stay. She then began to attempt to rebuild her business, but with limited success. Life was not easy in rebel Cork in the mid-1920s for a former British agent and she appears to have left for good sometime in the thirties.

The fact that nobody took a pot-shot at Mrs McKay during the rest of the twenties though the country was in effect an armed camp for over a decade after the Civil War is odd. Many loyalists suspected of giving information were either forced out or shot. It seems extraordinary that one of Cork's most notorious spies—who was known as such even to the urchins in the street—was allowed to live in comparative peace after 1923.

'It is a well known fact here in this city that I was a marked person by the Republicans, and even at the present time I cannot leave my own house to go to Town shopping or even to go to Church on Sunday, when immediately I am seen in the street, I will be followed by all the sympathisers of the Republican crowd and the Ragamuffins of the street who call out after me, words such as "Traitor", "Where is the blood-money you received for selling the Boys?" "Spy" "English Bastard" etc., and some not very complimentary remarks on my dear husband, who, as you are aware died suddenly, brought about by the persecution he and I received at the hands of the Republican mob. I do not leave my house at all now, not even to go to Church, for I could not stand the jeers of the people.' The pressure got too much for her and she did eventually leave.

Was Mrs McKay spared from retribution by her friendship with Conroy? Conroy was by then very close to Seán Moylan, one of the most important IRA figures in the post-Treaty period.[16] The curious thing is that in all the 50 or so pages of the literature surrounding her application for compensation, her 'dear husband' merits only that one mention. You have to read the submission very carefully to find a reference to her two children—she had two, a girl and a boy—who were aged 13 and 8, respectively, in 1921. There is no reference to the suffering they must have endured after 1921 and no sympathy for what her actions had caused her husband. The lady's affections, if she had any, appear to have been elsewhere.

Apart from being subsequently immune to retribution, she also did rather well out of her spying activities. All in all she asked for £16,190 in compensation, an enormous sum in those days. The IGC was having none of it and granted her £4,800. She had also received an *ex gratia* payment of £1,100 in the spring of 1921 on the recommendation of the GOC Cork Command for her part in the Rahanisky affair. This was from the resettlement fund put in place by the military to allow those who gave information to move abroad. A report was prepared for the British government by the military authorities in Ireland in October 1921 in reply to various statements made by Mrs McKay. This report is still secret. A former Dublin Castle official, however, said: 'I remember a good deal about this case but unfortunately the Dublin Castle papers which contain detailed reports cannot now be traced. There is no doubt that Mrs McKay did render very valuable assistance to the Crown forces in Ireland. The War Office gave her a grant of £1,100 for the information and assistance which she had given them.'[17]

Seven years later, the Irish Grants Committee was allowed access to Mrs McKay's War Office file, on condition that it be returned immediately after the IGC was finished with it. There it remains under closure. Her own words say it best: 'I got a gratuity from the Government for services rendered . . . No one have [sic] served the British Government better than I have.'

So here were two more loyalists who, along with George Tilson, had been banished by the IRA in the early spring of 1921. So Liam de Roiste was correct.

As for her motive: perhaps it was love; perhaps it was greed. The account she left and her choice of words suggest that she was a somewhat uncouth person. It appears she started out in good faith as an agent in 1919. The British thought she was unreliable, though she had good connections with the military. Maybe she fell in love with Conroy and wanted to hold on to him when his cover was blown. There is no evidence that Joseph McKay ever provided information to the British or had any part in this tale. He appears to have been typical of the kind of loyalist portrayed by Olga Pyne Clarke, who kept his nose out of political matters. Yet he paid a heavy price for his wife's shenanigans. As for Mrs McKay, somehow one feels that being taunted by the street children of Cork was no more than she deserved and that she was extremely lucky to escape a bullet.

Chapter 26 ∽

A COMPENDIUM OF
VICTIMHOOD

In all the myriad records available on the War of Independence there
appears at first glance to be no record of anybody called Parsons being
killed by the IRA; nor is there any mention of anything, at least outside of
YMCA records, to suggest that anything untoward happened to that
organisation in Cork. There was one series of records, however, that no
historian working on the period had thought of checking. These were the
records of the Cork courts, what are known as the records of the Cork Crown
and Peace, office registers and in some cases the actual records of individual
court cases. These are quite a treasure trove of information, in particular the
Criminal Injury Books, which deal with compensation cases for personal
injuries. There were hundreds of such claims heard by the Cork courts
between 1920 and 1923. There are many cases not listed in newspapers. In fact,
taken together, this is a vast résumé of IRA and British activities, a sort of
parallel history of what the war was actually like on the ground in the city and
surrounding areas. This is a compendium of victimhood, with all kinds of
compensation cases of soldiers, RIC men and civilians, both for personal
injury and property damage. It's all there, from the burning of Cork city and
the City Hall to the shooting dead of most of the 'spies' we have encountered
in this book.[1] But there is no sign of Parsons and no sign of other teenage
victims either.

However, there were five compensation cases claimed by the Cork YMCA
and the National Council of the YMCA based in London. They appear, on the
face of it, to be relatively minor issues and concern a cluster of raids on YMCA
stores and materials, mostly occurring in June/July 1921. There was also a
claim for £116 made by the YMCA for losses incurred in the raid on its store in
Cat Fort in April 1921 already referred to and for a previous raid there in June
1920, where a Ford car and a substantial amount of equipment was taken, as
a result of which Mrs Ward, the wife of the caretaker, died. Most intriguing
though was a claim for the loss of a second Ford business touring car which
was taken from Merchants Quay at 11.45 on the morning of the Truce, 15

minutes before the ceasefire came into operation.[2] There were also two apparently minor issues that occurred on 15 June and 22 June respectively on the River Lee 'between Cork and Haulbowline', when some persons 'did maliciously destroy' 80 dozen boxes of Doubleday cakes, the property of the YMCA.[3]

To one who had seen the lists of all the Freemasons in Munster gathered for use as hostages and the correspondence accompanying them, this was small beer. In the context of the time it was no surprise that the cream cakes of the YMCA had been thrown into the Lee.

But what if abductions had occurred during one or other of these raids? What if the taking of the YMCA touring car on the morning of the Truce, a car that could hold up to a dozen people, what would now be called a minibus, was a copycat operation of the kind that lifted the two Auxiliaries from outside Johnson and Perrott's in November 1920? If gunmen like the Grays were capable of strolling up to two Black and Tans and abducting them quietly in a city full of military activity, then surely it would have been even easier to walk on to a minibus of YMCA youngsters on the morning of the Truce when British activity was winding down and take them on a trip out the country? This could explain why Connie Neenan was able to say that the YMCA abductions had occurred 'just before the Truce', while Corry would have been right in saying that they were 'just after the Truce'. The abduction would indeed have taken place before the Truce, admittedly by only 15 minutes, while the executions would have been carried out afterwards. Both could have been telling the truth.

And what if Parsons or others had been taken during the raids on the launch which the YMCA had been using to travel on the river from the city quays to Haulbowline in mid-June? Remember, this was the same week the YMCA received the 'threat' found in the toilet of the youth club in Marlborough Street. Did the 'threat' arise directly as a result of these raids? Was a boy (or boys) taken as part of these raids? Did the abduction(s) on the morning of the Truce, if it (they) happened, also arise from this? The YMCA river excursions would have passed along the Lee directly under Corry's farmyard. There might be a connection. But this is all mere speculation.

Chapter 27 ~

| DUMPING STORES

The pattern of attacks on the Cork YMCA began on 11 July 1920, a year to the day before the Truce, when the association's store at Cat Fort was raided and a car, cinema projector and some foodstuffs to the value of £783 were stolen. Mrs Ward was to die as a result. As mentioned earlier, Cat Fort was raided again on 9 April 1921. Similar raids were carried out on the YMCA store in Warren Place on 1 June 1921, in addition to the two raids on the river and the commandeering of the Ford touring car on the morning of the Truce. This reflects an increase in the frequency of attacks on all organisations that were regarded as pro-British. As Michael Collins argued at the time: 'My chief desire is not to single out any particular institution, but to get at them all. No English connection should be tolerated, except a connection we could not get rid of, for instance the Post Office.'[1] While Collins's argument does not concern itself with loyalists or loyalist organisations, it could be interpreted as including agencies close to the British military, and that would have included the YMCA.

The attacks on YMCA facilities, however, follow a pattern. While the raid of June 1920 was almost certainly an attempt to acquire weapons, the later attacks were part of a campaign against anyone who provided the British military with supplies, everything from equipment to coal and food.[2] The RIC reported that, in the month of June 1921, there were 18 cases of robberies of military stores in the Cork East Riding area alone, many of these in the harbour.[3] 'In very few cases was any use being made of the articles stolen. They were either burnt or thrown into the sea.' 'On 25/6/21 the ss *Rostellan*, the property of the Cork, Blackrock and Passage Railway company, plying between Cork and Crosshaven, was raided by a party of armed men in a search for military stores. There was none on board and they left without doing any damage.'[4] Similarly, the chronological list of IRA activities in Cork city for the first half of 1921 lists many raids on military stores in the city and surrounding areas.[5]

The correspondence between the leadership of the 1st Division of the IRA and Collins and Mulcahy in the months immediately prior to the Truce refer to the dire position of the brigades with regard to provisions and the fact that some units were almost going hungry for want of food.[6] Yet IRA units were well catered for by 'the people'. Whatever deprivations men on the run suffered, hunger is rarely mentioned as one of them. If the Cork brigades were in a dire position with regard to food, then why did they toss all the provisions they captured into the sea? Was this just another line peddled to get authorisation to go after loyalists? Pressure was also being applied to prevent merchants from supplying the British military. 'It is time we got the Irish people, whoever they are, not to freely supply the Enemy. . . . It seems ridiculous to have the civilian population supplying the Enemy while the army is in the field to cut off supplies etc.'[7] GHQ staff 'desire to have vested in them the power to authorise the O/C of any particular area to forbid the supply of materials to Enemy forces in that area at any time and in any circumstances as GHQ staff consider necessary.'[8]

With its canteens and huts in all the major barracks supplying the British military with tobacco, cigarettes, confectionery, sweets and so on, this was precisely the position the YMCA found itself in.

Yet there is nothing in any of the surviving accounts of these raids to suggest that boys were abducted, either as the reason for the raids or as a result of them. Was the 'threat' issued to the YMCA and found in the toilet in mid-June about the supplying of goods to the military? If so, why did the YMCA cancel all its excursions owing to the 'unsettled nature of the country'?

Similarly, there is nothing other than coincidence to suggest that the commandeering of the YMCA's Ford touring car from the Cork quays resulted in deaths. While the commandeering of military vehicles regularly resulted in the deaths of RIC men and soldiers, there is no evidence that such was the case in this instance, though the possibility cannot be ruled out. So, while there was a lot of activity around YMCA facilities, in particular from April to July 1921, there is nothing bar geographical proximity to directly suggest that the boy or boys killed by Corry's execution squad were picked up as a result of the raids on the river. And while the commandeering of the car may very well be linked to the disappearance of boys, there is no direct evidence of it.

It was, however, when I reread Connie Neenan's account of the capture and killing of YMCA boys that something new suddenly jumped into focus: 'We did not know then that the British had organised the youngsters of the YMCA to trail our men. They were mostly from good families. It was then, 15 months after the murder of Tomás MacCurtain that we learned that a kid of 15 had tracked him that night.'[9] Neenan was in charge of the south city battalion at the time. If Neenan stated that a kid of 15 had tracked Tomás MacCurtain and that they only found out about it some 15 months later, then that has to be taken seriously.

But who were the three kids whom Neenan stated his group had shot? Was one of them Parsons? If so, why was he remembered and the others forgotten? Did it happen before or after the Truce? The identity of young Parsons should have been the easy part of the puzzle. After all, there was a J. and an S. Parsons named as being members of the Cork YMCA in 1919 and 1921 respectively. The problem with this was that S. Parsons was still a member during 1921/22, which means he must have been alive at the end of June 1921. While this does not preclude him from being one of the boys in question, it does mean he would probably have had to have been killed after the Truce. If that is the case, then who was the boy whose abduction was reported in *The Times* of 18 May? The other Parsons boy, J. Parsons, appears to have left the YMCA by 1920, probably because he had outgrown membership of the junior section. This suggests he was more than 15 by 1921.

It was then that things started to fall into place. John Borgonovo mentions a boy called William Edward Parsons, who was born in Cork in 1906 but for whom no death cert could be found.[10] There was no other evidence to link him to the case other than his age—he would have been 15 in 1921.[11] The discovery of an electoral register for Cork city in the courts records found only one family called Parsons living within the Cork city borough in 1913. A man called Joseph Parsons is named as having lived at No. 30 High Street on the south side of the city. According to the 1911 census,[12] Joseph Parsons had three sons in 1911: Joseph Jnr aged 10, Stanley aged 8 and Edward aged 4. It seemed likely that the J. and S. Parsons listed as members of the YMCA for 1919 and 1921 were Joseph and Stanley, who would then have been 19 and 18 respectively.

The younger boy, Edward, was 14 or 15 in 1921. A quick check of the Births, Marriages and Deaths Registers[13] established that he was William Edward Parsons. So John Borgonovo was right. This was the boy for whom no death cert could be found. He was born in Cork on 27 May 1906 to Joseph and Florence Parsons née Perman. Joseph Parsons was an Englishman who came to Cork some time between 1903 and 1911.[14] He worked as a cable electrical jointer. He described the family as 'Church of England'. The family hailed from Brighton, where Joseph and Florence had married in 1899.[15] Both older sons were born in England, while Edward was born after the family arrived in Ireland.

What evidence as could be found pointed to William Edward Parsons as being the boy abducted and killed by the IRA. His age was just about right; he was 15 in May 1921; he was the son of an Englishman. The location of his home also correlates with various strands of evidence. High Street is quite near the area where Mick Murphy and Peter Donovan lived. It is also no more than ten minutes' walk from the area where the *Times* reporter claimed that 'somebody's child' had been abducted—the city end of the Blackrock Road. The 'piece of open ground' at the city end of the Blackrock Road is the closest public green area to High Street. It would make sense for a 14- or 15-year-old to have been playing there.

On the other hand, it must cast doubt on Mick Murphy's assertion that

Parsons was watching Tomás MacCurtain's house on the night he was assassinated. Young Parsons would have been only 13 at the time of MacCurtain's death. He would have had to cross the entire city in the dead of night to the more or less alien environment of Blackpool, carry out his spying duties, call into DI Swanzy and get home again. It all seemed a bit far-fetched for someone so young. Be that as it may, the evidence now pointed to William Edward Parsons, who was probably only 14 at the time, as the Parsons boy, 'the son of an Englishman', picked up and executed by the Cork city IRA at some point in the conflict.

Chapter 28 ❧

ANOTHER MISSING TEENAGER

Because both Connie Neenan and Corry suggest that abductions of youngsters took place around the Truce of 11 July 1921, we need to look in detail at the days immediately before and after the imposition of the ceasefire. Luckily, the IRA's records for that week and succeeding weeks have survived.[1] The intelligence report of the Cork No. 1 Brigade of late July/ August 1921 dealing with lists of suspects states that 'all persons definitely identified [as enemy agents] have been dealt with'. This suggests that anyone the Cork No. 1 Brigade wanted killed was already dead by the end of July. We have seen how Major O'Connor was pulled out of bed on the eve of 11 July and shot. He had been on the wanted list since the spring. As one might expect, something of a 'mopping up' operation was taking place right up to the last moments before the ceasefire.

The only cases the report describes as being 'difficult to deal with' were those of Cruxy Connors, Monkey Mac and the 'spy' Stevens, a UCC student who joined the army to avoid capture. We have already seen the subsequent attempts of the IRA to track down and kill both Connors and McDonald.[2] Stevens had by then left Cork.[3] There are no members of the YMCA or Freemasons listed, suggesting that they had been either 'dealt with' already or they were not considered suspects, or at least not enough evidence was available to regard them as such. What is even more significant is that neither the YMCA nor the Masonic Hall is among the list of suspect 'enemy' organisations.[4]

The weekly reports for July of the individual companies of the Cork No. 1 Brigade also shed much light on the *modus operandi* of the brigade and how it was organised in the city.[5] It is the only surviving outline of how the companies of the city battalions operated on a day-to-day basis. It is an intriguing insight into how the guerrilla war machine in the city operated.

During the week leading up to the Truce, A Company of the 1st Battalion 'carried out patrol system as arranged by O/C Batt, for 4 men to be on duty each night on the look-out for enemy stragglers. Failed to get any.' o, e and f Companies were also on the look-out for 'enemy stragglers' and also 'failed to capture any'. On 9 July d Company had '6 men on the look-out for a soldier who was on active service in Cork Barracks and who was expected to visit a house in the area that evening. Unfortunately, he did not come.' h Company had better luck: 'On the 10th of July, 6 men and myself patrolled the Western Road from Donovan's Bridge west. We were looking out for a spotter but failed to find him. We held up four soldiers (Royal Engineers, 2 Staffs) and searched them but found no arms. We took them to a field in our area where they were executed before 9 pm.' These were the four soldiers that Connie Neenan claimed to have tried in vain to find before they were shot on the morning of the Truce.

g Company also found its target: 'On July 11th at 11.55 pm we captured Begley, a spy for whom we were on the look-out. He was executed on Saturday 16th.'[6] In this case the execution occurred after the Truce, though, as we'll see, the timing of the abduction was reported incorrectly and should have read 11.55 am.

What is interesting about these brief reports is the language. 'Enemy stragglers' is a military term straight out of the retreat from Moscow, and while guerrilla warfare as fought in Cork city in 1921 is far removed from Napoleon, the other term 'spotter' was widely used in Cork at the time. Clearly, just as the IRA was using women, Na Fianna members and others as scouts, 'the enemy' was doing the same. Words are important. It is a lot easier to kill an 'enemy straggler' or a 'spotter' than it is to kill a neighbour who may or may not be working for the other side. Quite clearly each company was given its quota of killings or abductions to be carried out if the opportunity arose. As we have seen, the 2nd Battalion, and g Company in particular, was spectacularly successful at this.

Outside the city the brigade was more lenient. On 8 July, for instance, the 6th Battalion captured a bugle boy called William Dickinson in Grenagh. Instead of being shot out of hand, he was deported to England on 15 July.[7]

It is clear that a plan was in place to hunt down and capture or kill as many spotters and stragglers as possible before the imposition of the Truce. The 'spy' Begley clearly belongs in this category. Was he a spotter or an enemy straggler? Was he a 'spy' or an 'informer'? Whatever the case, he was probably interrogated intensely over the four days between his capture and execution. If they caught Begley, they might have caught YMCA boys, but why do that when the YMCA was not even listed as a dangerous 'enemy' institution?

At least we can learn something about Begley, for his mother wrote to the Free State government over a year later:[8]

> 1 Rock Cottages
> North Mall
> Cork
> October 6th 1922

Dear Sir,
My son, John Begley, was taken by armed forces on July 11th 1921 at 12 noon. I interviewed the Liaison Officer for Cork city who informed me that he could not account for him. It is now over fourteen months since I have seen him, so I presume he must be dead. . . .

> Signed Annie Begley

The Department of Defence wrote back: 'As far as I can ascertain, [he was] shot unofficially as a spy. I have not been able to trace his burial place'.[9]

Annie Begley's address, 1 Rock Cottages, North Mall, was almost next door to an RIC station. This seems to have been a similar case to that of George Horgan. Begley was wanted because of his association with the RIC—indeed one of the most notorious Black and Tans, Charlie Chance, was stationed there. Begley was described by Connie Neenan to Ernie O'Malley as 'one of Shield's crowd', suggesting that he may have been connected to 'Saunders' and Dan Shields. This makes sense since 'Saunders' claimed he got information on Blarney Street, just up the road from the Begley residence.[10] Annie Begley had a notion that her son was in trouble and she had taken out 'a small insurance policy' in his name.[11]

The official list of disappeared persons mentions nobody else being kidnapped in the city during July. The last disappearance noted is that of one W. J. Nolan, who, according to that list, vanished on 11 June, a full month before the Truce. Nolan is variously mentioned as an 'ex-soldier'[12] and having been executed for applying to join the RIC.[13] There are various dates given for his disappearance.[14] In any event, in the few instances where Nolan is mentioned, the inference is that he was an adult, an ex-soldier who applied to join the RIC and was shot for doing so, and that he died before the Truce.

In fact, he was none of these things. The *Cork Examiner* of 14 July, some three days after the Truce, carried the story of the disappearance of one Willie Nolan which, though the statement is only four lines long and tucked away in an obscure corner of the paper, confirms the disappearance of another teenager:

A boy of about 17 years named Willie Nolan of Annemount, Friars Walk, Cork has been missing since about 11.30 am on Monday at which time he left his residence to post a letter. Nothing has since been heard of him. His father was previously a member of the RIC and a brother is at present serving with that force.[15]

Annemount is a terrace of houses on the south side of the city built for members of the RIC.[16] Nolan's father, originally from Carlow, had been a prominent RIC man in the city.[17] His younger son had applied to join the RIC, though he could not have actually joined because the minimum recruitment age was 19. The RIC also mentions the kidnapping: 'W. J. Nolan, son of an ex-RIC man, who had presented himself as a candidate for the force was kidnapped near his house in the City. Nothing has been heard from him since.'[18] Did he 'present himself' as a candidate in order to avoid IRA retribution? Did he too have a premonition that something unpleasant was in store for him? He was captured by members of E Company of the 2nd Battalion based in Friar's Walk.[19] There is no indication that the execution occurred in Corry's area.[20]

PART VI

Chapter 29

SERGEANT MAJOR MACKINTOSH AND MICHAEL WILLIAMS

According to the accounts gathered by Jim Fitzgerald in the 1970s, some 35 individuals were shot and buried in Knockraha and in Corry's farm between the summer of 1920 and the end of 1922. Recently released documents shed light on some of the cases. One of the questions that exercised us in Chapter 5 is: was Corry exaggerating the number of British military dead so as to cover up the large number of civilians that were executed in his area, especially considering that some of those killed in the area were picked up by the east Cork Battalion rather than coming from the city? These include several tramps picked up around Midleton. It also includes Eugene Swanton, an ex-soldier who was working for a farmer at Ballinacurra and who was taken at the end of June 1921 and never seen again.[1] For others such as 'Paddy the Painter' and the two women alleged to have disappeared in Carrigtwhohill and indeed the mysterious German watch thief who was shot rather than deported, they all seem to have just vanished.[2]

He says three undercover officers were executed.[3] While he stated to Ernie O'Malley that most of the spies he shot were soldiers in mufti, only these three could be described as intelligence operatives.[4] As we have seen, the British suspected something was going on in the area.[5]

Of all the soldiers Corry claimed to have shot, only one is actually named. He was a Sergeant Major Mackintosh. According to Corry,[6] Mackintosh, a Cameron Highlander based in Cobh Barracks,[7] was killed after the Truce as a reprisal for being a member of the 'murder gang', an undercover squad of Camerons who shot dead three 'young fellows' in Carrigtwohill in May 1921. This refers to the shooting of several Volunteers and civilians in Carrigtwohill.[8]

After the Truce, Corry claimed he and Mick Burke of the Cobh Company talked their way into the officers' mess at the military barracks in Cobh on the pretext that they were looking for Corry's cap which had been taken by raiding parties some months earlier. According to Corry, they were entertained and offered drinks by the officer they met, a Captain Morrison, who laughingly regretted that Corry had not turned up earlier when he was wanted. Morrison is also mentioned by Mick Burke as the intelligence officer who interrogated him after he was captured.[9]

The hat, Morrison said (in Corry's version of events), had been used as part of a disguise by members of his own raiding parties—it may even have been worn by members of the 'murder gang' while operating in the area. (IRA Volunteer Seán Healy left a very good description of hiding from that hit squad in a house in Carrigtwohill and listening to their Scottish accents as they searched in the darkness for IRA suspects.[10] So there is no question but that the squad existed.) Corry told Ernie O'Malley that Morrison asked about one of the undercover men sent into his area, only to be told he had been executed. Surprised that the IRA men wanted only lemonade, Morrison introduced Corry and Burke to a Colonel Cameron, who refused to speak to them. Then a 'very big man' walked into the canteen and was introduced as Sgt Major Mackintosh. All four sat down and had a drink together in the canteen.

A few nights later, according to Corry, Mackintosh was picked up outside Cobh, moved to Corry's house, tried with having killed the Volunteers in Carrigtwohill and executed.[11] All this of course was in breach of the Truce and if the account is true, it happened in late 1921 or early 1922, just before the Camerons left Cobh.

But is it possible that enemy combatants could simply walk into a British Army barracks less than six months after the end of such a conflict? The museum of the Cameron Highlander regiment in Inverness records only one casualty suffered by the regiment during its stay in Cobh in 1920/21. This was a Driver Hall, killed in an IRA ambush in August 1920.[12] No Camerons from Cobh are on the published missing list. In fact, no Camerons are among the casualty lists at all, suggesting that this might be an exaggeration on the part of Corry.

However, it soon became apparent that not all was as it should be in the regimental records. For at least one Cameron Highlander disappeared from Cobh between the Truce and the departure of the regiment on 3 February 1922. This was a Private J. A. C. (Arthur) Anderson, who was kidnapped on 26 October 1921 and described as 'believed to be buried in Knockraha'. There is correspondence in Michael Collins's papers from Anderson's sister in Glasgow writing for information on her brother's whereabouts.[13] The Cork IRA replied: 'We have to report that Pte Anderson QOCH did not fall into our hands and we have no information as to his whereabouts' and 'our forces are not concerned with his disappearance'. While this implies that Anderson was picked up and killed without official IRA sanction, it more likely denotes

O'Hegarty and O'Donoghue's capacity to deny anything that did not suit them.

It appears that his was another case of mistaken identity. For Anderson, who had not even been in Cobh during the conflict, was captured *in lieu* of another Cameron Highlander, a Lieutenant Anderson, who was blamed locally for the shooting of John O'Connell, a Cobh blacksmith also shot by the 'murder gang' in the belief that he was IRA company captain Jack O'Connell. So Anderson was killed in place of his namesake.[14]

Yet among the Camerons' regimental records[15] were details that lend at least come credibility to Corry's story. Among the officers of the 2nd Battalion based in Cobh was a Captain H. M'L. Morrison and a Captain I. C. Cameron, who was in charge of C Company. But it is the description of an action in Cloyne at the end of 1920 that was of most interest. After describing how the IRA men were cornered in a house before escaping, the regimental record goes on to say, 'Later on, as our detachment returned to barracks, it was seen that fifty or sixty rebels were lining a hedge along which the car would have to pass. Lieutenant Mackintosh thereupon promptly turned a Lewis gun on to them, upon which, very wisely, they all took to their heels, leaving one of their number dead behind them.'[16]

While the details of the siege in Cloyne are verifiable, what happened afterwards is pure hyperbole. For the dead 'Volunteer' was in fact a civilian, a boy called John O'Brien who was leading a donkey into the village and was shot dead in anger by the departing soldiers.[17] This episode alone would have been enough to put Mackintosh near the top of the east Cork IRA's most wanted list. A hardened junior officer, it is very likely he was part of the undercover patrols that caused such terror in Carrigtwohill in May 1921. Anecdotal evidence suggests that he was one of the most feared British soldiers in east Cork—almost a hundred years later he still gets a mention from those in the area who are interested in such things. But there is no evidence from the British side that he was shot.

The Army Lists suggest that he was a Sergeant Major Donald Mackintosh, born in 1885, served in the ranks for 12 years before being commissioned as a 2nd lieutenant in 1917 and at some time thereafter becoming a full lieutenant.[18] There is only one problem: he continued to serve in the army until he retired in 1930. Therefore, he could not have been shot by Corry.

So what actually happened? Did the Cobh IRA simply pick up a squaddie, Arthur Anderson, thinking he was Lieut Anderson, bring him to Corry's, execute him and then claim they had shot the much-wanted Lieut Mackintosh? Major General Douglas Wimberly, who commanded the Camerons at Cobh at the time, left the following fascinating account which has recently been republished:[19] 'As the whole civil administration of the country had broken down and ceased to work, a sort of martial law was in force. As a result . . . we had to take on the local registration of births, deaths and marriages and even hold all the inquests of which, at such a time, there were certainly plenty.' Wimberly goes on to describe one of these inquests:

> Another inquest I held was in a village near by called Carrigtwohill on the corpse of a man who was laid out in a cottage surrounded by lighted candles, while a lot of Irish women were holding a wake and wailing around the body. I came to the conclusion that the man had been murdered by some opposing Irish faction and returned a verdict of death by an unknown hand. Many years later it was revealed to me that the man had in fact been shot, or even murdered, by a certain Cameron, who had been out on his own secretly at night. I think the madman concerned was the same individual who was soon after removed from the regiment and the Army.

This was the inquest into the killing of Willie Bransfield, a young IRA Volunteer shot dead by 'a man wearing white breeches' on 5 May 1921.[20] It is very likely that this is the same man sought by Corry almost a year later. This account suggests that Mackintosh, if indeed it was Mackintosh, was soon drummed out of the army. Was Corry and Mick Burke's visit to the barracks a quiet way to get rid of him? While Wimberly's account states that it was to be years later before he found out that the man in white breeches was one of his own men, 'the madman concerned' had been quickly removed.

Is it possible that Wimberly, though o/c of the Camerons at the time, was not aware that some of his junior officers were going out at night in mufti to carry out unauthorised killings of IRA suspects? According to Mick Burke, 'It was around the end of May 1921 when I received information that a specially selected number of Cameron Highlanders were formed into a murder gang.'[21] Was the 'murder gang' operating behind the back of the officers in charge of the regiment, or was Wimberly just covering up?[22] Is it possible that Mackintosh was handed over to the IRA for breeching army discipline? Would the Camerons have handed over one of their own? It seems highly unlikely. There is no independent record of Mackintosh's death. There is, however, a paper trail on the disappearance of Arthur Anderson. The balance of the evidence suggests that it was Anderson who was picked up in place of his namesake and that Mackintosh was never caught. But because of his notoriety, the latter looked like a much better scalp for Corry and Burke.

Another recently released file also confirms that Corry's recollections, while occasionally flawed with regard to detail, are often very accurate. This is the case of the RIC man Williams, who was tried in Corry's house for his alleged part in the assassination of Tomás MacCurtain and who, it is claimed, confessed to being the third policeman up the stairs on that fateful night. Recently released Department of Justice files fill out the details of the Williams case.[23]

Former RIC constable Michael Williams, aged 37, who had served as a policeman in Newmarket, Co. Cork, was taken prisoner by republican forces on 15 June 1922, a month after being demobbed from the RIC, being abducted as he left Mass at his home village of Stradbally, Co. Laois. The men who captured him claimed it was in connection with the death of Lord Mayor MacCurtain. He was moved initially to Portlaoise, where his brother was allowed to visit him, and was relatively well treated. The Civil War broke out a week later and Williams was transferred south in advance of the retreat of republicans to Munster. In one account he was moved via Birr, Mallow and Cork city by a unit under the command of Seán Moylan, who had been the IRA commander in the north Cork area where Williams had served.

A week or two later he fetched up at Corry's farmyard. According to the subsequent Garda investigation, 'he was seen passing that evening in a lorry and the prisoner and his escort were covered in dust and appeared to be after coming a long distance. On the following day he was court-martialled and found guilty of taking part in the murder of Lord Mayor McCurtain [*sic*] of Cork and sentenced to death. Seán Hegarty of Cork acted as President of the Court. Mrs McCurtain [*sic*] was a witness there.'

This is similar to the account Corry gave to Jim Fitzgerald. The matter of Williams's guilt or otherwise is an important one. The confession extracted from him—by the usual means of promising him that he would be deported to Australia if he confessed, a local IRA man even straightening his tie 'for the journey'—was in the Corry family for many years afterwards. It seems pretty clear-cut. He confessed to having been a member of the assassination party and to having stayed at the Munster Hotel with the killers on the night before to the assassination. However, his sister in a sworn statement stated that, while Williams had been in Cork at the assizes on the night of the killing of MacCurtain, he had stayed with her and had not gone out.[24] She went to her grave believing he was innocent. Whether he was guilty or not we'll never know. What we do know, however, is that his name had been bandied about by the press during the public inquest into the killing.[25] The newspapers stated that Williams was in Cork that night, the insinuation being that he was part of the plot. He may have been, but it is far from certain.

The file goes on to state exactly where Williams was buried on the farm and that another 'spy' was buried 'in the same corner about a fortnight previous'. The best estimation for the execution of Williams is around the last week of June 1922. This account, from a local IRA man who was present, states that another man was buried in the same field some two weeks earlier, suggesting that at least one other 'spy' had been executed in mid-June. The Garda report on the matter also states that a third body was 'buried near the boundary fence of Corry's farm and an adjoining acre, the property of a man called Savage'. There is also a mention of the quarry at Ballinbrittig 'and our informant is of the opinion that there are bodies buried there also'.

This is the best independent evidence we have that Corry's farm was used as a 'veritable graveyard', as the Garda reports of the time called it. However, probably the most interesting item in the file is a letter to Williams's mother from an anonymous local woman. The details are almost certainly incorrect—for a start, Corry was not even present at the trial of Williams, and Williams was not hanged—but they are highly significant in the context of this narrative.[26]

> It is well known around here that your deceased son Michael was taken to Martin Corry's house near Knockraha, Cork and courtmartialled (mock) with another poor man, by this Corry and others and sentenced to death by hanging.
>
> The rope was procured, the victims bound, and the ropes fastened to their necks, the executioners throwing the end of the rope over a beam, pulled and pulled for hours, while the unfortunate victims struggled and struggled in their desperate agony. Oh! God what a death. The executioner, Corry, and his accomplices, having enjoyed this inhuman sport for some hours, retired for a rest and a drink, and then left the unfortunate and unhappy victims struggling in their half-strangled condition. When the executioners returned their victims were absolutely riddled with bullets and their bodies buried on Corry's Farm, where many other victims of his (Corry's) lie buried.
> Signed
>
> A Sympathetic Mother

This is an exaggeration of what had gone on at Corry's and was obviously written by someone in terror of Corry. It is not the execution of Williams, who was tried in the parlour of Corry's house by officers of the Cork No. 1 Brigade, including Seán O'Hegarty and Tom Crofts, and executed afterwards.[27] However, the details of it *are* similar to the account left by Corry of the killing of Parsons. The lady was right about the hanging but wrong about its victim—all the evidence suggests that Williams was shot in a military-style execution.[28] This is an important piece of information for it suggests that young Parsons was killed at around the same time as Williams or slightly earlier. It changes the whole context of the accounts left by Mick Murphy, Connie Neenan and others. It suggests that the versions given to the BMH and to Ernie O'Malley, where Parsons is described as having been killed during the Anglo-Irish conflict, were a smokescreen to cover up the fact that he was killed not just after the Truce but after the Treaty and well into the first year of the Irish Free State. This suggests that Parsons was killed a year after all the IRA survivors said he was.

What is also interesting about the Williams case is how quickly the cult of *omèrta* descended on the area in the aftermath of the killings. Kevin

O'Higgins, the Minister for Justice, directed that the 'Garda be instructed to search for [the] body and proceed generally as on the investigation of a case of murder. It must be remembered that prior to July 1922 a general amnesty had been given by the Provisional Government, so that the Indemnity Act does not arise.' When the gardaí attempted to do this, however, they quickly ran into difficulties. The local parish priest, Canon O'Leary, initially volunteered to help find the body. He then changed his mind and appeared to be avoiding the Garda investigating the case.

> When finally tracked down I was surprised to find that he now wished to have nothing to do with this case. I asked him why in view of his recent offer to hand over this body and his offer having been accepted. He would not give any reason but I have reason to believe he is afraid. I have also reason to believe he may have gone to some prominent Irregulars in this area with a view to their giving him this body and they refused to let him know where it was or to have the body touched. Anyhow, to use his own words on the matter, his attitude is: 'I wash my hands of the whole affair and I advise everybody concerned to let this dead body lie as no good can come out of lifting it or interfering with it.'[29]

The Deputy Commissioner of the Crime Branch of the Garda Síochána also cautioned:

> I am directed by the Commissioner to draw special attention to the circumstances connected with the death of ex-Constable Williams and to say that he is strongly of the opinion that should [the instruction to investigate the case] be carried out, it will undoubtedly have a most damaging effect. . . . Should the Gardai search for and find the body, an Inquest is almost certain to follow and such an Inquiry at the present time would have a very bad general effect . . . the arrests of any parties known to be concerned . . . would it is believed lead to a very serious situation. The Commissioner thinks that perhaps the results politically of pursuing this matter may have been overlooked and he asks that this aspect of the case be given further consideration.

The body was not in fact recovered and no further investigation appears to have taken place.

There was, however, one body recovered from Corry's farm during the Civil War period. At some point, probably after the internment of Corry himself, Free State Army troops arrived and proceeded to exhume a body from under the floorboards of Corry's house; this episode was witnessed by several people who were working at Corry's at the time. The body was that of a soldier or officer in uniform. Eugene Turpin remembered being shown one of the buttons found on the body. While locals had no idea who the body was, the chances are that it was Arthur Anderson since his is the only case mentioned in Free State military papers in connection with the area. Indeed the missing documentation from the Anderson file in the Department of Defence Papers may well be the 'red-stickered' confidential material relating to Corry.[30] The Irish State is still very sensitive about exhumations. Any request that I made in my efforts to track down missing persons through access to material on exhumations was politely turned down.

| MISSING SOLDIERS

The British Army, when contacted by relatives, is diligent on the matter of trying to establish the place of execution and burial of its men. The Irish National Army, as the Civil War was drawing to a close, was similarly diligent in its enquiries on behalf of the relatives of missing British personnel, even if they rarely got straight answers from republicans. The defence papers of the early years of the Irish Free State contain many lists of missing British military personnel and the correspondence relating to them. Among the Collins, Mulcahy and Department of Defence papers are several lists which contain the names of many more military personnel who disappeared than were published at the time.[1] In fact, it is much easier to track down missing soldiers and policemen than it is civilians.

Over a hundred soldiers, that is to say ordinary ranks, went missing in Ireland during the Anglo-Irish conflict, in addition to the officers named on the missing list of August 1921. This reflects the class-ridden nature of society at the time and the military in particular, in that a list of missing officers was published, while the names of 'other ranks' were not. Officers counted; soldiers could be ignored.

In addition, some 26 RIC men/Black and Tans/Auxiliaries went missing.[2] This is somewhat more than the 18 listed as missing by Richard Abbott in his book, *Police Casualties in Ireland 1919–1922*. The lists, particularly of military personnel, have to be approached with a certain amount of caution because they may also include deserters or those who disappeared for other reasons. However, National Army inquiries at the time were able to establish that only five of the 100 missing men were identified as deserters. Bearing in mind that the impetus for the search for information came from the men's families, it is likely that most of the names on the lists are in fact casualties.

So what do these lists tell us about Cork in general and east Cork in particular?[3] I have extracted the personnel listed as having gone missing in Cork.[4] The list (see Appendix 1) contains 26 names. This excludes the six officers whose names were published in 1921 and also three intelligence officers and a driver who were secretly executed and buried near Macroom in May 1922.[5] While the original list is called Pre-Truce Absentees, it contains six names of men who went missing after the Truce, two of whom, including Anderson, disappeared in Cork.

On the list are five names of men who may have ended up in Knockraha. These were Privates Anderson, whom we have already referred to, Ward and Walsh of the Cameron Highlanders, Sapper Still of the Royal Engineers and Driver Graham of the Royal Field Artillery.[6]

Is it possible that some of these were 'volunteers for intelligence work' and may well have included the three undercover men described by Corry? Walsh and Ward, for instance, disappeared within days of each other. Would the British Army have allowed these men to be subsequently labelled as 'absentees', with its hint of desertion, when they had in fact been carrying out intelligence work? Captain Thompson of the Manchesters who was killed by the IRA in November 1920 and Lieuts Genochio, Handy, Henderson and Dove, who were killed after the Truce, were all intelligence officers. The British Army in internal documentation had no problems admitting that the men were intelligence officers.

It is equally possible that some were off-duty soldiers out socialising in Cork. Corry stated that many of the 'spies' were soldiers dressed in mufti. In at least one case two young soldiers were arrested while out with girls in Tivoli and brought to Knockraha for execution.[7] The biggest single group of missing persons, however, came from the Manchester Regiment which was based at Ballincollig, some four miles west of the city. A total of ten men went missing from the Manchesters. Three of these were the drummer boys who were snatched on their way from the football pitch and shot and buried near Ovens. Six of the remaining seven cannot be accounted for.[8] If they had been killed by Corry's group, this would at least go some way to making up the numbers he claimed had been killed in the area. But Ballincollig was in the IRA's 3rd Battalion area. Geographically this bounds the 6th Battalion area to the north. The 6th Battalion, under the command of Jackie O'Leary and Frank Busteed, ran what Busteed called a 'death chamber' north of Rylane in what had previously been a training ground for the Volunteers. 'That country was immune from anything, from raids. There was a vast stretch of bog stretching into the Boggeragh Mountains and the Musheras.'[9]

Describing the capture and execution of Major Compton Smith, Busteed goes on to say: 'We moved him back to the death chamber where we had trained the column. It was away from everywhere in the wilderness. In Rylane parish in the townland of Kilcullen it was known as "The Cottage". He's for the Cottage, we'd say among ourselves, and that meant he was for execution.'[10]

This suggests that the missing Manchesters may have been killed in Rylane by Busteed and his men. Given Busteed's reputation as a killer, that would not be surprising.[11] However, there are a number of reasons which suggest that this may not have been the case. Busteed reports that Seán O'Hegarty visited the 6th Battalion area before Christmas 1920 and berated them for their relative inactivity. Two intelligence officers captured by the 6th Battalion in Coachford in November 1920 were moved to the adjoining 7th Battalion area and executed further west at Rusheen in Aghina parish.[12] This suggests that the 'death chamber' did not begin to be used as an execution area until the beginning of 1921.

Furthermore, the best estimation of the numbers killed out of 'The Cottage' is around 15.[13] These include Compton Smith, Mrs Lindsay and her chauffer James Clarke and, according to Busteed, five or six Protestant farmers 'as reprisals' and up to five other loyalists during the Civil War.[14] Anecdotal evidence suggests the former were Protestant farmers who were kidnapped in the Bandon area, moved to Rylane and executed.[15] Warder Griffin of Cork Jail was held by the company for some weeks in late 1920 before being released. He claimed he had been treated well.[16] As a result of the execution of Compton Smith, Mrs Lindsay and Clarke in April 1921, 'the area was honeycombed with lorries looking for them'. This suggests that the time window for the (pre-Truce) operation of 'The Cottage' was quite narrow.

There is no evidence as to where most of the Manchesters listed in Appendix III were killed. Nobody other than Corry has claimed them, though several bodies turned up at a farmhouse in nearby Killumney which the IRA had been using as a safe house.[17] While Rylane cannot be ruled out, given that Sing Sing and the Rea was the brigade's official prison and execution centre and that Corry claimed he shot ten Manchesters, there is a very strong probability that Corry is right again and that they ended up in Knockraha. Some of these may have been 'intelligence volunteers' or just 'enemy stragglers' who were simply picked up and shot. If they were abducted while on leave in Cork city, they very likely ended up in the Rea.

The disappearance of soldiers from Ballincollig Barracks is of more than academic interest, however, for there are several accounts of the IRA purchasing significant quantities of guns and ammunition from soldiers stationed at Ballincollig. There were friendly relations between certain soldiers and local IRA men. Busteed's brother, for instance, worked in the barracks and smuggled out 'a machine gun of sorts . . . and rifles, revolvers and grenades'.[18]

Curiously enough, as far as G Company [2nd Battalion, city] was concerned, our main source of supply of arms and ammunition was from British soldiers stationed at Ballincollig. . . . We secured quite a large quantity of rifle and revolver ammunition which we bought from soldiers, who were quite willing to do business at a price. It is interesting that a large quantity of .303 ammunition which we bought from Ballincollig was transferred by G Company to Tom Barry's flying column in West Cork immediately prior to the successful ambush at Crossbarry.[19]

The British military command was well aware of this. 'We have a number of very undesirable characters in the Ranks who are in close touch with the Sinn Féin movement and do not refrain from selling arms etc.'[20] G Company was involved in many of the killings described in this book and several ambushes and attempted ambushes. Perhaps their relationship with members of the Manchester Regiment yielded more than just .303 ammunition. Were some of the missing Manchesters defectors to the IRA?[21] However, knowing what we know about the southside battalion, if they had no more use for them, they were more than capable of shooting British soldiers after buying their guns and ammunition, thus scoring twice from the one transaction.

In any case, Martin Corry's claim that he shot up to ten members of the Manchester Regiment is quite credible. They were probably picked up in the city while off duty and in some cases involved in either smuggling arms to the IRA or perhaps investigating that smuggling. If so, this is an entirely forgotten aspect of the dirty war in Cork.

Chapter 31 ❧

A MURDEROUS
POSTSCRIPT

I was ready to send my book off to the publisher at this point because I felt I had exhausted all sources of further information. I was still uneasy about the YMCA story, however. While I had found three youths who had been abducted from the streets of Cork and executed by the IRA, they were not YMCA boys, nor were they from what someone like Connie Neenan called 'good families'. 'Good families' in the context of Cork in 1921 implies middle-class or even the better-off families in the more salubrious suburbs. Begley and Nolan were not middle class, nor were they Protestants. They could not have been the boys who 'confessed to their trackings and they were killed'.

Yet Martin Corry claimed that up to six members of the YMCA were executed on foot of Parsons' information in the months after his death. If this is true, it must have happened in 1922. Then there is the matter of the connection, if any, between the three boys killed and the YMCA. Edward Parsons had two brothers in the YMCA; he was probably a member himself, even if he is not on the list of subscribers. Then there is the curious absence of any references to such killings in the YMCA's own records of 1920–22 and indeed in the reports made by the Cork Brigade to GHQ around the time of the Truce.

The YMCA's record of meetings and AGMs suggests that the killings were small in number as they had little influence on the day-to-day working of the YMCA. Apart from the threatening notice of 22 June 1921 and the postponement of excursions, everything seemed to carry on pretty much as normal in the latter half of 1921. In fact the Truce and subsequent Treaty of December 1921 appears to have brought about a return to normality for the YMCA. Then there is the issue of who was 'somebody's child', the boy who was kidnapped in broad daylight at the city end of the Blackrock Road in May 1921 as reported in *The Times*.

Beset with these doubts, I decided to keep searching, initially using the street-level geography of Cork, much of which dates from the eighteenth and nineteenth centuries, in an effort to re-create a picture of what may have happened there 80 years ago. I set out on foot with a photographed copy of the street index of Cork city from 1921 in my hand.[1] As I walked, I checked out the residences and workplaces of many of the people whose names we have encountered. By taking this simple approach I uncovered some surprising new facts.

The first thing that was evident was that the 4th ward of the city south of the river, stretching roughly from Albert Quay southwards towards the Blackrock Road and on to Ballintemple and from there west as far as Ballyphehane, was inhabited mostly by middle- and upper-class loyalists of one shade or another, around 50 per cent of whom were Protestants. In some of the better off roads that had been developed as desirable places to live in the late nineteenth and early twentieth centuries, Protestants were in the majority. These included Victoria Road, Blackrock Road, the climbing terraces of Southern Road and the then wooded and semi-countryside expanses towards Douglas and Blackrock. In 1920 these were good places to live. But look at the street directory for 1924. Over half these people are gone; up to 80 per cent for some areas.

Farther west, in working-class and lower middle-class terraced housing, such as High Street and the red-bricked terracing of Summerhill South, Quaker Road and Friar's Walk, lived scores of RIC families. In fact the hills on both sides of what is now the Capwell bus depot constituted a virtual policemen's dormitory. If the north side of Cork city contained thousands of working-class families who could be deemed loyalists because of their connections with the British Army, then the hills to the south of the centre of the city were filled with policemen and their families. Whatever George Horgan, Edward Parsons and Finbarr O'Sullivan may or may not have done, they were surrounded by the forces of law and order—or the forces of lawlessness and disorder after the arrival of the Black and Tans.

But there were more specific hints that could be picked up by going around on foot with the geography of 1921 on hand. For instance, there is the fact that the headquarters of Thompson's bakery in MacCurtain Street (then King Street), which was managed by Alfred Reilly, was directly across the road from King Street RIC Barracks. This may be a mere coincidence until you look at an event of 1 June 1920.[2] On that day a large bomb was smuggled into the house beside the barracks and detonated, destroying the entire inside of the building, the damage even extending to a doctor's surgery next door. Miraculously, there were no casualties. According to the press statement issued by the police, the ten policemen inside rushed out on to the street on hearing a shot outside, thereby avoiding the blast. Did someone from Thompson's warn the police? Was Alfred Reilly in some way associated with this narrow escape? It is reasonable to suspect that the killing of Alfred Reilly as he left work may have had some connection with the proximity of his workplace to King Street RIC Barracks, which was in turn intimately connected with the shooting of Tomás MacCurtain.

And that wasn't the only item of interest to be found along MacCurtain Street. For around the corner, on Railway Street, in a building once owned by the Beale family's Cork Steam Packet Company (and now a car park) lay the remnants of what appears to be the YMCA's other premises. This building is shrouded in mystery. It appears that some kind of hostel was in operation there between 1919 and 1922, as it is mentioned several times in the YMCA annual reports of those years.[3] It was to have been a disabled soldiers and sailors home, a logical project in view of the many wounded and maimed ex-soldiers who roamed the by-roads of Ireland in those years after the Great War. However, it was either never finished or never fully opened, because the funding for it was not drawn down and the project appears to have been put in abeyance in the years after the revolution.[4]

Across the two streams of the River Lee, at the corner of Albert Quay and Victoria Road, can be found the remnants of the Sailors' bar, mentioned by Connie Neenan as the place where the 'spies' of the Anti-Sinn Féin League used to congregate. Owned by one William Markham, it was probably frequented by police and anybody who opted to hang around with them. At least four of those shot as spies in the first half of 1921 either worked as dock labourers or were picked up in the dock area.

The last place I visited was the Quaker graveyard off Summerhill South on Cork's south side. Quaker cemeteries are unique in that there are no family plots: each individual had his or her own grave, on the basis that each must stand alone before God. This is a cemetery of individuals. Even though many of these Quaker families, such as the Haughtons, Beales and Pikes, were rich by the standards of the time, there is nothing on their graves to distinguish rich from poor. There are no mausoleums or extravagant limestone monuments here. Quaker egalitarianism extends to the hereafter.

I soon found the row of graves of the Beale family, the main force behind the YMCA in the early twentieth century. There is the patriarch, Alfred Beale, president of the YMCA, who died in June 1932 aged 94, his son Alfred Jnr who died in 1951, and his nephews Charles E. Beale who, as we have seen, is sometimes mistaken for James C. Beal, and William Goff Beale. Charles and William Goff Beale were the owners of Harris Beale, the large hardware shop on Grand Parade. All were senior YMCA patrons.

One detail, though, almost leapt off the headstone: William Goff Beale died in March 1923 aged 52 years. This was during the Civil War. I had seen his name in a condolences notice in the YMCA Annual Report of 1922/23 and had assumed he had died of natural causes because he was not in the best of health. However, his death cert showed something different. For William Goff Beale had died in the South Infirmary Hospital on 23 March 1923 from 'heart failure resulting from gunshot wounds inflicted on him by persons unknown at his home, Elmgrove, Ballyhooly Road, on 16 March 1923'.

So one important YMCA member had been killed after all. William Goff Beale—not a well man—had been shot dead at a stage when the Civil War was almost over. Clearly, though the IRA was nearly finished as a fighting force in the spring of 1923, it was not finished with the YMCA.

And another thing turned up at this time. While perusing the records of phone-tapping that the IRA carried out on the British military barracks from August 1921 to their departure in 1922, I came across a curious little message: it was the transcript of a telegram from British military HQ in Parkgate Street, Dublin, to the British Army in Cork. Clearly HQ is annoyed with the coded intelligence messages it is receiving from Cork. The telegram reads: 'With reference to the three cases of chicken broth, relating to children. Are they children? Say children then in the report.'5

The transcript is dated 25/8/1921. In his Weekly Surveys of the State of Ireland, General Macready noted that there had been 14 civilians killed by the IRA in the week leading up to the Truce of 11 July 1921. However, in his next report he adds three more to the civilian death toll for the days after the Truce.6 Were these the three teenage friends killed in Cork by the IRA in connection with the YMCA? Macready mentions no more civilian deaths in July or August. This is the only British reference I have come across that suggests that kids may have been killed. Admittedly, the reference is vague, but it is the right number (three) in the right place at the right time. It may also confirm Neenan's claim that three teenagers were executed at around this time. Calling them children suggests they were at least younger than 16. Were these taken with the YMCA touring car on the morning of the Truce and killed afterwards? This appears to be the most logical conclusion.

Clearly my book was far from finished. It was time to go back to the archives again, this time to cover the period from the Truce of 1921 to 1924 to see what else I might uncover. What I found was surprising and even shocking. The War of Independence was only half the story. There was a lot more in the under-reported year of July 1921 to August 1922. For this truly was the year of disappearances.

PART VII

Chapter 32 ～

THE DISAPPEARANCE OF EDWARD PARSONS

S
o who was Edward Parsons? All we know about him is that he lived at 30 High Street, a street in which several other killings took place and which was at the heart of the area where the killers of the 2nd Battalion did most of their work. The first breakthrough occurred when I discovered Parsons' name in a Colonial Office card index of the names of thousands of those affected by the conflict in Ireland.[1] This needle in the haystack was a simple white card containing two lines and it suggested correspondence between the Colonial Office and the Free State on the case:

William Edward Parsons 031022
Inquiry re kidnapping of the above

This was confirmation from the British side that someone called William Edward Parsons had been abducted by the IRA. An equivalent card was found in the index to the records of the Governor General of the Irish Free State, Tim Healy.[2] A trawl through the newspapers found the next clue. The *Cork Constitution* and *Cork Examiner* of 25 March 1922 both contain the following sad little notice in the small ads column:

Missing since March 23, William Edward Parsons, 30 High St Cork. Age 15. Height 5ft 5in. Brown hair, hazel eyes. Was wearing black overcoat, blue jacket and green waistcoat, trousers and cap. Information gladly received by his parents.[3]

The main text of the newspapers of those weeks contains no further details. Clearly the abduction was not reported or, if it was, the report was censored. Parsons simply disappeared in March 1922, nine months after the end of the Anglo-Irish conflict and three months after the Treaty. This was peacetime, the year of the so-called 'Cork Republic'.

So William Edward Parsons, the supposed missing link in the puzzle as to the cause and effect of the killing of Cork city Protestants, was kidnapped and killed nearly 18 months after Mick Murphy said he was, and nine months after the latest of the other accounts suggested he was. He could have been no more responsible for the information that led to the others' deaths than I was. It does however tie in with one version of Corry's, where he states that immediately after Parsons' hanging and execution, 'three lorries came up the hill . . . and it was just after the Truce'.

While 'three lorries came up the hill' is meaningless in itself, there is a context in which Corry connected the two. For the three lorries refer to the trucks commandeered by the city IRA for the transport of the guns seized in the *Upnor*, a Royal Navy frigate boarded by the IRA in Ballycotton Bay soon after leaving Cobh laden with munitions. The *Upnor* episode on 29 March 1922—one of the most daring operations organised by the IRA in the post-Truce period—netted some 400 rifles, 700 revolvers, 30 machine guns and 25,000 rounds of ammunition.[4] Mick Murphy claimed it took a long time to get information out of Parsons. If he was captured on 23 March, he was probably not moved to Corry's farm until a few days later, when all attempts to get information out of him failed. This indicates that the attempted hanging and subsequent execution occurred in the last days of March, around the time the *Upnor* raid was carried out.

Corry also claimed that Parsons was brought to him by Peter Donovan. Donovan, one of Mick Murphy's most trusted men, lived on the Ballinlough Road, only a few hundred yards from Parsons' home. This strongly suggests that the abduction was organised and carried out by the men of C or D Companies of the 2nd Battalion of the city IRA. It may or may not have been sanctioned by Brigade HQ, though Mick Murphy claimed it was.[5] This was also the time that the British were in the process of withdrawing. Many barracks and police stations had been handed over at this stage.

The details of the case can be found in a number of files in the records of the Department of the Taoiseach and the Department of Defence.[6] The first contains a letter from Parsons' mother. It goes a long way to answering why young Parsons was killed and throws up some interesting facts about the case. The letter, sent from Brighton where the family originated and to where they returned in 1922, was written a year almost to the day after the boy's disappearance.

> Could you possibly do anything in the way of finding out what has become of my son, who was kidnapped in Cork on the 23rd of March, 1922? He was last seen alive at 9.30 pm when he said goodbye to his chum at the top of the Southern Road and within 50 yards of his home. He was 15 years and 10 months and had only just left school. He was in no way connected to any Movement; he belonged to the Boys' Brigade and the YMCA.

This suggests that Parsons was being followed and that the IRA knew what they were doing in that they did not seek to capture the 'chum'. The likelihood is that Parsons was held somewhere overnight before being brought before Mick Murphy for interrogation. Failure to extract useful information landed him at Corry's a few days later. Mrs Parsons showed considerable resolve in her attempts to track him down:

> I have made all possible enquiries, went to the Free Staters, Republicans, the Lord Mayor, RC Bishop, the Fathers and our own Bishop, and could get no satisfaction. The Republicans told me at Quinn[7] [sic] Quay Barracks to hold out no hopes as there were a lot shot. We advertised in the Cork newspapers, but the same cry, no news.

The letter also gives some details about the family's circumstances: 'My husband had to leave Cork where he was employed for 18 years at the Cork electricity works on account of my health which is broken. He went to Brighton from Cork and left with satisfactory character.' Mrs Parsons enclosed a photo of the boy, along with a description similar to the above. The photo appears to have been lost. The letter, sent via the Duke of Devonshire, arrived at W. T. Cosgrave's office from the Governor General, T. M. Healy. The Civic Guard in Cork could only conclude:

> Inquiries instituted in regards to the fate of this boy have not elicited any exact or reliable information, but that they [sic] see no reason for doubting a rumour which is current in the district of his home in Cork to the effect that he was shot by some person or persons unknown about March 1922 during some local disturbances which occurred about this time.

In his reply to the Duke of Devonshire, the Governor General modified this to: 'Conflicting rumours are current in the district to the effect that Parsons was shot during hostilities in March 1922 and alternatively that he was ordered by some persons unknown to leave the country and to remain away for twelve years.' Perhaps this consoled Mrs Parsons, just as similar half-truths consoled other families in such circumstances. However, Mrs Parsons was not given the full picture.

Free State forces, who were in control of Cork city by the time Mrs Parsons made her inquiry, carried out their own investigation into the kidnapping. A Colonel J. J. Murphy, reporting to the Adjutant General in response to Mrs Parsons' inquiry stated:

> The above-named was attached to the YMCA early in 1922. He was suspected as a tout for the British and for this reason he was kept under

close observation. He was arrested by members of the IRA on 23/3/22 in possession of two revolvers. He was tried and found guilty of being a spy for the British. Sentence was confirmed by Brigade Staff 1st Cork Brigade and his execution took place on 27/3/22. He was buried between Lehenagh and Ballygarvan on the Kinsale Road. The actual whereabouts are unknown.[8]

Some months later Colonel Murphy gave some additional information on Parsons' death and how the information about it was acquired:

> Original information on the trial, execution and burial of Boy Parsons was received by Sergeant Dorney of the Plain Clothes Squad attached to the 10 Inf. Bn. from a civilian called Stephen Harrington 'c' Coy 2nd Btn 1st Cork Brigade (Quartermaster). It was by members of this Company that Parsons was captured and executed. The names of the individuals cannot be stated at the moment. Harrington personally was not concerned in the matter. He has been neutral since the Split.[9]

This is obviously at odds with Corry's version for it states that Parsons was killed and buried somewhere off the Kinsale Road just south of the city. The other details in the statements are convincing though. The dates of Parsons' abduction and death are correct. The boy was captured by C Company, Mick Murphy's company, for spying in the area. The Lehenagh/Ballygarvan area was where the southside battalion buried many of its victims, just a few miles south of the city. Stephen Harrington lived down the road from Parsons, so presumably knew what he was talking about.

It is also possible that he was covering up for his former colleagues and gave the wrong place of burial so as not to attract Free State forces to Corry's. The fact that he refused to divulge the names of those involved and was not very specific about the place of burial suggests that this may have been the case. It seems highly unlikely that Corry would have come up with the name Parsons and the YMCA connection for the boy he had executed if it were someone else. The balance of probability is that the killing of Parsons was as Corry claimed and that the person shot and buried at Lehenagh was someone else (see next chapter).

While the account states that Parsons was acting as a spy, would he have been working for the British at a time when the British forces had all but pulled out and when its intelligence operations had largely ceased to function? Would a 15-year-old have been carrying two revolvers in his pocket? It seems that he came under suspicion early in 1922. The boy, however, did have leanings towards the military life:

We were trying to get him into the A.S.C, as an artificer. He sat for 2 exams, he passed the doctor and his papers with birth certificate and our consent were sent to the Woolwich Arsenal and we were waiting from them to send for him. His father served in the Royal Sussex 2nd and my son is now serving in India.[10]

Clearly the family had military links, not surprising in the years immediately after World War I. It is the connection to the Royal Army Service Corps, however, that is most interesting. This connects him with Lieut Green and also with George Horgan, Michael Finbarr O'Sullivan and Michael O'Brien (alias Ahern), all of whom lived on High Street and had also been shot as alleged spies.[11]

However, if Parsons had indeed been spying on MacCurtain's house on the night of the assassination, that would go a long way to explaining why the IRA went to such trouble to catch him and why he was so well remembered by the IRA men. A few other interesting details emerge from the Parsons correspondence though. What were the 'local disturbances which occurred about this time' that the Cork police referred to in their reply to the Department of Justice in 1923? And what about the statement the IRA in Union Quay made to Mrs Parsons to hold out no hope as 'a lot' had been shot around this time? Was the capture of Parsons part of something bigger that took place during the first six months of the Irish Free State? Were the half dozen other members of the YMCA whom Corry claimed were executed and buried on his land, killed in the immediate aftermath of Parsons' 'confession'? This would make sense, but there is no evidence of it in the newspapers.

The answers to some of these and related questions became possible with the release of new material at the end of 2007. But before we deal with these, we must look at another YMCA-related disappearance—probably the mysterious individual with the two revolvers who was shot and buried at Lehenagh. For Edward Parsons was not the first teenager with links to the YMCA to be abducted and secretly shot in March 1922. That dubious distinction goes to a 19-year-old ex-RIC man called Thomas Roycroft.

Chapter 33 ~

THE STORY OF THE ROYCROFTS

O n 11 March 1922, two weeks before the notice on Parsons, a similar notice appeared in the small ads of the Cork newspapers:[1]

Missing since about 8 pm on 9th March, Thomas R. Roycroft, Hazel Lodge, Douglas Road, Cork. Age 19 years; height 5 feet 9 inches; pale complexion; dark brown hair; medium build; eyes grey; wore a grey tweed suit, black boots, grey socks, light grey coat, soft collar and grey cap. Any information would be thankfully received by his parents at the above address.

Again the news stories of the newspapers of that week yielded no further information. Clearly, people were disappearing without their stories being printed.[2]

Thomas Roycroft and his father and brother were members of the city YMCA and their house on the Douglas Road was only a stone's throw from the Parsons home at the top of High Street. There can be little doubt that the two abductions were connected. In contrast to Parsons, we have no information as to what subsequently happened to Thomas Roycroft. No IRA man seems to have remembered him, though the likelihood is that he was the young man with the two revolvers who was killed and buried at Lehenagh.

However, William Roycroft, Thomas Roycroft's father, having been forced to leave Ireland owing to IRA intimidation, applied in 1927 for compensation from the Irish Grants Commission. William—he lived across the road from the Cork Workhouse where Seán O'Hegarty had worked and where Michael Walsh was first apprehended—was an RIC constable of 35 years standing. (In fact, O'Hegarty lived a few hundred yards away.) William Roycroft was 56 in 1921 and retired from the force in February 1921. Originally from west Cork, he had served in Clare, Limerick, Tipperary and Queen's County (Laois) before spending the last 20 years of his career in Cork city.[3] He was married, with three sons and three daughters.[4] He served, as he put it, right through the 'height of the Sinn Féin trouble'.

But if William Roycroft retired from the RIC in 1921, his second son Thomas joined the police on 21 August 1920.[5] According to Roycroft Senior's application to the IGC, Thomas was shot dead in Cork city on 9 March 1922.[6] As we have seen, a perusal of the newspapers around that date makes no mention of any such killing, though a pair of plain clothes policemen were attacked in Tuckey Street, an attack in which one of the men was killed while the other escaped to barracks.[7]

'He left his home at 8.15 [pm] on the 9th of March 1922 and informed his mother that he was going for a short walk. He has not since been heard of.' William Roycroft claimed that Thomas resigned from the RIC in July 1921 after less than a year in service which he spent stationed in County Monaghan.[8] This is incorrect, however, for he had been dismissed in June on disciplinary grounds, the offence 'being continually absenting himself from the barracks for long periods and failing to account for his absence'.[9] As we have seen, many of those who were abducted and shot and their bodies buried were doubly dishonoured by their own side by having 'dismissal' added to their record, when in fact they were lying in a bog somewhere.

But the questions do not end there, for Roycroft's older son was also on the receiving end of unwanted attention from republicans and may indeed have been the member of the family most wanted by the IRA.

> My eldest son, William, joined the British Army at the outbreak of the Great War and after demobilization returned to his post as Engineer at the Power Station Cork city and after remaining there four years was ordered out of the country and was fired at on four different occasions. He then came to Bristol but could get no work there. He then went to work in Harolds and Wolf [sic] Belfast Ireland but was followed there and after a hand to hand fight in the street he escaped and went to Canada where he still is.[10]

Clearly, William Roycroft Jnr, a fully paid-up member of the YMCA though not an RIC man, was also wanted by the IRA. Like many of the others connected with this case, he too had been a member of the RASC, probably as an engineer. To be tracked to Belfast, where he had a lucky escape, suggests he was high on the IRA's wanted list. An engineer in the Cork electrical company, he would have worked with Parsons' father. He was lucky to make it to Canada.

Subsequent to his retirement, William Roycroft Snr was also fired on and ordered to leave the country. This he did, leaving for Bristol in September 1922 and putting his house up for sale. As a result of the intimidation and the death of her son, William Roycroft's wife had a nervous breakdown and within a year or two had become an invalid. Roycroft, who could get no work in Bristol, a city in which he felt a foreigner, was reduced to the role of nurse and carer of his wife. 'I manage to do all the housework, cook and attend to my wife who can't do anything herself. . . . Any little money I had I gave to doctors to try and cure her feet but all was no use, to my sorrow as she was one of the best wives ever a man had, poor thing.'[11]

Roycroft does not state why the family was on the receiving end of so much intimidation, though implicit in his claim is that it was because of their connection with the RIC. He states that they had never claimed any compensation prior to the Irish Grants Commission because it was too dangerous to do so and because he had two daughters still living in Cork. He makes no mention of intelligence work. He does not appear to have been a member of the Crime Special Staff. All we can say is that the IRA wanted him out of the country and his sons dead. Since the younger Roycroft was stationed in Monaghan during the conflict, he could hardly have been a 'spy' in Cork. The likelihood is that he was picked up in March 1922 in an effort to extract information on his brother or else on Parsons who lived near by.

William Roycroft Jnr was still only 22 in 1921. Since he was an ex-soldier and a Protestant, it comes as no surprise that he was targeted in Cork. But to be shot at four times and then to be traced to Belfast, after having lived in Bristol, suggests that he was traced in the same way that Cruxy Connors or Monkey Mac were. There is only one conclusion: that William Jnr and Thomas Roycroft were regarded as serious enemies by the IRA and that this was connected to their association with the RIC and the RASC, three others with links to the RASC having been abducted and shot in the area in the previous year. It may also have been connected to their membership of the YMCA, but if so, why do all the IRA accounts see Parsons as the first YMCA 'spy' to be caught?

Chapter 34 ∾

THE HORNIBROOKS REVISITED

What has never been satisfactorily answered is what the IRA was doing raiding the Hornibrook home on the night of 26 April 1922, a month after Parsons had been captured. The locally accepted version of events is that men from the Kilbrittain and Ballinadee companies were drinking near by, and needing transport to get home, chose to raid the Hornibrook home to steal the family car. Entering the house in the middle of the night, Michael O'Neill was shot by Herbert Woods with a revolver that—so this account has it—was given to him for his own protection by Michael Regan, commandant of the local IRA battalion. Tom and Sam Hornibrook and Herbert Woods were then held for a week, being marched west where they were tried before being marched back east and executed in the middle of a field somewhere in the Newcestown area, north of Bandon.[1]

In this version of events, the execution of the Hornibrooks took place after the murders in the Bandon valley. This story may well be correct; certainly it is what is believed by locals in the Ovens and Killumney area. If true, it suggests that the Hornibrooks, Woods and Michael O'Neill were just the victims of an unfortunate sequence of events. But it also throws up a series of questions. First, the Hornibrooks had suffered many episodes of intimidation during the Anglo-Irish conflict, to the extent that Thomas Hornibrook resigned his position as Justice of the Peace and his role as magistrate at the Ballincollig assizes.[2] Unquestionably Thomas Hornibrook was a loyalist and had served as a JP at the Ballincollig court for many years, his son colourfully transporting him to the assizes in the sidecar of his motorcycle. However, he had ceased doing so by 1921, though that did not stop the pressure that was being applied to the family.[3]

Was the visit of April 1922 merely an attempt to commandeer a car or another chapter in the saga of cattle-driving and outhouse-burning that the Hornibrooks had suffered from the start of 1920? Or could there have been something else at the back of it? Others have claimed that the IRA was looking to borrow a dynamo,[4] but if this is the case, why choose to break into the house at 2.30 am, when it would have been easier to simply knock at the door and ask for it? According to the inquest into the death of Michael O'Neill, the members of the raiding party were coy about the reasons for the raid. 'We were on IRA business', was all they could say.[5] Free State investigators who looked into the case in March 1923 said only that the raid occurred 'for some obscure reason'.[6]

Surviving Old IRA men interviewed by Peter Hart in the 1990s claimed that the reason for the break-in was because the Hornibrooks were believed to be part of a loyalist conspiracy opposed to the republic. This was when the IRA was rounding up many of its old enemies.[7] It was only a month after the capture and execution of Thomas Roycroft and Edward Parsons, and was the very time that hit squads were sent to New York and England to hunt down known suspects like Cruxy Connors, Mrs McKay and Monkey Mac. If the IRA would go to the trouble of sending hitmen as far away as New York—'at a time when every man and every shilling was needed, we went to the trouble and expense of sending three men after him to America', according to Florrie O'Donoghue[8] (reflecting the eternal verities of IRA victimhood)—then what would it have done to suspected spies who were still in Cork?

No significant ambushes or attempted ambushes occurred in the vicinity of the Hornibrook farm to cast the finger of suspicion on the family for having given away some IRA operation. Peter Hart suggests that they were raided as part of the intimidation suffered by many loyalists at the time. If that was the case, you would expect that they would have been attacked by locals. The Hornibrook raid, on the other hand, was carried out by units from Kilbrittain and Ballinadee, from almost 30 miles away. Was this just a drinking bout gone wrong or was it a raid of serious intent, the plan being to catch the family at its most vulnerable?

It is my belief that this particular raid on the Hornibrooks was not on account of the Hornibrooks themselves, but on account of their guest, Herbert Woods. And if the car was to be commandeered, it was to be a by-product of the raid rather than its prime motivation. Herbert Woods had been decorated in the war, gaining a Military Medal and a Military Cross, and was apparently unlucky not to have earned a VC.[9] This was a war hero, a good target for a nascent enemy army bent on revenge. He lived when in Cork with his uncle Edward Woods on the Cross Douglas Road, just down the road from the Roycrofts and Parsons. Not only that, he also made a subscription to the city YMCA in 1920, though he is not listed as a member.[10] And there are other reasons for believing the IRA was primarily after Herbert Woods or else his uncle Edward Woods who was married to Matilda Hornibrook.

Edward Woods was a Cork city businessman and owned a wine and spirits shop in Cook Street, just off Patrick Street. He had married Matilda Hornibrook in 1908. They had two daughters, and also raised, apparently from childhood, Woods's nephew, Herbert. Edward Woods's first encounter with history occurred when his business premises was burned down on the night of the burning of Cork, 11 December 1920. His second encounter, however, was far more serious. On 5 June 1921 he got a note threatening him that if he did not leave Cork immediately, he would be shot as a spy. 'Spy Woods. You are shadowed as a spy, harbouring spies in your house. Beware of your tongue 48 hours will tell no more you are doomed to death spy.'[11] He immediately left and came back only occasionally to visit his wife, who remained in Cork until 1923.[12] This suggests that either the IRA regarded both Edward Woods and Herbert as spies or that Edward Woods, like James Beal, had British agents lodging with him. And, like Beal, he too ran a wine business in the city—and he was also a Freemason. So Edward Woods was driven from Cork for 'harbouring spies in your house', which would put him in the same category as James Beal. And there is another connection to the YMCA. The Woods home, Glenbrae, on the Cross Douglas Road, is listed in Guy's Directory for 1921 as being occupied by W. B. Lacy, an accountant and lay preacher and one of the vice-presidents of the YMCA.[13] In fact, it is probable that Herbert Woods's subscription to the YMCA for 1921 was because of his friendship with Lacy.

As a result of his expulsion, Edward Woods became depressed and, despite receiving £3,000 compensation for the burning of his premises which he used to purchase a farm in England, never managed to make a success of farming. (His wife, who had suffered considerably more, appears to have been better able to cope with the years of exile after the conflict.) So traumatised was Woods that in his claim to the IGC he was able to quote word for word the message he had received from the IRA in June 1921, though his claim was made in 1927.[14] Yet he does not claim to have provided information on IRA activities to Crown forces, nor does he claim to have been a spy, though to do so would have increased his chances of receiving compensation. Neither does his wife; they merely claim to have been 'staunch loyalists'. If Woods was on one of the IRA's wanted lists and if he was believed to have returned from England to visit his wife and family, then they would certainly have been on his tail. If his car turned up at Hornibrooks, they would have been there too.

It is my belief that the IRA was on the trail of both Herbert and Edward Woods in connection with providing accommodation for British agents. This of course conflicts with the perfectly plausible local version of events, as well as with the more generally accepted view that the Hornibrooks were targeted simply because they were loyalists. The timing, however, is crucial. The raid on the Hornibrook home was part of the IRA's tracking down of its old enemies as British forces were departing. The warning note received by Edward Woods was at the same time the YMCA also got *its* warning note. (This of course may all have been coincidental.) The Kilbrittain Volunteers may simply have been drinking on that night, but this story may also have been part of an IRA cover-up. As we shall see in subsequent chapters, there are good reasons for thinking that this was the case and that the killings we know about were only the tip of the iceberg of secret abductions and executions that took place during the spring of 1922.

Chapter 35

THE DUNMANWAY
MURDERS—A
REASSESSMENT

When we looked at the massacre of Protestants in the Bandon valley in Chapter 15, we came to the conclusion that they were killed not so much out of sectarian hatred, but because they had been friendly to the Auxiliary garrison that was billeted in the town during the Anglo-Irish conflict. Opinion on this, of course, varies. On the one hand, we have the claim that the motivation for their deaths was mainly sectarian and revenge for the shooting of Volunteer Michael O'Neill. On the other, we have more recent attempts to rebut this position and claim that they were shot because they were 'known spies'. The evidence for this allegation, that they were named in the so-called 'Black and Tan Diary', does not stand up to close scrutiny.

Old IRA survivors interviewed both by Peter Hart and Meda Ryan repeatedly claim they had nothing against Protestants *per se*. They are, of course, evasive about the killings, as one might expect. 'We had nothing against them', stated one of Hart's informants before going on to claim that the massacre was the result of anarchy, not republicanism.[1] The killings have recently been dismissed as the work of out-of-control groups within the IRA and were not 'officially sanctioned'. It is hard to reconcile this position, however, with the fact that the IRA garrison in Dunmanway made no attempt to stop the killings but allowed them to continue for three successive nights. Some of the murders had a lynch mob element to them, particularly those in Dunmanway; the shooting of James Buttimer, David Gray and Francis Fitzmaurice, and the narrow escape of George Appleby Bryan, William Jagoe and William Morrison were all part of a wild night of shooting in the town. The one murder of that week that can be easily traced to events of the War of Independence is that of John Bradfield who, though he was a cripple, was shot in place of his brother. However, there is plenty of evidence to show that at least some of the others were far from random. The motivation may well have been anger and the need for instant revenge for the killing of Michael O'Neill. Yet if revenge were the prime motive, one would expect the Kilbrittain and Ballinadee areas, Michael O'Neill's home patch, to have been targeted first, rather than Bandon valley and Clonakilty. So why did the IRA decide to seek its victims in Dunmanway, Ballineen and Clonakilty, rather than in Ovens/Killumney, where the Hornibrook episode took place, or in Kilbrittain and Ballinadee where the raiders came from?

We have already suggested that one of the main reasons was the poisoned atmosphere left in Dunmanway after the departure of the Auxillaries, where some local Protestants including David Gray, William Morrison and William Jagoe had been friendly with them.[2] It may also have been connected with the unveiling of a memorial to the local Church of Ireland men who had died in the Great War; this took place at the end of March, a month before the killings. The memorial was unveiled with great pomp and ceremony in Dunmanway by the Bishop of Cork, Dr Dowse, and attended by no fewer than seven clergymen from the surrounding area.[3] The Union Jack was unfurled— probably the last time this was publicly done in west Cork. This ceremony was not going to endear itself to the local IRA, which had just spent over a year on the run from the very same British Army.

It is when you look at the killings in detail, however, that another picture begins to emerge. Some of the IRA respondents recorded by Meda Ryan suggest that Rev. Ralph Harbord was, as they put it, 'the prime suspect'.[4] We have already seen the allegation that perhaps Harbord may have been suspected of setting up an anti-IRA vigilante group in the winter of 1920/21— unlikely given that Harbord was not even a resident in the area at the time. Both Reverend Harbords claim to have always been loyalists, but they do not claim to have been actively encouraging vigilantism. Yet some IRA men referred to Ralph Harbord as the person they most wanted to shoot.

Was the younger Rev. Harbord the minister referred to by Tom Barry who was gathering information on IRA activities and had to flee to Ballincollig Barracks and thence to England in the spring of 1921?[5] Barry is adamant that that minister, whoever he was, was never seen in the west Cork area again. The elder Harbord mentions having had to leave west Cork during the earlier crisis but then returned, while his son was at the seminary at the time.[6]

And then we have the curious anomaly that those shot during that week bear no resemblance to those listed by the IRA as suspected 'spies and informers' at the time of the Truce. Clearly, whatever 'evidence' was used to condemn these men was uncovered during the post-Truce period. And if it was not the Black and Tan Diary, then what was it? And were the killings unofficial, the result of the need for revenge for what was in fact the only killing of a Volunteer by a Cork loyalist in the entire period? Or were they, like the abductions of Thomas Roycroft and Edward Parsons and the attempt to capture Herbert Woods, quietly official and part of a plan to eliminate enemies left over from the Anglo-Irish conflict?[7]

We have seen that there was a connection between Herbert Woods and the city YMCA, the implication being that Woods was one of those on the wanted list as a result of whatever the IRA had extracted from Parsons, or else he had been wanted since before the Truce. Was Woods simply unfinished business? As an ex-officer who liked a bit of action, he had all the credentials to be a member of one of the shadowy undercover squads the British military were running in Cork. He was described as 'a bit of a ne'er-do-well and a bit mad but he had done splendid work during the war, a very active fellow, a great boxer and all that kind of thing'.[8]

If the Dunmanway killings appear on the surface to have had a random quality to them, then the same cannot be said of at least some of those that took place in Ballineen and Clonakilty on the following night. While Robert Howe and John 'Bertie' Chinnery of Kinneigh were shot dead while their horses were being commandeered, the others shot that night seem to have been part of a well thought out and premeditated plan. Indeed the reason the IRA wanted the horses from Howe and Chinnery in the first place was to get to their next victims, suggesting that they may even have been coming from as far away as Cork. After killing Howe and Chinnery at Kinneigh on the evening of 27 April, they arrived at the house of Frances Peyton in Ballineen village an hour or two later. When they knocked at the door, Ms Peyton refused them entry and tried to escape out the back, but another man lay in wait for her, ordering her back inside to open the front door. When she did so, she asked one of the intruders if he was going to shoot her. He said 'No. I don't shoot women.' While this exchange was going on, one or two other men went upstairs to the bedroom where Ms Peyton's 16-year-old grandnephew Gerald McKinley was asleep. They shot him several times in the back of the head.

Another young Protestant in the village, William Daunt, also had a narrow escape when his pony and trap was stolen. 'He was a young fellow at the time and was pretty sharp. He saw a rifle or a revolver and as he did he ducked and there was a chest of drawers inside the window and he [his attacker] fired and he hit the chest of drawers.'[9] Whether the intention here was to get Daunt or simply to steal the pony and shoot the owner is a moot point. Clearly the assailants needed transport, but they also knew enough about the locality to opt to steal it from a Protestant family. Soon afterwards, the nearby Murragh rectory was visited and Ralph Harbord was shot and wounded on the rectory steps.

At 2 am at Caher, a townland to the west of Ballineen, a farmer, John Buttimer, and his workman Jim Greenfield were shot in their beds in similar execution-type killings. Buttimer's teenage son, who had initially heard the knock at the door, made good his escape before the men entered.

The murderous rampage of that night did not stop there. For on MacCurtain Hill in Clonakilty, some ten miles to the south, there was a knock on the door of the house of Thomas Nagle at around 11 pm. Nagle was caretaker of the local Freemason hall and a clerk of the court at Clonakilty. When Mrs Nagle opened it, two men rushed in, saying they had come to search for arms and ammunition. As they searched the house, they proceeded to ask questions about the occupants. Thomas Nagle hid in a cupboard; his sons were asleep.[10] Further questioning of Mrs Nagle established that two of her sons were still at school but that 16-year-old Robert was a messenger boy at the Post Office. The men went upstairs and told Robert they had a warrant for his arrest. However, instead of arresting him, they shot him dead in his bed. At least two other Protestant homes were visited in Clonakilty that night, but either their occupants were out or they made good their escape.[11]

It is clear from the timing that the same group cannot have been at work both in Ballineen and Clonakilty. Taken together, though, it suggests significant planning. Both sets of killings appear to have been co-ordinated. The men who murdered Nagle were somewhat squeamish because they switched off the light before shooting him. These were not random acts of violence; they were carefully planned executions, and if innocent Protestants, such as Howe and Chinnery happened to be in the way, they too were shot. Other loyalists such as the Bradfields who, as we have seen, had been duped a year earlier by an IRA party,[12] were also attacked that night. Another branch of the Bradfield family was targeted the following night. In all, ten individuals were killed and another wounded.

Taken altogether it appears that the Ballineen and Clonakilty shootings were part of a plan to execute certain individuals and that others just happened to be in the wrong place at the wrong time. The movement of the assassination squad from Kinneigh to Ballineen to Murragh suggests that the prime aim was to murder Gerald McKinley, along with one of the Buttimers and Rev. Harbord. The others, Howe, Chinnery and Jim Greenfield, were shot simply because they happened to be Protestants. The assassins did not have their own transport but had to commandeer horses and traps along the way. This suggests that they probably consisted of a combination of outsiders and locals who knew what houses to target. Some of the Dunmanway killers were reputed to be locals[13] and known to their victims. These are said to be two IRA officers who served with both the 1st and 3rd Brigades, and would have come from Cork where both were staying at the time. The Ballineen and Clonakilty killers were not identified. In fact Mrs Nagle stated at the inquest into the killing that she did not 'know either of the men and did not think they were from Clonakilty or district'.[14] In Clonakilty, the prime aim seems to have been to execute Robert Nagle—though it is likely they were after the father as well. In all probability they would have shot both, had Tom Nagle been found. In fact his other sons, who worked for the Post Office in other parts of Ireland, were also targeted and driven out of the country.[15]

It is when we look in detail at the profile of those killed that a distinct pattern begins to emerge. Take first the case of Gerald McKinley. McKinley was 16 years of age and had been staying with Frances Peyton, his grand-aunt, since the previous July.[16] Up to then—the time of the Truce—he had been living 'elsewhere'. McKinley, whose parentage is difficult to establish since no birth certificate appears to be available for him, was described by local republicans as 'a friend of the police' and a 'precocious loyalist'.[17] But he did not live in Ballineen during the War of Independence. So where did he live?

One possibility, given how unusual the surname is in Cork, is that Gerald McKinley lived in Cork city, more specifically that he lived on Douglas Road, less than half a mile from where Edward Parsons lived, and that he was in some way related to Rev. Harold C. McKinley, the curate of St Nicholas's parish in the city, who lived on Douglas Road. Mrs Parsons, when looking for information on her disappeared son, stated that, in addition to being a member of the YMCA, he was also a member of the Boys' Brigade—most Protestant boys were members of the Boys' Brigade, the specifically Anglican branch of the Boy Scouts run in most Church of Ireland parishes. The Boys' Brigade branch of St Nicholas's parish, the parish in which the Parsons family lived, was run by Rev. McKinley, though most of its activities were suspended during the conflict. Reverend McKinley, a former British Army chaplain, left the parish within days of Parsons' disappearance to take up a position as chaplain in London and received a presentation from the Boys' Brigade before he did so.[18] This could of course be a coincidence; McKinley had been standing in for Canon Nicholson, the rector of the parish who was elderly and had been in bad health for several years. The move to London had been mooted in the press as early as February.[19] However, McKinley's friend Rev. Darling was somewhat circumspect in an address he made at the going away presentation for McKinley. Speaking 'as a personal friend of Rev. McKinley, they [the assembled guests] would understand the difficulty of one in [my] position that might not be able to say much'.[20]

The implication of this—and this is by no means proven—is that Gerald McKinley had to get out of Cork around the time of the Truce for his own safety. Was he too taking refuge in a relatively remote rural area and keeping his head down? Did this too apply in the case of Robert Nagle? Nagle, like Parsons, had just left school. Had all three boys been in school together in the city during the previous year? We shall never know because the records of Cork Grammar School for the period are missing,[21] but it is a reasonable possibility.

And the connection between the events of the last week of April 1922 and the pursuit of Protestant teenagers goes deeper. For two of the prime targets on the first night of the killings in Dunmanway were William Morrison and William Jagoe, neither of whom was at home. 'We'll get Jagoe yet', one of the killers called out as they searched his house.[22] Morrison was head teacher at the local Model School, while Jagoe had run the Boy Scout troops in the town—both, by definition, connected to young people. Two other young men were lucky to escape with their lives, John Buttimer's son and William Daunt in Ballineen.

So, far from being the work of an out-of-control maverick group within the IRA, this may have been a concerted and well-planned effort at revenge arising out of the capture of Edward Parsons. Many of the victims and potential victims were teenagers or adults associated with teenagers and were specifically targeted. Since their names do not appear on the lists of suspected informers submitted to IRA GHQ at the time of the Truce, they must have been marked down for retribution at some time afterwards. While the shooting of Michael O'Neill may have been the spark that ignited the pile of tinder that was the Bandon valley in those months, it is likely that some of the killings would have taken place anyway. For if young Nagle and McKinley were indeed connected to Edward Parsons, they would almost certainly have been quietly 'arrested', taken to 'an unknown destination', tried and executed and their bodies never recovered. It is very possible that, at least in these two cases, the only difference the killing of Michael O'Neill made was that these subsequent killings were carried out publicly rather than in the corner of a field.

What is also interesting is that neither William Morrison nor William Jagoe was at home on the night the IRA called for them. The only conclusion is that they were expecting unwanted visitors. Something prompted Morrison and Jagoe to live in fear of their lives. Jagoe, a Methodist, was a very staunch loyalist. There would also have to be a connection between Rev. Richard Harbord as curate of Murragh and the Boys' Brigade. Perhaps those shadowy deeds on 'the dark and stormy night' in Murragh churchyard in January 1921 were nothing more than a meeting of the Boys' Brigade. Certainly on the basis of the choice of victims, this may well have been the case.

It should also be pointed out that there were YMCA branches in Bandon, Dunmanway, Mallow and Kinsale, as well as in Skibbereen, Midleton, Fermoy and Youghal. Just as in Cork city, there would have been overlap between the membership of the Boy Scouts, the Boys' Brigade and the YMCA. It is likely that those shot in Dunmanway, Ballineen and Murragh were members of Dunmanway YMCA—Rev. Richard Harbord, as a clergyman, almost certainly would have been. Furthermore, the Bandon YMCA, the Allin Institute, was burnt down on 29 June 1921.[23] Taken altogether, the YMCA in its broader county context and indeed the Boy Scouts and the Boys' Brigade could be considered—for those who wished to so consider it—as a 'county wide Anti-Sinn Féin League', a 'nest of imperialism'.

I believe these killings, along with the attempt to capture Herbert Woods, were part of the targeting of members of Protestant youth groups in a witch-hunt of suspected spies in the wake of the killing of Edward Parsons. While some of the victims in the Bandon valley were probably murdered by men with city connections, the Hornibrooks almost certainly were. Michael Kenny was at the time a junior officer in the IRA's headquarters at Union Quay and remembered a group of IRA men returning one night 'after shooting the Hornibrooks'.[24] The sequence of murders suggests that, far from being random, this may well have been deliberately planned by Brigade HQ in Cork, but that the killers lost the run of themselves and the whole thing got out of hand. This is borne out by a comment made about a week after these events, by a local brigade officer, possibly Tom Barry, when he stated in a newspaper interview that 'this was an *outside* wave of human destruction'. The 3rd Brigade under Tom Hales subsequently offered protection to Protestants, which was gratefully accepted.[25] The trail to Cork city runs right through from the Hornibrook homestead and the link between Herbert Woods and the YMCA all the way to the killing of Gerald McKinley in Ballineen and Robert Nagle in Clonakilty. But, as we shall see, there are other parts to the puzzle as well.

Chapter 36 ~

PORTE OF CORK

In the winter of 1921/22 the Glenville company of the IRA received a circular from Brigade HQ instructing them to list any loyalists living in the parish and return it to Brigade Headquarters as soon as possible. A meeting of the company was convened in the local public house to discuss how to deal with this request—there were less than a dozen Protestant families in the area, none of whom was interested in politics. The meeting came to a head when the adjutant of the company, Jack Hickey, a moderate man and later a clerk of the court at Fermoy, stood up to speak. Hickey judged the mood of the meeting.

'We can fill in this form,' he is reported as saying, 'or we can choose not to fill it in. But we should remember one thing: if we give the names of our neighbours as loyalists, then there is a chance that the next orders we'll get will be to shoot them. Do we want to do this?'

The company filled in the form, stating 'there are no loyalists living here' and returned it to HQ.[1] Then they went one stage further: they set up a round-the-clock armed guard on the local demesne, that of Sir Edward Hudson Kinehan, whose family was well liked in the area. At the time, the armed guard was said to be a protection against 'the Grays'. This was the first time I ever heard mention of Jim and Miah Gray, two of the most prominent IRA gunmen on the north side of Cork city whose names were remembered with trepidation even 50 years later. It should be pointed out that this was not merely a matter of Civil War politics, for most of the members of the Glenville IRA Company took the anti-Treaty side. Besides, this all took place while the Treaty debates were going on and before positions on it had hardened.

However, it says two things: one, that anti-Protestant feeling was not rife in all areas of rural County Cork; and two, that local companies were well able to stand up to dictates from central authority. It also tells us that communities[2] were able to look after their own. Some credit is also due to the independence and basic decency of much of the Sinn Féin movement at that time and a general feeling that 'we cannot be seen to be fostering suspicion of a minority amongst us'.

This little debate was repeated in all battalion areas of the 1st Southern

Division of the IRA. The Anglo-Irish Treaty gave a general amnesty to all those on either side who had taken part in the conflict, including those regarded as 'spies and informers'. So one of the very first orders issued at the dawn of the new State was in breach of the spirit, if not the letter, of the Treaty—though of course that was not something that was going to worry the Cork IRA.

The orders issued by the IRA leadership in Cork were to list 'all persons guilty of offences against the Nation and the Army during hostilities and to date, and all persons suspected of having assisted the enemy during the same period'.[3] This is Florrie O'Donoghue's language. Many battalions did not respond, including those of Cork city, Bandon, Macroom, Ballyvourney, Kanturk and Newmarket. But many others did and 157 suspects were named, one-third of whom were charged with giving information to the enemy. Of the remainder, another third had simply been 'friendly' with the enemy in one way or another—girls going out with soldiers or policemen was the principal crime—while the rest were guilty of a wide variety of supposed crimes, such as having relatives in the RIC or British Army or working for military authorities or failing to subscribe to IRA arms funds or the Dáil Loan.[4] A few were named by other 'informers' in their confessions; one cheered British troops; another shouted 'Up the King'; others were simply described as 'hostile' or 'suspect'.[5]

One suspects that this list would be one of the primary sources of those marked down for subsequent killing during the late Truce period from March 1922 onwards and during the Civil War itself. However, in general this does not seem to be the case, though there were some on the lists who were targeted. There were, however, other lists being gathered at this time and these were lists that, if you were unfortunate enough to be on one of them, greatly increased your chances of dying or being expelled from Ireland during 1922 and 1923. These were the lists of Munster Freemasons that O'Donoghue began to gather in earnest in the autumn of 1921 and which include many of those killed or subsequently driven out of Cork.[6]

The obsession with Freemasonry seems to have begun with the shooting of James Beal, who was himself a Mason, in February 1921. As we have seen, the first of the lists may have been found on Beal himself.[7] There are many letters between the various battalions and between Cork No.1 Brigade and GHQ on the perceived dangers of the Masonic Order during the succeeding months.[8] All the indications are that this suspicion grew out of the killing of Beal and are connected with the notebook found on him when he was killed. Beal, if he was a spy as the IRA repeatedly suggest, was working for Lieut Green, yet Green does not appear to have been a Freemason.[9]

However, Beal's membership of the Masonic Order was probably enough to attract attention to the organisation as a whole—remember that in his intelligence circular of December 1920 Florrie O'Donoghue mentioned neither Freemasonry nor the YMCA; indeed he mentions no loyalist organisations, and neither organisation is listed among the 'suspect' organisations submitted to GHQ at the time of the Truce. It was only after the Truce that real attention was focused on the Freemasons.[10] Though there was little overlap between the membership of the Freemasons and the YMCA, in the IRA's view they were one and the same. A good example of this blind spot was the IRA's burning of the Bandon YMCA hall at the end of June 1921. This is invariably referred to by IRA men as the Bandon Masonic Lodge, though the real reason for burning it, it appears, is that British officers and men were entertained there, as they generally were in YMCA halls.

However, some prominent YMCA personnel were Masons, including James Burchill, who owned a stationer's shop on Patrick Street, Cork. Burchill ran the junior department of the YMCA of which Edward Parsons was a member and which doubled as the branch of the Boy Scouts that operated out of Marlborough Street.[11] There is no evidence that Burchill, like Charles Lane—a leading Cork solicitor who organised the Cork branch of the Boy Scouts and was also involved in the Boys' Brigade and was the secretary of the South Munster Lodges of the Freemasons—was ever targeted by the IRA. However, the very fact that both Burchill and Lane appeared on the IRA's lists of city Freemasons probably cemented the connection.

The IRA now found itself in the position where its very considerable resources in intelligence-gathering were put to work in raiding lodges and tracking the movements of Freemasons from all over Munster. A typical example of this was the way F. C. Porte, who ran an engineering firm in Cork city, was tracked from Cork all the way to a Masonic meeting in Tralee in April 1922. Porte's name appears on several of the lists found in O'Donoghue's papers:

> On Tuesday last, J. Benner, G. Raymond and F. McCarthy met some others at the Railway Station including Porte of Cork off the 12 o'clock train and proceeded to the Masonic Hall and remained there until 4 o'clock. There was a meeting of all the local Masons there that night.
> Signed, Kerry 1, 4/4/22.[12]

Sometimes this surveillance took ludicrous turns. Here is a report from Bandon on the mild and generally well-liked E. V. Carrette,[13] who was head postmaster in the town. Carrette, it should be noted, was also a member of the YMCA:

> I have been informed that Mr. Carrette (an extreme loyalist), PM, Bandon Post Office has received an increase in his salary; the amount is about £50 yearly, dating from 1st January 1922.[14]

This Stazi-like surveillance would be risible in a Keystone Cops kind of way—for lists were gathered from all over Munster—were it not for its often murderous outcome. Several lodges were attacked and burnt and members killed.[15] Over 200 Freemasons are listed in Florrie O'Donoghue's papers alone, mostly from Cork city. There are letters to the director of intelligence on the movements of Masons in many areas. Many of Cork's Protestant business people are named in the lists, along with other members of the establishment. These lists are an Aladdin's cave of suspicion and paranoia, and when taken along with the lists of suspect loyalists gathered in early 1922, they led to the situation where these groups were inevitably targeted as the country slid towards Civil War. It is no coincidence that many of the individuals listed as Masons for Cork city and whose names were collected by the IRA correlated closely with the names of families that disappeared off the postal registers over the next two years. This is a topic to which we shall return.

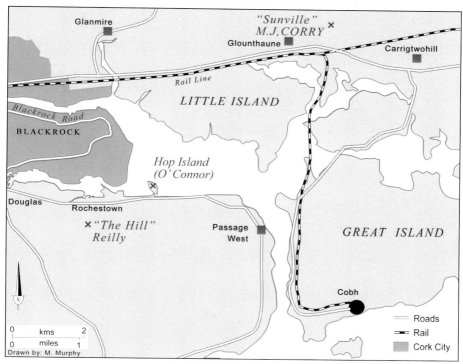

Map 1. The inner Cork Harbour area, showing Blackrock, Little Island and Martin Corry's residence at 'Sunville', Glounthaune. (Also showing the homes of Alfred Reilly, Douglas and Major George O'Connor, Rochestown.) (*Courtesy of Michael Murphy*)

Map 2. Old Blackrock Road, Cork, showing changes of occupancy between 1921 and 1924. The home of Josephine Marchment Brown is in green. Note the two fields of waste ground to the north of Old Blackrock Road with access between Elm View (Parker) and Rock Lodge (Cooke). (*Courtesy of Michael Murphy*)

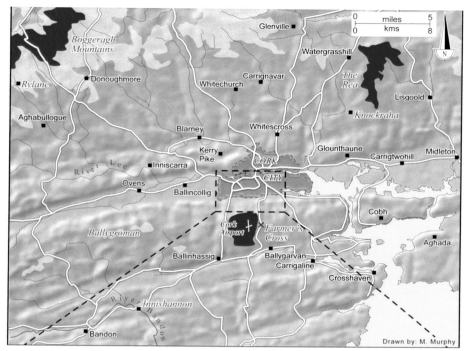

Map 3. The area surrounding Cork city, showing Knockraha, Rylane and the Farmer's Cross area south of the city (now Cork Airport).

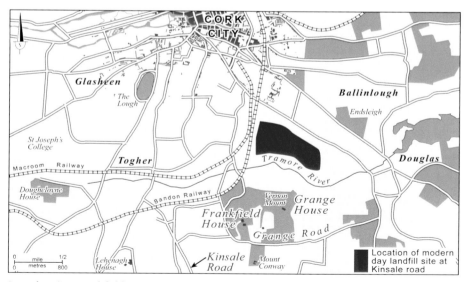

Inset showing Frankfield House, Vernon Mount and Carroll's Bogs—now the Cork Municipal Dump. (*Courtesy of Michael Murphy*)

Outer and inner views of 'Sing Sing', the vault at Kilquane Cemetery, Knockraha, Co. Cork, used by the IRA for holding prisoners during the War of Independence.

Two views of the Rea between Watergrasshill and Liamlara. The Rea was one of the three major execution areas used by the 1st Cork Brigade of the IRA. The top photo shows Carroll's Pond where several victims are believed to have been executed.

'Sunville', Glounthaune, the abandoned home of Martin Corry, as it looked in 2004.

The loft at Corry's where Edward Parsons was hanged and executed.

Fields at Corry's used as a burial ground during the post-War of Independence period.

Seán O'Hegarty, o/c Cork No. 1 Brigade, IRA. (*Courtesy of the National Library of Ireland*)

Martin Corry (*right*) with Éamon de Valera (*left*), Cobh, circa 1955. (*Cork Examiner*)

A photo believed to have been taken in 1926 of republican candidates of the newly set up Fianna Fáil party. Martin Corry is second from the right in the second row. (*Getty Images*)

Florrie O'Donoghue in the 1950s.
(*Courtesy of Fr Patrick Twohig*)

Members of the 2nd Battalion, 1st Cork Brigade, IRA, taken in 1922. Back row (*left to right*): Joe Wall, Lar Neville, Mick Murray, Tom Molyneux. Front row (*left to right*): Paddy Neville, George Sisk, Mick Murphy, Thomas Riordan. (*Courtesy of the National Library of Ireland*)

Josephine Marchment Brown, cutting from the *Evening Express.* (*Courtesy of the National Library of Ireland*)

Josephine Marchment Brown (*inset*: Reggie Brown), newspaper cutting. (*Courtesy of the National Library of Ireland*)

Rockboro Terrace, Old Blackrock Road, Cork. The middle house, No. 2, was the residence of Mrs Brown.

No. 1 Braemar, Old Blackrock Road, Cork (*nearer camera*), the residence of Frederick and James Blemens.

Volunteers of the 2nd Battalion enact a mock 'execution' on a hillside south of Cork city, 1922. Connie Neenan, on right, with hat and revolver. (*Courtesy of Pádraig Ó Murchú*)

Staff and officers of the 1st Southern Division of the IRA, taken at the Mansion House, Dublin, March 1922. Florrie O'Donoghue is third from the left in the front row with Mick Murphy immediately behind him. Liam Lynch, Liam Deasy and Seán Moylan sit immediately to O'Donoghue's left. (*Courtesy of the National Library of Ireland*)

A group of Auxiliaries on Union Quay, Cork, late 1920. Note the variation in uniform and the 'civilian' in the hat, with his hand on the machine gun. Was he a member of one of the death squads known as the 'Anti-Sinn Féin League'? (*Courtesy of the* Cork Examiner)

Major-General Colin McVean Gubbins in 1945. (*Getty Images*)

Michael Nolan's shop at 55 North Main Street, Cork, where Florrie O'Donoghue worked until April 1920. Nolan's name is still visible on the brickwork.

The clump of trees at Frankfield, Ballycureen, where three Protestant boys who were executed by the 2nd Battalion of the city IRA are believed to be buried.

Chapter 37 ~

HE KNOWS US ALL WELL

One of the more curious aspects of the accounts left by Cork city IRA men is how many of them remember Edward Parsons. They get the date of his killing wrong but several remember him. Why is this? It cannot be because of his youth. Several other teenagers were captured and shot as spies during the conflict itself, yet they all go unremembered, as if the shame of killing teenagers was enough to bury their names as well as the boys themselves. Yet this was not the case with Parsons. Why should he stand out? He was not the first YMCA member to be killed, nor was he the last. Why remember the boy who was captured nine months after the end of the war and forget those executed during the war? Why was Parsons so important that at least four IRA men backdated his capture so as to make it look as if he was killed up to a year and a half earlier when he could have been forgotten like the others?

The obvious answer is that his information was important and that it led to the uncovering of some sort of 'spy ring', even if that was only in the IRA's own terms. However, since the YMCA's own records contain no hint of clandestine goings-on, nor indeed do they contain any anti-nationalist or anti-Catholic sentiment, it is unlikely that, if such a spy ring existed, it was known to those who carried out the day-to-day operations of the organisation. Yet to be remembered many years later, young Parsons must have implicated others. The subsequent killing of Robert Nagle and Gerald McKinley and the attempts on the lives of those connected with youth movements in west Cork suggests that he did. Or did he simply provide a convenient structure that fed into IRA paranoia and suspicion? The confession extracted from him by Corry is accurate in its depiction of the workings of the YMCA. In fact, it is one of the few cases where you can correlate a confession with the reality of what the confession was about. The YMCA *was* structured into junior and senior sections. But does this mean that a spy ring existed in the YMCA? If Parsons is so important in this story, and all the evidence suggests that he is, then at least some of the killings that occurred after his capture occurred not just in west Cork but in the city too. A perusal of the historical record shows that this was indeed the case.

At 10 pm on 22 August 1922, a week after Free State troops had landed at Passage West and the IRA had fled from Cork city, 'six well-dressed young men' called to Rock Lodge on the Old Blackrock Road, the home of William Levingston Cooke.[1] Cooke, a well-known figure in Cork, was a 57-year-old Methodist and the owner of a plumbing business and cycle shop at the corner of Tuckey Street and Grand Parade. He was also a Justice of the Peace of long standing.

After talking to his wife and claiming to be collecting for Emmets Hurling Club, the young men asked for a donation to the club. Mrs Cooke went into the living room where Cooke was initially reluctant to give any donation saying he had already given enough. When she passed on this message to the men, their spokesman replied: 'Tell himself to come out as he knows us well.' Another said: 'He knows us all well. I bought a bicycle from him only last week and he will surely give us something.' Mrs Cooke went back to her husband: 'Do give them something. They look quite respectable and isn't it better that they be collecting for a hurling club than going around shooting people?'

Mrs Cooke's comment was oddly prescient. Cooke changed his mind and his wife got him a half-crown from upstairs. 'Take it out yourself. They will think more of it coming from you.' Cooke took the half-crown out to the men in the hall and handed it to them, whereupon they each pulled out a revolver and shot him several times before making their get-away across a nearby quarry, firing more shots at Cooke's daughter as she ran after them. Cooke died a few minutes later.

At the inquest his wife could see no reason why anybody would want to harm her husband, other than the fact that he was a JP. 'My husband was a magistrate and an honourable man who wished to do his duty and would not resign when I wanted him to. I think that is the reason why he was killed. It could be nothing else that I could think of.'

Yet Mrs Cooke did think of something else some years later when putting in a claim to the Irish Grants Commission. By then she had emigrated to New Zealand with her six children and had remarried. She stated that William Cooke had 'refused, under threats, to send in his resignation as a Justice to the Lord Lieutenant'. Moreover, 'he was constantly availed of by the ex-British soldiers, who called at his office to obtain his signature by way of certifying their identity and this fact also, it is considered, hastened the desire to take his life.'[2]

So here were two reasons why the IRA would want to kill William Cooke. Like Major O'Connor, he was one of those JPs who refused to bow to IRA threats and resign his post. Yet there were two dozen other JPs in a similar position in Cork city who, with three notable exceptions, were never harmed. The use of his office by ex-British soldiers would also be a cause for suspicion. Considering that most of those shot as spies in Cork city were ex-soldiers, whether guilty or not, any premises where they routinely called would, by definition, have been under suspicion. The implication of this is that Cooke, a stubborn man who took his role as a magistrate seriously, may have been using his office for collating information.

And there was another probable reason for his death. For William Cooke was registrar of the Order of the Temple, Grand Priory of the Freemasons of Ireland; in other words, he was the senior Freemason in Cork. He was also a member of the YMCA. The *Cork Examiner* of the day after the shooting stated that Cooke was a member 'of the Church of Ireland [*sic*] Young Men's Society, who by his death lost a benefactor and friend that cannot easily be replaced'.

In summary, there appear to have been many reasons for the shooting of Cooke: his role as a magistrate, his engagement with ex-soldiers at his work place and his connection with the Masons and the YMCA. Was Cooke one of the names of the 'Senior Spy Section' extracted from Parsons? Or was he just top of the lists of Freemasons gathered by O'Donoghue in late 1921 and early 1922? One thing is certain: of all the candidates we have met so far, he is the first killed in the city who might have been killed on foot of information extracted from Parsons.

Yet Cooke does not appear to have been in fear of his life. When asked at the inquest: 'Was your husband apprehensive of an attack previous to this murder?' Mrs Cooke replied: 'No, he never lost a night's sleep'.[3] This suggests he had no reason to be fearful. Republican sources in Cork claim that the IRA had long wanted to shoot Cooke as a spy and that he had absconded to America over a year earlier, returning after the Truce. This is borne out by his subscriptions to the YMCA, for Cooke and members of his family made membership contributions to the YMCA every year from 1919 to 1923, except for one year, 1921/22. Yet he was in Cork in April 1922 and his business continued operating as normal during the entire period as if nothing was happening.[4]

It is entirely possible that Cooke was wanted for carrying out some kind of anti-IRA activity and had long been on a wanted list for that reason. He may have been killed because he was connected to the YMCA. But if he was the organiser of a group of teenage spies, several of whom had disappeared, then what was he still doing living in Cork when retribution was sure to come knocking at his door sooner or later?

But there is one other thing that should be noted in the case of William Cooke: Rock Lodge, where he lived, is directly adjacent to 1 Braemar, where James and Fred Blemens had lived and from where they had been abducted. It was also three doors from the home of Josephine Marchment Brown.

Was Cooke, who was still a magistrate, likely to be involved in investigations into the disappearance of the Blemenses? Or was he linked to the Blemenses? Or was it because of his links with the YMCA? Yet Cooke had four sons who were teenagers at the time, none of whom was targeted.[5]

In summary, Cooke was a senior Freemason and a member of the YMCA; he was a next-door neighbour of the Blemenses; he may or may not have been involved in anti-IRA activity. His death may have also been part of the relentless pursuit of Freemasons which took place in 1922. And there is another factor: Cooke was a Methodist. As we shall see, the very fact that he was a Methodist and lived where he lived also had a significant bearing on his death.[6]

Chapter 38 ❦

THE SHOOTING OF
WILLIAM GOFF BEALE

Gentle in spirit and pure in heart, unselfish to the core, he is mourned by all who knew him. . . . God help the country when such things can happen to a harmless innocent.[1]

If there were many possible reasons for the killing of William Cooke, then there appears to have been none at all for the shooting and subsequent death of the second senior YMCA figure to be killed during the Civil War. Around 7 pm on Friday 16 March 1923, William Goff Beale, a Quaker and long-time member of the YMCA, was shot at point-blank range at the gate of his home, Elm Grove, Ballyhooly Road, by two men who appear to have followed him as he returned from work. He died from his wounds a few days later.[2] Beale, who was 52 and a stockbroker, was the most prominent member of the Cork establishment to be killed during the entire period. His family had been involved for generations in the business community in Cork, primarily in shipbuilding and engineering, and was among the leading Quaker families in the city. His uncle, Alfred Beale, was chairman of the YMCA; his cousins Alfred Jnr, Henry H. Beale and his brother Charles E. Beale were also senior YMCA members.[3] He was co-owner along with his brother of the hardware and seed company Harris Beale of the Grand Parade. So Connie Neenan and Frank Busteed were half-right. A partner of Harris Beale *was* killed, but he was W. G. Beale, not James Beal, and he was shot during the Civil War, not the War of Independence.

Being a Quaker and a pacifist and regarded as a quiet, rather inoffensive man 'who took no part at all in politics', Beale appears to have been an unlikely victim for a gun attack. The two men who carried out the shooting shouted that it was a 'reprisal for the executions'—in this instance referring to the executions of republicans by the Free State government, which was at this time going on apace in Dublin and in various barracks around Ireland. However, it is difficult to see what the Irish Free State executions could have to do with an apparently harmless Quaker on his way home from his workplace, unless of course he was shot simply because he was an establishment figure. Beale was not a notable Free State supporter, though he would have been pro-Free State in the sense that he would have been a supporter of the rule of law.

The most obvious explanation is that he was just a soft target, a well-known businessman who belonged to a minority religious group. His movements were well known. He returned from work at the same time every evening. There may also have been a geographical factor in his death: he lived near the Gray brothers, two of the most notorious IRA gunmen in the city, though there is no evidence that it was the Grays who shot him. If his killing had any political value, it would be to give public notice that the IRA, though on the run from Free State forces and facing defeat, was still capable of finding its victims.

There is no evidence on the face of it that the killing of Beale had any connection with his role, or the role of his family, in the YMCA. His brother Charles E. Beale, also prominent in the YMCA, said at the inquest that he knew nothing personally of the circumstances under which his brother was killed.[4] Yet it must have been a factor. The Beales were the most prominent family in the organisation. The Cork YMCA and the non-denominational Christian community in Cork in the late nineteenth and early twentieth centuries were synonymous with the name Beale. If you wanted to get back at the YMCA, then the Beales were a logical place to start, just as shooting William Cooke was an obvious way to strike at the Freemasons.

Of course Beale might have been shot simply because it was assumed by some within the IRA that he was related to James Beal. The accounts of Cork IRA men suggest such a blurring of the identities of the Beals/Beales that it is not difficult to see how W. G. Beale might be a target for an IRA revenge attack, especially in view of his connection with the YMCA.

There are some notable differences between the killing of Beale and that of Cooke, however. At the inquest into Cooke's death, the coroner J. J. Horgan said it was a very simple case 'up to a certain point'—the 'certain point' being the motivation for the killing. While Horgan, a well-known solicitor, 'knew Mr. Cooke well and noted that he was "a decent citizen and a good man", he went on to say that "as to the question of motive, the jury had no evidence and it was a terrible thing to contemplate that this was so."' N. J. Walsh of the Cork Civic Police said it was 'sad that in the city of Cork a number of men could go up to a house and murder the occupant without any effort being made by neighbours to pursue them . . . there were many people about and no attempt was made to stop these men'.

In Beale's case, the coroner in his summing up said this was 'an extremely painful one which disclosed a lamentable tragedy. The deceased was an exemplary citizen, well known in business circles. . . . It was very lamentable that such a man, pursuing his ordinary peaceful avocations, not mixed up in any other transactions, should be so injured that his death followed. I need hardly add that the relatives should have our deepest sympathy and, indeed, of everyone else in Cork.' The quotation at the head of this chapter by his friend John H. Bennett summarised the esteem in which William Beale was held.

There is a significant difference in tone between the two inquests. Cooke was a magistrate and clearly an enemy of the IRA at a number of levels. One can at least *read* into the inquest that there may have been unspoken and unacknowledged reasons for the killing. It is also interesting to note that neither the YMCA annual report of 1923 nor the AGM of late 1922 makes any mention of Cooke's death—an omission that is surely significant—while Beale was remembered with great affection. Beale, the only Protestant shot on the north side of the city appears to have been merely an ordinary decent citizen who was gunned down mercilessly. His crime? That he was well known as a member of the YMCA and that he appeared to share the same surname as an alleged spy.

And William G. Beale was not the last person with YMCA connections to be killed, even though by the spring of 1923 the outcome of the Civil War was a foregone conclusion. For on the afternoon of 19 August 1923, some three months after the official end of the Civil War, Theo Creber,[5] the son of the sexton of the Church of Ireland chapel at Carrigrohane, a few miles to the west of Cork city, was shot dead. Three young men were seen departing the scene of the murder on bicycles. Creber had worked at Kilcrenagh House, the home of Ebenezer Pike, a leading Quaker businessman, who had been forced to leave Ireland in May 1921 after watching from a stable while the IRA burnt down his house as a reprisal.[6] Creber had been shot once through the heart in what was an execution-style killing after having been beaten over the head with a blunt instrument. The hat he had been wearing was pulled down tight over his eyes.[7]

As usual there was no motive for the murder; though arson and the destruction of former loyalists' property was almost a daily occurrence, there was no suggestion of further damage to Pike's property. Rather, the killing appeared to be a straightforward execution, of the kind inflicted on Cooke and Beale. It was premeditated and well organised. One of the young men on the side of the road held the bicycles while the other two carried out the killing. 'The motive appears to be murder' was the best the Cork Civic Guard could offer by way of explanation. Creber was 27 years of age and worked as a labourer, his family having had a long association with the Church of Ireland parish at Carrigrohane. He was the last Protestant to be killed in Cork in the period and was one of the last victims of the Civil War.

Creber's family had long been associated with the Cork YMCA, along with Robert Heard, Pike's agent, who with his wife was one of the principal movers in the organisation. In the absence of any other explanation, Creber's association with the organisation seems at least a reasonable suggestion as to why he was killed.

So does this mean that the alleged YMCA 'spy ring' consisted of just five persons: Thomas Roycroft, Edward Parsons, Cooke, W. G. Beale and now Creber, along with several of those murdered in West Cork? This may well have been the case, were it not for Corry's statement that 'five or six' other members of the YMCA were shot and buried in his farm on the strength of evidence supposedly extracted from Parsons. It is clear that this is not the whole story.

Chapter 39 ～

| A BOULOGNE MYSTERY

ooke, Beale and Creber were not the only YMCA personnel murdered
by the IRA in 1922/23. In Chapter 51 we shall look in detail at the issue
of the targeting of Freemasons by the IRA in the post-Truce period.
One of the Freemasons who may have been killed by the IRA was Henry A.
Harris, divisional secretary of the Cork YMCA from 1915 to April 1921.[1] When
we last met H. A. Harris, he was leaving Cork on 3 May 1921 to take up the
position of general secretary of the East Bristol branch of the YMCA.

Harris would have made a good candidate as the leader of an alleged spy
ring operating out of the YMCA. He was a patriotic Englishman with a long-
time association with the Army and Navy division of the YMCA. A man of
enormous energy, he had received an MBE for his work during the war,
extending the YMCA in the South of Ireland from nine centres in 1915 to 110 by
the end of 1918, housing up to 60,000 troops in the process, 30,000 of these in
the hostel in Cork. He was exactly the kind of man whom the various
branches of British intelligence liked to recruit: reliable, energetic,
trustworthy and loyal. He had provided shelter and recreational facilities for
the troops for years. He was also greatly thought of in Cork and returned the
compliment on his departure:[2]

> He had now twenty years experience as YMCA secretary, having been
> stationed in almost every part of the world and he, as an Englishman,
> should say that to no part of the world he could look back to with greater
> pleasure than to Cork, where he had spent the last 5½ years. A more
> kindly, more heartening, more hospitable people he had never met and
> his prayer was that peace, contentment and prosperity would soon come
> to the country.[3]

These words are part of the speech Harris gave at a reception in the Metropole
Hotel on 2 May 1921 to mark his departure from Cork in order to take up his
role in Bristol, though it appears he had left the post at the YMCA some weeks
earlier. I have found no evidence from any surviving IRA men's accounts that
he was ever shot by the IRA or targeted or that his name was even known. But

he was the head man of the Munster YMCA during the War of Independence. Therefore, he would make for a logical target. The obvious conclusion was that if Harris was indeed a British spy and had organised some kind of spy ring among his charges, he left as a result of the first of his boy spies being captured and shot by the IRA. Except that if Parsons was the first of these to be exposed, that information did not become available until a year later.

There could still have been a link between the two, however. It is fair to say that if the IRA had information linking Harris to some sort of spy ring operating out of the YMCA during the conflict, they would have chased him to Bristol in 1921—both Cork newspapers stated that he was moving to the East Bristol YMCA—and shot him there two years before they did.[4]

On 26 March 1923, a week after William Goff Beale was shot, the Irish newspapers reported that an unidentified Englishman had been found washed up in the French port city of Boulogne. He was found floating in the harbour at dawn and was aged around 55. It was believed he was an Englishman because his underwear had been made by a Midlands manufacturer. His pockets had been turned out and his watch, wedding ring and pocket book were missing. Initially, the man was believed to be a ship's officer, later a London merchant called Gilhooly, and still later an American who had gone missing in Paris.[5] A few days later the Boulogne police received a letter purporting to come from the IRA which claimed that the dead man was killed as 'a traitor to the Irish Republic'. Under the heading 'A Boulogne Mystery' the *Cork Examiner* of 21 April 1923 summarised all that was ever to become publicly known about the case:

Boulogne Friday

According to a letter received by the police the Englishman who was found drowned here at the end of March and who was thought to be a British naval officer and subsequently a London timber merchant was killed by Irish Republicans as a traitor to the cause. The letter sent to the police is in English and made up of letters painstakingly cut out of an English newspaper and gummed side by side as required. The letter reads: 'The man found drowned was a traitor to the Irish Republic and it will be better for your own sake if you do not enquire about his execution'. It was signed I/O IRA. The police wonder whether the letter is a joke or not.[6]

Reuter

The Irish Times added the detail that the letter was posted locally and commented that because a direct steamer line existed between Boulogne and Ireland a 'good many Irishmen' were often seen in the town.[7]

The key to the affair may lie in the fact that the annual conference of the general secretaries of the YMCA was to be held that year in Boulogne. The British National Council of the YMCA had a substantial headquarters at Chateau de Falaise, near Boulogne. This had been acquired at the end of World War I for use as a receiving centre and hotel for people to visit the war graves of deceased relatives. The chalets in the grounds were used as a hostel until they were destroyed by the Germans in 1944. There was a lot of to-ing and fro-ing between Britain and Boulogne by YMCA personnel in organising the conference, which was held there from 16 to 23 June and which the then general secretary of Cork YMCA, George Bird, attended.

So what is the evidence that the mysterious Englishman was Harris? First, the age is about right: Harris was in his early fifties. The man was an Englishman, yet a 'traitor to the Irish Republic', which in itself is an odd combination. Then there are what facts as we can piece together on Harris's career after he left Cork. He did indeed serve as general secretary of East Bristol YMCA from May 1921 to the end of 1922. Then the trail goes cold because the records of East Bristol YMCA mysteriously end at 1922. However, at the June 1923 conference Harris's name was struck off, unusually without any reason given, and he never appears at the annual conference of the general secretaries again, nor does his obituary appear in the 1923 YMCA records.[8] He was also struck off the Freemason membership rolls at this time. So here he is, Henry A. Harris MBE, struck off two completely different data bases, that of the Freemason lodge of which he was a member and now the Association of General Secretaries of the YMCA.[9] If this is correct and if Harris was the man whose body was found in Boulogne, then he died the same week as William Goff Beale and his name should be included among the YMCA personnel killed in the aftermath of the capture and execution of Edward Parsons.

And there are other anomalies. Because on 23 April, two days after the Examiner piece appeared, The Irish Times carried a curious little report to the effect that the whole business of the note was a hoax and that the man found drowned in Boulogne Harbour had not been killed by the IRA at all, but was rather an Englishman killed by another Englishman, the 'evidence' for this being that the letters in the note were cut out of English newspapers. This has all the signs of a cover-up because, whatever about an Englishman blaming a murder on the IRA, it is unlikely such a person would know enough about IRA activities to sign it 'IO, IRA'. This was almost certainly an IRA job and has all the hallmarks of being the work of an IRA intelligence squad. The note published in The Irish Times looks very much like an attempt at dissimulation, as does the disappearance of East Bristol YMCA records post-1922. It suggests that somebody in Britain wanted to keep the facts of the drowning a secret.

So was Harris a spy? Was he hunted down, just as William Goff Beale, Theo Creber, Herbert Woods, the boys in west Cork and probably William

Cooke were because of information extracted from Parsons? The time-line suggests that this is likely to have been the case.

However, if the IRA knew that Harris was a spy in the spring of 1921, they could easily have shot him in Cork like they did many others or simply caught a steamer to Bristol, walked into the YMCA and shot him there. The fact that he left what was in effect a forwarding address in both Cork newspapers[10] and in the Cork YMCA's own annual report that was also publicly available suggests that he did not feel he was under serious threat in May 1921. Harris did not have any problem letting it be known that he was living at Bristol YMCA, despite the fact that during the very same month the IRA attacked the homes of at least half a dozen Black and Tans in Britain and assassinated an Irishman called Horace McNeill in London.[11]

And there is another intriguing angle to the story. It will be recalled that when Liam de Roiste was invited by Benjamin Haughton in March 1921 to a meeting in his house under the aegis of the American Committee for Relief in Ireland to discuss the political situation and the prospects for peace, Harris was present, apparently acting as secretary to the meeting.[12] (Eight American Quaker relief workers led by Clement France and John McCoy arrived in Ireland in February 1921 to administer the funds raised by what came to be called the American Committee on Relief in Ireland—*The Times* commenting that its members were a 'strange mixture of Anglophobes, idealists and radicals'. The fund was handled in Ireland by the Irish White Cross of which Haughton was a leading member.)[13] The Cork Distress Fund, which handled the ACRI relief in Cork, was led by Cork Quakers, all of whom were prominent YMCA personnel: Haughton, Beale and S. H. Newsome.[14] The meeting in Haughton's house, however, was clearly not confined to matters relating to the White Cross fund, but was a feeler being put out to Sinn Féin—both Liam de Roiste and Barry Egan were present, along with several city businessmen—in an effort to arrive at a peaceful settlement of the 'Irish Problem'. If the intention was to get moderate Sinn Féin politicians to come around to supporting negotiations, then the effort was successful because Barry Egan became one of the most publicly supportive Sinn Féiners of the efforts that ultimately led to the Truce. Was Harris the British government's eyes at this and similar meetings? Was Harris doing in Cork what Andy Cope was doing in Dublin, talking to Sinn Féin politicians in an effort to secure a settlement? If he was a military spy, he could easily have shipped Egan and de Roiste, who were high on the wanted list, to the army.[15] Or perhaps he was just a high-minded British Quaker administering relief work in Ireland. Harris's association with the ACRI makes it rather unlikely that he was a spy, if only on the basis that, if he was, Dublin Castle and the military in Dublin and Cork would not have had to go to the lengths they did to try to establish if ACRI friends were being used to buy guns for the IRA.[16]

It should also be pointed out that some of the attempts by Southern loyalists to broker a peace between Sinn Féin and the British government passed through the offices of Basil Thompson, the head of the Secret Service. Shane Leslie and Arthur Vincent of Muckross House in Killarney, both Southern Protestant nationalists, were in contact with Thompson, trying to secure peace.[17] Could Harris have been doing the same? Was he sending accounts of his meetings with de Roiste and Egan to England on YMCA-headed paper? Were these intercepted by the IRA? This is all possible, but the balance of evidence suggests that, if this had been the case, Harris would have been shot earlier.

When Harris left Cork for Bristol in May 1921, he did not think he was in danger from the IRA. Nor is there any evidence from IRA sources that Harris was exposed as a spy at that stage. In fact, at the time of the Truce, the YMCA does not appear to have been under suspicion (despite the attempts of Old IRA men subsequently to suggest otherwise). The most likely scenario is that he was targeted two years later on the basis of information extracted from Parsons and because he was in charge of the YMCA during the War of Independence. If Parsons had told the IRA of the junior and senior sections within the YMCA, he almost certainly would have told them that Harrris was the divisional secretary. Was Harris a spy? Was he acting as the British eyes at the meetings that led to peace negotiations? The fact that there appears to have been some sort of cover-up in Britain at the time of his death suggests this may well have been the case. We are not 100 per cent sure, of course, that the body found in Boulogne harbour was that of H. A. Harris, though the circumstantial evidence is strong. More information is needed to resolve this mystery.

And Harris was not the only Cork YMCA member who died outside of Ireland during 1923. Victor Wolfe, a young man with a small hardware business in the city, who sold his premises in the summer of 1921, also died under mysterious circumstances in Liverpool in April 1923. It is all suggestive of a long drawn-out process of revenge by the IRA.

Chapter 40

OLD FRIENDS AND OLDER ENEMIES

So were there any members of the YMCA besides Parsons, either city or county, who admitted they were spying for the British? The short answer is yes. Taken at face value, it could be argued that they might well constitute part of a spy circle operating out of the YMCA or even an Anti-Sinn Féin League of the type claimed by IRA members. However, closer examination suggests that this was probably not the case. The individuals concerned were William McNeill and John Willis, one a retired RIC man, the other a JP. Both were farmers and supporters of the YMCA. McNeill, originally from Fermanagh, lived outside the city but also seems to have owned a house on Thomond Square, just off Blackrock Road.[1] Willis, an Englishman, was a notable Methodist farmer and JP in Ballinhassig, some seven miles south of Cork city. Both had to leave Cork in the spring of 1921.[2]

They were close friends and were heavily involved in unionist political groups in Cork. William McNeill was secretary of the Cork Defence Union, while Willis was hon. treasurer of the Cork branch of the Irish Unionist Alliance.[3] The CDU would make a very good candidate for a putative Anti-Sinn Féin League. This was a profoundly anti-democratic organisation set up by Lord Barrymore—then mere Arthur Smith-Barry—in the early 1880s to protect landlords against boycotts by the Land League. Along with the Cork Landowners' Association, which shared much of the same personnel and operated out of the same address, 69 South Mall, it was still nominally in existence at the end of World War I and had as its leading members Lords Bandon and Barrymore and other unionist notables such as Savage French of Rushbrook, Captain T. R. Sarsfield and W. H. Beamish.[4] This was largely a rural organisation, but it was exactly the kind of organisation one would expect to take on the IRA, just as it had combated the Land League some 30 years earlier.

However, the case for making the remnants of the CDU into an Anti-Sinn Féin League does not quite add up. McNeill's story is the more interesting of the two. He was 60 years of age and an ex-RIC man. An Ulster unionist, he appears to be a perfect candidate for organising a spy ring out of the YMCA. In his attempt to get compensation from the IGC, McNeill stated: 'I occupied land at Riverstown and a large fruit garden at Ballyphehane, County Cork, all of which I was compelled to abandon on the 4th April 1921. Being an ex-member of the Royal Irish Constabulary and my occupation as already stated took me to various localities through the County Cork, which enabled me to supply information to the police as regards Republican gatherings and suspected ambushes.' So unquestionably William McNeill was an agent and had to decamp for Hampshire as a result. However, he states: 'Being Secretary of the Cork Defence Union which had to be dissolved owing to the trouble and on this account I lost my situation.'[5] This suggests that the CDU, like the military work of the YMCA, went out of business as the 'troubles' gathered momentum from 1919 onwards.[6]

So was the CDU the Anti-Sinn Féin League? If it was, then the IRA had its chairman, Lord Bandon, in captivity for several weeks in July 1921 and did not shoot him—which they would almost certainly have done had he been regarded as the head of a spy ring. Not only that, but no IRA man to my knowledge has ever referred to the capture of Lord Bandon as anything other than hostage-taking. Similarly, nothing untoward ever happened to Lord Barrymore or his estate or to the other prominent unionists who were members of the CDU.

Nor is there a strong case for making John Willis a major player in a supposed Anti-Sinn Féin League. Willis, a devious individual who spent a lot of energy gathering 'evidence' of anti-Protestant bias in public appointments in support of Ulster unionism during the Home Rule crisis of 1912–14[7] was a large farmer near Carrigaline, some miles south of Cork city. He refused to resign as a JP in 1920 and continued to supply the RIC barracks in Ballinhassig with foodstuffs in defiance of an IRA boycott. Three RIC men were shot while leaving his farm with supplies.[8] He was ordered to leave the country when a party of five IRA men entered his house on 31 March 1921—he was spared being shot only when he offered the men a 'substantial sum of money' to let him go. He was given 24 hours to get out of Ireland. He also stated to the IGC that he was more than happy to pass on any information he may have had on rebel activities: 'I informed the military of all that I knew which was going on by the rebels in the locality.'[9]

In summary, both McNeill and Willis had to leave Ireland within a week of each other, both supplied information to the British authorities, both were elderly members of loyalist political organisations, and both ended up buying farms in Hampshire. Neither, however, though happy to claim their information-gathering and their membership of the CDU and the Loyalist Alliance as evidence of their support for the Crown, mentions any form of Anti-Sinn Féin League or of organising anything out of the YMCA. They would have had every reason to mention it in order to boost their claims, for they were by then safe in England. If there had been an Anti-Sinn Féin League, that is to say a counter-revolutionary organisation of Cork loyalists operating against the IRA, then these two would surely have been members. Nor do they claim to have set up any sort of spy ring such as the one alleged to have operated out of the YMCA.[10] McNeill and Willis supplied information because that was what such men did out of loyalty to Britain. These were old school unionists cut out of the same cloth as people like Major O'Connor and Lord Bandon.[11]

PART VIII

Chapter 41

THE MANY GANGS OF GENERAL TUDOR

Probably the most successful organization was one consisting mainly of ex-officers who worked in plain clothes—mostly in the streets. They suffered heavy casualties and it was hard to get and train recruits.[1]

A lot has been written of the undercover intelligence campaign waged by the British military forces against the IRA in Dublin, from the Tudor Gang to Bloody Sunday and the Igoe Gang. Everything points to the Anti-Sinn Féin League being the Cork version of the Tudor Gang. There is much to be gleaned from the operation of these units which sheds light on the activities of the Anti-Sinn Féin League or Murder Gang as they were known to the IRA in Cork.

This shadowy organisation—'a rather hastily improvised Intelligence Organisation'—appears to have been set up initially by the military in the spring of 1920. After a short course of instruction at Hounslow outside London, at least some of its men were sent to Dublin in the early summer of 1920. According to one account,[2] 'The first batch were instructed to pose, initially as RE [Royal Engineers] officers but this rather futile procedure was soon dropped and the work consisted of getting to know the town thoroughly, tailing "Shinners" and carrying out small raids, with a view to collecting all possible information which would lead us eventually to stamping out the revolt.' What this account does not say is that part of the remit of these groups was also to eliminate known 'Shinners'. One well-known example of this was the assassination of John Lynch in September 1920 in the Royal Exchange Hotel in Dublin, when the intended target was Liam Lynch, and also the shooting of Seán Treacy in Dublin in October. The unit was transferred from the military authorities to the Chief of Police in the summer of 1920 and placed under the command of 'O', Ormonde de l'Épée Winter, chief of intelligence and Deputy Head of Police, who in turn reported directly to General Hugh Tudor, the newly appointed head of police. So these were army men, though technically they were called policemen. It is easy to see how they might also be called 'military police'.

Tudor was a friend of Winston Churchill and was, like 'O', an artilleryman. The intelligence department set up under Tudor was in many ways an old boys' network of former artillery officers. One of Tudor's units, consisting initially of only six men, was led on the ground by one Captain Frederick Harper-Shove. Four of his men worked undercover in Dublin, passing what information they could gather to the other two in barracks who then processed it. A letter written at the beginning of 1922 by Captain H. F. (Con) Boddington,[3] who replaced Harper-Shove, to General Boyd, the Military Commander of the Dublin district, tells us a lot about the kind of men who joined these units:

> That the undermentioned officers' record of service for the last two years be brought to the notice of the Higher Command and the War Office in conjunction with the results obtained for the Military Intelligence Branch in Ireland.
>
> The gentlemen have performed their duties with the utmost bravery and devotion to duty. For over 4 months they carried on the work at their own expense, and two of them for a period of 6 months . . . Although they were transferred to the Chief of Police they were at heart soldiers and not policemen, working for the Army to which they all belonged and for you [Boyd] as their original chief.[4]

Harper-Shove boasted of the killing capacity of his unit at a meeting with Churchill and Sir Henry Wilson in September 1920. 'Shore [sic] talks in the calmest way of murdering the sFs. He told us he had certain sFs marked down and at the slightest show of resistance they would be shot. Many amazing stories.'[5] The Dublin Castle mandarins were less than happy with this group. 'I had a file brought to me yesterday in connection with the employment of these *so-called* officers your "O" took over from Boyd.'[6]

It is clear from Wilson's diary that the prime minister, Lloyd George, was aware of and condoned Tudor's shooting of 'Sinn Féiners'.[7] 'Tudor made it very clear that the Police and the Black and Tans and the 100 Intelligence officers are all carrying out reprisal murders.' What is evident also is that these 100 intelligence officers and the units they belonged to were scattered throughout the country.[8] 'At Balbriggan, Thurles and Galway, yesterday the local Police marked down certain sFs as in their opinion the actual murderers or instigators and then coolly went and shot them without question or trial. Winston saw very little harm in this but it horrifies me.'[9] As Frank Crozier put it: 'Sir Neville Macready's idea of "restoration of order" [was] the secret murder gang and vice circle operating *sub rosa* with the avowed intention of out-murdering the Sinn Féiners.'[10]

The most extraordinary detail emerging from Boddington's letter is that these men were prepared to work at their own expense for long periods: for four months and, in the case of two of them, for six months. This suggests that they were adventurers, James Bond-types who loved the thrill of espionage work and were happy to carry out whatever killing was part of the job. They must have been relatively well-off to be able to afford it. These were recently demobbed junior officers from well-off families looking for excitement. They did not even need to be recruited, but volunteered for the work. Clearly, these were committed, dangerous men who simply wanted to have a crack at the Shinners and who were attracted by the thrill of working undercover. The semi-official policy of 'out-murdering Sinn Féin' created exactly the kind of environment in which such activities flourished. These were the equivalent of the various IRA hit squads on the ground, though they were vastly more experienced and probably even more ruthless. In those years such men had a free rein to do more or less exactly what they liked. Writing many years later, Crozier summarised the activities of these groups:[11] 'I resigned because the combat was carried out on foul lines, by selected and foul men, for a grossly foul purpose, based on the most satanic of all rules that the end justifies the means.'

Probably the most prominent artillery officer to die while involved in this work was Major George Osbert Smyth, who was shot through the door of the house of Professor Carolan in Drumcondra, Dublin on 12 October 1920 while trying to 'arrest' Dan Breen and Seán Treacy—Treacy was later shot by the same unit in a shoot-out on Talbot Street, Dublin. Smyth, a brother of Lieutenant-Colonel Gerald Bryce Ferguson Smyth, who as Divisional Inspector of the RIC in Munster was assassinated by the Cork city IRA on 17 July 1920, was widely regarded as being a member of the 'Cairo Gang'. This was a group of officers recruited from the colonies and brought to Dublin to carry out undercover intelligence work and assassinations for military intelligence. It is almost certain that 'Cairo Gangs' were in operation in other parts of the country, particularly in Cork city. Lieutenant George E. Green for instance, had come from Malaysia.

The case of Smyth is interesting because it shows how important personal vendettas are in a context like this. Smyth, who was stationed in Egypt at the time of his brother's assassination, vowed revenge for his death and succeeded in getting himself transferred to Ireland where he joined one of Tudor's undercover units. It also illustrates another element of the conflict and one that is surprisingly rarely commented on: the role of Irish unionist military men and particularly Ulster unionists in the fight against the IRA in the South of Ireland. From General Gough (a Wexford man) who refused to march against the Ulster unionists in 1914[12] to Sir Henry Wilson (originally from Longford), from Bernard Montgomery (County Donegal) to Brigadier

Higginson (County Tipperary), to local IOs such as Captain Kelly and Lieutenant Koe in Cork, Irish unionists in uniform were at the forefront of the fight against the IRA. This is a subject we shall return to, but we must look first at what connections, if any, can be established between these undercover units and activities in Cork.

Chapter 42 ～

THE CORK 'MURDER GANG'

My grandmother insisted on entertaining the military up to the last, even after having received repeated notes that she must not do so for her own safety. As a great treat she would take me up to the attic and show me in the trunk amongst the old uniforms and many other tattered treasures, the dress in which she had been presented at Court, complete with feathers. Then she would snap the trunk and, cupping my face in her hands, would say 'Some day you will wear that dress and make your curtsey.' This prophesy was never fulfilled because she was given twenty-four hours by the IRA to get out of the country. The entire contents of Ravenscourt were auctioned some months later.[1]

We know from British sources that in the summer of 1920 there were 100 intelligence officers in action in various parts of Ireland. That number was almost certainly doubled or even tripled by the summer of the following year. Connie Neenan is very informative on the effectiveness of these units. He describes how, in May 1921, he had to cross the River Lee downstream of Cork city in order to avoid roadblocks. 'I had barely set foot on land when I saw two civilians carrying Webley revolvers in their hands coming towards me. Immediately I ducked and luckily they did not spot me. I knew right away that these men were not IRA members but suspected them to be Black and Tans in mufti. And I was right in my assumption because, walking with great caution, I saw many more of them.'[2]

The picture Neenan paints is of an IRA under extreme pressure from the relentless harassment by these British units in the city, especially in the months immediately before the Truce. They were often quite well known to the IRA. 'On the way back to Cork . . . a big green car travelling at high speed suddenly passed us as we reached the Castle Tavern. I was very startled when I recognised it as the British Intelligence car which their "murder gang" normally used. However, since the car was fortunately going so fast, they did not take any notice of us.' According to Neenan, this was 'a relentless and most cruel British spy system whose members tortured, maimed and murdered mercilessly, running rampage among the civilian Irish population'.[3]

British sources are naturally very quiet about it, though General Macready, in his weekly summary to the Cabinet for 14 March 1921, was able to report (without a hint of irony) that 'a number of other murders occurred during the week which suggest that they are committed as reprisals for Sinn Féin murders of police and ex-soldier civilians'.[4] Some of these (murders not attributable to Sinn Féin) occurred in Cork. And while not much is known about the composition of these 'murder gang' units—the only ones we have been able to pin down are military men such as Lieuts Koe and Green—a few very prominent espionage types did have associations with Cork.

Two of the best known were Colin McVean Gubbins and J. C. F. (John Charles Francis) Holland.[5] Much of British espionage and counter-espionage activities during World War II, including the Special Operations Executive (SOE)[6] and the commandos, were set up by Holland and Gubbins.[7] Both had cut their intelligence teeth, so to speak, while serving in Ireland from 1919 to 1922. Gubbins, then a captain in the Royal Artillery, was attached—officially at least—to the 5th Division HQ in the Curragh from late 1919. Holland, a Royal Engineer, was stationed in Dublin. There is reason to believe, though, that their work was not confined to Dublin. Holland was certainly operating in Cork, for he was shot and wounded by an IRA squad in Cork city on 9 January 1921.[8] He was then removed from Ireland and given a senior intelligence posting at the War Office, where he was to remain until the outbreak of World War II.

In the case of Gubbins, there is, as his biographer (himself an intelligence operative) put it, 'no open source on Gubbins' sojourn in Ireland'.[9] Though he arrived in December 1919, the Army Lists do not pick him up until April 1921, when he is recorded as a captain with the 47th (Howitzer) Battery of the 30th Field Brigade of the Royal Field Artillery based in the Curragh. While there is no official record of what Gubbins was doing between the end of 1919 and April 1921,[10] he was very likely involved in intelligence work, since it was from his time in Ireland that he developed an interest in espionage that was to continue until the 1950s. The conflict suited one 'who had all the instincts of a good "I" officer; he settled in to learn all he could about clandestine warfare and the intelligence without which it could not function'. Gubbins and Holland were to remain close friends for the rest of their lives.

Gubbins too had connections with Cork. His wife Norah had been raised in Cork by an aunt who was married to Canon Alexander Jackson Nicholson, the Church of Ireland rector for the St Nicholas parish on the south side of Cork city. This is the parish in which many of the events described in this book, including the shooting of four alleged spies and the abduction of Edward Parsons, took place. In fact Rev. McKinley, who ran the Boys' Brigade, was standing in for Canon Nicholson during those years. This may of course be a mere coincidence, yet the fact that Holland—who may also have had family connections in Cork—was shot when working undercover in the city, while Gubbins had close family ties with the area, suggests a link between the two.

Thanks to Tudor, many artillerymen were involved in intelligence work in Ireland in 1920/21. The majority of officers decorated for bravery—and these were usually intelligence officers—were from the RFA and the RGA, most particularly in the 5th Divisional area.[11] At least 11 members of the artillery corps were shot during the conflict.[12] Five of these were lieutenants and almost certainly intelligence officers.[13] Given the manpower priorities and needs of the army at the time, it is almost inconceivable that someone like Gubbins, with a growing interest in intelligence work, would not be engaged in actually doing it.

It is interesting to note that the shooting of Holland went unreported in the newspapers. It is equally clear that the IRA knew who he was, getting his rank and initials more or less right. Was Holland operating out of barracks? Or was he, as is much more likely, lodging with civilians? Given that Green was also known to the IRA when he was shot, the latter is much more likely. While it is clear from the case of Sgt Major Mackintosh that such killers were sometimes recruited from the serving soldiery, operatives such as Holland and Green (and possibly Gubbins) were far more likely to be staying in civilian accommodation while on their missions. This would fit the pattern of the Bloody Sunday killings in Dublin where all those shot were staying in boarding houses or other residences.

And we know that these undercover units were carrying out unofficial killings right up to the Truce. Some stayed at hotels—Green was travelling from Cork's Imperial Hotel on the night he shot himself during his altercation with Auxiliaries. Two other officers in mufti—members of o Company of the Auxiliaries, cadets Agnew and Mitchell—were snatched shortly after they left the Imperial Hotel in November 1920 and were shot as spies.[14] Koe was also staying in the Imperial in the post-Truce period. 'Saunders' stayed at the Salvation Army hostel off Patrick's Quay.

But of all the places in the city, the most likely refuge for British officers, whether undercover or not, was the YMCA. YMCA buildings around the country (including the one in Fermoy) were at the time commandeered for use by Auxiliaries and troops[15] and were again commandeered by Free State forces during the Civil War. The facilities, both at the YMCA hostel on Railway Street and the organisation's HQ on Marlborough Street, would always have been open to members of the British forces. The YMCA building in Bandon was burnt down for that very reason. It is inconceivable that the YMCA facilities in the city were not being used by undercover agents, if only behind the backs of those who ran it on a day-to-day basis. It is but a small step from that to using the boys themselves to ferret out information on the IRA.

The implication of this is that the British military authorities, at least from the spring of 1921, had started using teenagers as spies—and the RIC may have been using them as early as March 1920. We have seen several examples of this. However, there is nothing in contemporary IRA reports to suggest that the IRA suspected the YMCA of being a spying centre in the months before the Truce.[16] The balance of evidence suggests that the YMCA only really came to the attention of the IRA with the capture of Parsons in the spring of 1922 and that this came about because of the pursuit of alleged spies in the High Street area going back to George Horgan in December 1920. Horgan and the Roycrofts had been members of the YMCA at one time or another. But Parsons appears to have been the first that the IRA recognised as such.

If undercover agents were staying at the YMCA and with Cork Protestant families such as the Beals and the Woods, this would not go down well with the IRA. In fact, there is reason to believe that the proprietor of at least one well-known city hotel where IOs regularly stayed was also abducted and shot by the IRA. These 'military policemen' lodged anywhere they could in the city. Anybody who put them up was inevitably going to suffer as a result.

However, Green and Holland were serving officers. The British Army intelligence report on the rebellion stated, on the other hand, that 'probably the most successful organisation was one consisting mainly of ex-officers who worked in plain clothes—mostly in the streets. They suffered heavy casualties and it was hard to get and train recruits.' This is normally taken as merely referring to the operations of the Cairo Gang in Dublin. However, there are good reasons to believe that ex-officers, many of them Irish, were also involved in undercover operations in many other parts of the country. Some were attached to the Auxiliaries and Black and Tans; others were not. These certainly constituted a significant proportion of what came to be called the Anti-Sinn Féin League in Cork. These were the 'selected and foul men' remembered by F. P. Crozier. It is time to look at one of its possible members.

| WARREN PEACOCKE

On the evening of 31 May 1921 retired Lieutenant Colonel Warren John Peacocke was sawing wood in a shed at his home at Skevanish, Innishannon, Co. Cork. Two young men approached the house and one of them walked up to the shed and asked Peacocke for directions for the road to Bandon. 'Keep straight west, young man', Peacocke is said (according to his killer) to have replied, whereupon the 'young man' pulled out a revolver and shot Peacocke twice in the chest. He was to die of his wounds at home the following morning.[1] The 'young man' was a local IRA man, Tom Kelleher. This is one of the most celebrated IRA assassinations in all the lurid history of the period and has surrounding it a complex mythology in the Bandon area and in republican circles. The assassins escaped on foot.

Warren Peacocke, the son of an English army captain, was more than a mere retired British Army officer. He was one of the most decorated veterans of the Somme, having on the first day of the battle at the Schwaben Redoubt rallied his men when they were about to be overwhelmed by a German counter-attack. In fact, Peacocke's bravery was one of the few good things to come out of that day of slaughter and was to make him one of the most celebrated war heroes in Ulster. For the men he led, members of the Inniskilling Fusiliers, who had 568 casualties in the first minutes of the battle as a result of German machine gun fire, were part of the 36th Ulster Division, comprised almost entirely of Ulster Protestants. Commanded by the self-same F. P. Crozier, later to lead the Auxiliaries in the Irish War of Independence, the division had been raised in Ulster by the simple expedient of converting the militant UVF into a division of the British Army.[2] It could be said that Peacocke was a senior figure in the most determinedly unionist section of the British military machine.

Was he shot by the IRA for that reason, as a symbol of British military might and Ulster intransigence? As one of the most decorated war veterans in the South of Ireland and a national hero in Britain, he would have made a prime target for an IRA trying to get back at its all too successful enemies, more specifically for the vicious campaign being run in west Cork by the RIC, the Auxiliaries and the Essex Regiment where impromptu roadside executions were the order of the day. According to Crozier, Peacocke continued to live in Innishannon 'for the fishing', the Bandon river along that particular stretch being a famous trout and salmon run. Crozier is generally accurate when it comes to matters pertaining to the Tans and Auxiliaries. He claimed that Peacocke was shot because of his association with Lieutenant Colonel Gerald Smyth, the RIC Divisional Commander, who was shot at the County Club in Cork city in July 1920 for his inflammatory speech made to the RIC. In Crozier's words, Peacocke was killed because he assented to these views and because of the 'tactless and arrogant things he said and did (all repeated in the servants' hall and village) which sealed his fate months before he met his maker at the hands of his assassins'.[3]

The IRA, however, had a different angle on Peacocke. According to Tom Barry he was an extremely dangerous man. 'This Britisher was not only an important organiser of espionage against the IRA but guided in person raiding parties of the Essex Regiment.' This refers to the killing of the Coffey brothers in February 1921, who were killed by 'civilians' and to two other military-style executions of Volunteers in Timoleague at the end of January. In the case of the Coffeys, 'the murderers on this occasion were led directly to the room where their victims were sleeping by two masked civilians, obviously local men and members of the British espionage circle'.[4]

According to Tom Barry, Peacocke dressed as a civilian and wore a mask during these raids but was identified one night when the mask slipped. 'From that night . . . we wanted him very badly, but he knew he was in danger and practically lived with the British Military Officers in barracks. When on occasion he ventured to Innishannon, he was invariably guarded by Black and Tans and his movements were most irregular.' Barry states that, on the evening he was shot, he was being guarded by four Black and Tans, who fired after the two men as they escaped.

Tom Kelleher was even more fanciful on Peacocke's supposed role. In a dramatic account entitled 'The Shooting of Intelligence Officer for Munster', he says:

There lived in Innishannon a retired Lt. Col. of the British Army. He was Intelligence Officer for Munster and he visited Belfast once a fortnight. We also believed that he led raiding parties of the Essex Regiment. Now he was heavily guarded by 4 RIC men around the clock. Myself and another Volunteer were given the task of disposing of him. His movements were very irregular and with the heavy security he was a difficult nut to crack. Around the end of May 1921 we got a report that he was sleeping at home. Carefully we entered in daylight his house which was right on the edge of the river. I hid in the laurels near the house to put him under surveillance. While I waited, he crossed from the house to a garage where he had some sort of workshop or power house. Leave him to me, I said to my companion as I approached the garage. The door was slightly ajar and I could see he was taken aback when I entered. I was afraid he might raise the alarm as I was too far away from him and I only had a short [revolver]. I knew I had to get near him without alarming him. I took the initiative and said could he direct me to Bandon . . . 'Keep straight west, young man . . .' Whipping out my gun I let him have it. He spun backwards and fell. I now had to escape before the RIC guarding him could catch me. On hearing the shots, they rushed to a window and opened fire on me with rifles. Some of their bullets winged me as I jumped over a ditch and fell into a drain. Both of us were then out of the line of fire. We were not followed, and I escaped back to the west through Innishannon village to my own country.[5]

The two accounts are quite at variance with each other. For Crozier, Peacocke was shot because of his 'mistaken and arrogant loyalty' and because of 'vulgarity masquerading in the Union Jack'; in other words, because he was a loudmouth who boasted of his pro-British views in front of the servants and in the village. In Barry's and Kelleher's view he was an 'Intelligence Officer for Munster', who visited Belfast once a fortnight, presumably for briefings or to pass on his information. According to Connie Neenan, Peacocke was the 'Head of the British Murder Gang in Munster'.[6] This all amounts to the same thing: the Anti-Sinn Féin League.

So was Peacocke a major intelligence officer, the head of the British 'murder gang' in Munster? Was he back and forth to Belfast every few weeks with his findings? Or was he just a cocky ex-officer going about his business in a particularly supercilious way? On the run up to Peacocke's assassination, Richard Russell of the local IRA company was given instructions to follow his movements and report them back to the Brigade 10. He followed Peacocke to Dunmanway where he was going on a fishing trip. 'But then, he was doing nothing other than that; he was enjoying a fishing holiday.'[7] It is difficult to prove if Peacocke was in fact an intelligence agent. What we can do is compare Barry's and Kelleher's account of his killing with the official British inquiry. This should shed light on a number of telling details. Was Peacocke being guarded by four Black and Tans? Did they shoot at Kelleher and wing him? Who else was staying at the house?

According to the RIC District Inspector of Bandon, who investigated the case:

I proceeded to Innishannon on the 1st of June to investigate the case. I found bloodstains in an engine house near the residence and blood tracks leading to the house. I questioned the household but could get no evidence of anyone having seen two men spoken of by Col. Peacocke. Col. Peacocke was a loyalist, was extremely popular with his tenants and the neighbourhood in general. He is reported to have refused subscriptions to the Rebels' arms fund. He is not known otherwise to have taken any part for either side in the present disturbances.

Clearly there is a discrepancy between the RIC's account of the killing and that of the IRA. Far from shots having been fired at the departing men, the DI could find no witnesses to the fact that two men were involved in the killing, though Peacocke said before he died that he had seen two men. According to the DI, Peacocke was killed because he refused subscriptions to the IRA's arms fund. There is no hint of intelligence work.

Two days later, however, intelligence work did get a mention in the House of Commons in a debate in which the killing came up:

Col Boyds: 'Can the right hon. gentleman assign any motive for this dastardly and cowardly crime?'

Sir Hamar Greenwood (Chief Secretary for Ireland): 'The only motive I can assign is that he was a loyalist and an ex-officer of His Majesty's Army.'

Col Allen: 'He served in the Ulster Division. That is why.'

Col Willoughby: 'Can the right hon. gentleman say whether this officer was known ever to have given any information to the Government as to any action of the Sinn Féin Party?'

Greenwood: 'None. I can speak for that. He had no connection whatever with the Government or any public office or any political movement in the country in which he lived.'[8]

The House of Commons debate puts the quandary in a nutshell: Peacocke was killed either because he was organising a spy ring or simply because he was a loyalist with strong Ulster affiliations. There is no room for ambiguity. Either Tom Barry and Tom Kelleher are both lying or the DI for Bandon was covering up and Sir Hamar Greenwood was lying. What must be significant, though, is that the subject of Peacocke's role in intelligence work was ever even broached in the House of Commons.

Luckily, the transcript of the military inquiry into Peacocke's death has survived. What it suggests is that there were not four RIC men present in the house on the evening he was killed—that was Tom Kelleher gilding the lily— and they did not fire back.[9] There was one though, a Constable John E. Deacon, who was a Black and Tan rather than a regular RIC man, though he had been in the Royal Engineers. So Peacocke was being guarded. Deacon's account is worth recording:

At Innishannon about 18.30 hours on the 31st May 1921 I was in Col. Peacock's [sic] house. One of the maids came into me saying, 'Did you hear the shots fired in the roadway?' I went out and met Col. Peacock running down the passage. He said 'Deacon, they have shot me.' He stumbled. I took him to his room and put him on a bed. He then said: 'I was fired on by two strange men.' I stayed with him about five minutes, locked up the house and having searched it went out to look for the men who had fired. I could not find them.

Signed John Edward Deacon Con 71044

So there *were* RIC men staying with Peacocke, and while only one officer was present on the evening he was killed, there may well have been four guarding him around the clock. That lends weight to Tom Kelleher's account, though the return of fire was just an exaggeration. The conclusion of the inquiry was the standard one in such cases: that Peacocke died as a result of wounds caused by 'shots fired feloniously, wilfully and with malice by some person or persons unknown and that such persons are guilty of wilful murder'.

The inquiry, however, was curious in a number of ways. The maid who had summoned Deacon, saying that she had heard shots, was not called as a witness, nor was any other member of the staff who worked in the house. The only witnesses called were the local doctor, Deacon, the RIC DI and a Mr Sweetnam. The reason for this could well have been that the inquiry was held at Bandon Barracks, and Peacocke's staff would have been too frightened to attend. However, this is in contrast to most of the other inquiries I have read about where there are usually a greater number of witnesses called. Moreover, there were no next of kin among the witnesses. If Peacocke was living with his mother, then why was she not called to give evidence? Perhaps she wasn't there at the time, but it is still a curious omission since the next of kin are usually the first people called in such cases, if only to identify the body.

And then there is the very odd statement in the RIC's daily summary on the day after Peacocke's house was burnt down (15 June) to the effect that his younger brother had moved to England as a result of the shooting and subsequent arson attack.[10] So why was the brother not called as a witness? Whatever the case, Kelleher was not shot at by four Black and Tans; nor was he winged; nor was Peacocke armed when he was shot.

So what evidence is there that Peacocke may have been an undercover intelligence officer? First of all there are the connections with Ulster. As we have seen, members of the Black and Tans and Auxiliary detachments in the Bandon area were blatantly sectarian in their operations and portrayed some of the worst characteristics of their northern co-religionists. Kelleher stated that Peacocke was making regular visits to Belfast. There was no reason for Kelleher to make up this part of the story, since it is not self-aggrandisement. In fact, Peacocke had just returned from Dublin on the day before he was killed.[11] It is likely that Peacocke was in the habit of regularly visiting Belfast, for whatever reason. Peacocke was very close to the former UVF men of the

36th Division. Ulster unionists had a prominent role in the Irish War of Independence on the British side, from DI Swanzy to Gerald and Osbert Smyth, from Sir Henry Wilson to Bernard Montgomery. It is fair to suppose that Warren Peacocke, though not an Ulster unionist in the strict sense, was another one.

And Peacocke, who was utterly fearless, would have had another motivation for such a role if he was close to District Commissioner Smyth. Just as Smyth's own brother had returned from Egypt to avenge his death, it is very possible that Peacocke had a similar motivation: revenge for Smyth's death at the hands of the Cork IRA. If English officers were signing up for the secret intelligence squads and paying their own way for up to six months at a time, then how much more likely is it that this particular officer, who had more motivation than most, was not doing the same?

There were, however, a number of other events that took place around the same time that, while not connected directly with Peacocke, go some way to suggesting that he may indeed have had a role in the intelligence system that was guiding raiding parties to their targets.

One was the burning at the end of June 1921 of the Bandon YMCA, otherwise known as the Allin Institute.[12] The reason usually given for this building being torched was that it was used as a social centre for British forces in the area. But the same could be said of the Bandon Masonic Hall and indeed of the Bandon Orange Hall. Yet these were not harmed, while the Allin Institute was gutted.

Tom Barry said his men entered Bandon town only on three occasions in the months before the Truce. One of these incursions was on receipt of instructions to shoot an alleged spy. This was one George T. Webb, who was fired on at the door of his house on 20 June. Webb was employed as Lord Bandon's agent, but his son George Innes Webb was the honorary secretary of the Bandon YMCA. Immediately after the shooting, both Webbs were transported under armed escort to Cork Barracks and thence to Plymouth. George Webb Snr received £4,000 in compensation, an enormous sum for the time, particularly when the bullet only grazed his knuckles. Neither man lived in Bandon again.

George Innes Webb—the same could be said of his father—was a well-known Protestant and loyalist. He took a leading part in recruiting and 'in my business capacity used to supply the military with maps and information about the configuration of the surrounding countryside'.[13] As long-time secretary of the YMCA, he would probably have used such maps for scouting purposes with the boys in his care. Whether the intention was to shoot him or his father is unclear. What is highly likely, though, is that Peacocke was a regular incumbent of the Allin Institute, as were his friends in the Essex Regiment and his Ulster friends in the Auxiliaries and the Black and Tans.[14]

When the British Army compiled its intelligence report as part of the

Record of the Rebellion in Ireland in 1922, it stated that 'in the south the Protestants and those who supported the Government rarely gave much information because, except by chance, they did not have it to give'.

> An exception to this rule was in the Bandon area where there were many Protestant farmers who gave information. Although the Intelligence Officer of this area was exceptionally experienced and although the troops were most active it proved almost impossible to protect these brave men, many of whom were murdered, while almost all the remainder suffered grave material loss.[15]

There can be little doubt that this refers to the half a dozen or so loyalist farmers who were shot as informers by members of Tom Barry's column and others who were driven out in fear of their lives. And while the 'exceptionally experienced' intelligence officer mentioned is usually taken to be the notorious Major Percival of the Essex Regiment, it may also have been Lieutenant Colonel Warren J. Peacocke, who was even more experienced and exceptional than Percival.

Peacocke's army service record, while weeded of anything that might imply that he had a career in intelligence, consists of three registers: one dealing with his career in the Inniskilling Fusiliers during World War I. This ends in 1918 with the cessation of hostilities. For most officers serving in the Great War, this would have meant the end of their career of active service. However, Peacocke has another register that runs from 1918 right up until the end of 1919.[16] Virtually the entire contents of this second register were removed and destroyed in 1930, suggesting that Peacocke may well have been working for the military after he officially left the army. Far from being retired, he may well have been on active service of a kind whose records merited destruction.[17]

After his death and the destruction of his house, the military authorities in Cork were urgently concerned about his estate—an honour they did not bestow on any of the scores of other residences burnt out at the time.[18] What's more, Peacocke's mother, an Englishwoman and a diehard unionist, had been nominated by the Irish Command for decoration and received an MBE from the King on 23 April 1921 as a tribute for patriotic work she had been carrying out.[19] Was this why she was not called as a witness during the inquiry into her son's death, even though she stated to the Irish Grants Commission that she had been living in the house at the time? She was doubly compensated for her losses suffered during the war, receiving £10,000 for the loss of her property from the Compensation (Ireland) Commission and, in breach of the rules governing the IGC, a further £1,800 from the IGC—the only case I have come across where the IGC compensated someone for losses incurred before the Truce.[20]

Perhaps the last word should be left to Frank Crozier, who was well placed to make an objective assessment, when he stated with no small amount of insight that 'most of the Colonel's co-Unionists suffered and were expelled for that which was said and done by the Englishman who, after all, was enjoying Irish life because it suited him'.[21] What this says is that the Protestants of the Bandon valley, and perhaps outside of the Bandon valley, suffered enormously because of what was said and done by Peacocke, the English Ulsterman among them. The implications are clear enough: Peacocke was probably central to British military intelligence operations in Munster. The IRA men, in this instance, appear to have been right.

Chapter 44 ~

CLERICAL ERRORS

In its intelligence summary, written when the War of Independence was over, the British Army was quite clear as to its best sources of information. It lists, in order of importance, women, clergy, bank managers, shop owners and employees, military contractors, farmers and civilians employed by the military or police. Some, though not many, of those shot belong to these groups. (It is also worth noting that ex-soldiers and tramps, two of the IRA's main victim groups, do not figure. Nor do loyalists.)

In the context of the YMCA in Cork city, one would expect the clergy to be the most important. It is quite clear that in the eyes of British military intelligence, clergymen (of whatever denomination) 'who are generally safe in Ireland whatever their religion' were second only to women as useful sources of information. This is an important statement from two points of view: one, that clergymen were significant sources of information on IRA activities; and two, that they were unlikely to be shot by the IRA, even if they were unlucky enough to be found out. From his analysis of those suspected by the IRA, shot by the IRA and actually informing on the IRA, Peter Hart has found no evidence that clergymen were targeted as informants. He found that, out of a total of 38 informants (from various sources), just three were clergymen.[1]

The immunity of the clergy to retribution was no doubt because of the deeply religious nature of Irish society at the time. It is often pointed out that Mrs Lindsay and her chauffeur were shot for their role in reporting the Dripsey ambush and that Father Shinnick, who was equally culpable—the aim of both was to save lives—was not. This is seen as an example of the sectarian nature of much of the IRA campaign. The IRA would almost certainly have shot Shinnick if he were a lay Catholic. It was the collar that saved him, not the fact that he was a Catholic. Similarly, when an RIC sergeant, who was playing both sides, told the Carlow IRA that a Protestant clergyman was his principal informant, the local O/C 'did not consider it advisable to take drastic action at the time'.[2]

Yet this does not appear to be true everywhere. Tom Barry wryly noted that in west Cork a Protestant clergyman was acting as a British agent: 'A Protestant Minister, head of an Intelligence group, [was] the organiser and transmitter of all information collected by his section to the British. One night, three members of the Flying Column went to shoot him but, observing their approach, he got out by the back door and made his escape into the darkness. Before morning he had made his way to Ballincollig Military barracks, where so often he had given his information and within twenty-four hours he was escorted to England. To our knowledge, he never returned to Ireland.'[3] Did the clergyman escape or was he quietly allowed to escape? We'll never know. With one exception,[4] this appears to be the closest the IRA got, so far as we know from the public record (apart from Rev. Harbord in 1922), to actually shooting a clergyman.

So who was Tom Barry's clergyman? One possibility is Rev. Frederick Girling, rector of Drinagh, who left west Cork for England during 1921 and never returned. Drinagh rectory was subsequently attacked during the Civil War. According to the Church of Ireland Bishop of Cork, however, Girling left because of ill health.[5]

Flor Begley of the Bandon company and an IRA intelligence officer gives an account of this affair: 'The minister from Bandon was evidently the local contact and he would be next on the list. So Percival sent word that if he was shot or a hair of his head touched, the PP or a neighbour (or a brother) of the Bishop would be shot. Even then he was in danger, for one night he heard sounds in his house and he woke to find men looking over him who were armed with revolvers.'[6] The two ministers listed for Bandon for 1921 were Rev. J. C. Lord and Rev. V. W. Darling. Darling, as we have seen, was a close friend of Rev. Harold McKinley and is the leading candidate to be the clergyman in question.[7] If so, this points to another intelligence connection between west Cork and the city.

All this suggests that at least some clergymen may have been agents for British military intelligence. This was not simply the passing on of scraps of information that may have come their way in their day-to-day life, but actually gathering, collating and transmitting such information. There is no reason to disbelieve Barry's account—the would-be victim escaped; this was not a well-known execution in search of an excuse; there is no reason why Barry should make up the story. The clergyman was probably uncovered as a result of raids on the mails or watching his movements or through interrogation of suspect informers. The role of some clergymen as conduits of information is beyond dispute. The 'Irish Coastal Patrol' network run by 'Blinker' Hall from the Admiralty during World War I lists five Church of Ireland clergymen among its agents, including one in County Cork, Rev. Richard Hodges, rector for Youghal.[8] Were McKinley and Darling working as agents? The evidence—at least three boys dead—at least gives grounds for suspicion.

An analysis of the transfers of clergymen within the main denominations between the years 1920 and 1923 yields some extraordinary results though.[9]

Leaving aside deaths and movements within the diocese, the Church of
Ireland lost only one clergyman from the city and three from the county out
of a total of 113 between 1921 and 1923 (4 per cent)—and two of those resigned
on grounds of ill health.[10] The Presbyterians replaced only one clergyman out
of 14. McKinley and Darling apart, there is only limited evidence that some
kind of organised intelligence-gathering system existed among Church of
Ireland clergymen and none at all for Presbyterians. Much of the intimidation
suffered by Church of Ireland clergymen was inflicted on rectors who were
blameless. One of many examples of this was the experience of Rev. Leonard
Henry of Newport, Co. Tipperary, who was threatened with death and had to
leave the country in June 1922. 'This to him was a shocking calamity. He had
done nothing to deserve such treatment.'[11] There were many examples of this
kind of intimidation all over the south of Ireland, at least six in County Cork
alone.[12]

The most striking changes of all, however, occur among Methodist
clergymen. Of the 18 ministers listed for 1921, twelve (66 per cent) had left
Cork by 1923. Of these, four left in 1921 and the remainder in 1922. The
turnover rate of Methodist ministers was always going to be higher than that
of other denominations since it was a missionary Church in the South of
Ireland and clergymen did not remain at their posts for long periods. With its
'circuit system', Methodist stations were changed every few years. However,
these are still very striking figures. What is more, the four who left in 1921 were
all associated with areas where Methodists had been kidnapped or shot
during the conflict: Reverend Kell[13] with the city (Alfred Reilly), Rev. Shire
(Youghal, John Cathcart), Rev. Beacon (Ballineen, Tom Bradfield) and Rev.
Clarke (Skibbereen, E. A. Swanton, W. G Wood and Jasper Wolfe). Two of the
civilians targeted during the Dunmanway massacre, James Buttimer and
William Jagoe, were Methodists. Furthermore, Rev. James Alley, who was to
become president of the Methodist Congregation of Ireland in 1923, was on
the general committee of the YMCA and was, along with Rev. Mercer Wilson
of the Church of Ireland, removed from his chaplaincy of the YMCA in June
1921.[14]

All but one of those who left Cork were transferred to other centres in
Ireland by 1923. It is probably safe to say that there is no question mark over
these, for if they were British agents of any kind, they would have been
removed to England or elsewhere for their own safety. To remain anywhere in
Ireland, even in Northern Ireland, would mean they would still be targets for
IRA retribution. There was, however, one clergyman whose name disappeared
off the clerical list and who does not appear anywhere among the Irish
Methodist clergy for the next few years. He was Rev. George Kell of Blackrock
and Passage West.[15] Kell did not leave the ministry; he may not even have left
the country. It appears he went off to train as a teacher. He married a Cork
girl, Irene Musgrave, the daughter of W. P. Musgrave, owner of the Metropole

Hotel, a few years later and served in Youghal in the late 1920s. After a stint on missionary work in India, he returned as Methodist minister of Dun Laoghaire.[16] At the Methodist Synod of September 1921 Rev. Kell is described as having been transferred to another centre in Ireland,[17] yet he is not publicly named as being at any of those centres over the next two years until he turns up in Belfast in mid-1923.[18]

When I consulted experts on the workings of British intelligence, they expressed no surprise that Anglican ministers might have been carrying out intelligence work, but thought that Methodists were far less likely to have been doing so. This was because of the Low Church and non-political nature of Methodism relative to the Church of the establishment. However, far more Methodists were shot (proportionally) by the Cork IRA than were members of any other denomination. Considering that Methodists made up only 10 per cent of the Protestant population of Cork,[19] the high number of them among IRA victims requires some explanation.

And there were some other very odd things going on around Kell's ministry. Kell, who hailed from Lisburn, Co. Antrim and was pastor of Blackrock and Passage West, should have been the natural person to preside at Alfred Reilly's funeral in February 1921 and at the memorial service held for him a few days later. Yet, though three other Methodist clergymen were present and most Methodist notables from the city's business community were there, Kell is not listed as having attended.[20] Bearing in mind that he regularly gave the Sunday service in the Methodist chapel on Military Hill— where Reilly was organist—even giving it on the Sunday before Reilly's death, and ran the service in Passage West on the following Sunday, his absence at the funeral that week is strange, to say the least.[21]

Furthermore, Kell officiated at one or other of the Methodist services in Cork on almost every Sunday from the beginning of 1921 until the day before the Truce, 10 July, when he returned to the Theological Hall, Methodist College Belfast, to complete his training. However, with five Methodists shot in County Cork during the War of Independence and up to half a dozen others disappearing in 1922, there may well be a connection between the two.[22]

Florrie O'Donoghue claimed that loyalists in Cork had set up a civilian branch of the British Secret Service in the city and county. He said five or six were shot in 1921 and that that put an end to their activities. This may refer to the YMCA or to the Freemasons or to activities surrounding one or two clergymen. Consider the number of Methodists shot: Reilly, Cooke, John Cathcart in Youghal, Tom Bradfield of Enniskeane, Gilbert and Fred Fenton in Bandon[23] and others such as Edwin Swanton, William G. Wood and Jasper Travers Wolfe of Skibbereen who were kidnapped, as well as self-confessed informants such as John Willis, who was lucky to escape with his life, and others such as James T. Mulligan and William Hosford, fired at or otherwise intimidated, and you have almost what amounts to a pogrom on Methodists in Cork. In addition to which, several Methodist families with connections in the city YMCA Cork left in 1921.

In an attempt to understand the background to this, we need to look briefly at the history of Methodism in Ireland in the twentieth century. Methodism was an evangelical faith, being little more than 150 years old at that stage. Its members tended, in general, to be more committed to Christian ideals than members of more traditional Churches. Irish Methodists found themselves in an invidious position with the advent of the revolution. Methodists, and Protestants in general, had traditionally been opposed to Home Rule. In a wide-ranging analysis of the relationship between Methodism and the Irish movement towards independence, published in 1931, Rev. Alley stated: 'Traditionally and by conviction, Irish Methodists . . . stood in overwhelming numbers for the continuance of the legislative union with Britain. It is safe to say that not two percent of the Methodists of Ireland desired Home Rule. They had lived under British rule since birth and had no complaint to make against it. Home Rule, most of them honestly believed, meant Rome Rule and as staunch Protestants they were prepared to resist to the death.'[24]

However, as the Home Rule issue reached its crisis in the years before 1914, 'there grew amongst some of the younger Ministers and Members of the Church the conviction that, whatever their personal predilections might be, it was not possible to meet the persistent demand of Southern Ireland for self-determination and self-government with a policy of blank resistance'.

As a result, there was a split in Irish Methodism between the older generation, people like John Willis who were vehemently pro-Union, and the younger generation such as Jasper Wolfe who were pro-Home Rule. This was a very serious issue for southern Methodists and threatened to tear the Church apart. 'For a time,' according to Alley, 'it seemed like the church might be rent asunder.' When William O'Brien set up his All For Ireland League in 1909 which campaigned for Home Rule on the basis of 'Conference, Conciliation and Consent' between Irish Catholics and Protestants, he won widespread support among non-conformists. Leading Methodists such as Joseph Hosford, who owned one of Cork's largest bakeries, and other non-conformists such as Thomas Farrington, professor of chemistry at UCC and a leading figure in the YMCA, ran for election under the All For Ireland banner. The O'Brienites, who roundly defeated the Redmondite Home Rule Party in Cork in the 1910 general election, got much support from the merchant classes of Cork and other Munster population centres, many of whom were Methodists. In fact, Methodists put down to divine intervention the 'change of heart' that saw southern Protestants begin to support the League's stance on Home Rule rather than the increasingly bellicose and isolationist Ulster unionist position.[25] 'Unionism was declared to be a discredited creed.'[26]

The curious thing is that many of the Methodist businessmen targeted by the IRA between 1920 and 1923 appear to have been pro-Home Rule or at least took out advertisements in the *Cork Free Press*, the organ of the O'Brienite Party. While you could argue that this was merely good business practice, if they were serious unionists of the traditional variety they would hardly pay for ads in a partisan Home Rule newspaper. Jasper Wolfe and his brother Willie, who was a Skibbereen councillor for the AFIL, campaigned vigorously for Home Rule from 1910 to 1912. Jasper roundly condemned John Willis for his campaign of vilification aimed at showing that Roman Catholics in the south were excluding Protestants from positions of power. In this he was supported by R. H. Tilson, the brother of George and newly elected O'Brienite High Sheriff for Cork city.[27]

Rev. Alley is equally unambiguous on the matter of passing on information on IRA activities: 'Some of them [Irish Methodists] who on conscientious grounds felt compelled to inform the British authorities of things that were being done in their districts were foully murdered. It made it no easier for their relatives that those responsible for the deed of crime called it an execution.' These men felt compelled because of their Christian beliefs to pass on any information they may have had on what they saw as a campaign of murder. As an uncompromising Christian, Rev. Alley may have contributed to the sufferings of his flock. His sermon on the Sunday a week before the Truce was entitled 'Our relationship to, and duty in, the present crisis'. If that duty entailed passing on information on IRA activities, then it is easy to see the dilemma in which Cork Methodists found themselves.

In fact there had been a long history of targeting Methodists and members of minority evangelical groups in Cork. Street preachers were regularly pelted with rotten fish and vegetables and sometimes even stoned in the streets. In February 1920, Rev. Alley, by all accounts a brave and upright man, was stoned by a mob in Blackpool—he was lucky not to lose the sight of one eye in the affray.[28] The very fact that Rev. Alley had been attacked in this manner at this time suggests that he had gone back to street preaching, something that would not have endeared him to the locals.[29]

And there was another factor. Methodism was very closely associated with the army. In fact, Methodist chapels were very much part of barrack life all over Britain and Ireland. There were no fewer than 15 Methodist clergymen assigned to the Curragh camp in 1919.[30] The chapel on Military Hill in Cork served the nearby Victoria Barracks; the one in Passage West served the naval and artillery communities of the port's naval and army bases. In fact, on the occasions when Kell did not give the service, his place was sometimes taken by one Sergeant Major Adams of the Royal Garrison Artillery.[31] 'Our Ministers never flinched in their duty to the English Nonconformist troops quartered in Ireland during "the troubles".'[32]

Was this what Florrie O'Donoghue referred to as a 'garrison clique'? It is fair to assume he meant this in the literal sense. These men saw their role as looking after the spiritual well-being of 'the troops'. It is quite clear from YMCA records that some Protestant groups, in particular Methodists, were very involved in proselytising among the soldiery. Many Cork Methodists were also related to northern Methodists, if only through marriage. It is very possible that Methodists such as Alfred Reilly, church organist in the military chapel, were killed for no other reason than that they *were* a garrison clique. In fact, referring to someone such as George Kell as a 'spy' is as ridiculous as referring to a British army chaplain as a spy. Kell was Methodist chaplain to the British forces in Victoria Barracks and the Artillery forts in Templebreedy. Given that he was a Northern Protestant, he was hardly going to be a friend of republicanism. Such close contacts between civilian groups and the military were not going to be popular with the IRA. Yet he was not a member of Cork YMCA, nor did he ever make a subscription to that organisation.

And there was also fear and a certain amount of defiance in the position of Cork Methodists. The very first British soldier killed in the conflict in Cork was a Methodist—killed when Liam Lynch's 2nd Brigade ambushed a party of soldiers on their way to Sunday service at the Wesleyan chapel in Fermoy in September 1919. 'When British soldiers were shot down at our church door in Fermoy, it was the Minister's wife who first tended them, when every other door in the street was closed in terror.'[33] Such ministrations to injured British soldiers were not going to help Methodists either. And the baiting of Tom Bradfield in January 1921 only added fuel to the fire.

Yet it was Cork city Methodists (led primarily by Alfred Reilly himself) who signed and delivered a petition to the British government for the release of Terence MacSwiney in the autumn of 1920. Allied to this is the fact that in the case of those shot in early 1921, such as Fenton, Reilly and Cathcart, the opinion of the army's Record of the Rebellion in Ireland is that there was less than a one in ten chance of any of them working for military intelligence.

There is perhaps no contradiction between the Methodists campaigning for the release of Terence MacSwiney and reporting on IRA activities. For men like Alfred Reilly and others like him were profoundly Christian. Reilly was described as a man of blameless integrity; Richard Jagoee was 'held in saintly estimation by his Roman Catholic neighbours';[34] and Musgrave's Metropole Hotel was 'dry' during those years and for decades afterwards.[35] Families like the Parkers, Merricks, Musgraves and Jagoes were held in high esteem by Cork society. Musgrave Park was called after J. G. (Jimmy) Musgrave. On the other hand it requires very little imagination to see that, from a fundamentalist Christian perspective, there is not much difference between trying to save human life by intervening in a hunger strike and saving life by trying to prevent others from carrying out killings, particularly if such killings were seen as murder.

And, of course, Protestants in general were very fearful of a 'free' republic.

One Church of Ireland member executed by the west Cork IRA said as he was about to die: 'I am a Protestant and the King of England is the Head of my church. You are fighting to drive out his soldiers and himself. If you do this, you will drive out the Protestant religion too and so I, being a Protestant, was right to help the English against you.'[36] Tom Barry, to whom this confession was made, goes on to quote the 1916 Proclamation guaranteeing religious freedom and lists the many Protestants who were significant figures in nineteenth-century nationalist history. It is quite clear from his writings that Tom Barry could not have cared less what religion the man was. However, this indifference was not shared by all his colleagues, as is evidenced by the many attacks on rectories and churches and other Protestant institutions that took place in 1922/23.[37] And if members of the Church of Ireland felt vulnerable, then how much more vulnerable must a minority faith such as the Methodists, with close links to the army, have felt?

Minority evangelical groups were always going to be in the line of fire, if only because they were marginalised from the majority faiths. The suffering of non-conformists came up in the House of Commons in May 1921, when it was clear that something amounting to a pogrom was taking place in Ireland.

> Mr. Pennefather asked the Prime Minister whether his attention had been drawn to the recent well-substantiated reports from Ireland to the effect that organized attacks were being made by the rebels on the persons and properties of peaceful and inoffensive individuals because they were Protestant Nonconformists and would he consider what steps could be taken to protect these people on account of their religion?[38]
>
> In reply, one Lieut Croft stated: 'Is the Right Honourable Gentleman aware that in the last three months the murder of farmers who are in no way connected with Crown forces numbers something like 40?'

The number of attacks on Methodist chapels far exceeded those on Church of Ireland or Presbyterian churches. While there were no serious attacks on Church of Ireland or Presbyterian churches in the city, there were four on the two city Methodist chapels in 1922 and the one in Cobh was damaged in 1923.[39] 'A false step, however innocently taken, a concocted story by someone who hoped to profit by their removal, might lead to the meeting of a secret and perhaps self-constituted court, the condemnation of one or more members of a family to death and the carrying out of the sentence without any reason assigned or any opportunity of proving one's innocence. Yet night after night thousands of our people [faced] such dangers.'[40]

'Some were entrapped into giving information to members of the Republican forces who came wearing the uniform of British military officers and then were shot for their simplicity and their homes burnt. Not a few were compelled to fly the country in order to save their lives. Others had their property destroyed and some, growing hopeless of settled conditions in their lifetime sought in Northern Ireland, in Britain, or in lands beyond the seas, a happier home.'[41]

Methodists then compounded their guilt in republican eyes by enthusiastically supporting the Free State once it was set up. Rev. Alley stated in 1922 that 'every member of the Methodist Church wishes God-speed to and is prepared to do his best to further the interests of the Free State of Ireland',[42] thereby finding themselves doubly damned in the eyes of republicans during 1922 and 1923. Ballineen Methodists even convened a meeting around the time of the Treaty and voted to give their support to the Irish Free State.[43]

By the end of the decade, Alley was full of praise for the tolerance shown to minority religions by the Free State: 'There is a spirit of tolerance abroad in the land today which few a decade ago hoped to live to see. In the Free State today, it is now generally felt that not only has a man a right to his convictions but that he has a perfect right to give expression to those convictions as long as he does it without causing needless harm to his neighbours.' Alley was nothing if not grateful for 'the herculean task which these "nine very young and inexperienced men" [the ministers of the Free State Government] set their hands . . . there is probably no country in the world freer from serious crime today than this which has so recently emerged from chaos'.[44]

Alfred Reilly, John Cathcart, Tom Bradfield, Gilbert Fenton and William Cooke, all Methodists, were all assassinated, the last also a very senior Freemason. It seems that war was effectively declared on Cork Methodists. William B. Hosford, who farmed at Bishopstown just outside the city, was on the receiving end of a relentless campaign of intimidation from the Truce right to the end of 1922, with corn being burnt, cattle and horses driven off, windows being broken and shots being fired at his house. He and his wife both had nervous breakdowns as a result.[45] There are also many Methodist family names among those who disappeared off the YMCA membership lists in 1921 and 1922. As the Methodist Notes column of *The Irish Times* of 17 June 1921 stated: 'Having heard with deep distress of the tragedies that have grievously affected Methodist homes we express our abhorrence at all such crimes.'[46] Even as late as February 1923 Cork Methodism again noted 'the large number of co-religionists who had left the district in the past year'.[47]

The balance of evidence supports the thesis that some Protestant clergymen did provide information to the British military in the fight against the IRA. The clergymen involved had usually been attached to the Forces during the war or else had Ulster connections. And some Methodists did pass on information on local activities on foot of their religious beliefs, though only one of those publicly shot, William Cooke, was associated with the YMCA. Cork Methodists found themselves caught between a rock and a hard place, believers in thrall to their faith and clergy faced by an implacable and deadly enemy. In a situation like this, the people with the guns would always win.

PART IX

Chapter 45 ∼

LIFE IN PROTESTANT CORK, 1922

A number of years ago a friend of mine was driving along one Sunday morning, listening to the car radio, when a piece came on *Sunday Miscellany* about a researcher from UCD who was working for the Irish Folklore Commission. This gentleman related a tale of how, in the 1970s, he had to make his way to Carrignavar in County Cork to pick up some fragments of old Gaelic documents from an elderly man in the village. My friend, who was himself from Carrignavar, took a great interest in the story and was amazed by what he heard.

According to the researcher, the documents were very old and believed to be valuable. The old man he was visiting, Timmy Owens, had been a foreman at the estate of the McCarthy family just outside Carrignavar village. The papers had come into his possession in a most extraordinary way.

The McCarthys—represented by two old Protestant ladies then in their seventies—were part of the old Gaelic aristocracy; the family had converted to Protestantism in the seventeenth century in order to hold on to their lands. Despite this, they still saw themselves as keepers of the Gaelic and bardic traditions of pre-planted Munster and were patrons of Gaelic art and poetry. As a result, Carrignavar remained a *breach Gaeltacht* right until the end of the nineteenth century and had its own school of poetry, with poetic luminaries such as Tórna, Seán an Raithíneach and Micheál Óg Ó Longáin. The result was that the family had in its possession a priceless hoard of Gaelic documents gathered over centuries from scholars and most particularly from An Cúirt Filíochta, run by Seán na Raithíneach during the eighteenth century.

It was, however, the story of how fragments of the documents found their way into Timmy Owens's hands that interested my friend. It happened during the Civil War, according to the UCD man. More specifically, it happened during September or October 1922 when there was a skirmish between Free State forces and the IRA in the area. The IRA was approaching Carrignavar village. Standard practice at the time was for IRA detachments to use any big house in the area as billeting quarters. This meant they would likely be staying with the McCarthy sisters.

Such was the terror of the old ladies at the prospect of the former freedom fighters staying in their house that they instructed Timmy Owens to pull out sheaves of documents and to light a big fire in the glen below the house and burn the lot. The surprising thing was that the ladies, who were as Irish as the IRA men themselves, would opt to burn their collection rather than let them fall into the hands of people whom by this stage they clearly saw as their enemies. The ladies, who would be in favour of Irish political independence and presumably had been as pleased as anybody else at the announcement of the Truce in July 1921, were now terrified. They were old and vulnerable; two neighbouring farmers had been murdered in cold blood while working in a turnip field. But the main reason they were frightened was because they were Protestants. Whatever they had done to promote Gaelic culture was as nothing compared to the fact that they were now of the wrong religion. There are shades of George Tilson here and his 'not to be done in by them'. These elderly ladies would have preferred to see their Gaelic poetry go up in flames than let it fall into the hands of the IRA. These were people living in the shadow of impending apocalypse. It says more about the terror with which the IRA were perceived at the time than a hundred compensation claims by pro-British loyalists.

In the event, I do not think the IRA ever stayed at the house, though Timmy Owens took his drawers full of documents down the glen and burnt most of them. But for some reason he saved a few papers from the flames and kept them for the rest of his life. Somehow the Irish Folklore Commission got to hear of them and our UCD researcher travelled south, found Carrignavar and Mr Owens, and the few scraps of paper are now apparently in the files of the Irish Folklore Commission in University College Dublin.

For my friend—we had been in school together and marched as 10-year-olds dressed in Volunteer uniforms for the 50th anniversary of the 1916 Rising—this did not fit with the image of brave flying columns fighting impossible odds that we had celebrated in 1966. This was a new perspective on the IRA. The glorious flying columns had become somehow inglorious in the space of a year. In fact it was a view that was to become all too common as the Truce moved to Treaty and Treaty moved to Civil War. And while some of this picture was the result of one-sided propaganda on the part of pro-Free State newspapers during the autumn of 1922, it would be hard to stand on a hill anywhere in County Cork and not see a fire burning as a Big House or a rick of hay or a Protestant residence went up in flames.[1]

For Protestants the change in perspective had begun earlier than the outbreak of civil war. Willie Kingston, a young solicitor in Skibbereen and a junior partner at the office of Jasper Travers Wolfe, had in early 1921, as a result of the disturbances in west Cork, taken a year off to travel the world.[2] Kingston, a fair and broad-minded Methodist, reckoned that after the Treaty Ireland had become sufficiently stable for him to return to his job. Reading the papers in South Africa where he was staying, he felt with the arrival of what looked like permanent peace that this was an opportune time to come home. Kingston, who welcomed the aims of Sinn Féin and the movement towards independence, though he abhorred violence, had represented many clients at Sinn Féin courts before his departure. There would be plenty of court work in the new Ireland. When offered a partnership in a practice with Francis Fitzmaurice in Dunmanway, who was already in partnership with Wolfe, he deferred his decision until he returned home. He was lucky.

'I was firmly convinced that, following the Treaty and once the British removed their forces, Ireland would immediately go back to its usual peaceful condition. But I was not long home before I discovered my mistake, as the country was more upset and dangerous than when I left.' It was now apparent that 'there was no real authority at this time to which to appeal for protection, and any man with a gun was a law unto himself . . . it was obvious to me that we were sitting on a volcano about to erupt, so I decided to clear off to Dublin on 29 April 1922'. This was the week that Fitzmaurice and the others in the Bandon valley and Clonakilty were shot. Kingston left again for South Africa in the summer of 1922. He finally returned to Ireland in the spring of 1924, when he was able to ply his trade with Jasper Wolfe, the former Crown solicitor, who now became renowned for defending many of his former adversaries in the IRA, serving as a TD for West Cork in the late 1920s.

The aim of the final sections of this book is to look at what happened to Cork Protestants during 1922, which changed them from being largely irrelevant players in the fight for independence to having to flee in large numbers in fear of their lives. For one of the most striking things I had noticed when I first became familiar with Guy's Postal Directories for Cork city was the change in the population of parts of the city that took place during these years, 1922 in particular. There are whole streetfuls of names that have not survived, hundreds of families that left, amounting to an exodus of several thousand individuals, almost all of them Protestant. Did these simply leave or were they pushed? How many of them left in fear of their lives? Or did they leave for economic reasons because, being part of the British administration, they left along with it?

This is an important question because, on the one hand, does it represent the expulsion of a large segment of the population or was it simply a case of regime change and its inevitable consequences? After all, Cork had always been a Protestant city and it was largely Protestants who had built it. And what of the widely held belief that, as John A. Murphy put it, 'there was no ethnic cleansing on the South Mall', in other words that the old Cork establishment continued as it had done from British rule right through the years of the Irish Free State? The question at issue here is did the revolution make any difference in Cork city's Protestant inhabitants and was there any real change between 1918 and the mid-1920s? Was the old order simply re-established after independence? Even the most cursory examination of the postal directories of those years suggests it was not.

Of the 52 Protestant-occupied homes along the Blackrock Road at the start of 1922, 28 had left by 1926.[3] The figures are similar for the Douglas and Ballinlough roads and also for Ballintemple, Blackrock and Douglas itself. In the same period, some 31 solicitors left the county as a whole (including the city), 21 of whom were Protestant;[4] 24 commissioners for oaths departed, 18 of whom were Protestant; while 8 accountants left, 5 of them Protestant.[5]

It is generally accepted by historians that, whatever about places like west Cork, Ballinasloe, parts of Tipperary and Laois, urban Protestants were largely untouched by the revolution and maintained their hegemony and their control of the professions right into the years of the Free State. And while this is true for those of them who survived until the end of 1923, the above figures suggest that it was far from true for areas of Cork city, particularly the south-eastern suburbs. Comparisons between the 1911 and 1926 census figures show that the Protestant community in Cork declined by 50 per cent in Cork Borough and 40 per cent in the rest of the county.[6] This compares with an average decline of 32.5 per cent across the 26 Counties as a whole for the same period. This is somewhat surprising, given the widespread evacuation of Protestants from much of west Cork in the wake of the Dunmanway massacre. Many of these, however, being farmers with a stake in the land, returned after 1923—and a lot of west Cork Protestant farmers sold up and bought land in north and east Cork during those years. Yet proportionally more Protestants left the city than the county.

What the figures hide is the fact that most of the urban decline occurred during 1922 and mostly in one specific area. And when these families left, they never returned. Some 90 families left the Knockrea townland, consisting of the area between the Blackrock Road and the Douglas Road in 1922 alone.[7] The Cork courts records for 1922–24 show hundreds of lesser forms of intimidation, such as homes being burnt and property stolen.[8] Comparing the postal directory listings for many of the more salubrious and indeed working-class areas of the south of the city, in particular the Blackrock Road, Douglas Road, Turner's Cross, Capwell and Friar's Walk areas, shows a very significant change of home occupancy. Hundreds of homes changed ownership between the start of 1922 and 1924 and hundreds of Protestant names disappeared for ever. Cork city had around 9,059 non-Roman Catholics in 1911. That had dropped to 4,400 by 1926. Analysis of the change in house occupancy on a street-by-street basis suggests that most of this decline occurred in 1922 and was most severe in the south-east corner of the city, between the Blackrock Road and the Douglas Road. This is a large and sudden displacement of population for such a small city. What is most surprising is that this substantial change in the fabric and make-up of Cork society has hardly been commented on, appears to have gone unnoticed and is completely forgotten about. The ghost-like evacuation of these areas of Cork is the biggest single displacement of a portion of a city's population anywhere in the British Isles since the seventeenth century. Apart from those who submitted claims to the Irish Grants Commission, there is no record as to why these people left, but the reasons are not hard to fathom.

Interestingly, the area in the county with the least decline in Protestant population was Skibbereen, where between 1911 and 1926, a drop of 33.2 per cent reflected that of the country as a whole. This no doubt reflects the fact that Skibbereen was under the control of pro-Treaty forces loyal to Michael Collins for much of 1922. In May 1922, the local IRA issued a proclamation condemning threats to Protestants.

One gets the impression from the accounts left by city IRA men that more alleged 'Anti-Sinn Féin League' members were killed than can be accounted for by the historical record of the pre-Truce period. However, if the Anti-Sinn Féin League is taken to mean those Protestants killed after the Truce and into the Civil War period, then these accounts can be seen in a much clearer light. It is obvious, in particular from Mick Murphy's account, that it was the confession extracted from young Parsons that led to the so-called 'spy circle' that allegedly operated out of the YMCA. If we are to extend this to include the Boys' Brigade and branches of the YMCA outside the city, as well as the perceived evils of Freemasonry, then we are well on the way to a fully rounded conspiracy theory.

There were elements of reality in it. Edward Parsons may well have been spying, and possibly out of the YMCA, if only for the simple reason that, along with the soldiers and sailors' homes and the Salvation Army, it was what might be called a 'safe house' from a British military point of view. Yet the British were gone before Parsons was caught. McKinley and Nagle may have been connected to their local branches of the YMCA, though we have no proof of it, as was Herbert Woods. McKinley's need to flee to Ballineen after some years living 'elsewhere' is also cause for suspicion, if nothing else.

It is clear that Protestant Boy Scout groups were also now targets. William Jagoe, William Morrison and Rev. Harbord all seem to have been targeted because of their association with such Protestant youth groups. Jagoe was also an avid loyalist and had Auxiliaries over for tea; David Grey allegedly went drinking with them. It is the death of Francis Fitzmaurice, though, that gives us an insight into another motivation for the killing.

Francis Fitzmaurice, a moderate man, was a solicitor who had once been a Freemason. Thomas Nagle was a clerk of the court and looked after the Masonic hall in Clonakilty, which was raided and burnt on the night he was shot. Taken along with the Boys' Brigade and YMCA connections, it is easy to see how clergymen, youth workers and professionals with Masonic links could all be grouped into an 'Anti-Sinn Féin League'. Further fuel for the conspiracy was the fact that clergymen of all denominations had been a source of information for British forces during the conflict and also that Protestant clergy, even if they were keeping their heads down, were strong supporters of Britain and British interests—witness the unveiling of the war memorial at Dunmanway in March 1922, attended mostly by clergymen. Taken altogether, you have a cocktail of suspicion that would fuel the minds of gunmen right until the end of the Civil War.[9]

'They [the names extracted from Parsons] were shot one by one and in groups', Mick Murphy said. This statement makes little sense in the context of the Anglo-Irish conflict, when only six Protestants were killed in the city and none of them was killed 'in groups'. It does make sense, however, in the context of the later killings: we have five members of the YMCA—Thomas Roycroft, Parsons, Wm Cooke, Wm G. Beale and Theo Creber—all shot 'one by one' and others in west Cork shot 'in groups'. We have at least two others killed in France and England. At least some of the west Cork killings of 1922 were carried out by men from the city. And the witch-hunt did not stop there. Some 38 members of the city YMCA failed to renew their subscriptions in the summer of 1922, with 30 more dropping out in the following year. Some were business people; others were professionals; some were boys. The experience of some of them makes for interesting reading.

Take, for instance, Charles Lendrum, another solicitor and long-time member of the YMCA and a Freemason.[10] He was 'always a loyalist and persecuted as such'.[11] In his IGC application he stated that his house and premises were raided 'and in the July following [1922] ... my wife and younger children were advised to be sent to England. In the August following—1922— I was living away from my house and I was further raided and intimidated', from whence he finally left for England, putting his home up for sale. He spent the summer of 1922 in hiding while he arranged for the sale of his property and his departure for England.[12] Lendrum was lucky. Charles Geeve, a builder and another long-established member of the YMCA who lived on Boreenmanna Road, had to get out on 20 April 1922 since 'I was to have been one of the victims of the conspiracy to murder or drive out Loyalists from Co. Cork.'[13] Accountant Samuel Beamish of Douglas had his house raided on numerous occasions between September 1921 and September 1922 and was called an 'Orange Dog' and other derogatory terms.[14] Ernest Allen of Passage West was ordered out on 13 July 1922 because he refused to join the IRA.[15] Henry Chamney, a senior officer in the telephone service, suffered a nervous breakdown as a result of intimidation experienced during the summer of 1922 when he found himself constantly under surveillance and had to decamp for Dublin. '[Since 1922] he has been in a truly pitiable state through some nervous affliction impeding his walking—he is indeed a cripple ... [having passed] through some severe experiences during the troubled times in this country.'[16] Chamney's subordinate at the Post Office, Walter Hailes, another Freemason, was shot and severely wounded in September 1922.[17] And this is just a fraction of those who disappeared off the YMCA membership lists in those years.

According to recent attempts to justify the west Cork killings of 1922 and to play down their significance, it is claimed that the killings were immediately 'stamped out' by the IRA in the area. And it is true that Seán Buckley and indeed Tom Barry did carry out internal investigations into the killings, and they were stopped, at least in that area. However, far from being stamped out, the murders merely went underground and went on sporadically until the end of the Civil War.

We have already seen the killings of William Cooke, W. G. Beale and Theo Creber in the vicinity of the city during the Civil War. The Hornibrooks appear to have been shot by city men. Similarly, Edward Williams, a native of Liverpool, was shot dead in the centre of the city on 14 September.[18] Was he too believed to be a spy or did he simply share a name with a prominent Cork accountant[19] who also left Cork around this time? Others were somewhat luckier. Walter Hailes—the only loyalist in the Cork GPO, according to Henry Chamney[20]—was shot near his home on the Lough on his way from work on 12 September but survived his wounds. Was he 'the spy in the GPO'? As we have seen, two girls sent in from England were the actual spies in the postal system. Hailes claimed he was shot simply because he was a loyalist and a Freemason.[21]

The killings during this period were not confined to the city. David Lee O'Gorman, a Nationalist Home Ruler, was shot and wounded in Fermoy in October 1922.[22] Also in December near Kilworth, outside Fermoy, solicitor Robert Baylor was fatally wounded and his driver John Joyce wounded in an assassination attempt. This was despite the fact that Baylor too had been a regular attendant at Sinn Féin courts.[23] And intimidation of loyalists and members of the legal professions also extended to old-style nationalists: barrister and newspaper owner George Crosbie's residence at Montenotte was burned down in January 1923, as was the Blackrock residence of Maurice Healy, brother of Tim Healy, the newly appointed Governor of the Free State. Denis McGrath, the manager of the *Cork Examiner*, was shot at the corner of Victoria Road and Blackrock Road on 19 January.[24] The home of Denis O'Connell, former clerk of the Crown and Peace in Skibbereen, who had been taken hostage in July 1921, was burned down in February,[25] as was that of Frank Pitt, the manager of the Cork Opera House.[26] Jasper Wolfe, partner of Francis Fitzmaurice who was kidnapped twice by the IRA and narrowly avoided an assassination attempt, owed his survival on one of these occasions to the intervention of Eamonn Duggan, the IRA's chief liaison officer in Dublin.[27]

A related murder took place on 17 December 1922 when Eric (Bonnie) Wolfe, a 'well-known figure at point-to-points and at agricultural shows, particularly in the jumping enclosure', was shot dead on his way home from a night in a public house in Kinsale. The murder of Wolfe, who appears to have been a popular figure locally but was an ex-officer, appears on the face of it to have been largely motiveless.[28]

And these are just the killings and other forms of intimidation that went reported. There are 26 missing persons whose families wrote to the Department of Justice after the Civil War looking for information as to their whereabouts, at least 12 of whom disappeared from Cork.[29] What are we to make of the case of Josephine Keevlan of Bridge Street, Mallow, who went missing along with her two sons Victor and James sometime during 1922? Were these buried at Corry's? Was William Savage another one? And these were only the cases where relatives contacted the Department of Justice in later years. What happened to J. F. Williamson, clerk of the Peace for Mallow and another member of the YMCA? Was he expelled from Cork or did he too disappear?[30] Was this why the army was extremely concerned about the fate of loyalists in Mallow towards the end of 1921?[31] There are almost certainly many other missing persons. Oral accounts from various parts of the county suggest that this adds up to a very significant number.[32]

The period for which the least amount of information is available is from mid-March 1922, when the British Army was leaving and the RIC disbanding, to the beginning of September of that year when Free State troops had consolidated their hold on the city. We have seen from the Roycroft and Parsons cases that kidnappings went largely unreported. On 8 July William Ludgate, the editor of the *Cork Constitution*, wrote in a brief editorial: 'It is a fact that the IRA has established a censorship over the *Cork Constitution*. The Republican authorities wish us to state that their censorship is merely for the purpose of securing impartial reports.'

The claim for impartiality is fair enough. Some elements of the press, in particular the *Freeman's Journal* and the *Irish Independent*, were at this stage savagely anti-republican.[33] The *Cork Constitution*, however—amazingly, it seems for a so-called 'staunch' unionist organ—was, during the War of Independence and Truce periods, surprisingly even-handed. It set out like the *Cork Examiner*, in so far as it could, not to offend republican sensibilities. It did of course reflect its loyalist readership, reporting on YMCA and Church of Ireland matters and keeping its eye, like the *Skibbereen Eagle*, on affairs in London as much as Dublin. However, it could not at that stage be accused of the kind of one-sided anti-republican ranting that was going on in the *Freeman's Journal*, nor indeed in profoundly anti-Irish conservative London dailies like the *Morning Post*. What the *Constitution* did do, however, in contrast to the *Cork Examiner*, which shamefully ignored the whole episode, was report in detail the events of the Dunmanway massacre. This suggests that Ludgate was very brave to defy the republican censors who had been controlling the content of the papers from the beginning of the year.

There were at least a dozen shootings, some of them fatal, in the city during the first three months of 1922—most of them of former RIC men. Publicly reported killings did not appear again in the newspapers until the last week of August. It is very unlikely that there were no shootings or abductions in the city between the end of April and the middle of August. Are we to take it that during this period when the IRA was in undisputed control of events in the city and county, when Seán O'Hegarty was sending hit squads to England and as far away as New York to shoot former enemies and known spies, that the same was not happening in Cork? Or that the IRA, after the interrogation of Roycroft and Parsons, was to wait until the Free State forces had arrived in Cork to shoot William Cooke and the others who were subsequently killed? It is inconceivable that there were not further abductions and secret killings going on during this period. The half-dozen or so other YMCA members that Martin Corry claimed were executed and buried around his farmyard may well have been killed at this time.

This brings us back to the inconsistencies in the statements of IRA survivors many years after the events. Mick Murphy stated—twice—that Blemens and his *two* sons, not one, were killed.[34] Connie Neenan said the Blemenses had good shoes and their executioners took them. Yet Connie Neenan was in jail in England when James and Fred Blemens were executed and did not return to Cork until three months later. He had nothing to do with their deaths. Could they have been referring to another father and two sons who were abducted and killed? Maybe the reference is to Mrs Keevlan and her two sons. There are several groups of persons with the same surname who disappeared off the YMCA membership lists, including two Leslies, two Roycrofts, two Williamsons, two Warners and three Wolfes.[35]

Then we have the almost incredible statement made by Mick Murphy to the effect that 'all the spies that were shot in Cork were buried, so nothing was known about them; they simply disappeared'. If this has any truth to it, then it cannot apply to the War of Independence period, where less than a quarter of those killed disappeared. It is far more likely to apply to the period when the IRA was the sole authority in Cork during the spring and summer of 1922. What other way can we explain Connie Neenan's extraordinary statement about Mick Murphy's time in charge in the city:

> Mick used to smoke cigarettes. Pat Hayes came down to him with the list of the spies from the Anti-Sinn Féin League. Most of them were in the Seaman's Bar. Mick would blow smoke out of his mouth and say: 'Just you shoot them,' and as the names went on 'and you shoot them also' and he'd let out a puff of smoke.[36]

Was Charles Geeve right to claim he was 'to have been one of the victims of the conspiracy to murder or drive out Loyalists from County Cork'? The statistics support him, at least for certain sections of the city. Clearly, something dreadful happened to Cork city Protestants in 1922.

If you were a Protestant living in Cork in the summer of 1922, you would be forgiven for thinking that a process was in place to drive you out. The IRA turned on Cork Protestants during 1922 and right through the Civil War because it believed that a conspiracy had existed in the YMCA and other Protestant institutions. As we saw in the case of Warren Peacocke and at least some clergymen, there may have been grounds for suspicion in some instances. None the less, Protestant communities took a disproportionately high amount of blame for what British military intelligence had been doing during 1920/21. There is a lot that remains to be written about 1922, the *annus horribilis* in the Southern Protestant mind.

Chapter 46 ~

THE YEAR OF
DISAPPEARANCES

When it comes to the killing of Protestants, the accounts left by various IRA survivors of the conflict in Cork make little sense when compared with the actual historical record. We have Connie Neenan claiming that ten Cork city merchants were shot in February and March 1921, with three others in June of that year.[1] We have Mick Murphy stating that the Anti-Sinn Féin League spies were shot 'singly and in groups'. Yet there is nothing in the historical record—that is to say, in the newspapers of the time or in any British record that I have been able to access, or in the wide variety of compensation claims—to suggest that these events took place during the War of Independence. The RIC's summary of everything that was going on in the country on a daily basis is available. It contains nothing to suggest that prominent merchants were shot in Cork either in the spring or early summer of 1921. Nor is there any evidence of groups of loyalists being rounded up and shot.

Then we have Mick Murphy's ominous statement to the effect that 'all the spies that were shot in Cork were buried, so nothing was known about them; they simply disappeared'. Again, when seen in the context of the War of Independence, that simply is not true. About a quarter of those shot as spies were abducted, executed and buried. Even Murphy, with his penchant for exaggeration, is unlikely to go so far as to say that they were all buried when he himself was involved in shooting many of them in the street. What is more, he was either gone from Cork or in British custody from May 1921 onwards, when at least some of these supposed killings took place.

Connie Neenan's statement that the boys of the YMCA shot as spies came 'mostly from good families' also asks for explanation. It suggests that there were significantly more than Parsons and Roycroft shot; that the boys killed were middle class or at least from what might be called 'respectable' families.

In addition to this, we have all the accounts of various killings and secret burials. We have Corry stating that he executed five or six members of the YMCA in addition to young Parsons; we have Frank Busteed claiming that six or seven loyalist farmers from the Bandon valley were moved to Rylane for execution during the War of Independence. This is confirmed by local sources.[2] Busteed also states that three or four other loyalists were brought to Rylane for execution during the Civil War. Yet neither during the War of Independence nor the Civil War is there any independent evidence that such abductions and killings took place. It is fair to assume that if 13 prominent merchants had disappeared, there would be some record of it.

Then there is the bewildering gathering of lists of Freemasons by the IRA, mostly from city lodges. Two hundred and eighty individuals are named in these lists, many of whom had left Cork by 1924. Furthermore, we have the reactions of Protestants themselves. Many city Protestants applying to the IGC claimed there was a campaign to drive loyalists out of Cork. Their own abandonment of middle-class suburbs and the fact that they fled these areas in significant numbers suggests that the threat from which they were fleeing was real. A leading city businessman, Sir Alfred Dobbin, stated that he 'had to leave Ireland in June 1922 owing to the continuance of the conspiracy . . . to drive loyalists out of Ireland . . . [for I was] a member of the class against whom the conspiracy was directed'.[3] People who live comfortable lives in what had always been a comfortable and friendly environment do not simply walk out on these lives without good reason.

Is it possible that all these other killings, from the six or seven west Cork loyalist farmers to the five or six loyalists shot supposedly during the Civil War to the five or six members of the YMCA claimed to have been shot by Corry, took place during the year from July 1921 to August 1922? Throw in for good measure the four ex-soldiers claimed by Stan Barry to have been shot and buried in Clogheen,[4] another three mysterious civilians buried at a farmhouse in Killumney, and more again at Farmer's Cross, Douglas, Blackrock and Turner's Cross, and you have far more than can be accounted for by those listed in the first half of this book. Add to that all the rumours of people buried in this or that bog and it all adds up to a lot more than can be explained by the historical record.

Common sense suggests that the majority of these disappearances must have taken place during the year when the IRA was in charge of Cork and when its men had time on their hands. However, this is the least well-documented period of the revolution. It was a period of flux. The British administration was winding down and handing over responsibility for running the country to the provisional government. The RIC was being disbanded from March 1922. The Treaty negotiations and subsequent Treaty debates and developments took up much of the newsprint. Even loyalists, as evidenced by *The Irish Times* and the *Cork Constitution*, were optimistic, at least initially, even if they had to grin and bear the new changes. Many of them were glad the British were going. British excesses in the conflict, such as the burning of Cork and the campaign of murder and arson carried out by the

Black and Tans and Auxiliaries, had turned all but the most entrenched unionists against the forces of the Crown. Was it a case of nobody wanting to spoil the party by playing up apparently random sporadic abductions?

When Arthur Griffith offered what amounted to an amnesty to all loyalists, including those who helped the British forces during the conflict, and both de Valera and Michael Collins moved quickly to assure loyalists that there was a place for them in the new Ireland, it looked like all was well, and God—be he Protestant or Catholic—was in his heaven.

However, this was an illusion. For the priority of the Cork IRA for much of the coming year was not to prepare itself for the inevitable conflict that would become the Civil War. Rather, its resources continued to be poured into attacking the remnants of the British presence in Ireland. Ex-soldiers, RIC men, ex-RIC men and loyalists were all still in the line of fire. It was as if the IRA had nothing in its collective mind but revenge—'vengince byjasus', as Collins once put it, though by this stage Collins himself had moved on well beyond the luxury of vengeance for its own sake.

So what is the evidence that multiple disappearances took place in Cork between the Truce of 11 July 1921 and 10 August 1922? Well, the evidence, though skimpy and altogether lacking the same level of detail as is available for the Anglo-Irish conflict, is there. It is rarely, if ever, written about. This is a catalogue of secret skulduggery, of people being lifted in the middle of the night, of torture, execution and secret burials, where the only thing you can say for certain is that nobody ever told the truth or left anything like honest accounts of it. Nobody sang about this afterwards; there are no rebel songs to commemorate the 'brave deeds' carried out in bogs in the small hours of the morning. There are no detailed accounts given to the Bureau of Military History about what happened during *that* year. For all the heroics occurred before 11 July 1921; there was only silence afterwards. And then the shame of the Civil War put another layer of silence on it all again. This was the most secret year in Irish history. It can truthfully be called the year of disappearances, when even the disappearances themselves disappeared owing to a combination of clever organisation by the IRA and a blind eye being turned by the newspapers, the new government and even Britain in its own political interests. There is a saying that in the house of the hangman nobody talks about the noose. This was a year when black deeds were done, when nobody but the families directly involved knew anything about them. But enough has leaked out from various sources to give us some picture of what happened. This will be the subject of much of the rest of this book.

Chapter 47 ◠

WEEKLY SURVEYS

It is often claimed that truth is the first casualty of war. In the case of the Anglo-Irish conflict of 1919–21, the truth is, ironically, not that difficult to establish, at least from a historical perspective. Because the functions of civil administration, such as newspapers, the courts (for the most part) and the registration of births, marriages and deaths, continued almost as they would in peacetime, there is a wealth of sources to draw on in addition to those accumulated by the military forces. Add to these the reminiscences of IRA survivors given to the BMH, to Ernie O'Malley and in local histories and you have the resources to build a good picture of the conflict.

However, in the case of the Irish revolution, the truth, far from being the first casualty of war, was in fact the first casualty of peace, or at least of that uneasy peace that lasted (in Cork) from the Truce of 11 July 1921 until the arrival of Free State forces over a year later. When it suits everybody concerned to stay quiet about what happened, a spectacular void forms in the historical record. All that can be said with certainty is that lies and half-truths and denial are all that remain of many of the events of that poorly documented year.

So what can we establish for the 13-month period when the IRA was the undisputed authority in Cork and over much of Munster? This was the so-called Cork Republic when, for the only time in its history, the IRA was not living outside the law but rather constituted the law itself. The provisional government was marooned in Dublin, unable to establish its authority over much of the country. Reading British Army correspondence of the spring of 1922 it is clear that departing military leaders such as General Macready were of the view that the Free State government would not be able to establish any authority and that the IRA would win out in an ensuing conflict. The tone of pessimism in Macready's weekly reports to the British Cabinet is palpable.[1]

However, it is to Macready's reports we have to go in order to establish the level of violence during the Truce and early post-Treaty period. These weekly reports are a continuation of those issued by Dublin Castle during the War of Independence and are the best source of statistics for the later period. Their drawback is that, while they give the statistics for violence such as murders, attempted murders, kidnappings, raids and ambushes, they give very little detail about these events. Their other drawback is that while the reports *per se* continued until the summer of 1922, they cease to contain even this level of reporting after the end of January. This reflects the fact that the army was in the process of pulling out, the intelligence services were being wound down and the RIC had ceased to be a source of information. So their principal value lies in the light it sheds on the six-month period from July 1921 to January 1922.

So what does it tell us? Well, for the first few months of the Truce, the IRA was assiduous in maintaining the peace. Macready is quite happy with his dealings with the Sinn Féin leadership, even if he is appalled by the bellicose attitude of Tom Barry, the IRA's new liaison officer for much of County Cork.[2] IRA discipline was good, though illegal drilling was continuing, as one would expect. From September, however, things begin to get frayed; violence in its many manifestations started to break out between the IRA and the army and police. Shoot-outs became common and a general air of lawlessness began to prevail. On 1 October an exasperated Macready reported: 'The work of the [peace] Conference may well be interrupted and possibly jeopardised if the Truce is not better observed by Sinn Féin . . . There are two police forces in Ireland: the RIC and the Sinn Féin Police—hence the obvious danger.'[3]

It is accepted by historians that the Truce was uneasy and that there was a continuous risk of the peace running aground as a result of tit-for-tat skirmishes. Both the British military and the IRA maintained their forces on a war footing, ready to go back fighting in the event of the Truce breaking down. This is the context in which we have to view the events of the last six months of 1921. You had an explosive peace, which was only put out, albeit temporarily, by the Treaty of December. There was a myriad of small-scale raids and attacks across the country, most particularly in west Cork, during the fall of 1921. However, what interests us here are the statistics on kidnappings.

The favoured weapon in the IRA's armoury in this period when it came to suspected 'spies', or anyone believed to have helped the British war effort, was kidnapping, execution and secret burial. To shoot down somebody in the street, as had been standard practice during the War of Independence, would have been in breach of the Truce. Secret abductions, on the other hand, now that transport could move unhindered by roadblocks, were hardly even noticed. The 'bog job' as a military strategy reached its peak during this period. It is interesting that while in his Weekly Surveys Macready noted no new political 'murders' in the six months after the Truce, from early September onwards he reports dozens of kidnappings and 'illegal arrests'. So while on the surface everything appeared peaceful, underneath there was much activity as the IRA began to round up its former enemies. (The number of kidnappings and illegal arrests of civilians from the Truce to the end of

January 1922 on a week-to-week basis are given in Appendix v.)

These figures have to be approached with a certain amount of caution. The Weekly Survey tends to divide the kidnappings into those arrested in connection with the operation of Sinn Féin courts and arrests of witnesses and court officials to prevent them from appearing at traditional courts where cases concerning IRA activities were being heard. The reports also list in some instances whether or not the individuals concerned were subsequently released. What we are most interested in here are those cases that do not belong in either of these categories; in other words, people who were kidnapped, not as criminals or as witnesses in British courts, and who were not released. As can be seen from Appendix v, there were 213 such arrests from August 1921 to the end of January 1922. Of these, 132 were not reported as having been released or of not belonging to the above categories. And these are just the cases reported to the RIC and British Army. It is reasonable to assume that many of these people simply disappeared.

It is clear from Appendix v that there were several weeks of peak activity when many abductions took place and other weeks when no abductions at all occurred. The peak weeks were the first week of September[4] when 20 illegal arrests took place, the last two weeks of October when 38 took place, the first two weeks of November with 40 abductions, and with 56 more before the end of November. It appears to tail off then, with another small peak of 13 abductions at the end of January 1922. This is the last week when Macready lists the statistics for violence in his reports. It is fair to assume that the level of abductions of the various categories was unlikely to decrease thereafter. In fact, with the mass release of imprisoned IRA men at the end of 1921 and the split over the Treaty looming, the opposite was far more likely to be the case, something that the British military authority took cognisance of at the time when they withdrew their most important intelligence officers in the light of likely reprisals.[5] Of a total of 132 unaccounted-for abductions, how many of these ended up in bogs or in the middle of fields in various places in Ireland? (The middle of a field was a favoured burial place apparently—it is much more difficult to stumble on a freshly dug grave in the middle of a field than it is around the perimeter.) The short answer is that, with the paucity of information in the newspapers and the general deterioration of conditions in Ireland when fewer records were now being kept, we do not know. What we can say, however, is that the IRA was only getting into its stride when British statistics ceased at the end of January 1922.

However, the statistics from January to March can be augmented to some extent for Cork city because the records of the IRA's Chief Liaison Office in Cork have survived. These paint a very troubled picture of the state of the city during that period. From early January to the end of March there were 13 kidnappings reported to the office, three of whom are known to have been released, and one escaped. There were also 20 other attacks on civilians, including assaults, threats and raids on houses and other forms of intimidation. What is interesting is that, as the months pass, the numbers of reported incidents peter out, with 19 for January, and seven each for February and March. Since the liaison office mainly processed complaints from the British military, this no doubt reflects the gradual disengagement of the British military from Cork.[6]

What is also interesting is that the kidnappings reported are almost certainly only a fraction of the total number that took place in the city, particularly in March. Only three kidnappings are listed for the city for March; the real number was at least four times that.[7] Neither the capture of Edward Parsons nor Thomas Roycroft, for instance, is listed. In most cases the names of victims are not given in these statistics since the supporting literature was not passed up the line. However, some names do appear in State papers because relatives subsequently wrote to the Free State government for information as to the whereabouts of various individuals, while others are listed as merely missing (see Department of Justice missing persons lists compiled in Appendix III and Appendix IV). As can be seen from Appendix III and Appendix IV there were 31 individuals listed by the Department of Justice as 'missing', while 41 other individuals had enquiries made as to their whereabouts. Many of these were from Cork. The letters pages in the *Cork Examiner* reflect the general state of chaos pertaining in the city during this period. One correspondent called on 'our worthy Lord Mayor' to set up a Citizens Watch in an effort to 'check the efforts of [the] evil disposed persons who now infest the city'.[8]

The next few chapters will attempt to piece together the story of the expulsion of loyalists and the hunting down of alleged loyalist 'spies' in Cork city during the second half of 1921 and the first half of 1922. Some of these may be connected with other abductions, such as the capture of boys in the Shankill/Bray area south of Dublin and in south Tipperary,[9] Limerick[10] and other parts of the country where there was better reporting to the Dublin newspapers.[11] It is, however, to Cork that this discussion must, by definition, be confined.

Chapter 48 ~

BEWARE THE IDES OF MARCH

The Anti-Treaty faction have a regular spy section; we see their detectives watching our movements just as the old Dublin Castle detectives used to watch in days gone by.[1]

In late 2007 a memoir and related papers written by Connie Neenan, who was in charge of the 2nd Battalion of the city IRA in the months leading up to the Truce, were released by the Cork Archives Institute. This is quite the most detailed record of these events we have because, from March 1921, Neenan was involved intimately in the campaign on the south side. While there are significant deliberate evasions in his accounts, none the less they provide a number of useful details in addition to what he gave to Ernie O'Malley. On the matter of loyalist 'spies':

In the autumn of 1920 a member of the Cork Post Office was arrested by the IRA. During questioning he confessed his association with the Black and Tans, with the nightly raids and with the Sinn Féin [*sic*] Murder Gang. It took some months of investigation in checking not alone his confession but also the activities of a number of so-called British loyalists in Cork City, practically all of them merchants. The first one to be dealt with represented a well-known firm in the Grand Parade in Cork and on this person was found a cheque for £1,000. However, our people did not entertain the idea that these people committed 19 murders for the sake of money. Our people felt that these men had such an intense hatred of the Irish people, whom they successfully exploited, nevertheless they sided with the enemy in the most barbarous fashion. Inside the next few days the balance of that murder gang was adequately dealt with. One, who escaped, committed suicide on a train bound for London.[2]

This looks, on the face of it, to be perfectly plausible. Clearly, it appears to refer to the cases of Beal and Tilson. But it has a number of fundamental flaws. Chief among them is the simple fact that there is no evidence that any merchants were shot in February 1921 in the days after Beal was killed. In fact no merchants at all were shot by the Cork city IRA during the conflict, if you exclude Alfred Reilly, and he was a bakery manager rather than a merchant. In his memoir, Neenan also states that 'his [Beal's] companions, 10 of them in all, were eliminated soon afterwards and the only one who managed to escape our net committed suicide on a train bound for London'. He also says, however, that 'the elimination of the Anti-Sinn Féin British Murder Gang in Cork, late in March 1921 and our detection of the British policy of using young boys of the YMCA to trail some or our most important IRA members caused the British grave concern'.[3] There is no evidence for any of this in the actual historical record of 1921. Neenan then states that three more merchants were shot in June 1921, for which there is no evidence either.

As regards the 'grave concern' that this caused the British, there is no sign of that either in any available military or RIC records. It is not until August 1921 that we have any suggestion from British forces that anything untoward may have taken place around the YMCA and that is the mention of the 'three cases of chicken broth'.[4] It seems obvious that the 'elimination' of 13 city merchants would at least be mentioned in the intelligence accounts left by the military and police if it had happened during British rule.

And then we have the reference to the Post Office official captured in September 1920. Who was he? According to John Borgonovo, quoting from Neenan's earlier accounts and from the BMH witness statements of Ballincollig Volunteers, this was a man called O'Sullivan or O'Callaghan, captured in the city on the basis of information leaked around Ballincollig.[5] Yet the only Post Office official that we have on record to have been shot by the IRA was Walter Hailes, who was indeed from Neenan's own parish of the Lough. Hailes, a Freemason, was shot in September, but it was September 1922, not September 1920. Could it be that Neenan is broadly correct in his various accounts but that he has moved his version of events back by a year or sometimes two so as to make it look as if they took place during the War of Independence rather than later?

As the next chapter will show, this supposition is essentially correct and it suggests that IRA survivors backdated these events to grant them the legitimacy of having taken place during the conflict with Britain. It is extraordinary that, apart from Corry making one slip that Parsons was executed just after the Truce—though he changes his story elsewhere—and Frank Busteed mentioning the execution of 'three or four loyalists during the Civil War', there is no mention in any of the multiple accounts left by IRA men that significant numbers of Protestants may have been killed in the post-Truce and post-Treaty periods. In fact, if you were to believe these accounts, nobody at all was shot after the Truce.

Yet it is clear that Neenan wanted these 'spy hunts' recorded. A further irony is that the historian is dependent on the accounts of the perpetrators of these killings to put together a picture of what actually happened, since the press and the families and community of the victims themselves either stayed silent or fled in fear of their lives.

What contemporary records can tell us is that, if the IRA did not regard the YMCA as a serious threat at the time of the Truce, it did think so by the end of August 1921. Whether this was because of the capture and execution of the 'three cases of chicken broth' in the days after the Truce or for some other reason we cannot be sure. We know that the YMCA was under surveillance by the start of September because on 14 September a Sergeant Edward O'Sullivan, an ex-soldier and a well-known boxer, was abducted from his house on Shandon Street by a group of armed men. He was taken to Blarney where he was questioned and badly beaten. O'Sullivan was lucky, for he was a Sinn Féin supporter and was released. He subsequently refused to co-operate with the police on the reasons for his abduction, stating only that it was because he had assaulted a Sinn Féin policeman.[6] O'Sullivan, who worked in the War Pensions office, was the soldier who had requested access to the YMCA's gym in early September, only to be turned down 'with regret'.[7]

It is unlikely that O'Sullivan was able to give any information to the IRA as to the inner workings of the YMCA for he would have known very little about them. The fact that he was released suggests that he had nothing to tell. His importance to us lies in the fact that he is a direct connection between the public record and that of the YMCA. Here is a man who was in contact with the YMCA and who was interrogated violently by the IRA and the event was recorded by the newspapers and the RIC.

Then on 17 September the *Cork Constitution* reported that an unnamed city bookmaker had vanished—the paper suggested he may have disappeared to avoid bad debts, but no more details appear on the case.[8] A week later another ex-soldier, Edward Callaghan, was kidnapped by the IRA in Ballincollig.[9] There is nothing to connect Callaghan directly with the YMCA. However, the link between individuals in Ballincollig and the Anti-Sinn Féin League has been made several times.[10] Callaghan was described by the RIC as a 'man of rowdy nature, dishonest and a general nuisance in the locality. It is believed that owing to his conduct he was arrested by the IRA and carried off probably for trial.' So there were three recorded kidnappings in the city in September 1921, the first of which was certainly linked to the YMCA. On 24 October the IRA gave orders that no children were to be allowed on to the streets after 9 pm.

The next recorded abduction connected to teenagers took place on 23 November when a 14-year-old unnamed policeman's son was picked up by four men while going to school through Peacock Lane on Cork's north side.

He was blindfolded, taken a considerable distance to an unoccupied house and held for five or six hours. He was then driven back to within three miles of the city, released and thrown into a shallow stream. Like Edward O'Sullivan, he was not prepared to talk about his experience and the RIC could assign no motive to the abduction—or if they could, they did not report it.[11] Given where he was captured, near the North Monastery, he was likely to have been a Catholic. Would he have been released had he been a Protestant?

Then on 12 December a boy called Walters was forced to take refuge in Union Quay RIC station. Walters, from Shanballymore in north Cork, was held by the police for a few days until such time as his parents travelled to Cork to collect him.[12] He is not listed as a member of the YMCA, though he probably was a Protestant. It was the British Army's reaction to Walters' narrow escape that is most interesting. For a few days later a telegram was sent by the 6th Division in Cork to the 21st Brigade relaying a request: 'GHQ wants to know the number of Boy Scouts in your Brigade. Please wire reply.'[13] This suggests that what the IRA had been after since the raid on the Riverstown Boy Scouts hut in early May were Boy Scouts rather than members of the YMCA per se. However, since the YMCA doubled as a Boy Scout troop for non-denominational Protestants, this amounted to the same thing. Cork Boy Scouts ceased to function and had abandoned their office at 11 South Mall by the end of 1921.[14] While the Church of Ireland Boys' Brigade and the YMCA continued into the early years of the Free State and beyond, the Boy Scouts' Cork headquarters closed down. It also suggests that there was at least some affiliation between Boy Scout troops and the military. There is nothing in British records to suggest they were used against the IRA, but they may well have been. The weeks from mid October to the end of November was a peak time for IRA kidnappings, with 77 people abducted whose fate is unknown (Appendix v). It is reasonable to suggest that at least some of these were boys picked up on the streets of Cork.

The snatching of the boy on Peacock Lane may have led to other boys disappearing in the following days. For on 28 November the 6th Division sent the following telegram to GHQ: 'The police have been making inquiries from the Liaison People. You know we won't do anything about it. A well-known IRA officer has been making inquiries around here.' GHQ replied: 'We got a letter from someone anonymously about the matter.'[15] It was at this time that the YMCA annual report for 1920/21 stated that 'several of our younger members have recently gone abroad; we have given them letters of introduction to YMCA branches in the various cities in which they have settled'.[16] You would have to wonder how many of them actually went abroad or how much of this was a cover-up. Either way, the very fact that the IRA was deploying its considerable resources in hunting down Boy Scouts over a prolonged period says as much about the attitudes of the Cork leadership as it does about the YMCA or indeed about the Boy Scouts.[17]

Chapter 49 ∾

A TIME FOR REVENGE

That the account of the killing of city loyalists as alleged spies in Connie Neenan's memoir is backdated to make it appear as if they occurred during the War of Independence is clear from his version of the Anti-Sinn Féin League story:

> The elimination of the Anti-Sinn Féin, British murder gang in Cork, late in March of 1921, and our detection of the British policy of using young boys of the YMCA to trail some of our most important IRA members caused the British great concern. The leader of this Anti-Sinn Féin murder gang—which was notorious for its vicious campaigns of terrorism and murder—was living in G Company, 2nd Batt, area. He was dealt with in a more civilized manner than the poor victims he and his companions maimed, tortured and killed had experienced and suffered from him and his henchmen. His companions, 10 of them in all, were eliminated soon afterwards, and the only one to escape our net committed suicide on a train bound from Fishguard to London.[1]

Clearly this is meant to be read as a reference to Beal and George Tilson. We shall take the account at face value for the moment—there are clear contradictions in it—and focus on what it tells us about the IRA's view of the contact between the 'murder gang' and local loyalists. In Neenan's view there was no difference between the undercover assassins and those with whom they associated. We know that Lieutenant Green and another intelligence officer lodged with James Beal and his wife. Undercover men may also have been staying with Edward and Matilda Woods. But who were Beal's companions, ten in all, who 'were eliminated soon afterwards'?

We know that Beal's pocket book was taken when he was shot and that it contained a list of names. It is clear from his account that Neenan remembered ten individuals, mostly merchants, as having been killed by the end of March, and elsewhere he states that three more were killed in late June. But who were they? There is no indication from contemporary accounts of other Protestant loyalists being killed or abducted in the city at this time. It is clear that Neenan is referring to Cork merchants when talking about those who associated with the 'Anti-Sinn Féin Murder Gang' and not with the ragbag of suspected informers publicly shot in February and March 1921. So who are these people and when did they die, if indeed they did die?

So if the 'leader of the Anti-Sinn Féin murder gang'—'notorious for its vicious campaigns of terrorism and murder' was not Beal, then who was it? Who was the companion to those who 'maimed, tortured and killed'? Was it the accountant whose pocket book was taken or was it an actual officer, a member of the real Anti-Sinn Féin League?

It is far more likely that this is a reference to the only actual intelligence officer who was executed by the IRA within the city bounds. This was Lieutenant Henry Genochio, who was abducted a year almost to the day after Beal. Genochio, a Londoner of Italian extraction, who was nominally attached to the Royal Engineers, left Victoria Barracks dressed in civilian clothing on 15 February 1922. He was found shot dead in the grounds of the city asylum some two days later. The inquiry into his death held by the military came to the conclusion that he had been executed because 'he had been very active in rounding up rebels' during the War of Independence.[2]

Did the IRA get information out of Genochio? Did they get names of loyalist contacts he may have had? Were some of his companions 'eliminated soon afterwards' and 'inside the next few days'? Well, again, given the paucity of information and the gag placed on the newspapers in the spring of 1922, and the inability or reluctance to report kidnappings, there is nothing reported on the disappearance of city loyalists in the days immediately after the discovery of Genochio's body.

What is interesting, though, is the manner in which the killing was reported. Genochio's body was discovered on the morning of 17 February. The *Cork Examiner* of the following day carried the story and it was the major headline in the *Examiner* on the Saturday and the Monday. However, it went unreported in the *Cork Constitution* until 21 February when a tiny piece of five lines mentions the fact that there would be no inquest into the killing of Genochio because the British military authorities refused to release the body. This seems odd because the *Constitution*'s reporters usually acted as stringers for *The Irish Times* and for British newspapers, and *The Irish Times* did carry the story on 18 February. So the *Constitution*'s own reporters must have had the story, yet the paper chose not to print it. What we can say is that if there was a round-up of loyalists in Cork during that weekend, it probably would not have been reported either. What is also clear is that the military authorities did not want a public inquest into the killing of Genochio.[3] Could it be that the *Cork Constitution* did not print the Genochio story because of pressure from the British military authorities? It seems likely. Either that or it was trying to protect somebody closer to home.

And there is another possibility. Who was the mysterious civilian who was caught by the IRA on the same day as Genochio and held in the grounds of St Mary of the Isle? This was in the heart of the area controlled by Neenan's group. Was this the businessman referred to by Neenan? Was there a connection between the two?[4] This capture also went unreported in the press.

One shooting in the area, though, was reported some two weeks later. This was the assassination in broad daylight of an RIC constable called Dudley O'Sullivan and the wounding of his colleague Patrick O'Sullivan on 9 March. Both appear to have been members of that most shadowy of units, the plain clothes policemen, technically attached to the RIC. Dudley O'Sullivan was a former British Army officer. Was he 'murder gang' material?

Both O'Sullivans, dressed in plain clothes, were making their way from the RIC barracks in Tuckey Street when they were ambushed while passing through Hanover Street, suggesting indeed that one or other of them may well have been living in the G Company area.[5] The intention appears to have been to target Dudley, for Patrick O'Sullivan, though wounded, was able to make his way back to barracks without being pursued. Were these detectives or members of the Crimes Special Squad? Or were they 'military policemen', in other words members of one of the Anti-Sinn Féin hit squads? Another interesting aspect of the killing of O'Sullivan is how General Macready reported it in his Weekly Survey of 13 March. He states that there was only one casualty that week in Ireland: a constable fired upon and wounded in Cork on 9 March—clearly a reference to Patrick O'Sullivan.[6] He neglects to mention that another 'constable' was killed in the affair. They were almost certainly shot by Neenan's men. This lends credence to Neenan's account, even though the tendency is still to blame local loyalists for the crimes of departed hitmen.[7]

At eight o'clock that same evening, Thomas Roycroft left his home on the Douglas Road never to be seen again. The big difference between the two episodes is that the killing of O'Sullivan was reported, while the Roycroft abduction was not. Two weeks later when Edward Parsons was abducted, this was not reported either. Clearly, whether through censorship or otherwise, a different view was held of the shooting of former policemen and that of YMCA members. And there was one other figure who was shot dead during this period who lived in the area. This was retired RIC Sergeant Arthur Gloster. But before we deal with his case, we first have to look at the mysterious happenings of St Patrick's Day 1922.

Chapter 50 ⌒

ST PATRICK'S DAY PARADE

In the passing of time a great number of these [Cork city merchants] are enjoying the fruits of prosperity in the Republic of Ireland. Never at any time have they been conspicuous in coming forward, telling of the wonderful freedom they are enjoying in the 26 Counties. Openly, they enthusiastically support a 'Poppy Day' on November 11th, but never at any time have they come forward to support any cause connected with Irish Nationalism, or Ireland's efforts to obtain complete freedom for the entire 32 counties. Instead they represent a solid barrier, which has all the implications of hostility in its most severe form.[1]

It had long been the tradition in Cork that St Patrick's Day would be played in at midnight by the Fair Lane brass and reed band marching from the Grand Parade through Patrick Street. On St Patrick's Eve night 1922, which was a Friday, the band, consisting mostly of ex-servicemen, had assembled and was about to begin its march when it was attacked by a large group of armed IRA men—described by one source as 'Irish Republican Police'.[2] A riot ensued in which two band members were shot, one of whom, Patrick Horgan, died as a result of revolver fire and another man was badly wounded. This was duly reported in detail in the newspapers on the following day.[3]

What was not reported next day, however, were a number of other events that took place around the city during the same night. For, though the exact timing is unclear, there is reason to believe that the attack on the Fair Lane band was a ruse designed to divert the attention of the remnants of the police and military remaining in Cork. For that night the IRA raided the homes of 'a number of strong supporters of a certain political party' and took them away to 'an unknown destination'. For four days the city was awash with rumours. A number of prominent citizens had gone missing. It was not until the following Tuesday, 21 March, that the Irish newspapers carried some hint of what had happened. Indeed, were it not for the Press Association, the story might never have made the newspapers at all. *The Irish Times* stated the following Tuesday:

Confirmation, says the Press Association, is forthcoming of a rumour current in Cork for the past few days that some prominent local supporters of the Treaty were recently kidnapped by armed men and moved to an unknown destination. The kidnappings took place on St Patrick's Day. The only information that the families of the men have received is a telegram stating that they are well and in custody. The reason for the kidnapping is unknown.[4]

The *Cork Constitution* and *Cork Examiner* of 21 March were able to give a few more details. The *Examiner* stated that 'the rumours have proved correct', that the kidnappings had taken place on St Patrick's night at around 11.30 and that, according to one statement, the number of men kidnapped was six. The *Constitution* stated that those abducted were 'strong supporters of a certain political party' and that 'there was much anxiety as to their whereabouts'.[5]

No reason was set forth for their detention. Though the kidnapping took place on St Patrick's Day, there was no hint of any untoward occurrence; but in the passing days the rumour spread of what is set out above. To many, the names of the men seem to be well known but there is no definite information on that point.[6]

The implications are clear. At least six well-known and prominent citizens of Cork city, pro-Treaty supporters—many Protestants and merchants could at this stage be described as pro-Treaty supporters—had been kidnapped on the night of 16/17 March. And far from the men being 'well and receiving every care',[7] there is every reason to believe that by then they were dead and buried either in Martin Corry's land or elsewhere in County Cork.[8] It is interesting that only one of these kidnappings appears to have been reported to the Truce liaison office in Cork.[9]

Were these at least some of the merchants mentioned by Connie Neenan? They were indeed shot before the end of March, though it was March 1922, not March 1921. Were these the 'Anti-Sinn Féin League spies' so often referred to in IRA reminiscences? Though they were indeed shot 'in groups'—one group then and another group the following June, they were probably not the Anti-Sinn Féin people. Were they targeted because they were either believed to have helped the covert British military hit squads or because they were associated with the YMCA and/or the Freemasons? They were at least six in number, though Connie Neenan states the number was ten, and they were almost certainly all Protestants.

On 22 March, the IRA issued a statement through the press:

> The headquarters of the IRA in Cork inform us that the report of the kidnapping or arrests of men for being pro-Treaty supporters in Cork is absolutely without foundation.[10]

The implication of this is clear: it denies the arrest of the men as pro-Treaty supporters, not their arrest *per se*. This was to be the last time this particular incident was reported in the press. The level of co-ordination and organisation involved in this operation and its cover-up suggests that these disappearances were carried out by direct order of Brigade HQ. It is fair to say that by this stage the men were probably dead. They simply disappeared.

What's more, another attempted murder took place on St Patrick's Day. This was the shooting of Sergeant Patrick Curran of the RIC, who was shot four times in the back in Cornmarket Street. Curran's shooting is likely to be in connection with his arrest of one John Francis O'Mahony for the shooting of former nationalist lord mayor of Cork, P. H. Meade, at his premises on South Terrace the previous December. Curran survived his wounds.

The killings did not end there, for a few days later, on 26 March, Arthur Gloster, a retired police sergeant, was shot dead at the foot of Barrack Street while on his way home. Ten revolver bullets were fired into his body by a group of young men.[11] Gloster, who was a Church of Ireland member from Farranfore, Co. Kerry, had lived in Elizabeth Fort, a disused military depot, since his retirement some two years earlier. He had been in charge of College Road police station for many years and had a reputation for vigilance as an inspector under the Food and Drugs Act.[12] Gloster was popular and his family were well liked in Cork. The reason for his killing can be traced back to evidence he gave at the inquest into the assassination of Tomás MacCurtain when he stated that all RIC men in the city had been in their barracks that night.

Of course, the IRA also did their best to distance themselves from this killing. Denis Barry,[13] the head of the Irish Republican Police in Cork, stated at the inquiry into Gloster's death that 'in no way had the occurrence anything to do with the IRA. They had nothing whatsoever against him and would do all in their power to bring the guilty parties to justice. They (the IRA) condemned it as strongly as anyone else did.'

The coroner at the inquiry, however, spoke for many when he said: 'He [Gloster] had been killed under circumstances of great deliberation. The citizens of Cork were greatly alarmed and there were men going around passing sentence of death on individuals and using their own judgment mainly.' Just as in the case of more recent killings in Northern Ireland, nobody saw the occurrence, according to the Republican Police.[14]

This was of course the same week that Edward Parsons was kidnapped by C Company of the 2nd Battalion. Not only that, but Parsons was not the only teenager targeted during that period. Thomas Telford was an Ulster

Presbyterian—and the only Cork-based loyalist I have come across who claimed to be an Orangeman—who ran a laundry business on Evergreen Road on Cork's south side. His chief customer was the British Army at Victoria Barracks. In October 1921 the IRA forced him to give up his work for the army after intercepting him and threatening him on several occasions on his way to the barracks. For a while he sent his 15-year-old son in his place, until he too was intimidated into staying away.[15]

In the spring of 1922, Telford got a warning from the local Roman Catholic priest that the son was in immediate danger. He had barely sent the boy to London when a group of IRA men called to the house looking for him. It is probable that young Telford would also have ended up in Corry's farm were it not for the intervention of the priest. Indeed, the number shot in those two weeks may have been even greater than this, for when Mrs Parsons inquired at republican headquarters at Union Quay, she was told to hold out no hope because 'a lot' had been shot during that period.

Kidnappings and resultant executions were not the only forms of intimidation going on during these weeks. Rita Curran, who had been employed as a typist at Victoria Barracks and whose father was the RIC sergeant shot on St Patrick's Day, was badly beaten and forced to leave for England.[16] 'Only yesterday [20 March] the wife of one of our most respected citizens was attacked in a most savage manner by one of these armed highwaymen in a very lonely and unfrequented part of the city.'[17] Presumably, this lady and her family had to leave for England too.

Indeed it seems that several batches of individuals from the south side of the city may have disappeared during the first half of 1922. The businessmen taken on St Patrick's Day were in all probability distinct from 'Anti-Sinn Féin League' individuals taken by the 2nd Battalion. The latter appear to have been lower middle-class Protestants from the south side of the city who were deemed guilty of a pro-British stance and possibly of fraternising with British officers and men in places like the Seaman's Bar on Albert Quay.[18]

It appears that the men taken on St Patrick's Day were not the only Protestants to disappear in Cork city during the first half of 1922. This is borne out by the statistics from the Department of Justice's 'whereabouts' list for the post-Truce period—up to 40 missing persons, half of whom appear to come from Cork[19]—which suggests that there was a second significant round-up of loyalists in Cork at this time. For those taken on St Patrick's Day are not even named in that list. Indeed they are probably only the tip of the iceberg. Add to this the 31 individuals listed in the earlier Department of Justice missing persons list,[20] many of whom had Cork connections, and you have what amounts to a purge of Cork loyalists in the post-Truce and post-Treaty periods. And there are probably many others for whom no record is available. In other words, you have a lot of people disappearing. The number of kidnappings during the Truce for which no motive has been ascribed, 132 up to the end of January for the country as a whole and another 25 for Cork city for the first three months of 1922, gives credence to this. And the Cork IRA was only getting into its stride at that stage.

The secrecy and censorship in place in Cork from February to the end of August 1922 makes a space in which it is possible for all kinds of people to have disappeared. It appears that the reaction of the families involved was in effect to collude with this silence out of fear of attracting even more violence. While a year earlier the Blemens family and George Horgan's mother were able to communicate with Collins and Mulcahy, the community was by now so terrified that there is little reference to most of these disappearances in Irish State papers.[21] Of those kidnapped in Cork city in March 1922 it is ironic that the only one for whom an information trail exists is an English boy, Edward Parsons. As for the rest, the Cork Protestant community, with its legendary reticence, is as silent as the grave.[22] 'All those who were shot were buried, so nothing was known about them. They simply disappeared.' This has the ring of grim truth about it in the context of 1922.

Interestingly, in Telford's account Roycroft and Parsons are described as having been taken together 'as they left the YMCA'. Strictly speaking, this is incorrect but it shows that Parsons and Roycroft were friends and their kidnappings were seen, in Protestant eyes at least, to be connected with each other and with the YMCA. As regards the men taken on St Patrick's Day, they may correspond to the six members of the YMCA executed and buried at Corry's. However, they cannot have been taken on the basis of information extracted from Parsons for he was captured a week later. They are probably just another batch of disappeared 'spies'.[23]

What is most significant is the reaction of the Protestant community to these events. The initial reaction seems to have been that the killings and kidnappings had been a response to violence in Northern Ireland, where several particularly brutal killings of Catholics had taken place during the previous few weeks. Indeed there is likely to have been a connection between the two. For it was only days earlier that the Northern Ireland government officially declared war on the IRA. The Patrick's Day abductions and the possible abduction and execution of half a dozen loyalist farmers from west Cork the same week all took place within days of the Northern government proscribing the IRA. In fact, General Macready expressed his misgivings about the Northern decision and effectively predicted that something bad would happen to Southern loyalists as a result.[24] The IRA had taken 42 loyalist hostages in the border counties over the previous two months to secure the release of republican prisoners held in Northern jails. It is entirely possible that the Patrick's Day abductions and the abduction of loyalist farmers in west Cork may have been a response to Northern policies and may also have been in retaliation for the killing of Catholics in Northern Ireland and the forced expulsion of Catholic workers from Northern Protestant firms. This was the culture of revenge that led to the killing of Sir Henry Wilson two months later and raids on the Intelligence Branch of the Irish office in London at the end of March.

Frank Busteed stated explicitly that the '5 to 6 loyalist Protestant farmers' who were moved from the Bandon valley to Rylane were executed as 'reprisals'.[25] The only logical object of reprisals during those weeks—the British were departing and the Civil War was still some months away—was the Northern Ireland government, which was by then beginning to clamp down savagely on the IRA. This is particularly the case when it appears that at least some of those taken in the city were from families with Northern connections. If the intention was to get a message across to the Northern authorities, then it appears to have got through, for in mid-March Sir Henry Wilson, recently appointed security adviser to the Northern Ireland government and himself to die soon afterwards, wrote that the South of Ireland had been reduced to 'a welter of chaos and murder, difficult to believe and impossible to describe', a claim that was disputed by Southern Unionists.[26]

However, if the March 1922 abductions were an attempt to put pressure on the Northern authorities, no IRA survivor apart from Busteed ever hinted at the connection. Yet the newspapers of the next few weeks are filled with columns from various Southern, mostly Church of Ireland, Protestant communities condemning the Ulster killings of Catholics while at the same time claiming that relations between Catholics and Protestants in the South were nothing short of rosy. While Church leaders were in the habit of condemning killings, it marks a new departure when business and community leaders publicly begin to do the same. Southern Protestant communities also went to considerable lengths to distance themselves from anti-Catholic pogroms in Northern Ireland.[27] Typical of these was the statement of Sir Charles Barrington, Vice-Lieutenant of County Limerick, whose daughter had been shot dead in an IRA ambush in 1921, who stated that his community 'never suffered from intolerance of any kind and lived in perfect harmony with their Catholic neighbours'. His deputy William Waller stated that 'any sort of religious intolerance was abhorrent' before going on to challenge Sir Henry Wilson's claims of wholesale skulduggery in the South: 'The letter of Sir Henry Wilson on the situation in the North, he [Waller] had no hesitation in saying, was written for a political purpose because it asserted that the Protestants of the South are not allowed to conduct their business in an orderly manner.'[28] Yet Wilson was not for turning. On 20 March he stated: 'Tell them, and get others to tell them, the real truth of what is going on in the South and West and what is really passing in Ulster.' On 5 April the British Cabinet was so concerned at receiving a letter from Lord Midleton describing the difficult situation facing unionists in the South that it envisaged that 'they may be compelled to fly to Dublin or the sea. The aid of the Navy may have to be invoked to remove them from certain points on the coast.'[29] This was a whole month before the massacre in Dunmanway.

Over 50 Cork business leaders whose relatives and friends were among those who disappeared on St Patrick's Day signed a declaration condemning the Northern atrocities and linked, by implication, the deeds in the South with the expulsion of Catholic workers from companies like Harland and Wolff in Belfast. The denial of the events of St Patrick's Day was absolute:

> Representatives of fifty of the principal commercial firms in Cork, who are not Roman Catholic, have signed a statement in which they express abhorrence of sanguinary methods for political purposes and or reprisals or the use of violence in the supposed interests of any religion. They deny that they have been subjected to any form of oppression or injustice by their Catholic fellow citizens and they called on the Northern Ireland Government to carry out the agreement for the re-instatement of expelled Catholic workers.[30]

The signatories of the above letter comprise a list of the great and the good of Cork business society of the time, the majority of whom almost certainly had no truck with any form of spying operation. Nor were the missing men among the most prominent officers of the YMCA. The composition of the YMCA general committee remained unchanged over this period and kept on meeting as if nothing had happened. Indeed, there is no reference to any of these 'sanguinary methods' in YMCA minutes.

It is also clear from this that, for the Cork business community and for Southern Protestants in general, suppression was the price of survival. This denial was to continue in the aftermath of the Dunmanway killings some weeks later. Rev. Alfred Harbinson, the Methodist minister of Dunmanway, stated in *The Irish Times* that on the night of the killings,

> The manse was neither visited nor attacked and there is no truth whatsoever in the statement that I had to seek refuge in the fields or elsewhere. Never at any time have I been molested or interfered with in any way. I have always received the utmost courtesy from the people of this town and surrounding country.[31]

All the evidence from a variety of sources suggests that Rev. Harbinson did in fact flee. Both Methodist and Church of Ireland clergymen fled.[32] The victims of the St Patrick's Day operation appear to have been largely Methodist and Quaker businessmen. In a message to Cork Methodists the Church synod said: 'Our heartfelt sympathy goes out to all those who have suffered and in particular to the members of our own church in the district in the severe testing which they have been called to endure.'[33] It is equally clear that both communities closed the book on this event and that every effort was made to suggest that the abductions had never taken place. Several were the proprietors of agricultural firms, who continued to import and sell British-made 'binders, mowing machines, horse rakes, swathe turners, hay trolleys (rick shifters), ploughs, harrows, corn drills and root cutters' in defiance of an IRA ban that came into operation from the end of March 1921.[34] The ban was reinforced in March 1922, 'seeing that conciliatory measures have failed to end the inhuman atrocities committed by Orangemen'. Another was a member of a family of importers who owned one of Cork's largest hotels and who continued to put the hotel at the disposal of British forces right through the conflict. If, as seems likely, the civilian held in St Mary of the Isle in February 1922 was the first of the group to be captured, then why did Connie Neenan need to associate them all with James Beal, who was shot a year earlier? Beal *was* associated with British undercover agents; others were shot on foot of 'evidence' found on him, but it seems that these 'prominent supporters of the Treaty' were not among them.[35] Or was part of the reason the fact that, along with being generally pro-British, they had refused to obey an IRA ban on the import and sale of British goods during the War of Independence? It seems they were also 'guilty' of reporting these threats to the British military. Such reporting would in all probability have been noted by people like Josephine Marchment Brown in the barracks. It may even have been a combination of all these reasons. My own view is that when the IRA wanted to give a signal to the British and Northern Ireland authorities, they selected these men because they had Northern connections, they had defied the IRA and were perceived to be 'anti-Irish' in the IRA's terms. They may also have suspected them on the basis of whatever was extracted from the mysterious individual captured in mid-February. Given the attitudes of activists such as Connie Neenan, as evidenced at the start of this chapter, it is easy to see why they might decide to 'eliminate' these poppy-wearing enemies of the Republic since 'they represent a solid barrier, which has all the implications of hostility in its most severe form.'

But these were but one of several groups who disappeared. 'All the spies shot in Cork were buried, so nothing was known about them. They simply disappeared.' They were all called 'spies', though they were different groups. We have one group in the summer of 1922, another in March 1922 and those we have already seen, the YMCA members—Roycroft, Parsons, Cooke, William G. Beale, H. A. Harris, Theo Creber—and probably several others.

As regards the three businessmen from the Blackrock Road whom Neenan stated were killed in late June by the 2nd Battalion, again it is likely they were killed in June 1922, not June 1921. For there is no evidence that they disappeared during the War of Independence; there is no trace of them in the (relatively complete) records of June 1921; nor do they appear in any compensation files. Indeed, it is probable that these were among the '4 or 5' loyalists that Frank Busteed claimed were executed and buried in Rylane during the Civil War—the Civil War having started by that stage, even if it had not reached Cork.[36] We can even speculate that these killings were carried out in Rylane because Corry's had by then become a security risk on account of the execution of Michael Williams having become known in the area.

It should also be pointed out that the targeting of Protestant institutions took place all over the country at this time. The Orange Hall and the YMCA in Kingstown (Dun Laoghaire), County Dublin, were burnt out and raided, respectively, on 7 April.[37] The Masonic Hall in Limerick was burnt out and the Protestant Cricket club in that city raided, leading Sir Charles Barrington to make another public statement at this time that 'the Masonic body is a purely philanthropic and social body . . . our aim is to live in peace and love and harmony with all men'.[38] As late as January 1923, Salvation Army personnel were attacked on the streets of Cork, and when they fled into the YMCA building, the building itself was damaged.[39]

Some of the men taken on St Patrick's Day, such as those mentioned above, can be identified from various contemporary records.[40] For instance, nine men, eight of whom were Protestants, were among those who disappeared from the postal directories in 1922 and are listed in the Valuation Lists for the Blackrock Road/Douglas Road area as having their homes transferred to a next of kin, usually a wife, between 1920 and 1923. Yet their deaths were not registered. Obviously there are many reasons why someone would transfer their property to a next of kin, and it is unlikely that all these men were killed. However, death is the most common reason. It should also be pointed out that right through both conflicts the deaths registers were quite assiduously filled in if only for probate reasons.[41] On the other hand, disappeared persons are rarely if ever registered.[42] And these are of families who remained in Cork. Of the many families who left, it is fair to assume that at least a certain number of these also had missing persons. Six persons in the area are listed in Florrie O'Donoghue's notebooks, none of whom was still living there by 1924.[43] These include Mrs Stoker of Douglas Road—'daughter married to Cook [sic]', Stanley Hunt and Thomas R. Holland, both near neighbours of Josephine Marchment Brown. Hunt, a manager at McMullen's mills, very likely disappeared, while Thomas Holland may well have been the magistrate mentioned by Connie Neenan as having been among the three businessmen shot there in June. Holland, the owner of another flour milling business, was a JP and lived in a large house across the road from Roxboro Terrace. Another probable victim is one Thomas Manley. Manley's name appears on the Department of Justice missing list and he is also among those whose YMCA membership lapses in 1922. There are also several names in both the Department of Justice missing persons lists who may have been among those who disappeared in Cork around this time, but in the absence of the files themselves being released, we have no firm information as to the dates and circumstances of the disappearance of these individuals.[44]

Aside from alleged spycatching, there is also reason to believe there was intimidation going on in the area for personal gain. It appears, for instance, that at least two market gardeners (Catholics) in the Ballinlough area may have disappeared and three others had to sell up and leave. Also several homes abandoned by Protestants were subsequently occupied by republican families.[45]

It is also clear that a decision was made by the various communities involved to suppress this story, and many of these families never wrote to the Free State authorities at all, let alone apply for compensation. It is clear from Rev. Alley's account of the sufferings of Methodists that, in some instances at least, families were informed by the IRA that their men had been executed and that some families had more than one family member disappear. It is also clear the families believed that in many cases the suspicions may have arisen out of spite or out of a desire to clear out what were successful businesses owned by Methodists.[46] It is possible from family trees, valuation records, street directories and the registry of deaths to identity some of these, but this does not constitute proof. One group, however, whose disappearance can be largely authenticated and who constituted the largest group of the so-called Anti-Sinn Féin League 'spies' will be the subject of the next chapter.

In the meantime, it appears that the unfortunate Methodists—including the Methodist farmers who disappeared in west Cork the same week—were left to their fate, not just by the British government and the Irish Free State, but also by the Church of Ireland. For a few days after the St Patrick's Day disappearances, the Church of Ireland Bishop of Cork, Rev. Dr Dowse, was asked about the desirability of holding a public meeting of the Church of Ireland and members of the other Protestant Churches in Cork to give public expression to the horror and detestation with which they all regarded all these awful atrocities (naming the murder of Gloster and the McMahon killings in Belfast, but not the events of St Patrick's Day).

> I have been approached about that and on reflection it seemed to me that such a meeting might suggest that there was some necessity to create such a feeling. Knowing that there is no such necessity, knowing that every member of our various communities view these happenings with loathing and dismay I do not think any useful purpose would be served by such a meeting.[47]

So much for interdenominational cross-community support. Clearly, Dr Dowse did not want to associate himself or his Church with disappeared Methodists, whatever the reason for their disappearance. This of course is perfectly understandable: he did not want the contagion of suspicion to be visited upon his own community. In an unstable and uncertain environment it was simply a matter of survival. He might as well have condemned the abductions though, for it was only a matter of weeks before his own community was to experience a similar fate with the events in west Cork in late April and the fall-out from the capture of Edward Parsons. As for the Catholic community, they ignored it, though Dr Dowse was later to receive letters of support from the Catholic Young Men's Society. In a sinking ship, it was a case of every man for himself.

Chapter 51 ～

| THE MISSING MASONS

Of the groups of Protestants taken in the spring of 1922 by the Cork city IRA and shot, only one group can be identified with any certainty. These were the alleged 'spies' known as the Anti-Sinn Féin League who were executed by the 2nd Battalion on the basis of the notebook found on James Beal. These killings could have occurred at any time from the shooting of Beal in February 1921 to the end of the Civil War, though the chances are that most of them took place in the spring and summer of 1922. In contrast to those taken on St Patrick's Day, these were not particularly well-known figures and most appear to have been lower middle-class Protestants. All they had in common was that they were Freemasons. Connie Neenan's statement is worth repeating:

> Mick used to smoke cigarettes. Pat Hayes came down to him with the list of the spies of the Anti-Sinn Féin League. Most of them were in the Seaman's Bar. Mick would blow smoke out of his mouth and say: 'Just you shoot them' and as the names went on 'and you shoot them also', and he'd let out a puff of smoke.[1]

The membership rolls of the six Freemason lodges that existed in the city from 1900 to 1923 shed interesting light on the lives of the men of Protestant Cork at this time. While many leading city Protestants were Masons, including the Church of Ireland bishop, many others were not. The notion that Cork was in effect run by a coterie of a few hundred Freemasons is a fallacy. The majority of Cork Protestant business people and senior figures in political, legal and economic life were not Masons at all. In fact, the YMCA was more representative of the Cork establishment than were the Freemasons. While there were still many prominent figures in the Cork lodges, the vast majority of the membership were clerks, accountants, small business people, shop assistants and some former policemen and soldiers, though serving policemen are notable by their absence. It is also evident that many people who went on to become senior figures in Cork city in later life had been Freemasons in their twenties, only to resign in the first two decades of the century.

The most striking thing about the membership rolls of the lodges is the number of resignations that took place during the years of the revolution. Some 60 Masons resigned between 1921 and 1923, mostly from two lodges, No. 1 and No. 71. While some 29 are listed as having died, including Beal and William L. Cooke, the total number of deaths recorded during the period is not especially high and were mostly from natural causes. Some deaths, however, are unregistered and may be significant, though there is no proof of that.[2]

It is clear from the annual reports of the Munster grand lodges that very few meetings took place during the revolutionary period. In 1921 the secretary of the Munster Lodge, C. J. Lane—also a leading figure in the Boy Scouts—reported that owing 'to the very disturbed condition of the Province in the earlier part of the year the Brethren thought it wise to meet as little as possible and few meetings were held'.[3] In 1922 Lane stated: 'I regret to say that owing to the conditions of things in this Province it has not been thought advisable for regular meetings of the Lodge to be held during this period and accordingly the meetings that have actually taken place are very few and only when considered absolutely necessary.' Looking back in 1923, Sir Charles Barrington, the leading Mason in Munster, noted that 1922 was 'a period of considerable unrest over the whole area . . . our activities were considerably curtailed and some lodges had no meetings at all. During the past five years considerable numbers of our members have left the country, some of whom, I regret to say, will never return to live permanently amongst us.'[4]

Yet despite all this and despite the slew of resignations, C. J. Lane was able to claim in 1922: 'I am glad to say, however, that there has been little evidence in the Province of hostility to the Order, though two of the Lodge rooms have been destroyed by fire.' This refers to events in west Cork where in late 1921 and in May 1922 Bantry and Clonakilty lodges were raided and burnt out. One of those raids was reported by the IO of the 3rd Brigade in November 1921:[5]

> This Brigade has a strong hostile civilian element organized in Freemason lodges to contend with. Our men have got a good grasp of the significance and danger of this and so much attention has been devoted to it that its service to the enemy is now slight. Our Intelligence Department may be said to satisfactorily control the area. The men generally are efficient and keen on their work. Close touch with Divisional HQ is always maintained.[6]

Despite this declaration of IRA paranoia, there is no evidence that Freemasons in west Cork were secretly shot and buried. Francis Fitzmaurice had been a Mason in the early part of the century but had long since resigned. Robert Nagle's father Tom had been the caretaker of the Clonakilty lodge, though he was not a Mason himself. According to a Volunteer interviewed by Peter Hart who had been involved in the raid on Clonakilty lodge some 70 years earlier, 'it had the queerest things in it', which, it has to be said, would not be an unusual reaction on first exposure to Masonic symbolism and paraphernalia.[7]

So Lane was correct so far as west Cork was concerned. However, with regard to the city, he appears to be making the best of a bad situation. Walter Hailes, for instance, who worked in the GPO, was shot by the IRA in 1922 largely due to his membership of the Masonic Order which 'was particularly distasteful to the Sinn Féiners.'[8] The key word here is 'evidence'. Lane was one of Cork's leading solicitors. There was indeed little 'evidence of hostility', mainly because the evidence did not make it into the public domain. Just because there was no 'evidence of hostility', though, did not mean there was no hostility.

The conclusions are pretty straightforward, at least on the surface: in contrast to the YMCA, where meetings took place right through the revolutionary period, in the case of the Cork Masonic lodges very few meetings took place at all. It is also clear from the annual reports that the Grand Order of Freemasons of Ireland swung right in behind the provisional government as soon as it was set up. 'It is our bounden duty as Masons to be good citizens and to support the Government under which we live, so long as that Government protects us.' As stated earlier, when the Dublin Freemason hall was occupied by the IRA in 1922, the officers of the Grand Lodge of Ireland were treated with 'the utmost courtesy and consideration' by Michael Collins and Arthur Griffith. 'They seem to realise that, far from being a dangerous body, we are a body—as we are—bound to support and give all the assistance we can to any legally constituted government of the country in which we live.'

However, something else becomes apparent when we look closely at the membership rolls of the Cork city lodges. For when the lodges began to meet regularly again in 1925/26 what is surprising is the number of Masons whose names were struck off the membership rolls (see Appendix VIII). A total of 32 Masons were struck off, all but one of them in 1925/26. But the most extraordinary statistic is that all but four of these were struck off from just one lodge, No. 71. This was the lodge of which James Beal was a member. Were these were the 'Anti-Sinn Féin League spies' shot by the south city battalion of the IRA?[9] (See Appendix IX.)

Of course, there is no way of proving how many of them were actually killed.[10] There are any number of reasons why someone might lose his Freemason membership—the most obvious one being that he did not attend Masonic meetings. They could, for instance, have been struck off because they were associated with Beal and because this was a political matter which was not allowed under the rules of Freemasonry. However, most were struck off in 1925/26, well after the event, suggesting that this was not the case. I believe many of these were the names found on Beal when he was shot at Dennehy's

Cross in the spring of 1921.

The list also sheds some light on the kinds of persons the IRA were targeting.[11] There is the relatively high number, nine in all, of people with military and police links. Five of these were soldiers/officers and could conceivably be undercover members of the British plain clothes squads who operated in Cork, which would of course have made them 'colleagues' of the real Anti-Sinn Féin League, which would in turn make them legitimate military targets—that is if they were killed during the actual conflict. On the other hand, they may have been merely ex-soldiers. Another was John Beecher, an ex-RIC sergeant, two of whose sons had been in the Canadian Army and whose names were also struck off. It is likely that Beecher, who lived on Quaker Road—who was also a YMCA member—and his sons may well have been the father and two sons that Mick Murphy said were shot and that the father was 'dead drunk' and who, according to Connie Neenan, had their shoes taken off them after they were executed. (Murphy and Neenan ascribe these details to the Blemenses, but the Blemenses, like Beal and Parsons, appear to stand in for everyone else in these recollections.)

Four of the remainder could technically be described as merchants/manufacturers, but they are minor figures. The one described as a merchant, Charles Wolfe, the only Mason struck off in 1922, was a pawnbroker rather than a merchant in the strict sense. Quite clearly, if these were the Anti-Sinn Féin League members shot by Mick Murphy's men, they were not the merchants mentioned by Connie Neenan. Nor were they the 'prominent supporters of a certain political party' taken on St Patrick's Day 1922. The Freemasons were more likely to have been picked up in ones and twos over a longer period, as Mick Murphy said they were. Some, no doubt, fled the country and were part of the Protestant diaspora from the south side of the city who left in the spring and summer of 1922. It is impossible at this stage to determine who fled and who disappeared.

I am of the view, however, that the majority of these men probably disappeared. There are several reasons for thinking this: all but one of them listed in Guy's Directory prior to 1921 were gone by 1924. Most Freemasons who left Cork at this time simply transferred to other lodges in their new homes. It is clear from Freemason records that many transferred to Dublin, Wicklow, Belfast and elsewhere in Ireland, but mostly Northern Ireland, while others transferred to lodges in Britain, the US and the colonies. Masonic membership was a useful introduction to a new country and was much availed of by Cork Masons who departed during those years. It is also important to bear in mind that being struck off did not simply mean you were no longer a member of that particular lodge; it meant you were no longer a member of any lodge because you were no longer a Freemason.

If Masonic membership was a distinct advantage when starting out on life in a new country, it was a distinct disadvantage if you decided to remain in

Cork. It is clear from Appendix VIII that there was a veritable flood of resignations from the city lodges during those years, most of which occurred between 1921 and 1923. The reasons for this are not difficult to discern. When your fellow Masons begin to disappear, you no longer want to remain a Freemason. This also goes a long way to explain the bland affirmations of the annual reports of the Munster lodges where a tone of stoic acceptance was maintained and where nothing of a serious nature is claimed to have happened. The number of resignations alone suggest that this is simply not the case and that C. J. Lane's claim that very little hostility was shown to the Masonic Order is simply another example of Protestant *omèrta*.

And there are other reasons for thinking they were shot. One or two are even in the public record. We have already seen the case of H. A. Harris of the YMCA, though Harris was a member of Lodge No. 95 and is unlikely to have been associated with the Beal group. Francis McMahon was abducted in late May 1921 on his way to work, taken into the countryside, shot and his body buried. John Moore, a 70-year-old retired accountant 'of delicate appearance and wearing a dark body coat with brown muffler and bowler hat' and 'thought to be suffering from memory loss' left his house on Friar Street on Sunday 1 May 1921 and was never seen again.[12] Stanley Hunt, yet another neighbour of Josephine Marchment Brown's at the city end of the Blackrock Road and who worked as a manager in McMullen's Mills, was, as we have seen, on one of Florrie O'Donoghue's wanted lists. Apart from Harris, others such as the Beechers, John Cottrell and Edward Owens had connections with the YMCA. Of all those on the list, only one, Nathaniel Todd, who was chief steward at the Cork Club, is still listed as living in Cork in 1924 and he is named as living at the club. Considering that a Major Phillips, a retired army man who lived at Carrigrohane, was nearly abducted at the City Club in May 1922 when the club was effectively laid siege to, one wonders whether Todd was in fact still living there by 1924, for his death was not registered subsequently. Apart from the two mentioned above, all the rest had either left or had disappeared. And the strain on those remaining was enormous. Fifty city Freemasons resigned during the revolutionary period. One prominent Mason was so terrified that he died, having accidentally overdosed on narcotics 'for the purpose of attaining sleep'.[13]

So were all or some of these men actual spies? As we have seen, Harris may well have been some kind of British agent in Cork. In the case of those with army or police links, including the three Beechers, it is entirely possible they were members of the various military intelligence units that passed themselves off as the Anti-Sinn Féin League. This lends credence, at least in part, to the IRA version of events.

The majority of those on the list, however, were clerks, accountants and other petty officials such as shop assistants and, in one case, a commercial traveller. Could somebody like John Moore, a doddery 70-year-old, have been a spy? Did these constitute a substantial 'spy ring' as claimed by members of the 2nd Battalion? There are a number of reasons for believing that this was not the case. For a start, one of the basic rules of Freemasonry, then and now, is that Masonic activity was not to be of a political or sectarian nature. Then there is the fact that Masonic activity in Cork came to a virtual standstill during those years. If there were very few meetings of the various lodges, and none at all of some lodges, then it would be very difficult to use 'the Masonic cement', as Florrie O'Donoghue called it, to organise a spy ring.

Interestingly, there were no Masons struck off the west Cork lodges during this period, suggesting that, despite the 'evidence' of a Masonic conspiracy there, common sense prevailed and Masons were not targeted merely on the basis of paranoia and suspicion. However, the fact that the 3rd Brigade believed it had 'a strong hostile civilian element organised in Freemason lodges to contend with' no doubt fed into the murderous tendencies of the 2nd Battalion in the city, especially considering that 'close touch with Divisional HQ [was] always maintained'.

These clerks and accountants of Lodge No. 71 are likely to have been those named in the Treasury notebook taken from Beal when he was killed and were probably Beal's friends and contacts. We have plenty of evidence that this list was guarded jealously by the IRA through a number of raids and passed on through a succession of IOs. It was hidden under a bucket at Vernon Mount during a British raid in early 1921 and retrieved afterwards.[14] Beal may of course have been a spy, but what kind of spy would go around with a list of his fellow agents in his pocket? It is hard to believe that British military intelligence would be so incompetent as to reveal the names of two dozen of its agents to one of its own and then allow him to go around the streets with a list of those names in his pocket.

Perhaps the 'captured' list of Freemasons that can be found in Florrie O'Donoghue's papers may shed some light on this matter, especially considering his role as Brigade IO and later as a leading member of Divisional HQ. The reader will remember that there are a number of lists of Freemasons in O'Donoghue's papers, most of which appear to have been taken in the raids on the lodges in late 1921 and 1922. These are the rolls of various Cork lodges for 1920 and appear authentic.[15] (The very fact that they were membership rolls for 1920, though captured in late 1921 and 1922, in itself suggests that there had been very little updating or meetings during the intervening period.) The other list is different. This is a list consisting of 181 Masons from various parts of the county, though mostly from the city. It is in alphabetical order and can be found in MS 31, 200 in O'Donoghue's papers, described as documents 'captured' between January and April 1921.[16] The obvious conclusion to come to is that this is the list of Masons found on Beal because he was the only Freemason shot in Cork during this period.

The list itself, however, tells a completely different story. For a start, not a single person of all the 181 men on the list was ever harmed by the IRA, let alone shot. None of those listed as 'struck off' in the Grand Order of Freemasons rolls is named. While many of those named were Masons and correspond with those named in the 1920 lists and with the membership rolls of the Grand Order of Freemasons, there is a significant minority who were not members at the time. Closer examination of the list leaves little doubt that this was not captured in 1921 but was compiled sometime between 1928 and 1934.[17] You would have to ask the question: what was O'Donoghue doing compiling lists of Freemasons in the early 1930s—and for whom, seeing as he had officially resigned from the IRA in 1922? And what is it doing masquerading as a 'captured' document supposedly found in the spring of 1921? The only conclusion is that this list was compiled around 1930 and slipped into the file of captured papers so as to give the impression that this was the list found on Beal. Is this a subtle way of saying that nobody in such a list was ever killed by the IRA? Because by implication it exonerates the IRA from ever having shot the members of 71 Lodge and, given that the whole unseemly business was carried out in absolute secrecy, it almost succeeds. 'Very real anxiety exists among members of the Masonic Order at the determined hostility being shown to their brethren in Southern Ireland.'[18] In short, this document appears to be a very clever fabrication, but then O'Donoghue was nothing if not a clever fellow. So why was it drawn up? The most likely explanation is that families were asking questions around Cork in the late 1920s or writing from England looking for information on their missing relatives and that this was part of O'Donoghue's cover-up. It may also have been planted to put historians off the scent and to suggest that it never happened. O'Donoghue, as a diligent historian himself, would have been in no doubt that questions would arise on this at some stage. Perhaps his own words say it all: 'They were in the main intelligent observers with rich business and social contacts and the Masonic cement kept them all well integrated.' 'Those who showed signs of becoming dangerous were quickly eliminated.'[19] What he does not say is that they were 'quickly eliminated' well after the event and in all probability on the merest suspicion. They were eliminated because their names appeared on a list.

Chapter 52 ～

REACTIONS AND
RESPONSIBILITIES

One of the thornier questions running through this narrative is who made the decisions to pursue and execute these men and teenagers, particularly since the IRA was so heavily involved at the time in national issues. One would have thought that with the post-Treaty split and the various manoeuvrings to avoid the drift to civil war, senior officers in the Cork brigades would have had more than enough on their plate not to be chasing old enemies. As we have seen in Part II, during the War of Independence there was a huge discrepancy between the numbers of civilians shot by the two city battalions of the IRA, with the 2nd Battalion outshooting the 1st by a factor of five to one. It is also clear from Connie Neenan and Mick Murphy's accounts that almost all the loyalists shot in Cork city were shot by the 2nd Battalion. So the question at issue is: were these killings carried out by the 2nd Battalion acting on its own, or were they sanctioned and planned by Brigade HQ, in other words by O'Donoghue and O'Hegarty?

It is difficult to assign responsibility but, on the basis of the accounts left by various individuals, the 'Anti-Sinn Féin League spies', that is the Freemasons of No. 71 Lodge, were shot by the 2nd Battalion. While it is not clear who ultimately gave the order, it is clear that O'Donoghue organised a cover-up by inserting fake lists of Freemasons into his papers. The merchants snatched in February and March 1922 were taken by Connie Neenan's group, either acting on its own initiative or under orders from Brigade HQ. The YMCA business is much more complex, occurring over a longer period and over a much wider area. All we can say about it at this point is that it originated on the south side of the city and that Parsons and perhaps half a dozen others were executed by the Brigade's official executioner, Martin Corry. It appears to have started just after the Truce but gathered momentum only with the capture of Parsons. Connie Neenan appears to have been intimately associated with it. The role of O'Donoghue and O'Hegarty is more difficult to establish.

Clearly O'Donoghue is being somewhat disingenuous when he writes about the five or six loyalists, the 'garrison clique', who he claimed were organised as a civilian branch of the British Secret Service, when the real number of dead loyalists may be up to ten times this figure. These, he states, were quickly eliminated and as a result caused little damage. Does this refer to the Methodists shot during the conflict: Reilly, John Cathcart, Tom Bradfield, Gilbert and Fred Fenton and some of the other farmers shot in west Cork, or to the men abducted on St Patrick's Day 1922? Or does it refer to the YMCA or the Freemasons, the so-called Anti-Sinn Féin League, a term that O'Donoghue, incidentally, always refrains from using? Elsewhere, O'Donoghue refers to the 'Masonic cement' binding the group together, so it appears to refer to the Freemasons who disappeared. But we cannot be sure.

What's more, O'Donoghue never mentions anything about the YMCA or indeed that a vendetta against city loyalists was still running as late as 1923. Indeed, he never mentions the pursuit and killing of teenagers at all in his writings. But then, he never alludes to the taking of the Blemenses either or to the shooting of Beal, though he almost certainly ordered both. The Blemenses, Cooke and several of those shot in 1922 lived on the Blackrock Road and were all near neighbours of Josephine Marchment Brown—only 50 yards separate all their homes. It is inconceivable that he did not have knowledge of these latter killings. In fact, the area immediately around Roxboro Terrace was the most dangerous place in Cork to live if you were a Protestant between 1920 and 1923.[1] The fact that he never once refers to the disappearance of his neighbours suggests that he knew a lot more than he was prepared to let on.

Another thorny question is ascribing levels of guilt to those shot. Taking the word of the IRA men themselves—and they are our main source—is fraught with difficulties. After all, nobody in the situation the IRA veterans found themselves in was going to admit that individuals might have been innocent or shot in the wrong or shot for a crime that might have fallen far short of actual spying. Therefore these accounts have to be treated with scepticism. Ernie O'Malley was the only IRA survivor to suggest that O'Hegarty was careless about the evidence against the 'spies' his men shot, though it is clear from his correspondence that Richard Mulcahy believed the same thing. Corry praises O'Hegarty for never asking awkward questions about those killed in Knockraha, suggesting that others may not have been so accommodating about turning a blind eye to what was going on. O'Hegarty and O'Donoghue in their own reports to GHQ claimed to be certain of the guilt of those shot, but then, they would say that, wouldn't they? It is impossible to believe that all those shot were guilty. But it is equally impossible to believe that they were all innocent. The problem in dealing with this dichotomy can be illustrated by the few cases where we know both sides of the story.

We have seen earlier that at the time of the Truce the 1st Brigade reported to GHQ that all those suspected of spying in the city had already been dealt with, with three notable exceptions: Cruxy Connors, Monkey Mac and the 'spy' Stevens. Connors, as we have seen, was shot in New York in April 1922; McDonald was tracked down in England only for Connie Neenan to discover he was already in jail for theft.[2] Stevens was never found and the weekly report of the week of the Truce suggested that he had joined the RIC. In fact, he had joined the British Army. What is more, he left an account of his experiences in Cork with the IGC which is quite at odds with the versions left by IRA men.[3] According to Seán Healy, Stevens was a student at University College Cork and was operating as a British spy. Healy seems to have been pursuing Stevens around the Western Road area with no small amount of diligence and, if he is to be believed, Stevens was pursuing him with similar deadly intent. When Healy was captured, Stevens identified him when he was incarcerated in Victoria Barracks.

According to his own account, Stevens, the son of a captain in the British Army Medical Corps (and an English Catholic), received a scholarship to study engineering at UCC in 1920. 'My father was stationed at Victoria Barracks and I was approached by members of the IRA with a view to joining that body. This I absolutely refused to do, with the result that three attempts were made on my life and after the third attempt it was impossible for me to return to my studies and I was forced to live in Victoria Barracks for protection.' After the Truce, Stevens joined the British Army and subsequently served with the Staffordshire Regiment.[4]

It is probably true to say that Stevens recognised Seán Healy at the barracks. But was he working as a spy? Or was he simply approached to act as a spy for the IRA, refused to do so and was targeted as a result? It is his word against Seán Healy's. If he was doing espionage work for the British Army, then why not say so, to increase his chances of compensation? As a serving soldier, he would certainly have nothing to lose (and much to gain) by this approach. If indeed he was a spy, he would have jumped at the chance of joining the IRA. The most logical conclusion is that events transpired much as Stevens himself described them. He was approached, refused to work for the IRA, was threatened, and then passed on whatever information he had on the men who tried to recruit him, identifying Healy in the process. You could say he was a spy. But you could also say he was forced into the role of 'informer' by the circumstances of his attempted recruitment. Many Protestants, in a form of not-very-subtle intimidation, were similarly 'recruited' into the IRA after the Truce, only to be branded as 'spies' and driven from the country or shot when they refused to join.[5] And Stevens is one of the most vilified of British so-called 'spies' in Cork. What about those who were less vilified and merely shot? For one thing is sure: if Stevens had stayed in Cork, he would have been murdered and pencilled down as another extremely dangerous spy.

These stories and that of Henry Forde that we saw earlier illustrate the dangers of relying on one side's version of events. (British reports are equally full of inaccuracies and misconceptions and have a similar tendency towards self-glorification.) It is human nature to build up one's own role in a conflict and, unfortunately, in many instances we have only one side to rely on.

There is little doubt that many of the men listed in the previous chapters died simply for befriending various British military personnel or because they were listed in the pocket book of one who did. It is interesting to compare what happened to them with what happened to a Catholic guilty of the same crime. In September 1921 Tim O'Mahony of Brown Street was taken to the seashore at Blackrock and beaten with a whip handle. When the congregation emerged from Mass in Blackrock Catholic church, they found O'Mahony chained to the railings with a label 'Blackguards beware' attached to his chest. O'Mahony's crime was to go drinking with Black and Tans.[6] He was not shot, however, nor did he disappear. Protestants who did the same thing were never seen again.

There are a number of reasons for thinking that Brigade HQ and not just the 2nd Battalion was behind many of these killings. Connie Neenan stated that the British were very concerned about the targeting of loyalist 'spies'. This is because, when many of the killings took place in March 1922, the IRA was in a perfect position to judge exactly what the British military thought about it, because from the previous August they had managed to place a tap on the telephone lines into Victoria Barracks. The IRA eavesdropped on all communications entering and leaving Cork Barracks. They knew exactly what the British were thinking during this period, and if the British were concerned at the killings, the IRA would have known it.

Florrie O'Donoghue kept most of the transcripts of these communications and they paint a fascinating picture of how the army viewed the situation in Cork at the time. But guess what? The transcripts end on 16 March, the day before the abductions.[7] Clearly, O'Donoghue dumped those records made after 17 March so that he would have us believe that these events also never happened. The British were no doubt concerned when pro-Free State former loyalists went missing—but we do not know what form that concern took.

And there is another reason for believing that O'Donoghue was party to the decision to eliminate these men. He kept a couple of small notebooks with occasional entries in his tiny, insect-like handwriting over the winter of 1921/22 and spring of 1922, one of which we have already mentioned. These notebooks, though the detail is sketchy, have enough information in them to suggest that the plan to track down and execute city loyalists had been in place for some time before the actual killings took place.[8] For instance, Arthur Gloster is listed, as is Constable Williams, as is Mrs Stoker of Douglas Road[9] and Thomas Holland and Stanley Hunt. Even Dan Shields gets a mention and is listed as living at an address at Eason's Lane. In an entry marked

'Douglas'—where several of these disappearances took place—O'Donoghue makes the following statement: 'Intelligence to be especially dealt with. Police work to be done in stages.'[10] As stated earlier, none of those listed in these diaries was still living in Cork by 1924. It is clear that the regular surveillance network built up during the War of Independence was still very much in operation, having been augmented with the arrival of peacetime. It was now the real law in Cork, a Stazi-like surveillance system where suspicion fed upon itself: 'The Anti-Treaty section have a regular spy section; we see their detectives watching our movements as the old Dublin Castle detectives used to watch in days gone by.'[11] If this sounds ominous, it probably is, for it is suggestive of carefully planned schemes to track down the 'enemies of the Republic' and eliminate them. If you go looking for enemies, you are sure to find them. As Liam de Roiste stated in his diary during the week of the March disappearances: 'A few of the officers of An tOglaigh [the Volunteers] think nothing of taking human life, but the majority of the boys are in no way bloodthirsty.' Liam de Roiste clearly knew where the responsibility lay.

This is further evidence that the upsurge of shootings of civilian 'spies' that took place in Cork city during the War of Independence from February 1921 onwards may well be connected to the fact that this was when O'Donoghue took over the effective day-to-day operation in the city. Most of these killings took place in February, March and April when O'Donoghue was in charge— they dropped again in May and June with his departure for 1st Southern Division duties in Cork and Kerry. These killings were indeed carried out by the south city battalion, but O'Donoghue was also living on the south side in various billets and safe houses but also at Josephine's house on the Blackrock Road. Seán O'Hegarty, Florrie O'Donoghue and Mick Murphy lived within a stone's throw of each other in the Blackrock and Douglas Road areas. It is surely no coincidence that the majority of the killings of loyalists also took place in these areas. In fact, most of the Protestants living within a few hundred yards of Josephine Brown were gone by 1924 (see Map 2).

O'Donoghue is very careful in his writings to avoid giving too much away on the matter of the execution of suspected spies. In fact, he goes to some lengths to distance himself entirely from decisions and to give the impression that O'Hegarty was a lot more bellicose on the matter than he was himself, giving the example of one 'gentleman' who survived because of his own intervention, but who would have been shot had the decision been O'Hegarty's. O'Donoghue has always got an easy ride from historians on this matter, while O'Hegarty is painted as a ruthless backroom conspirator. Yet they were almost like father and son. It is fair to say that their views were largely shared. In fact the evidence here suggests that O'Donoghue may have been even more ruthless than O'Hegarty. O'Donoghue rarely if ever has a good word to say for Cork Protestants. While Mick Murphy could see city loyalists for what they were and that they did what they did out of patriotism,

O'Donoghue is never less than bitter about the Protestant minority.

Lifelong republicans like Connie Neenan who did not 'compromise' by being pro-Treaty or later becoming members of Fianna Fáil, could always justify these killings:

> It must be made quite clear here and right now that such executions were by no means 'wanton murder' nor could they even be called 'reprisals'; they were nothing but a form of simple desperate defence against a relentless and most cruel British spy system whose members tortured, maimed and murdered mercilessly, running rampage among the civilian Irish population until such time as we were finally able to hit back and match their effectiveness and efficiency. Up to that time many of our young companions had fallen victim to the more experienced and ruthless British spy system who, one regrets to admit, were aided in some cases quite considerably by Irish informers.[12]

There is some truth in this, though whether the British killing system was more effective than that of the IRA is open to question. None the less, there is more than an element here of the kettle calling the pot black. The fact that, 'up to such time as we were finally able to hit back' was nine months into peacetime and that the war was well and truly over and the British had effectively left, is not mentioned at all. After all, whatever they may have done during the conflict, the British did not abduct and murder people during the post-conflict era.

The IRA now had a new and ultimately far more deadly enemy. Indeed, the intelligence war was to continue right into the Civil War, for Neenan states that in July 1922 'a young Dublin boy was arrested as a Free State agent which, in turn, soon led us to arrest a well-known footballer who in 1918 was attached to Sinn Féin.'[13] Who was this boy? Who was the footballer? Were they attached to the undercover squad that the Free State set up in Cork city in the summer of 1922 in a direct imitation of the British undercover activities of a year earlier and which was very efficient at picking up IRA men, particularly on the south side?[14] Both, presumably, ended up in a bog somewhere. Seeing as Neenan was himself a well-known GAA personality, it is likely that he knew what he was talking about. What this suggests is that this story is even murkier than whatever reconstructions we can attempt to make from the sources available. Many IRA accounts, even those given under oath to the BMH, are a minefield of misinformation. All we can be sure of is that there will always be as many lies as truths.

Chapter 53 ❧

CLAIMS AND COUNTER-CLAIMS

The most controversial aspect of writing on this kind of material is the issue of collaboration with British forces. The term 'spy and informer' was used to good effect by the IRA as a description of espionage, but it was also used to frighten a whole population into silence. Yet spies and informers did exist, though the term was extended to cover anybody who helped the British war effort in a variety of ways. Yet there are grades of culpability. Is a British agent working undercover, infiltrating a flying column, the same as a Volunteer who is captured, gets the tar beaten out of him and as a result betrays his comrades? Is a loyalist who sees his friend, the local District Inspector of the RIC, about to be shot and picks up the phone to warn him the same as the petty thief who gives away his IRA comrades for monetary gain? For that matter, is the clergyman who views the IRA as a gang of murderers and feels honour bound to pass on any information he may have the same as a clergyman working as an agent gathering and collating information?

These are complex issues and while it would be easy to dodge them, some effort must be made to address this matter. It is simply not good enough, as some have done, to say that it is impossible to determine who was guilty of informing and who was not. British records, so it is said, are too fragmented and incomplete to make any stab at establishing if those whom the IRA shot as 'spies' were in fact guilty. This leaves us in the situation where, on the one hand, all those shot were simply loyalists—of whatever denomination—and were shot because of their loyalist/unionist views, all of whom were, by this definition, innocent of any wrong-doing.

And the opposite view is also held: that all those who were shot were shot because they were spies; that the IRA never shot anyone in the wrong; that all those Protestants, tramps and ex-soldiers executed supposedly as 'spies' were just that. Both these positions represent black and white views and are nothing more than the manipulation of history to suit particular political viewpoints. I call this the Alias Smith and Jones[1] theory of history. On the one hand, all IRA men were little more than a gang of murderous villains; on the other, IRA officers were the epitome of honour, men of flawless character, who were incapable of taking life needlessly, who fought bravely until dragged down 'into the mire' by British brutality.

The truth of course must lie somewhere in the middle. Some tramps, some Protestants, some ex-soldiers did give information. Others from these groups were shot though they were entirely innocent. Peter Hart is surely right in claiming that the biggest threat to IRA security came from within its own ranks or from the families of those within the ranks. But the issue here is the perceived paucity of information in British records that—so it is said—makes it impossible to establish who was guilty and who was shot out of convenience or out of revenge or from a combination of suspicion and the need to make a political point. (It could be argued, for instance, that many of those killed or otherwise targeted during the Civil War were picked on to advertise the fact that the IRA had no intention, as they saw it, of letting the situation slide back to the status quo that had pertained before the revolution.)

However, British records are not that fragmented. In fact, they tell us quite a lot about who might have been a 'spy' and who was not. In some cases they are definitive; in others we can get a pretty good idea as to who gave information and who was an innocent victim. For instance, the Record of the Rebellion in Ireland,[2] detailing the performance of the 6th Division in the Munster area, discusses two of those described in this book in some detail: Mrs McKay and Cruxy Connors. It also mentions a girl who had a relationship with a policeman in the Victoria Cross area of the city and who provided information that led to an arms find. Cruxy Connors' own brother told reporters in New York that he had 'revealed secrets of the Irish Army'.[3]

The British Army's intelligence report also has to be taken seriously. When it states that in February 1921 the IRA 'began a series of murders of persons whom they believed might have given information. In every case but one the person murdered had given no information', there is no reason not to take that statement at face value.[4] The intelligence officers who wrote it presumably knew what they were talking about. There was no need to invent such a statement in an otherwise detailed, reliable and indeed confidential report. The question is, which was the one case where, the report goes on, 'the murdered man was an agent known to be untrustworthy, but the terror created was such that all who had been giving information previously were silenced'. The guilty man could have been any of those killed during February 1922 both in Cork or elsewhere. Speculation as to who it might be is probably pointless—there is less than a one in ten chance of being right. As Colonel J. E. S. Brind, who commanded the intelligence staff at British Army HQ in Dublin, put it in June 1921: 'The murder of civilians shows no sign of abatement and the pretext that the victims are Government spies is, in most cases, purely fictitious.'[5]

This implies that the IRA, as Florrie O'Donoghue effectively stated, was terrorising the population into silence and that many of those killed were simply useful targets to get across the message of terror.

> Numbers of ex-soldiers and others have been murdered during the rebellion, not so much because they were ever discovered in active espionage—indeed, few of them had ever given information—but they met their deaths partly because there was a possibility that they might become informers and partly in order to keep alive the terrorism which it was considered important to impose. The outside public knew not whether or no the man who had been foully done to death was an agent or not. By the customary notice pinned to his back, it was informed that he was, and, when cases of this kind were numerous, the layman concluded that the rebel organization had almost miraculous facilities for tracing a betrayer.[6]

This at least is what the top brass believed and in many cases it is undoubtedly true. However, there is another source we can turn to in an attempt to distinguish between the hapless victim and the putative 'informer' and, while it is by no means foolproof, it can give us some indication at least as to how the families of such victims felt and where they stood.

This is the register of compensation cases for personal injuries heard by the Compensation (Ireland) Commission, which we have seen earlier and which was set up in 1922 by the governments of the UK and the Irish Free State to compensate civilian victims of the conflict.[7] In this, the cases are divided into categories depending on who was to be responsible for paying out compensation. Some cases are clear cut. For instance, civilians shot down by British troops are clearly a case of British liability. Similarly civilians shot by the IRA should, one would expect, result in Irish liability, and indeed many of them do. In cases where there was a doubt as to responsibility, both sides were prepared to accept 50:50 liability. The most interesting cases, however, are those where the victim was clearly killed by the IRA, yet the family accepted British liability. What this means, in effect, is that the family believed the victim had been shot because he had been helping the British in some way. In other words, that it was because of loyalty to Britain that he or she was killed. (There is a possibility that some families may have accepted British liability in the hope that they would receive higher compensation from the Treasury than from the Free State. However, there is no evidence from the amounts handed out that this was ever going to be the case. There is also the possibility that some, particularly the families of ex-soldiers, claimed British liability because those killed were ex-soldiers and for no other reason, the logic being that Britain was liable because of who they were, not because of what they did.)

This of course is not the same as admitting that the person was actually a spy or an informer. What it does suggest, though, is that the family was aware that he or she was probably killed for helping British forces. And there is a further category: where the person is described as a 'British Supporter'—clearly a euphemism for loyalist, though not necessarily stating that they actually gave information. This classification was backed up by the police. 'Generally in the cases where the details of the outrage did not in themselves imply active support for the Crown Forces, a certificate of loyalty by the police was held as sufficient to justify payment and many such payments were made.'[8]

So how do the figures pan out in the various theatres of this vicious little war? Well, of the 19 killings of 'spies and informers' in west Cork, ten describe the victim as either a British supporter or as accepting British liability. In north and east Cork, of the ten IRA victims who sought compensation through the committee, six claimed British liability. In the city, of the families of the 22 victims who put in claims, only seven claimed British liability and two of these were military employees and would have got British liability anyway, while two others are described as British supporters. This supports the statements from the British intelligence community that only one of those shot in February 1921 was an actual agent. None of the February victims in the city claimed British liability; nor did the Blemens family, suggesting that James and Fred Blemens, and indeed James Beal, were not active spies.[9] Indeed, of the Protestants shot in the city, only George Horgan and Major O'Connor—'definitely a loyalist'—accepted British liability. Of those shot in the High Street area, only George Horgan fits into this category. (Those who claimed British liability in the city and environs were John Sherlock, Edward Hawkins, Major O'Connor, Christy Sullivan, George Horgan, David Nagle and Denis O'Donovan. John Hawkes is listed as a British Supporter. Those whose families received compensation with Irish or 50:50 liability were Alfred Reilly, James Beal, M. F. O'Sullivan, William Sullivan, John Sullivan Lynch, Patrick Ray, Tom Downing, P. J. Poland, James and Fred Blemens, John O'Callaghan, John Begley and Michael Walsh.)

Taken all together, from all parts of the county, the figures suggest that around 50 per cent of those killed may have been helping the British in some way. In the city, however, this drops to under one-third. IRA intelligence seems to have been more accurate in rural areas than in the city. This no doubt reflects the atmosphere of suspicion that existed in the urban environment, combined with the ruthlessness of the city battalions, particularly in the south city area. It also reflects the fact that in the city the British forces had been more successful than in rural areas. One possible explanation for the high level of killing of so-called 'spies' in the city might be the need to find scapegoats for British successes. These figures add to the 'shoot first and ask questions afterwards' reputation of the 2nd Battalion of the city IRA.

As Florrie O'Donoghue put it: 'We put some of them out of action for their proved guilt, as a stern warning to others and to let their paymasters know that we were aware of their activities.'[10] Clearly this implies that men were shot as a 'warning to others'. The question is what exactly constituted 'proved guilt', especially in the case of people gunned down in the street or those from whom dubious confessions were extracted under torture.

However, there may be another explanation. It is difficult to reconcile the ruthless campaign against suspected 'spies and informers' in the city, over 60 per cent of whom were likely to be innocent, with the often-stated belief of Florrie O'Donoghue that all those shot as spies had been proven guilty. In his writings O'Donoghue comes across as being both fair minded and astute. Yet there are substantial omissions in his records—the campaign in the city during 1921, when he was *de facto* in command is notable by its absence. Then we have his letter to HQ of June 1921 when he claims that all those shot as spies were guilty.

Was this simply a case of terrorising the population into silence—a strategy that appeared to work? Or was there another factor in this? As we have seen, there are grounds for suspicion that British military intelligence may have wanted to get rid of Tom Downing, suspecting him of being an IRA spy, although he was an army employee. Christy Sullivan may be another instance of this. Sullivan had been working as a civilian employee with military transport. When it was discovered in the spring of 1921 that he had been working as an IRA spy in Victoria Barracks, he lost his job.[11] Six weeks later he was found dead in the western suburbs with an IRA notice 'spy' attached. Why was he (apparently) killed by the IRA when he had been an IRA spy?

Is it possible that at least some of those shot as spies by the IRA in the city in the spring of 1921 had their names quietly slipped to the IRA by British military intelligence? If so, what would the British have gained by this? Was it simply a means of protecting the identity of those who were the real agents in the city?

Pat Margetts, one of the IRA's informants in Victoria Barracks, warned Seán O'Hegarty that there was significant leakage of information from within the IRA ranks to the British military authorities and that they knew an awful lot more about IRA activities than the IRA realised.[12] 'It would have been better for him and his command if he looked more closely at his own men, for they needed looking and some of them were giving information as well as Connors.' O'Hegarty ignored him and refused to believe that his own men might have been anything less than totally dedicated to the cause. In fact O'Hegarty was more inclined to shoot the messenger, and Margetts himself came under suspicion by O'Hegarty. It is entirely possible that Percival and Kelly were passing on false information to the IRA. They would certainly not be above passing on the names of those they might have been suspicious of themselves—William Sullivan, for instance, had a brother in the IRA—Cork ex-soldiers of dubious loyalty were as expendable to the British as they were to the IRA.

However, just taking the figures for the city alone, those who applied to the Compensation (Ireland) Commission account for only around half of those killed. The rest were probably those families who were either unaware that such compensation avenues were available or for whom the prospect of financial remuneration was not worth the pain of revisiting the period when their lost ones were either killed or disappeared. And no British source can help us when it comes to the culpability or otherwise of those shot after the Truce and in the post-Treaty and Civil War periods—many of whose identity we don't know anyway. However, seeing as most of these killings were carried out by members of the south city battalion, it is fair to assume the latter were as accurate in their suspicions of guilt after the Truce as they had been before it. Thus the Freemasons shot by Mick Murphy's men were shot in all probability because their names appeared in Beal's address book and the YMCA men were shot on the basis of a dubious confession extracted from a 15-year-old. We also have the not unexpected scenario that most of those responsible for actually passing on information on the IRA had fled in fear of their lives, particularly in the spring of 1921. People like John Willis and William McNeill cleared out and never came back. There were others like them. This would suggest that the most serious informers had left, if only on the basis that they knew that sooner or later the IRA would come looking for them. There is evidence that several YMCA members departed from Cork in the autumn of 1921, suggesting that those who remained, and this may include some of the businessmen taken in March 1922, did not consider themselves at risk. It was not as if they could not afford to leave: these were very well-off men and could start up again with little difficulty in Canada or Australia. 'The fact that they sacrificed their lives to their slave masters was something they, apparently, had never thought nor expected to do.'[13] Given the terror under which many Protestants lived, they would have been extremely foolhardy to have remained on in Cork had they been active spies. The sudden departure of what look like the real British agents in Cork—who appear to have been neither Protestants nor natives of Cork—in early April 1922 in the wake of the St Patrick's Day abductions suggests that the IRA was once again looking for the wrong people in the wrong place.[14]

It is also possible that some were shot in the post-Truce and post-Treaty periods in order to prevent awkward questions being asked about neighbours and friends who had disappeared during the earlier conflict. William Cooke, for instance, according to his wife, never lost a night's sleep in the months before his death, though at least six of his fellow merchants had disappeared some months earlier. He may have been a spy; he may have provided facilities for ex-soldiers to drop off pieces of information. He may have been killed because he was Grand Master of the Munster Freemasons and a member of the YMCA, in other words a figurehead of two organisations that the IRA was targeting. But it is no coincidence that he too lived almost next door to Josephine Marchment Brown and (by then) Florrie O'Donoghue.

Henry A. Harris may have been killed because he had run a spy ring out of the YMCA or perhaps because he was a British presence during peace feelers. But it was far more likely he was killed simply because he had been head of the YMCA during the conflict and that the IRA got his name from Parsons.

The inoffensive William Goff Beale was almost certainly killed because he was known to be a senior committee member of the YMCA. And he had the wrong surname. You could be shot because of who you were just as much as because of what you did. But you could also be killed because of where you lived.

PART X

Chapter 54 ～

'PREPARE FOR EXECUTION'[1]

It is perhaps appropriate that this story should end up where it began, with a series of unmarked graves. This book was almost finished when I chanced upon an elderly Cork city man who had a lifelong interest in the War of Independence and who knew, or so I was told, where at least some of the bodies were buried. He lived right in the heart of the area where many of the events described in this book took place and had a vast knowledge of the history of the south side of the city.

His father had been a Volunteer, a lifelong republican who had worked for a prominent Protestant firm in the city with the result that he also had a great affection for the Cork Protestant community. This 89-year-old man confirmed much of what I have already described in this book. His stories were remarkably similar to those I had heard in east Cork: body parts turning up under the plough in fields along the Tramore Road, a lane on the high ground near Cork Airport that was said to be haunted by the ghost of a dead RIC man. But the first really useful piece of information was that the Carroll's Bogs referred to by Mick Murphy was not part of the Rea east of Knockraha—though bodies were buried there too—but was rather the area immediately south of the city and west of Douglas village which is now the Cork municipal dump on the Kinsale Road. This was immediately adjacent to what Florrie O'Donoghue grandly referred to as the brigade billets at Vernon Mount where the list taken from Beal was hidden to avoid detection during a British Army raid. If the Blemenses and the 'Anti-Sinn Féin League spies', that is to say the Freemasons shot by the 2nd Battalion, are buried in this Carroll's Bogs rather than in the other one, this means that the Cork municipal dump is in effect a mass grave with well over 20 individuals—and these are only the ones we know about—buried there.

Yet my man had never heard of the YMCA *per se*, nor of any 'spies' allegedly operating out of it, though he knew a lot of what had happened on the south side. He knew about the shooting of Sergeant Gloster for instance who, he said, was believed locally to have been shot in the wrong. He was also able to list the names of many RIC men who tipped off the IRA when raids were due. But most importantly, despite having never heard of the YMCA, he was able to provide new details that helped make some sense of the puzzle that was the IRA's interaction with Protestant teenagers during 1921 and thereafter.

For it was when I asked him about secret burial spots that he began to recall what older people had told him about the fate of some Protestant youngsters in the High Street area. One night a friend of his remembered hearing a boy pleading for his life in the lime quarry at the foot of Windmill Road. The boy was trying to tell his interrogators that he had not tried to warn 'the two above'. It was said locally that the boy, who was a local Protestant of about 15, was executed and his body buried in the quarry. His family were said to have departed for England soon afterwards. As for the 'two above', one of them disappeared and was never seen again, while the other managed to escape to America. Many years later this man returned to Cork and tried to find out what had happened to the other two, apparently to no avail.

This quarry—it is now Capwell bus depot—is just a hundred yards down the road from High Street. This episode almost certainly refers to the case of Parsons and the Roycrofts and, if correct, it suggests that the IRA's prime target was William Roycroft Jnr, who did manage to escape, albeit to Canada rather than the US. It also suggests that Parsons was caught because he had warned Roycroft that the IRA was on his trail. Roycroft was only one in a long line of suspect 'spies' targeted in the area which also housed at least a dozen RIC men in commandeered houses. George Horgan, Finbarr O'Sullivan, Michael O'Brien (alias Ahern), Edward Parsons and William and Thomas Roycroft all lived within a hundred yards of each other, while William Sullivan was just around the corner on the South Douglas Road. These were all shot because the IRA believed, whether rightly or wrongly, that they were associated with this group of (probably undercover) RIC men.[2]

Were Parsons and the Roycrofts among the boys who confessed their trackings and then were killed'? Whatever the case, this is the right area and the right number; they were friends, even if one managed to escape. Except of course, this happened in 1922, not 1921.

It also sheds light on what happened to Parsons after he was snatched. The men who caught him brought him down the road to the quarry, interrogated him, probably with force, before moving him to Corry's for further interrogation. The implication is clear enough: the IRA had wanted to get their hands on the Roycrofts. William Roycroft is warned and manages to escape, but they get his brother instead, whom they shoot and bury. Then Parsons is blamed for warning his friends, so he too is caught and shot and buried, but not before a dubious confession is extracted from him concerning the YMCA. William Roycroft returned years later to try to find the body of his brother and the boy who saved his life. He had two sisters married in Cork who remained there for many years afterwards. It would have been easy enough to come back after the Civil War to try to get some closure. In this, it seems, he failed.

But the story was never going to be that simple and it is the cell-like structure of the urban IRA during the War of Independence that makes it so hard to separate truth from lies. Different groups in different parts of the city were often operating independently of one another and pursuing their own wars with only a handful having the big picture. Also many of the gunmen operating in the city, in contrast to the local Volunteers who acted as scouts and dispatch carriers, were from rural areas, often from other parts of the country. Men from Tipperary, Kerry, Offaly, Galway, even Dublin, spent some time serving in Cork.

It quickly became apparent that the High Street boys were not the only trio of Protestant youngsters targeted on the south side of Cork city, for my man was able to point out to me where three other boys were shot and buried. The story, told to him by a Volunteer who waited until all connected to the event were themselves dead, was that three other Protestant youths were executed in the corner of a field at the foot of Grange Road near what is now the Touchdown roundabout, not far from the aforementioned Carroll's Bogs. According to him, the three kids—'they talked, you see'—were taken into the field by just one man and executed there and their bodies buried. These would appear to have been the 'three cases of chicken broth' killed in the summer of 1921 reported by the British Army to HQ.

During May and June 1921 the south city IRA had a dugout or some kind of hidden billet near the shrubbery of Frankfield House off Grange Road. They had been forced out of the nearby Vernon Mount in February when the British Army raided and subsequently burned down the lodge there which they had long used as a base and where O'Hegarty and O'Donoghue had been seen heading when they were spotted by Major O'Connor.[3] Now they moved up the hill to the woods surrounding Frankfield House.

Frankfield House, now Frankfield Golf Club, was an ideal vantage-point from a military point of view and was to be used on and off until the end of the Civil War when it was finally burnt out. High over the city, it offers a panoramic view of all the approach roads, both from the city itself, from Kinsale to the south and from Ballincollig to the west. It was the perfect hiding place from which to run operations in the city. Sherrard Ronayne, who lived in Frankfield House and ran the Norwich Union office in Cork, had been driven out in May. His wife gave a detailed and colourful account of the intimidation she suffered. Her letter is worth quoting in full.[4]

At the time the trouble began [3 May 1921], a very respectable man called one night to see my husband, talking on behalf of the IRA, demanding rates. My husband told him he would not and could not conscientiously give it and after some talk the IRA asked him if he was prepared to take the consequences. My husband, all honour to him, replied 'I am.' Two or three weeks passed by and one night after 11 o'clock I and my little boy and the maid were in the house alone as my husband was in Waterford all week and would not be back till next day, Saturday. We heard the knock, known and dreaded at that time in Ireland, at the hall door.

The maid, with a face as white as a sheet, came in to me and asked me what she was going to do. I told her to open the hall door wide and answer all their questions and call me. There were two men outside; one of them was hung [sic] since for the murder of Sir Henry Wilson in London.[5] She told him the master was not at home and then she called me. I knew well they might shoot me instead, if they found he was not at home. So I told the maid to keep the child in the parlour till I came back to them.

It was a clear moonlit night and I walked right out the hall door onto the gravel. One man, who evidently came to do the deed, was an awful-looking fellow; the other man was better. He asked me if Mr Ronayne was at home and I replied 'No, but he always comes home on Saturdays.' But I said, laughing, 'I will not promise that he will come home next Saturday.' Then he asked me again if I was sure he was not in the house. I replied they could look if they liked but that, as I was his wife, I ought to know. Then I asked them if I would not do as well and after a few words about that I said: 'Tell me at least what you want him for.' He opened his coat and putting his hand on a revolver looked into my face and said: 'That's a matter between him and me and can be settled in a few minutes.' 'Oh well' I said, laughing, 'I can do no more. Good night.' He lifted his hat and I walked into the house.

The maid and I then went around the house and barred and bolted all the windows and doors. When that was done I called her into the parlour and said to her: 'Now, Mary, I must tell you, we are in great danger; we must stay up all night; we are cut off from all help until morning.' She was an R.C. but she knelt with me as I commended our souls to God's care.

But as the night went on I began to lose courage and longed for someone with us in the house. So at last I decided I would run across the lawn which was a good distance from the house and in full view of the avenue where I knew a lot of these men were hiding. I wanted to get down to the lodge and bring our man up to stay with us. I caught up an overcoat of my husband's and put it on, telling Mary to lock the door after me and open it quickly when I came back, DV. I went out. The night was clear as day. I had no fear. I was no coward—I say that to show how God saved me—and was just about to leave the shadow of the house and come into full view of the avenue when a sudden peculiar fear came over me and I turned and ran back and got in the door. I know it was God put His hand between me and death. For had I gone out into the moonlight with that coat on, they would have been sure it was my husband and I would not be alive to [live ?] with this.

Morning came at last and without having tasted anything since they came the night before I drove into town to a friend's house and he wired to Waterford to stop my husband coming home but found he had left for home earlier and was then in the train. This friend hid us in his house for a few days till we could get away to England. And while waiting there three days I stole out of the house and walked by the back roads out to our house to say goodbye to it. When I was crossing the lawn, my dog bounded down to meet me, barking furiously and at once three shots in succession were fired over my head. We got off to England at last and had to remain there for 2 years and 3 months during which time our furniture and cattle were sold for little or nothing. When at last we thought we could come home again in safety our home of course was gone and my husband's business completely shattered.[6]

Sherrard Ronayne was lucky he did not return to Frankfield that night. It is clear that the IRA was prepared to shoot him and label him a spy for not having made a donation to republican funds, though the real reason would appear to be that they wanted the family to clear out.

Not so lucky, however, was Michael Harrington, a farmer's labourer who lived across the road in Ballycurreen. Harrington had encountered the work of the IRA before, for he was 'the herdsman', as Mick Murphy called him, who in February 1920 came upon the body of Quinlisk on the farm of Thomas Good in Ballyphehane where he worked. Good ordered Harrington to report the body to the RIC at Blackrock Road. This he did, probably thinking at the time—after all, Quinlisk was the first civilian death of the conflict in Cork—that there was no good reason for not reporting the body. This was carried in the newspapers and Harrington became a marked man.[7] However, it was his proximity to the Frankfield hideout that was a bigger factor in attracting the IRA than the fact that he had reported Quinlisk's body. In any case, he disappeared on 29 June 1921, less than two weeks before the Truce.[8] And he may not have been the only one.[9]

What links all these events is the mind-set of the men hiding in the Frankfield area. Most of the IRA units had been driven out of the city by this time, many safe houses had been raided and scores of city IRA men were in jail. As the British Army intelligence report stated, the IRA was effectively defeated in the city and its most active units had moved into the countryside, even if it could still carry off some operations in the city. At the end of April 1921 Macready was able to report: 'This Battalion which supplied most of the "murder gang" has suffered very heavy casualties during the past month and is at present completely disorganised.'[10] The men at Frankfield were desperate men who would kill anybody who posed even the slightest threat. This is the likely context in which three Protestant boys, who had been captured for whatever reason, found themselves. Perhaps they had been 'talking'; perhaps they had been scouting and had just stumbled on the men in the woods.[11]

Then my elderly informant told me that down the hill from the entrance to Frankfield Golf club, I would find a small clump of trees. The three Protestant boys, he said, are buried there and the ground has never been disturbed. After parking my car, it took just five minutes to find it. There it was, a clump of three trees. By my guess, the trees were some 30 to 40 years old, suggesting that someone may have returned in the 1960s or 70s and planted them to mark the spot. Were these the boys whom Connie Neenan said were killed around the time of the Truce? These boys were either picked up near by or were taken with the YMCA touring car that was stolen from the Cork quays on the morning of the Truce. We have to treat Neenan's claim that they confessed their trackings with a certain amount of scepticism on the basis that the overall evidence suggests that the YMCA was not recognised as a 'spy centre' until sometime afterwards. None the less, there is a reasonable possibility that these three had either been scouting or 'talking'.

They were executed, apparently, by one man, who simply took them over the ditch and shot them and buried their bodies. While there is no evidence that they were killed by Neenan personally, he probably ordered it as he was the O/C in the area at the time. Neenan goes to considerable lengths to leave it in the public record that he spent the day of the Truce searching Togher for the four young soldiers who had been taken on College Road the previous evening, and the following day sleeping off the exertions of having been out all night. There is no reason to doubt him. But just as in the Togher case, there were several practised killers in the 2nd Battalion who were more than capable of carrying out such an execution, though many Volunteers would probably have been uncomfortable with it.[12] Mrs Ronayne's account above gives a good picture of the kind of men who were hiding there. If it was done behind Neenan's back, the likelihood is that he would have been told that a confession had been extracted from the boys.[13] According to Neenan, this was just before the Truce. But if they were captured along with the YMCA car on the Cork quays on the morning of the Truce—and remember this is the only link we have that directly connects the Truce to the YMCA—their killing took place afterwards and the case for claiming they were spies is nil.

And there is another possibility. Frankfield House had been occupied up to 1920 by Dr A. W. Sandford, a well-known ophthalmologist and founder of the Cork Eye, Ear and Throat Hospital. Sandford was District Commissioner of the Cork Boy Scouts.[14] It is entirely possible that the three boys had gone on a scouting expedition with the advent of the Truce and had, wittingly or unwittingly, stumbled on the IRA encampment in their old haunts. Either way, they 'confessed their trackings and they were killed' and may have set in motion a whole witch hunt fuelled by suspicion and paranoia that led to dozens of deaths.

Chapter 55 ❦

| ON ACTIVE SERVICE

On 12 May 1921, Florrie O'Donoghue wrote from west Cork to Josephine, his new bride whom he had married a month earlier. O'Donoghue was on a four-month tour of duty of Munster as part of his new role as Adjutant of the 1st Southern Division of the IRA. He was in good form. The weather, he said, was 'gloriously fine and bracing'. These letters are vivid, colourful and well written. 'On every roadside primroses and violets made a riot of delicate colour along the green and mossy banks.'[1]

But like a lot of O'Donoghue's writings and correspondence, they conceal almost as much as they reveal. We have debated whether O'Donoghue actually knew anything about the YMCA business or whether it was all carried out behind his back by members of the southside battalion of the city IRA. We have seen nothing at all to connect O'Donoghue to these abductions. But the sanctimonious tone adopted throughout his papers belies a far more cunning and devious mind than you would guess from reading of his concern for, and understanding of, British officers and his self-proclaimed inability to hate the English. In fact, O'Donoghue may have been a lot more intimate with the YMCA business than he let on.

For one of the things we have not been able to establish is who was 'somebody's child', that mysterious youngster the *Times* reporter noticed being abducted along the Blackrock Road in May 1921. The *Times* article stated that the boy, assuming it was a boy, was playing on a piece of open ground at the city end of the Blackrock Road and that the car in which he was taken drove off in the 'direction of the town'.[2] This could be interpreted as meaning the car drove off into the city or that it headed off in the direction of Blackrock. If the 'mysterious individual' who drove the car was a British intelligence operative and if 'somebody's child' was an IRA captive, then it would make sense for the car to make for the city. If, on the other hand, the car was an IRA commandeered car and 'somebody's child' was captured by the IRA, then the town in question would be Blackrock, away from the roadblocks that festooned Cork city. Would the British military have gone to that much trouble to capture a child? It is extremely unlikely.

The most extensive piece of open ground at the time lay directly to the north of the Old Blackrock Road, between the gasworks and the rear of the Park View row of houses on Victoria Road (see Map 2). This was at the time a wide area of almost 20 acres consisting largely of waste ground and would have made an ideal place for teenagers to hang out. It was also directly behind Josephine Marchment Brown's house in Rockboro Terrace.[3]

Despite having the names of those who left the YMCA in 1921 and again in 1922 (see Appendix IX and Appendix X), I am not in a position to identify who was taken on the Blackroad Road in May 1921. In fact, we don't even know if the child (or children) was even a Protestant, let alone a member of the YMCA. All we can say is that the IRA went to some lengths to cover it up, even to the extent of dumping the copies of the *Times* which reported on the matter into the river after they arrived in Cork.[4]

While the identity of 'somebody's child' is unknown, it is easier to pin down the date on which the abduction took place—because of a claim for compensation put in by Robert H. Parker to the Compensation (Ireland) Committee for an injury sustained on 12 May 1921.[5] For Robert Parker, a well-known Cork builders providers merchant, lived adjacent to the stretch of waste ground on which the abduction took place. In fact, to leave the open field, a car would have to drive through the narrow lane right by Parker's house, Elm Park, and also past William Cooke's house and out on to the Blackrock Road. (The beginning of the laneway can be seen at the lower left-hand corner of the picture of the Blemens house.) If anyone were to witness these events, the most likely person would have been Robert Parker or members of his family.[6] Even the weather, so poetically described at the beginning of this chapter by Florrie O'Donoghue writing from Kerry, is similar to that described by the *Times* reporter in Cork. If this is correct, then 'somebody's child' was picked up on 12 May 1921.

What this means is that at least one abduction of a minor took place in the vicinity of the house of Josephine O'Donoghue, as she was now—she and Florrie having got married in early April. This was also where the abduction of the Blemenses took place in November 1920—also the work of mysterious individuals in a motor car, the alleged disappearance of three Protestant merchants in July 1922 and the shooting of William Cooke in September 1922. Yet Florrie O'Donoghue was away in Kerry in May 1921, so he could not have been involved directly in the abduction. Neither could Mick Murphy, who was by this time serving with the brigade column in mid-Cork. Yet the whole thing seems to follow the same sickening trajectory that we saw in the case of the Blemenses.

First of all, it happened while O'Donoghue was away—he had gone for several months as part of his new role as Adjutant of the 1st Southern Division and was writing back to Josephine almost every day.[7] The reader will recall that James and Fred Blemens were lifted on 29 November 1920 and shot a few days later, again while O'Donoghue was away, this time in Liverpool, London and Cardiff, organising the springing of Reggie Brown. The Blemenses were lifted by Mick Murphy and his men on information received 'from a Mrs Brown who lived next door'.[8] So there is no question that it was Josephine who provided the information in the case of the Blemenses.

Now some six months later, a few weeks after O'Donoghue departs, this time for mid-Cork and Kerry, we have another near-neighbour, 'somebody's child', lifted from the field where local kids play, and which is over the wall of Josephine's back garden. And other boys may have been lifted too.[9] It is extremely unlikely that Josephine did not have some part in these operations, if only, as in the case of the Blemenses, by providing the information that led to the kidnapping(s). Was she 'the mysterious individual in a motor car' who was involved in the actual abduction? The use of the word 'individual' rather than 'man' is itself interesting.

There might be a simple reason for the abduction. On 7 May the military reported that they had made a series of arrests in the area the previous evening. Four suspects were arrested at an unnamed address on Old Blackrock Road, another in Ballinlough and three more at Fitzgerald's Place, also on the Old Blackrock Road. It is clear that these raids were well co-ordinated: there were no shoot-outs and the men were simply rounded up. If the men captured were IRA men, and they presumably were, then the army seems to have been working on good information. This was just one of a series of raids by the military in the Blackrock area in April and May.[10] Clearly the RIC and the military were working on good intelligence. Did the local IRA believe these men had been given away by some neighbouring kids? Did this constitute some sort of 'spy ring'? Did the local kids identify the houses to the raiders?

One possible scenario is that a few days after the raids a boy is picked up, driven away to Blackrock and executed and buried, like George Horgan, in Lakelands. Except that Lakelands had been burnt down on 9 April by the military since it had been known to the RIC for some time as a 'Sinn Féin prison' and was no longer available as such.[11] According to the RIC, 'the Sinn Féiners were very incensed that one of their strongholds was found out and set on fire', and they in turn burnt out a local Protestant, C. J. Young's home, as a reprisal.[12]

It is clear that during those weeks O'Donoghue was very worried about Josephine because he had not heard from her for some time and expressed his concern in his letters.[13] O'Donoghue's preoccupations during those months, as is clear from his correspondence, are almost entirely concerned with his efforts to organise the newly formed divisional structure of the IRA. This is also something of a one-sided conversation as O'Donoghue chose to release only his own letters among his papers (Josephine's replies are not included). There is very little from this one-sided correspondence to suggest that dramatic happenings might be taking place near Rockboro Terrace in

O'Donoghue's absence. There are, however, one or two hints, and if what they suggest is correct, then they cast a new and extraordinary light on the matter.

In his letter of 17 June, written from west Cork a month after these events, O'Donoghue makes one cryptic reference to matters in the city: 'Well, to return to more personal matters again, some friends from Cork were here today and told me that you were, so to say, on active service one day a while ago. But there was nothing doing apparently.' O'Donoghue goes on to chide her: 'Only that I feel you are so well able to take care of yourself, I would be tempted to indulge in a lecture. You'll be careful, won't you?'[14]

This, of course, could be interpreted to mean anything. For instance, it could mean that she was back to her role of bringing information out of the barracks. But she was bringing information out anyway. Moreover, both she and O'Donoghue always maintained that nobody in the Cork Volunteers knew about her role in the barracks. Indeed, Mick Murphy's account of the Blemenses kidnapping supports this: Josephine is described as 'a Mrs Brown who lived next door' to the Blemenses, not as Florrie O'Donoghue's partner. So seeing as the information came through a third party, 'some friends from Cork', almost certainly IRA men, it can only mean what it appears to mean, that 'active service' refers to an active role in IRA operations. The reference to 'nothing doing' suggests that whatever operation she was involved in on that particular day did not come off.

Three days later, on 20 June, O'Donoghue makes another rather odd statement. Given that 90 per cent of the contents of O'Donoghue's letters concern military matters, it is strange to see him referring to something that appears on the face of it to be completely unrelated to things military: 'By the way, I have just seen in the paper that there was a boating accident in Cork on Sunday, and that there was a youngster in it. I am wondering if it was your party. Ye seem to have a pretty taste in accidents of that kind. Glad to see, however, that nothing worse than a ducking befell anybody.'[15] This may be merely a flippant comment. However, considering that we have already speculated that boys may have been taken and thrown into the sea along with YMCA provisions during raids on the harbour in mid-June, and also that Harris may later have been drowned in Boulogne, this is a striking coincidence.[16] Also, its tone is identical to the sort of gallows humour that passed between Martin Corry and his wife when they discussed such matters and indeed the sort of 'fun' exemplified by members of the 2nd Battalion when they staged mock executions for the camera (see photo).[17] With Lakelands now out of bounds as a holding facility, was the boy (or boys) taken across the river to Corry's or simply drowned in the harbour?

Considering that Josephine O'Donoghue regarded herself as an intelligence officer within the IRA, the implication of these statements is clear: that she was involved in operations over and above her role as provider of information from Victoria Barracks and that at least some of these operations may have involved the hunting down and capture of kids in the Blackrock Road area and/or around Cork Harbour. She was also able to drive and was a keen sailor. This puts a rather new slant to O'Donoghue's note to Mulcahy written during these weeks where he tries to scotch the suggestion: 'I think GHQ has somehow got the idea that in the Cork Brigades and especially in Cork No. 1, men are being shot as spies more or less on suspicion.' O'Donoghue's denials are absolute: 'Instead of this, as I am aware myself, the greatest care is taken in every instance to have the case fully proved and beyond all doubt. As a matter of fact, the men shot have in most cases admitted their guilt before being executed.'[18] Apart from the fact that men shot dead in the street have little chance to 'admit their guilt before being executed', teenagers picked up and beaten will admit to almost anything to avoid being shot.

If this is correct it is likely to have been the work of a small, tightly organised group, probably consisting of no more than two or three individuals. Did Josephine, with her love of sailing, lead some of the raiding parties that intercepted YMCA provisions as they sailed down the harbour to the British naval base in Haulbowline? Was something other than cases of Doubleday cakes taken or thrown overboard? We have no direct evidence for it other than these cryptic statements from O'Donoghue and the fact that he is otherwise silent on all matters relating to the execution of juveniles by the IRA. It is clear, however, that this was kept a secret even from most within the IRA—Mick Murphy was so surprised a year later at Parsons' confession that he wanted to bomb the YMCA, only to be ordered not to do so by O'Hegarty. As Sandow Donovan put it many years later: 'The O'Donoghues were, and I suppose still are, the most secretive family ever born.'[19]

Were these the half-dozen or so members of the YMCA whom Corry claimed were executed and buried on his land? It is possible that this was the case and that the Parsons' confession, which was extracted a year later, was added on retrospectively to justify the killings. Yet the belief in the Corry household was that Corry did not return home until three days after the Truce, his home having been the target of constant raiding during the conflict. If they were killed by Corry, it is more likely they were held in Sing Sing and executed and buried in the bogs of Knockraha. Does O'Donoghue's reference to the near-drowning of a teenager in the *Cork Examiner* report imply that they were simply drowned in the harbour?[20] His letters suggest that he was only too well aware of it; but the reference to 'your party' suggests that this was his wife's work.

At the general committee meeting of 18 May the general secretary of the YMCA stated that the summer camp, which had been held for many years at Crosshaven, was cancelled for 1921 'owing to the very distressed state of the country'. This was also the week when the Boy Scouts hall near Riverstown was raided. Was there a connection between these events and 'somebody's child'?[21] The British Army reported that week that the Riverstown area was being 'plundered by members of the IRA. The residents are not reporting these events.'[22]

There is another possibility: that some boys were taken and held as hostages against the British executions of IRA men that were pending during those weeks, the last of which occurred on 16 May. Connie Neenan stated that four ex-soldiers were held and executed and their bodies buried as reprisals for the execution in February of a number of IRA men. Mrs Lindsay and Major Compton-Smith were similarly shot after executions in April. Was the same strategy tried again? Did O'Donoghue and O'Hegarty decide to up the ante by this time taking Protestant teenagers as hostages? O'Donoghue stated in *No Other Law* in connection with these weeks that 'it was recommended that this counter reprisal offensive should be sufficiently heavy and persistent either to put an end to British reprisals or clear the country of its active resident civilian enemies'. The British military, and presumably the YMCA, had their own view on the matter, at least initially. In his Weekly Survey of 9 May 1921, the Chief Secretary reported that 'in order to increase their numerical fighting strength in some districts they [the rebels] are known to have resorted to the conscription of youths of sixteen years of age or upwards'.[23] On 13 May the issue of organised attacks on the 'person and properties of Nonconformists' even came up in the Commons.[24] The other place I am aware of where the term 'conscription' was used in connection with the IRA was with the forced enrolment of Protestant young men in the IRA in west Cork in the latter half of 1921. The IRA never had to conscript anyone and certainly not youths, considering they already had Na Fianna acting as scouts and dispatch carriers. As O'Donoghue put it at the time: 'we have more men than we can possibly utilize.' This reference is most likely to be to Protestant youths. A decision had been taken on 29 April, after the previous British execution of IRA prisoners, to carry out general shooting of all British forces as reprisals. Did this include Boy Scouts or YMCA members 'of 16 or upwards'? By the end of the following week, after the executions had taken place at Cork Detention Barracks, things seem to have been clarified from the military's point of view, for the Chief Secretary in the text of his Weekly Survey of 16 May stated that 17 civilians had died as a result of violence over the weekend.[25] Yet only ten of these can be found in the newspapers and in RIC records. The connection to Cork Harbour is reinforced by the fact that the military and Admiralty forbade the sailing of civilian boats within the harbour on the same day.[26] This was also the day that Dan O'Brien, the last IRA man to be officially executed by the British, was put to death at Cork Jail.

Since the publication of the first edition of *The Year of Disappearances*, I have been contacted by several families who had a member disappeared in Cork city or the surrounding area during those years. One of them was the family of a Protestant youth, one of those listed as having 'left' the YMCA in 1921 (see Appendix x). This young man, though from the Ballinlough area, was abducted while camping in Crosshaven. He was never seen again. This must have been before 18 May 1921 since the YMCA banned its members from camping in Crosshaven from that date. In fact it is likely that this abduction was the reason for the YMCA's cancellation of its summer camp at Crosshaven. And it is highly unlikely that he was camping on his own. So there is no question that Protestant youths 'of 16 and upwards' were disappearing on the south side of Cork city during those weeks.

Interestingly, Florrie O'Donoghue published General Strickland's Weekly Intelligence Survey of the British Army's 6th Division for the week of 17/5/1921 as an appendix in *No Other Law*. Like a lot of O'Donoghue's records, this one is useful as much for what it leaves out as for what it puts in. Although the abstract states that 'the long expected rebel offensive took place on Saturday', there are no details of the actual offensive itself.[27] Similarly, there is little reference in it to matters that occurred in the city or the harbour over the weekend; the activities of the 1st and 2nd battalions are not mentioned at all, though those of the 4th and 5th battalions and the rest of the brigades are reported. All this is very odd because over the weekend of 14/15 May three RIC men were blown up in Blackpool, an attempt was made to rescue prisoners from Cork Jail, three Volunteers were shot dead in Carrigtwohill and Fr O'Callaghan and Pat Sheehan were murdered in the city. Yet, apart from the three Blackpool RIC men being mentioned in the statistics, there is no reference to any of these actions in this version of the Weekly Survey. Also missing is the civilian casualty list, despite the fact that in Fr O'Callaghan and Winnie Barrington in County Tipperary, Strickland had two of the most high profile civilians to die in the entire conflict. Did Strickland neglect to mention these events or was the report subsequently censored? Considering that British GHQ in Dublin knew about all of these occurrences as evidenced by the Dublin Castle Weekly Survey for the same week, the latter seems much more likely.[28]

If the intention was to take Protestant kids as hostages as part of a plan to prevent further British executions of IRA prisoners, then the strategy appears to have worked, for Dan O'Brien was the last prisoner to be officially executed during the War of Independence. The fact that O'Brien was captured only five days before being executed, having been immediately sentenced by drumhead court martial, suggests the u-turn in British policy was sudden. And if the arm of the British military authorities was twisted by this, they too wanted to stay quiet about it, for only four of the 17 violent deaths of civilians mentioned in the text as having occurred over the weekend were included in the Chief Secretary's statistics for the week.[29] However, it has to be said that political developments at this time also had a significant role to play in this.

And there is another connection to the YMCA: kids of the Blackrock Road area who were members of the YMCA spent the summer evenings for many years playing tennis at Citadella, a few hundred yards east along the Blackrock Road. Citadella, then a rambling residence and now a ruin, was a former lunatic asylum with a couple of tennis courts and was owned by Thomas Wolfe, one of the leading members of the YMCA.[30] Yet the abduction(s) appear to have had little bearing on the running of the tennis club, and Citadella continued to be used by the YMCA boys right through the summer of 1921, with Wolfe attending YMCA meetings as usual. The house was, however, temporarily abandoned between 1922 and 1924, and Wolfe suffered what appears to have been a nervous breakdown in the second half of 1922.[31] This supports the idea that whatever about boys being snatched on the Blackrock Road in May 1921, the supposed espionage link with the YMCA was not made in 1921 but rather as a result of the capture of Parsons in the spring of 1922.

If this is the case and Protestant youths 'of 16 years of age and upwards' were used as hostages against British executions or simply shot as reprisals, it betrays an extraordinary ruthlessness on the part of O'Donoghue. One of his own intelligence officers, Michael Kenny, witnessed one example of O'Donoghue's ruthlessness. In September 1920, Kenny was out after curfew along with another Volunteer on the trail of an alleged spy, Michael Walsh. Both were armed. Going up Gardiner's Hill they noticed a curfew patrol coming around the corner. The other Volunteer gave Kenny his gun and made a run for it. Kenny, now with two revolvers in his possession, decided to duck into the nearest house. As he did so, a young lad of around 15, who had also spotted the curfew patrol, ran in ahead of him.

A musical evening was in progress in the parlour and an elderly man was playing the piano. The young lad dived in behind the piano. Kenny told the family to stay calm and keep their mouths shut while he concealed the two revolvers inside his jacket and took off his hat. When the knock came to the door, Kenny brazenly answered. The officer in charge of the party demanded to know if anyone had seen the man who had just ducked in. 'There he is,' Kenny said, pointing to behind the piano. The soldiers pulled the youngster from his hiding place, handled him roughly and and took him away, ignoring his pleas of innocence. While this was going on, Kenny made his escape through the back door.

A few days later word got back to him from Victoria Barracks that the youngster had been beaten into confessing that Kenny had been the Volunteer in the house. Kenny was shocked to hear that the boy was now marked down by O'Donoghue for execution as a 'spy'. Kenny went straight to IRA HQ, slapped his revolver down on the desk in front of O'Donoghue and said that if the boy was shot he would immediately resign from the IRA. 'That boy saved my life.' The boy would have been shot as a 'spy' but for the intervention of Michael Kenny.[32]

This unforgiving mind-set was not true of all or even of a majority of officers within the IRA. Both Liam Lynch and Seán Moylan deported loyalist prisoners who had admitted to passing on information. Liam Lynch, no doubt mindful of what had gone on over the previous six months, went to considerable lengths to try to limit the amount of shooting of 'spies' during the Civil War, instructing his forces, as Mulcahy had done earlier, not to shoot civilians without sanction. All the prominent loyalists taken by Tom Barry's men in west Cork, and held as hostages before the Truce, were released—even though they could subsequently have identified their captors. (They chose not to do so, of course; they were too terrified. Besides, as they acknowledged, they had been treated as well as could be expected in the circumstances.) Jimmy Brennock, one of Lynch's men who ran a flying column in north-east Cork, had his dugout discovered by the British Army the very same week these events were going on in the city. Suspicion fell on Willie Ginn, a local Protestant, who admitted, according to Brennock, that he had been grilled by the military but claimed he had told them nothing and that the two events must have been a coincidence. Giving Ginn the benefit of the doubt, Brennock ordered him to be taken to Cobh and deported. Ginn, who was probably innocent of the charge, at least lived to tell the tale.[33]

Another example of this is the account left by Flor Begley, intelligence officer of the 3rd Brigade, of the spying activities of a member of the brigade that led, so it is alleged, to the setback experienced by the west Cork IRA at Upton Station. The man was tried and sentenced but was not executed because the sentence was passed after the Truce. Like Ginn, he was deported, though he returned to the area subsequently.[34] There are several other accounts of alleged informers around the county having their sentences commuted on the arrival of the Truce. By contrast, there is to my knowledge no record of the men on the south side of the city ever releasing a prisoner, at least not in 1921.

If Josephine Marchment Brown was capturing youngsters as spies or as hostages, then that must surely make her one of the most implacable of the IRA operatives in the city. There is other evidence that she was a very tough operator. In the spring of 1922, as part of the effort to track down Cruxy Connors, she travelled to Cobh with her sister to identify Connors' family as they embarked for the US.[35] Towards the end of May 1921 the War Pensions office on South Terrace was targeted. Francis McMahon, an accountant (and one of the 'struck off' Freemasons) who worked there, was abducted on his way to work, taken into the countryside, shot and his body buried. Richard W. Cooper, a retired army officer in his sixties and the former head of the pensions office, was to have been kidnapped on the same day and executed, had he not been warned by a priest.[36] It was through Cooper's kindness that Josephine O'Donoghue got her first job in the War Pensions office, where apparently the pair got on well. Indeed, it was also Cooper who recommended her for her post in the barracks. Clearly, sentiment was not going to stand in the way of this kind of justice. It is clear from the high regard in which she was held by people like Sandow Donovan just how important she was in the IRA's scheme of things.[37] Along with the behaviour of the 2nd Battalion, this also casts a new light on the disparity between the killing rate for civilians between the north and south sides of the city.

And then there are the other rather odd disparities among those shot in Cork. Josephine O'Donoghue claimed she knew many of the British Army intelligence officers and even taught the piano to some of their children.[38] She brought lists of the living quarters of most of the officer class who lived outside barracks and passed them on to O'Donoghue. Yet no British intelligence officers were assassinated in Cork city, apart from Genochio in the spring of 1922.[39] The victims of the espionage war were usually small fry: ex-soldiers, Protestants and teenagers. The whole thing simply does not add up in the terms put forward by various IRA survivors.

Chapter 56 ∿

A PRIVATE BAND OF AVENGERS

Much depressed as Penrose Fitzgeralds have gone, never to return, a heartless and cruel end to a good straight life spent in the town's welfare, a great blow to our community here.[1]

When I began researching this subject, I expected that, if I ever got to the bottom of it, the taking of Protestant teenagers would be the work of maverick elements within the IRA. I expected it to be an 'unofficial operation' or series of operations and the perpetrators to be some of the wild men on the margins of the movement. Indeed, this may well have been the case for the three shot at Frankfield. Not for one moment did I think that some of these deaths might have been associated with someone so close to the centre of IRA and indeed IRB activities. Not only that, but that it was associated with two of the icons of the revolution. For Josephine and Florrie O'Donoghue have almost mythical status in the history of the War of Independence in Cork. What is more, most of what O'Donoghue wrote on the history of the period suggests a fair-minded and reasonable man who had no shortage of sympathy for his military opponents. These were cultured and intelligent people. Josephine, after all, was teaching piano to the children of British officers. Unravelling this kind of stuff felt like a form of sacrilege.

The suggestion that elements within the Cork city IRA had a campaign to round up and kill Protestant boys as spies or, worse, as hostages is so serious that it is necessary to review the evidence before making any attempt to come to a conclusion. It might be argued that, while two or three such kidnappings may have taken place, it does not merit the conclusions arrived at at the end of the previous chapter. It could also be argued that the 2nd Battalion were more than capable of doing most of this on their own. In 1918 an outside Volunteer officer found the men of the battalion in the Pouladuff area, where many of these events took place, to be of a low calibre. 'The Company officers were very backward, even the captain knew very little . . . Of course we couldn't tell him [Richard Mulcahy] that the Battalion staff were looting all round the place. We would have been ashamed to confess it.'[2] Men like the Grays were capable of almost anything. Was O'Donoghue, as the primary historian of the period and the guiding hand behind the Bureau of Military History, merely protecting the excesses of his men? Or was he, rather, the instigator of much of the terror experienced, especially by Protestants, on the south side of the city?

The simplest explanation is that Harris or perhaps William McNeill set up a surveillance system using the boys of the YMCA and that O'Donoghue uncovered it and that all the boys picked up and shot over a two-year period were part of that. The only hint from British sources that there may have been some Secret Service involvement in the YMCA is the apparent attempt to cover up the fact that the drowning in Boulonge was carried out by the IRA. Nor does McNeill hint at such a surveillance system, declaring rather that he passed on any information on IRA activities that he picked up in his travels as a market gardener around the county.

If O'Donoghue had been aware of a spy operation being run out of the YMCA, then why did he not pass on that piece of information to his replacement as IO of the brigade when he went off to serve in the 1st Southern Division in April 1921? Denis Kennedy, who briefly took over from him as brigade IO recalled the importance of these lists of suspects many years later: 'Finally, you will probably recall you handing me over your record of suspects when you went to the Division.'[3] Yet YMCA personnel must not have been on that list of suspects because they do not figure among those who were still wanted at the time of the Truce. Neither is the YMCA named as a suspect loyalist organisation at that time.

Could it be that he did not trust the men of the intelligence department of the brigade to round up teenagers and kill them and kept it in-house in the most literal sense of the term? In other words, that it was an IRB job rather than an IRA job. This is a possibility and the extremely tight nature of IRB structures would mean that the secret would never get out among the general body of the Volunteers. However, we have to follow the evidence. His correspondence with Chief of Staff Richard Mulcahy during those months suggests that O'Donoghue wanted to target two groups, Freemasons and those who supplied provisions to the military, which would have included the YMCA. There was also the tendency to extrapolate from one suspect 'spy' to tar a whole organisation with the same brush. Thus Beal, who provided accommodation to undercover agents, was the starting point of a process whereby up to 30 Masons were mysteriously struck off the Freemason membership rolls. Similarly, Parsons in the spring of 1922 was the starting point for the targeting of up to 20 Protestants in the city and elsewhere.

Parsons, in turn, came out of a spy hunt in the High Street area that began with George Horgan but which included several who now appear to have been entirely innocent.

There also is no question that the IRA, particularly in the harbour area, carried out many raids on military supplies during June 1921. The RIC recorded that 18 such raids took place during that month.[4] The army reported that seven such raids took place in County Cork, four of them in the harbour area in the week to 11 June alone.[5] As we have seen, the District Inspector expressed his surprise at these attacks, which he records were 'very prevalent of late. In very few cases was any use being made of the articles stolen. They were either burnt or thrown into the sea.' Some of these attacks were on a comparatively large scale, involving up to 20 men, who in at least some instances left without doing any damage, suggesting that they may have been after something other than stores.[6] It is also likely that for most of the 18 raids, nothing worse than the dumping of quantities of groceries, beer and in one case coal, took place and that the bulk of these attacks were merely military operations carried out by companies in the vicinity of the harbour. We can see from the case of Thomas Telford's son what would happen even to 15-year-olds who were caught supplying services to British Army barracks.

The minutes of YMCA meetings also make clear that the first two weeks of May was not the only time that unwelcome things were happening to YMCA members. On 17 June the ladies committee recorded: 'The secretary explained that since the last meeting [13 June] circumstances had arisen which he thought made it inadvisable to proceed with the American Tea [a sale of work planned for midsummer]. Mrs Gates strongly supported the idea of having no such functions just at present owing to the very dangerous state of the country.'[7]

Along with the decision to cancel the YMCA summer camp in Crosshaven and the raid on the scouts hut at Riverstown in May, this is one of the few references to the revolution to be found in YMCA records. Given the extremely reticent nature of the Cork Protestant middle class, this is likely to be significant. Taken together, the two statements suggest that the YMCA was afraid to go on any form of excursion or even to hold a 'sale of work'. This was the week that the first of the June raids on the YMCA launch took place in Cork Harbour. It was also the week when the 'threat' was left by the IRA in the YMCA toilet.

So what was going on? Did the IRA begin by targeting YMCA provisions bound for the military and then up the ante by capturing YMCA personnel into the bargain? Or did they capture some youngster who confessed to being a scout for British forces? If so, why did nobody remember his name, considering that they all seem to remember Parsons, who was caught a year later? Or did O'Donoghue intercept some letter from H. A. Harris to British

Intelligence that suggested he was a British spy? O'Donoghue claimed that an attempt was made to set up a branch of the British Secret Service in Cork and that its members were 'bound by the Masonic cement'. The YMCA may be the source of this comment, for Harris was indeed a Freemason. However, it is more likely that O'Donoghue was referring in this instance to those lifted and shot on the basis of the list found on Beal.

O'Donoghue claimed that the decision to 'clear the country of its active resident civilian enemies' to force the end of British reprisals and executions was taken at a large meeting of IRA officers of Kippagh at the end of April 1921. Yet neither Tom Barry, Seán Moylan or Ernie O'Malley, all of whom attended that meeting and left detailed accounts of it, mention this. Indeed, it is in the section devoted to the Kippagh meeting that O'Malley makes his statement about east Cork shooting a lot of 'spies' and O'Hegarty not being too concerned about evidence.

O'Donoghue goes on to claim that GHQ gave its sanction for the targeting of loyalists. Yet that sanction was not issued until 22 June, little more than two weeks before the truce. And it concerned loyalist properties and came with very strict provision. 'For the purpose of such reprisals no person shall be regarded as enemies of Ireland, whether they be described locally as Unionist, Orangemen etc., unless they are actively anti-Irish in their actions.' O'Donoghue puts this in italics to emphasise that this was how the Cork IRA operated. The very fact that the statement had to be issued in the first place suggests otherwise.[8]

There are a number of reasons for believing that boys were taken from the area south and east of the city and used as hostages: Sing Sing was by far the most secure place for the IRA to hold such hostages; it was just a hop across the river from where the abduction(s) took place (see Map 1). Seán O'Hegarty was also in Knockraha during these weeks.[9] Despite spending ten years investigating this subject, I was not able to reconcile the numbers alleged to have been killed north of Knockraha—27 at the very least—with the number of actual disappeared persons who might have ended up there. According to my calculations, no more than 11 military personnel ended up in Knockraha—and it could well have been half that—and three RIC men. This means that the remaining 13 (or more) were civilians. This ties in with Martin Corry's account to Jim Fitzgerald when he stated that 11 'spies and informers' were buried there. However, of the 19 civilians whom we know to have disappeared in Cork city, only three were buried in Knockraha.[10] This leaves eight or nine who are not accounted for. I believe that some of these were hostages and may include the four ex-soldiers mentioned by Neenan. Corry also mentions Seán O'Hegarty personally escorting prisoners to be executed in Knockraha. Would he, as Brigade Commander, have been doing this if these were mere spies—especially when during 1921 'spies' were simply shot down in the street? Informers would have received short shrift and would hardly have been escorted to their place of execution by the Brigade commander. What's more, Sing Sing was the 'official' Brigade prison and was the most secure place in the Cork city region for the holding of prisoners.

After the Kippagh meeting of late April 1921 the two main problems facing the rebels in the South, in Florrie O'Donoghue's words, were the British policy of executing prisoners and the policy of official reprisals 'whereby Crown forces arbitrarily selected and destroyed, by fire or explosives, dwelling houses and business premises in the vicinity of army activities'. In response, the IRA then set about burning loyalist mansions. Some of the most notable big houses in the county went up in flames as a result, including Convamore in North Cork, the home of Lord Listowel. 'It was recommended that this counter reprisal should be sufficiently heavy and persistent to put an end to British reprisals or clear the country of its active resident civilian enemies.'[11] However, reprisal burnings had begun earlier, in early April in, of all places, the Blackrock Road in Cork city, which had to have been O'Donoghue's decision as he was the most senior officer in Cork city at the time.

But the execution of prisoners of war was also being addressed and the solution was to be found in the same place: the targeting of loyalists. One of the first letters the 1st Southern Division HQ sent to Richard Mulcahy, the day after O'Donoghue arrived, shows that a response to the British policy of shooting prisoners was going to involve the 'faithful civilian garrison' as O'Donoghue called them.

> In view of the fact that the enemy continues to shoot our Prisoners we suggest that for each prisoner shot in future we shoot one loyal loyalist— prominent Freemason Officers to be the first to suffer. It is proposed to notify the loyalist to this effect and by so doing we hope to get them to prevent the enemy from shooting our prisoners … The above actions is suggested in view of the fact that in the Cork 2 Brigade area where the enemy burned houses as a reprisal, we burnt loyalist houses in counter reprisals with the result that the local loyalists approached the enemy authorities immediately asking them, for God's sake, to stop reprisals. It is thought that the threat of taking action against the lives of loyalists will have the effect of making them do their best to have the shooting of our prisoners stopped in order to save themselves.[12]

It is clear from the letter that these actions were predicated on getting a positive response from GHQ. GHQ delayed making a decision. Mulcahy wrote back: 'I want you to stay your hand on this matter.'[13] Lynch and O'Donoghue replied: 'Your instructions on my suggestion of 4th inst are noted. Hope some will be sanctioned in a few weeks when the present situation changes'.[14] The interesting word here is 'noted'; the instructions might have been noted but they were not being obeyed. For loyalists—and they were all Protestants—

including 'prominent Freemasons' were already being targeted on the south side of Cork city. At least two Freemasons—and these are only the ones that we are certain of, the number may be significantly higher—Francis McMahon and John Moore disappeared during May. Others, including Robert Parker and J.T. Mulligan, were shot and wounded, while R.W. Cooper was lucky not to suffer the same fate as McMahon on the day the latter disappeared. What most of these have in common is that they lived in the Blackrock Road and Douglas areas. At least nine other prominent loyalists, all but one of them Protestant, disappeared from the Blackrock Road at some point in 1921/22. (See Chapter 50) Most of the Protestant properties burnt as reprisals in Cork city during April, May and June 1921 were also in this area. For the following week, the 3rd Brigade took the first of its prominent hostage/prisoners in west Cork. What is more, the 1st Brigade had already shot Mrs Lindsay, James Clarke, Major Compton Smyth and at least four unnamed ex-soldiers as hostages, without looking for any sanction.

It has to be said—and no historian is going to argue with this—that, going all the way back to Soloheadbeg, the IRA brigades of the South rarely waited for approval from GHQ before embarking on a course of action. In fact, if they contacted GHQ at all on such matters, it usually meant they were already doing them. Just as in the case of the counter-reprisal burnings—for which the brigades did not get sanction either until the end of June—the shooting of hostages had begun even before the Kippagh meeting. It is fair to assume if the shooting of 'loyal loyalists' in reprisal for British executions was being urged on GHQ that it was already taking place on the ground. It was around this time that 'somebody's child' was abducted on the Blackrock Road and the YMCA member was snatched near Crossshaven.

The 1st Southern Division correspondence leaves us in no doubr that loyalists were now going to take the brunt of IRA reprisals for British actions. The expulsion of the Wallace sisters from Cork and the closure of their shop which had long served as a headquarters for the 1st Brigade in the city was to be countered by the closure of six branches of English firms in the city 'and director or manager [to] be ordered to England or Carsonia as the individual deserves—we can enforce the order by boycott or destruction.'[15] It is quite clear from the detailed analysis of the military conflict in Cork by William Sheehan that, in the months leading up to the Truce, the IRA war in Cork had changed from being a guerrilla campaign to a campaign of terror, and that loyalists, mostly Protestants, were being placed on the front line.[16] This was partly a propaganda exercise—'the greater the strain imposed on the enemy in the presence of his own partisans [loyalists] the more speedily he will lose those partisans.'[17] But it was also born out of military necessity: 'It is sound military policy to hammer away at his civilian side. It gives us fresh objectives and discounts the Enemy reinforcements in advance. At the worse, it ensures that we can place against any military losses we may suffer the serious civil losses we inflict ... reprisals against Enemy Officers—or, failing that, Officials—will eventually result in stopping murders of prisoners'. Burning of loyalist properties was such 'an unquestionably useful weapon' that it 'should be organized systematically at once'.[18]

From the point of view of the 1st Southern Division, Cork city was central to this strategy. 'The more effort we set forth in Cork city and the more strain we place on the Enemy in and around it the greater relief we offer to outlying areas. To obtain the best result this "gripping of the throat" in Cork should be extended and backed up by as complete a development as possible in the surrounding area ... deliberately tackle the Enemy where it would suit him to have his hands free ... Hostile territory or neutral is the place to operate, friendly territory the place to base operations.'[19] On the matter of the execution of prisoners of war, Lynch and O'Donoghue noted the success of the offensive of the weekend of 14/16 May. 'Even with counter-reprisals only in the 1st and 2nd Divisions the enemy seems to have tired of the game as they have more or less stopped official executions; they may have realized that they have lost far more than we did within that period. We also realize it has demoralized some of the rank and file who continually fear death and cannot move about freely.'[20]

Indeed, British cabinet papers suggest this was a significant factor in bringing the British Government to the negotiating table. In a well-known memo to the Cabinet on 24 May General Macready reported how demoralised the troops were becoming. 'Events lately have shown that the rebels stick at nothing in order to carry out their policy of endeavouring to secure their ends by outrage and murder, under the impression that the further they go, the more chance there is that the British Government and public will be cowed into submission.' Macready warned that 'I am convinced that by October, unless a peaceful solution has been reached, it will not be safe to ask the troops to continue there another winter,' and that the men 'for the sake of their morale and training should be removed from the Irish 'atmosphere''.[21] This is the context in which the letters from Florrie O'Donoghue to his wife written during these months have to be read.

As we have seen, O'Donoghue wrote to Josephine on 16 June 1921 that 'some friends from Cork were here today and told me you were, so to say, on active service one day a while ago. But there was nothing doing apparently.'[22] A few days later, having read of an account of a boating accident in the harbour near Blackrock, 'and that there was a youngster in it', he wrote: 'I was wondering if it was your party, ye seem to have a pretty taste in accidents of that kind. Glad to see however that nothing worse than a ducking befell anybody.'[23] This is stating, pretty unambiguously it seems to me, that Josephine was organising 'accidents' of some kind, and that youngsters were involved.

So who were the 'friends' who informed O'Donoghue that Josephine was 'back on active service one day a while ago'? This can only refer to Seán O'Hegarty or Joe O'Connor, Brigade Quartermaster and brother of Fr Dominic. These were the only people who knew of Josephine's role in the IRA or who knew that Florrie and Josephine were now married. Both were core IRB men. 'Of course the person who told me is one of the best, and you need not fear it was just gossip. Nell would know. He called to her. Only that I feel you are so well able to take care of yourself, I would be tempted to indulge in a lecture. You'll be careful, won't you?'[24] This suggests it was Joe O'Connor who, like O'Donoghue himself, was regularly making trips into and out of Cork city during these months. Both O'Connor and Josephine were able to drive—something that was highly unusual for a woman at that time. ('I've been worrying about my forgetfulness in regard to that motorcar ever since,' O'Donoghue wrote to Josephine two weeks after the Truce. 'I promised that you should have it and I hate breaking a promise.'[25]) The well-known IRA drivers in the city, such as the Grays and Jack Cody, were on the run in west Cork at this time, but we don't have to look very far to find candidates for that 'mysterious individual in a motorcar' involved in the abduction that was reported in *The Times*.

On the matter of reprisal burnings, O'Donoghue wrote to Josephine on 15 June: 'Official reprisals are certainly at an end, which is a big victory for us. The message which has been circulated to enemy police concerning the matter is sufficiently doleful. And no doubt only a very pressing necessity compels the enemy to abandon this weapon.'[26] There is no question that the targeting of civilians was part of this strategy. 'All this takes no account of what the civilians may do in the way of making peace in the meantime … Already she ["England"] is trying to placate us somewhat in the matter of our prisoners. I think the shooting of men for carrying arms and levying war is at an end, or nearly so. Presently she will recognize our prisoners as prisoners of war and treat them as such.' I believe that the 'threat', signed by the 'CO, IRA, Cork district' that was found in the YMCA toilet the very same week that O'Donoghue was making this remark, was in connection with the hostage-taking of 'loyal loyalists' or members of the YMCA, what O'Donoghue called 'active resident civilian enemies'. These were the same weeks when members of the YMCA were afraid to go outside the door; the same week that their stuff was being dumped into the River Lee; it was the same week that the *Irish Times* noted 'with deep distress' the 'tragedies that have grievously affected [Methodist] homes'.[27] My view is that a small number of core IRA/IRB activists were taking Protestant youths 'of 16 years or upwards' in the Blackrock Road and surrounding areas and holding them as hostages against British executions or else simply killing them as reprisals. I believe Josephine was involved and that a car was stashed away somewhere for that very purpose and that she was promised the car after the Truce. Some may have been shot; others may have been released and they and their families ordered out of the country—which would go some way to explain the sudden evacuation of the Blackrock Road area by much of its Protestant population.[28] In its annual report for 1921 the YMCA recorded that 'several of our younger members have recently gone abroad' and the organisation had given them letters of introduction to YMCA branches in the various cities in which they had settled.[29] Others had a more dubious fate. It is even possible the three boys mentioned by Connie Neenan as having been shot around the time of the Truce were simply hostages who had overstayed their welcome.

Tom Barry, who was appointed chief liaison officer for the Cork IRA upon the cessation of hostilities and who allowed his own hostages to be released, did not see such kidnappings as a military matter but rather as a civilian one. In a letter to O'Hegarty, written near the end of July 1921, Barry complained:

> I have instructed the Liaison Officers concerned that complaints received affecting the IRA and the civilian population should be forwarded to the o/c Brigade or CI of Police. The reason for my doing so was that a number of complaints not affecting this office, such as commandeering of motor cars to the Truce, shooting of spies, kidnapping, etc are being referred here.[30]

Clearly Barry, who saw himself as a straightforward military man, was unhappy to have these complaints dealt with by his liaison office. Either he did not regard them as worthy of military attention or his office was overwhelmed by the sheer number of such complaints, which, with the sudden outbreak of peace, is what one would expect. The very fact that he suggested that the County Inspector of the RIC should deal with them shows just how exasperated he was and that he saw the 'shooting of spies' and kidnappings as a civilian matter. Either way, he washed his hands of the affair, suggesting that the 'o/c Brigade' was the man responsible and that O'Hegarty should deal with the issue himself.

So Barry—himself far from being a moderate—was at the very least uncomfortable with the scale of secret killings of civilians around the city, something he shared with his future enemy, Richard Mulcahy, then Chief of Staff, who never subsequently trusted O'Hegarty or O'Donoghue.

So was this largely a vendetta against Protestants on the part of O'Hegarty and the O'Donoghues and a handful of gunmen close to them? While the O'Donoghues had no great love for Protestants, it is far more likely that at this stage it was merely a strategy to extract concessions from the military or from the British government. The most logical explanation is that the YMCA members were simply taken and killed because they were perceived as British —'active civilian resident enemies'—in an effort to ramp up the pressure on the British government in the months leading up to the Truce.

Chapter 57 ⁓

SAYING GOODBYE TO THE HOUSE

For two weeks there wasn't standing room on any of the boats or mail trains leaving Cork for England. All Loyalist refugees, who were either fleeing in terror or had been ordered out of the country. Frank Hayes went to see his boy off by the Cork boat and he said he felt quite choky to see them all, young and old, many of whom he knew personally, all leaving the country. Poor old Mrs Williamson for instance, who is a Cork woman born and bred and has lived here all her life and is now 75 years of age and her husband Colonel Williamson were given 6 hours to leave the country. Frank said it was sad to see the old woman, standing on the saloon deck with tears streaming down her face . . . Noel Furlong has been ordered out of the country and is gone.[1]

One of the most striking statistics to emerge from this investigation is the large number of Protestant families who had to flee the south-eastern corner of Cork city during these years. It is likely that the departure and widespread expulsion of Protestants from the Blackrock Road and Douglas areas in 1922 was at least in part an attempt to cover up the killing of teenagers in both areas a year earlier. All we know about the boys who died is that 'they mostly came from good families'. At least some of those 'good families' were the families mentioned in YMCA records as having left in the second half of 1921: the Hosfords, Warners, Williamsons and Julians among others.[2] But most appear to have left in 1922. It would be incorrect to describe this as 'ethnic cleansing' since the departed Protestant families were often replaced by other Protestants, but it was one of the most dramatic expulsions of non-Catholics seen in the South during these years and it occurred mostly between March and July 1922. The Blackrock and Douglas Roads lost a third of their original residents, almost all of them Protestants, during 1922. Other compelling evidence of the sudden nature of the departure of Protestants from the south-east ward of Cork city comes from what subsequently happened to their properties.

Out of 178, mostly Protestant homes that changed hands in the Douglas Road, Blackrock Road, Ballintemple and Ballinlough areas between 1921 and 1926, only 47 or 26 per cent had the title deeds officially transferred to the new owners during the same period.[3] It could be argued that there may be any number of reasons for this: many people were renting; transfers of deeds may have been registered later; solicitors' offices may have been slow to submit their returns—though if that was the case, then what about the 47 that were returned; some may even have bought properties without going through the legal niceties. (This state of questionable ownership is a common phenomenon all over the south of Ireland, especially where departed ascendancy types left behind a legal mess when it came to various portions of their properties.) This however appears to be different. These were often substantial family homes in better-off areas and were the property in most cases of members of the professional classes. It is doubtful if accountants, solicitors, barristers and doctors would have sold off their family homes without doing so legally, had they been given the opportunity to do so. Some of these properties were owned by the men who disappeared in 1922; many of the others were almost certainly expelled.[4]

This is a contentious subject; there are many reasons cited for the calamitous collapse of the Protestant population in the South of Ireland during the post-revolutionary period, and direct intimidation is only one of them. However, in certain areas it was the most important reason and the area to the south of Cork city is a case in point. When one compares two long-established and traditionally better-off suburbs, the Knockrea area south of the city, which comprises the area from the Blackrock Road to the Douglas Road with its equivalent, the Montenotte area north of the city, the contrast is striking. According to valuation records, 155 properties changed hands in the Blackrock Road and Douglas Road areas between 1921 and 1924. (And this does not include Wallace's Avenue, the entire population of which virtually changed in 1922.) This contrasts with just three changes of occupiership for the Montenotte area for the same period, eleven for the College Road/Magazine Road area west of the city and 12 for the Wellington Road to Gardiner's Hill area north of MacCurtain Street. These are all areas that had a similar population profile; in other words, they all had significant populations of better-off Protestants.[5] It is sometimes said that there was no ethnic cleansing on the South Mall. Certainly, if you were a Protestant from the north or west side of the city, that was the case. If you came from the south-eastern corner of the city though, from the area from Blackrock to Douglas, you might beg to differ.

It has been argued that many former loyalists left because they no longer felt they had a stake in the country. Yet one group who had a stake in the country, who owned their land and who would not have left had they not been forced to, were farmers. Yet of the 13 Protestant landowners listed for the parish of Douglas in 1921, nine had left by 1924.[6] This no doubt reflects the kind of intimidation suffered by the Ronaynes on account of IRA activities in the area. If nothing else, too many foul deeds had been committed; there were too many bodies in too many fields.

Admiralty correspondence also suggests that there was a daily exodus of loyalists from Cork city during the late spring and early summer of 1922 and that some of these may have been evacuated with British help—despite Churchill's fear of a mass evacuation of Southern Protestants leading to a refugee crisis in Britain. It is also clear that the British authorities were only prepared to evacuate those whose lives were in danger.[7] In reply to a question from the Admiralty concerning rumours of large numbers of refugees leaving Dunmanway in the wake of the April killings, the Admiral at Queenstown was able to report that despite some 200 refugees leaving Dunmanway in the last days of April, 'just normal numbers [were transported] by ss *Puma* from Cork on Friday night and tonight. None from Queenstown.'[8] While Cork was no Saigon, this reference to 'normal numbers' suggests there may have been a clandestine military-backed evacuation of some civilians along with military personnel and ordnance out of the South of Ireland and out of Cork city during March to May 1922.[9]

It is also clear from Alice Hodder's account that youngsters were being forced out. She refers to Frank Hayes, a landowner, and JP from Carrigaline, seeing his son off by the Cork boat. Hayes had only one son. He was 10 at the time. Noel Furlong, a Cork mill manager, who was also ordered out, also had a 10-year-old son, probably in the same class as Hayes's boy. Colonel Williamson, whom she also mentions, was a leading member of the YMCA.

There was also property-grabbing going on. Alice Hodder was speaking for many when she wrote of those months: 'There is a frightful lot of land grabbing everywhere and the Provisional Government say they are trying to put it down and in many cases have turned the grabbers out but you never know when you've been reinstated what will happen next.'[10] Whatever the reason, the facts are that for 131 (or 74 per cent) of the 178 family homes that changed hands in that area, an area that is now (and was then) prime real estate, the property transfers had no basis in law, at least not at that time. While many such changes were almost certainly changes in tenancy, you have to ask yourself: how many of the new residents simply moved in?[11]

Where did those loyalists go? Some went to Dublin, County Wicklow or Northern Ireland; YMCA members emigrated to Canada, the US or Australia; but the majority moved to the place nearest to home, the western and southern coastal towns of England and Wales. From the IGC papers, it is clear that many of the former residents of Cork who had to flee in 1922 did not move far from where they landed but ended up in cities and towns such as

Swansea, Bristol, Plymouth, Portsmouth and the smaller towns of Devon and Cornwall.

> The local papers bear melancholy testimony to the exodus that is in progress. Their advertisement columns are filled with notices of sales of farms, residences, furniture, shops and businesses.
>
> The extent of the exodus that has already taken place is difficult to gauge. It is naturally more marked in some places than in others. For instance, upwards of 80 families, all refugees from Cork city and county are now living in Bournemouth. A friend of mine recently received a letter from a Cork lady now resident near Bristol, in the course of which she mentioned: 'Last Sunday it seemed quite like home, as there were nearly 20 refugees from Bandon in the house.'[12]

Either way, what all this suggests is that these people left in a hurry. Most of the changes took place in 1922 and 1923 in the area where Florrie O'Donoghue and Seán O'Hegarty lived.

It is clear from his account to Ernie O'Malley what Florrie O'Donoghue's attitude was to Protestants. He was convinced of the existence of a substantial Freemason intelligence organisation which comprised most of the businessmen of Cork. Indeed it is clear he equated the very existence of Freemasonry with intelligence gathering. He claimed he had the 'master list' to prove it—though that master list was compiled in the late 1920s or early 1930s. Indeed, it is equally clear from O'Malley's notes that he himself was sceptical of O'Donoghue's claims. While one or two Freemasons such as James Beal or Edward Woods may (or may not) have been spies, there is no evidence to tar the entire organisation with the same brush. O'Donoghue's attitude to Cork's Protestant community can be summarised in another comment he made to O'Malley: 'They got control on the business of Cork but recently they are intermarrying with Catholics. It is a question of time now before they disappear.'[13] Given these views, is it any wonder that so many Protestants had to get out of the Blackrock Road?

There is no evidence that anything even remotely like this exodus took place in the 1st Battalion area on the north side of the city, despite it having a large population of loyalists who lived in the vicinity of Victoria Barracks. When it comes to the expulsion and killing of Protestants, the 1st Battalion seems to have clean hands. Even on the south side, the highest rate of departures occurred in the Blackrock and Douglas Road areas. All the evidence, from letters to the press by Protestants and submissions by clergy and other leading establishment figures, suggests that the majority of these people left in the six months from March to September 1922 and that the homes changed hands afterwards.

I think it can be taken as read that further undocumented teenagers (and adults including many of the 'struck off' Freemasons) disappeared from April to August 1922, necessitating the widespread clearance of Protestants from the area. Much of this took place around youth organisations. Several prominent members of the YMCA, including four clergymen, departed in 1922. Others, including Tom Wolfe and W. B. Lacy, appear to have been living in terror of their lives and had nervous breakdowns in the latter half of 1922 and early 1923. Most of the staff of Cork Grammar School changed during 1922. And this was related to the fact that they were Protestants, not that they were necessarily loyalist. Even Hugo Doak, the poet and nationalist-leaning headmaster of Cork Grammar School, and his *Gaelgeoir* French teacher William Glynn were forced to leave. The Grammar School's own school rolls disappeared, suggesting the management was afraid they might fall into the wrong hands and be used to compile further death lists. Doak and Glynn make extremely unlikely spies. Doak was so mild he was barely suited to being a schoolmaster, let alone a spy master, while Glynn, a Quaker and an Irish language enthusiast, liked to teach Teilhard de Chardin through Irish. Another school teacher, Robert Fleeton, headmaster of St Nicholas National School which many of these boys had attended, may well have been poisoned in the summer of 1923. Fleeton was a member of No. 71 Freemason lodge and his son was one of those struck off the Freemason rolls.[14] Of the 15 members of Cork Grammar School junior rugby team of 1921, only three lived in Cork subsequently.

What evidence there is available from the Registry of Deeds suggests that many simply abandoned their homes and were not too worried about legal niceties. This is what you do when your children begin to disappear for whatever reason. As an appeal for help for Southern refugees put it in early June 1922:

> There is no record of the number of murders which have taken place since the Treaty but it is well known that there have been very many more murders of loyalists, ex-soldiers and ex-policemen than have been reported to the House of Commons. The terror is so complete in many districts that resistance to evacuation would be perfectly futile and men have had to fly on the first intimation that their presence is undesirable.[15]

As Macready, who was by then reporting directly to the British Cabinet and who had been quite optimistic some six months earlier, put it in late February, 'in a few districts the conditions prevailing are something of a military tyranny'.[16] The Leader of the House of Commons, Joseph Chamberlain, stated on 10 May: 'It [the Dunmanway killings] is but one startling and concentrated flashlight on the many semi-political murders that are being committed up and down the country week after week.' Kidnappings and murders occurred every day 'with the most complete and contemptuous impunity'.[17] Lest we be in any doubt as to the origin of the decision to target Protestants in Munster, Florrie O'Donoghue repeated his earlier instructions to all units on 26 April 1922:[18] 'You will compile a complete and detailed list of all Unionists in your Brigade area.' But it was the disappearance of youngsters both in 1921 and 1922 that truly traumatised the Protestant community.

All this ended abruptly when Free State forces took over Cork city and the men of the 2nd Battalion were quickly rounded up—suggesting that the people of the south side were glad to be rid of them and provided plenty of information to the new authorities on their tormentors.[19] In fact, during the Civil War, when mansions all over the country were going up in flames, Cork city was to become something of a safe haven for Protestants. By then, of course, O'Donoghue and O'Hegarty were no longer part of the Anti-Treaty IRA, and their men were in jail. Besides, despite its reputation, the Anti-Treaty IRA was not near as vengeful against Protestants as O'Donoghue and O'Hegarty had been.

An interesting postscript to this took place in the autumn of 1924 when a group of leading members of the ultra-unionist Irish Unionist Alliance, which had long since split with the more conciliatory majority of Southern loyalists led by Lord Midleton, went on a tour of west Cork. Their intention was to stir up mischief for the Free State by reporting on the mistreatment of Protestants in the area during the War of Independence and Civil War. It is easy to dismiss *Notes From Ireland*, the official organ of the IUA, as paranoid propaganda designed to paint as negative a picture as possible of the Free State during the first decade of its existence.[20] None the less, what they found says much about the experience of former loyalists in Cork and the silence that was to descend on the community when it came to its experiences during the revolution.

There were no loyalists of the poorer classes left in the locality now. All had been driven out. The only loyalists left belonged to the well-to-do farming class. They had suffered too but not enough to compel them to go as yet.

The Rector of the parish told us that two years ago the Republicans had torn up the floor of his parochial hall but he took no notice of this or other such things and he believed that on this account only were he and his family alive today. Nobody ever discussed local conditions with him and everybody appeared to live in a state of mutual suspicion. He mentioned one family in particular who had suffered. We called to see them but the daughter would tell us nothing. She was obviously afraid to trust anyone.

In a rectory further on the Rector's wife told us she knew nothing whatever about her husband's work or affairs. She appeared to be afraid that the servants would hear our conversation.

Twenty miles further south of this we called to the house of a friend. He said he would prefer not to discuss the conditions prevailing there as they found it safer to keep their mouths shut.

We had some conversation with a Nonconformist minister there who seemed afraid to speak. He told us however that he hoped that men who had been driven out of the country for an expression of opinion might be able to 'sneak' back into their old homes some time or other.

At one house we saw the relatives of a family whom we knew had been driven out. They told us that when the head of the family had been murdered the doctor who had been sent for to attend him before he died had refused to go, so prevalent was the terrorism at the time.

Nobody would speak freely to us. The impression we formed was that in the small towns and villages the poorer loyalists had been practically wiped out.[21]

Silence had now become the fallback position of the Protestant communities of Cork. They were caught in the middle, particularly during the Civil War. 'Some few Protestant clergymen recently have shown a new-born enthusiasm for the Free State, thereby placing many of the lay members of their flocks in a position of great difficulty as all their actions are being closely watched and noted by the Republicans.'[22] They dared not open their collective mouths out of fear that even worse might happen. One thing is certain though: 178 families could not all have had members who were spies.

Chapter 58 ～

| WITH GOD ON OUR SIDE

Florrie O'Donoghue moved to Cork as a 16-year-old in 1910 and was to spend the next ten years working as a draper's assistant at the shop of his cousin Michael Nolan at No. 55 North Main Street. He left Nolan's employment on the assassination of Tomás MacCurtain and spent the next year and a half on the run. He continued his intelligence work for the IRA out of the shop of the Wallace sisters just around the corner, while his own sister Agnes moved into the flat over Nolan's shop and effectively acted as O'Donoghue's secretary, processing vast amounts of paperwork all the way through the conflict.[1]

There was another IRA connection with No. 55 North Main Street, for in 1914 Walter Leo Murphy also came to work there, reflecting the habit of city retail premises of picking their sales staff from various parts of the county in the hope that they would attract customers from their own areas into the shop.[2] O'Donoghue and Murphy were to become best friends. O'Donoghue and Seán O'Hegarty, however, were concerned about security at the shop, for there was no access out the back or to the rooms upstairs—the place was a 'bloody rat trap', according to O'Hegarty. O'Donoghue and Murphy hid lump hammers under the counter in the hope that they could break their way out of the back of the shop in the event of a raid. Murphy was ordered to cease working there at the end of 1920 and was forced to engage in 'whole time service'.[3] This did not save him when some six months later he was captured at Waterfall and summarily executed by members of the Manchester Regiment.

O'Donoghue had a rule against IRA correspondence coming into the shop and also against persons calling there indiscriminately.

> There were two reasons—first because I was beginning to realise the need for covering my activities from the eyes of the police and second because I know Michael Nolan would disapprove. I was determined to give him no cause of grievance, either by neglect of my work for him, or by what he would regard as undesirable callers. He had ceased to talk about it, but I felt his silent hostility.

In connection with the first reason there is a curious thing. The shop was on the corner of North Main Street and Castle Street. Police were still doing ordinary patrol duty. One policeman on this beat, McCoy, was a customer of mine and occasionally he would come in for a smoke and a chat and on a wet day would stand in out of the rain. Leo Murphy and I never knew whether he was friendly or otherwise. He knew we were Volunteers, was frank about the fact that he knew, but never made the slightest effort to get information. Later in 1920 and 1921 he had a bad name. It was well known to them [the RIC] that I had gone on the run, but I was still around town and saw him on several occasions in circumstances in which he would hardly have failed to see me. He was the one policeman who unquestionably would have been able to identify me, and I always believed that had he set out to get me that he would have been successful. I gave him credit for having a good streak in him.[4]

It is the second reason, however, that concerns us here, for Michael Nolan was, and had been all along, an RIC informer. More specifically, he was an informant run by Sergeants Jack Maliff and T. J. Ryan of the detective unit of the Bridewell, whom we have already met in connection with the activities of the Special Crimes division of the RIC. Nolan admitted as much in his application for compensation to the Irish Grants Committee some years later. In fact, it seems that he provided substantial information that led to the capture and killing of Leo Murphy, whom he regarded as extremely dangerous. Not just Murphy, but Charlie Daly was also shot dead a result of the round-up. 'Mr. Nolan gave me every possible assistance with this man [Murphy]'.[5]

Nolan appears to have been something of a sad case. He had no children and his wife had a long series of miscarriages that brought great unhappiness on their home, with the result that he turned to drink. He was also afraid of the Volunteers. 'He had the honest if foolish conviction that my association with the Volunteers would injure his business. I honestly believe that it brought him more business than it lost him.' This however cannot be correct because the IRA became aware of Nolan's spying activities and he was subjected to such hostility in the post-conflict period that he lost one of his shops, his home was regularly raided and he was nearly put out of business.

The question is: was O'Donoghue aware of Nolan's role as a British spy? The answer is probably yes. T. J. Ryan was captured by the IRA, held in Sing Sing, and was only released because he promised to pass on some 'titbits' to the IRA. Was Nolan's identity one of those titbits? Despite stating that the IRA brought more business to Nolan that it lost him, in the very next sentence O'Donoghue, who was prepared to make allowances for Nolan's alcohol problem, goes on to say that 'God be good to him, he died in near poverty. He said to me some years before his death that he never had a day's luck since I left him. Of course, it was not altogether a question of luck.' Nolan's home in Blackrock, where he had moved around 1914, was repeatedly raided by the IRA from the end of 1921 to 1925, with the result that it further wrecked his health and that of his wife. He was not, however, shot or kidnapped and executed. Clearly, if O'Donoghue knew about Nolan's treachery, he was not treated in the same way as the Protestants of the Blackrock Road.

However, this throws up many other questions: if he did suspect Nolan was a British agent, why did he make no attempt to warn Murphy? Were the orders Murphy received to go on the run an implicit recognition of the dangers posed by his employer? Was Murphy sacrificed in the interests of IRA security? If Nolan was a spy and the IRA knew about it, then why was he not shot or even threatened until the end of 1921? Why did McCoy ignore O'Donoghue despite having a 'bad name'?

Nolan's importance to us in this narrative is that he lived in Blackrock and that most of the intimidation he suffered in the post-conflict period occurred in Blackrock. We don't know if he provided the information that led to the many raids in Blackrock and the Blackrock Road in April and May 1921—in fact it is more likely that the information came from within the IRA since there were no shoot-outs and nobody was killed in these raids. However, his main contacts in the RIC lived or were stationed in the Blackrock Road area. McCoy, for instance, was the sergeant in charge of Blackrock Road RIC barracks until it was burnt down by the IRA. Sergeant Thomas Flynn, who was in charge of the district that included North Main Street, stated of Nolan: 'I am aware that he assisted representatives of the Government in ways that I am not disposed to commit to paper fearing it may get into the hands of undesirable persons before leaving the country.'[6] Flynn, who was one of Nolan's principal referees in his application for compensation from the IGC, lived at No. 16 Rockboro Road, just around the corner from Rockboro Terrace.

So were some of the killings of Protestants along the Blackrock Road part of an attempt to divert attention away from the real spy in Blackrock? Was the 2nd Battalion let loose on the Protestants while Nolan was spared? The fact that he was not shot reflects the control the IRA had over its men. The experience of Michael Nolan gives the lie to the idea that it was the wild men of the 2nd Battalion acting on their own who were responsible for the huge disparity between the rate of killing of civilians north and south of the River Lee. If that were the case, they would have simply shot Nolan as a spy. This strongly indicated that the orders, especially in the post-Truce and post-Treaty periods, came from higher up. From the level of intimidation suffered by Nolan between 1921 and 1925, it is clear members of the IRA were aware that he had been supplying information to the police. Yet he was not shot, nor was he forced out of Cork. It is fair to assume that if Mick Murphy and his men were making *ad hoc* decisions to shoot informers in their own area, they would have shot Nolan rather than simply threaten him. This implies that the guiding hand for the high rate of civilian murders on the south side of the city, both during the War of Independence and subsequently, was that of O'Donoghue. You could be a spy and get away with it so long as you were related to the top brass, but if you were a Protestant and lived in the Blackrock or Douglas areas, you were shot or driven out on the merest suspicion.

So how do we square this with the obviously fair-minded O'Donoghue whom we encounter in his writings? The 'moral responsibility undertaken in killing our enemies' was something to which O'Donoghue gave considerable thought. 'I could not accept any plausible or pseudopatriotic sentiment as sufficient [for killing], nor could I dismiss it on the grounds that one would be merely obeying orders. I felt it as a personal responsibility; I wanted some rock-solid ground for the moral authority of those who issued the orders.' O'Donoghue got this 'moral responsibility' from a not entirely unexpected source:

> With Father Dominic's wise guidance I found the principles in Catholic teaching which satisfied me completely. Put in the briefest and simplest terms, they are that a nation which is unjustly invaded has the right to resist the invader and the right to use any lawful means to try to eject him. That reason is not extinguished by reason of the fact that the invader, by superior force, has annihilated the lawful government of the invaded country and established himself as the supreme and unquestioned master. It still lives on in the people. Nor it is extinguished by reason of the length of time the invader maintains his conquest, nor by the fact that his government of the invaded country is temperately administered. It still lives on in the people. Not merely have the people the right to combine for the purpose of trying to eject the unlawful invader but when his superior forces makes combination possible, they still have the right in small groups and even as individuals to resist injustice, to resist unlawful occupation and if need be to kill the invader. There is even more of a right to resist. There is a duty. It is the moral duty of the people to resist and endeavour to eject the invader; and that duty again extended down to even one lone man who stood for the right against injustice on behalf of his people.[7]

When you have this sense of 'moral authority' you can do almost anything. Richard Mulcahy described O'Donoghue as 'one of the impeccables without whom the Civil War would not have taken place'. Considering that in O'Donoghue's view the local loyalist was more 'the enemy' than the British themselves, this has obvious implications. For Fr Dominic made another interesting theological intervention in which kidnapping featured prominently:

Kidnapping, ambushing, killing, ordinarily would be grave sins or violations of Church law and if these acts were being performed by the volunteers as private persons, they would fall under the excommunication ... [However] these acts performed by the Irish Volunteers are, not only not sinful, but are good and meritorious. And therefore the excommunication does not affect us.[8]

This is the kind of quasi-theological rhetoric that is used in every theatre of conflict to justify unspeakable deeds. And while O'Donoghue could say it came with the imprimatur of the Catholic Church in the form of Father Dominic, it is not a doctrine with which the Bishop of Cork would have agreed.

Florrie O'Donoghue went to considerable lengths to either cover up or ignore the unsavoury episodes of the War of Independence and its immediate aftermath. While his papers are an invaluable source for historians, they have to be approached with caution. They are what O'Donoghue decided posterity could be allowed to see. All the rest he burnt before he died. Who knows what secrets went up the flue of the O'Donoghue home in the mid-1960s. In his writings he focused only on the heroic and on those like Liam Lynch and Tomás MacCurtain who were unquestionably idealistic. He was the first revisionist of the revolution, at least as it was played out in Cork city. What's more, we have no idea what role his wife played in all this, since O'Donoghue was careful not to include her half of their correspondence in his papers. A quotation from Goethe that he used in *No Other Law* says more about his position than a hundred pages of his own sanctimonious accounts of the revolution: 'The doer is always conscienceless; no one has a conscience except the spectator.' The supreme irony of this is the brigade leadership hunting down 15-year-olds, while a far greater threat to IRA security lay much closer to home.

APPENDIX I

Pre-Truce Absentees from British Troops in Ireland
(Cork only, from Department of Defence Papers MA A/07304)

Royal Garrison Artillery

1018368	Driver Pike, A. J.	14/3/20	Fermoy
278872	Gunner Earl, R.	21/6/21	Fermoy
1018886	Driver Graham, J.	18/11/20	Spike Island

Royal Gloucestershire Regiment

| 5174827 | Pte Chappell, G. | 17/6/21 | Kilworth |

King's Own Scottish Borderers

| | Heggarty, Johnson and Heggarty | 9/4/21 | Bere Island |

Manchester Regiment

3513058	Boy Chapman, G. A.	5/6/21	Ballincollig
3514271	Pte Caen, G. H.	24/6/21	Ballincollig
3513066	Pte Tinehes, B.	20/2/21	Ballincollig
35187590	Pte Murphy, R.	14/8/20	Ballincollig
35185108	Pte Rodgers, J. J.	28/8/20	Ballincollig
35190198	Pte Clarke, H.	26/8/20	Ballincollig
3513908	Pte Mason, A.	19/2/21	Ballincollig
————	Pte Roughley, F.	01/4/21	Ballincollig
————	Boy Carson, M.	5/7/21	Ballincollig
————	Boy Cooper, J.	5/7/21	Ballincollig

2nd Btn Cameron Highlanders

29234714	Pte Walsh, J.	9/8/20	Cork
29233713	Pte Ward, H.	13/8/20	Cork
2923325	Pte Anderson J. A. W.	26/10/21	Cobh

King's Regiment

3758253	Pte Hughes, E.	7/7/21	Bantry
3757583	Pte Foley	9/5/21	Bantry
103391	Pte Clifford, M.	12/8/20	Bantry
117865	Pte Burdsall, W. H.	21/8/20	Bantry
99967	Pte Fitzmaurice, J.	2/9/20	Kenmare

Royal Engineers
2309868   Spr Still, G.   2/11/20   Cork

RASC
M121964   A/cpl Belchamber   15/2/22   Buttivant

Essex Regiment
5999596   Pte Saunders   6/9/2   Courtmacsherry

APPENDIX II

Post-Truce/Civil War Killings of Civilians in Cork City and Environs*

Three Protestant Boys	Frankfield	11-15/7/21
Thomas Roycroft	ND	9/3/1922
Patrick Horgan	Grand Parade	17/3/1922
Six 'Prominent Citizens'	Glounthaune	17/3/1922
Wm Edward Parsons	Glounthaune	23/3/1922
Arthur Gloster	Barrack St	25/3/1922
Herbert Woods	ND	26/4/1922
Thomas Hornibrook	ND	26/4/1922
Samuel Hornibrook	ND	26/4/1922
Michael Williams	Glounthaune	June 1922
Three 'Merchants'	Rylane?	June 1922
William L. Cooke	Blackrock Rd	22/8/1922
Denis McCarthy	Barrack St	29/8/1922
Jeremiah Coleman	Crookstown	3/9/1922
Edward G. F. Williams	Bridge St	14/9/1922
Patrick Clancy	Leitrim St	13/10/1922
John Patrick Walsh	Gerald Griffin St	16/10/1922
Patrick Griffin	Patrick's Bridge	30/10/1922
William Aherne	Bishopstown	7/11/1922
James Murphy	Lady's Well Hill	10/11/1922
Madge Daly	Mulgrave St	20/11/1922
Katherine Fehily	Bachelor's Quay	7/12/1922
James Malone	Gerald Griffin St	22/12/1922
Robert Tobin	Washington St	5/1/1923
William G. Beale	Ballyhooley Rd	16/3/1923
William Murphy	Patrick St	24/4/1923
Theophilus Creber	Kerry Pike	21/7/1923
Abina Murphy	Gerald Griffin St	18/8/1923

*__Bold__ denotes individuals who disappeared

APPENDIX III

List of Missing Persons, Department of Justice Files: H16, 1922–26

Name	File	Source of inquiry	Location of disappearance	Other details
Peter Wahbrot	H16/3	J. Hayes, Cork	Cork	German citizen
Wm Ed. Parsons	H16/7	Mrs J. Parsons, Brighton	Cork	See NA/S 3033
Wm Nolan	H16/9	Mrs Burke, Carlow	Cork	
Wm Savage	H16/13	B. H. Smith, Shepherd's Bush	Unknown	Native of Liverpool?
Edward McGann	H16/22			Army deserter?
Robert McGarrity	H16/23			
Daniel Flanigan	H16/24			Native of Belfast?
Wm Frazier	H16/29			Special constable RIC
T. L. Gallagher	H16/29			Special constable RIC
Ml J. Dempsey	H16/31			Sergeant, National Army
Patrick Keogh	H16/42 and 46	Mary Hayes, Cork	Cork	Ex-soldier, native of Waterford
Mr McCarthy	H16/52	Nurse C.J. Wright, Surrey	Cork	Native of White St, Cork
Joseph Coonan	H16/54			Cloughjordan
Patrick Kelly	H16/55			Killarney
Josephine, Victor and James Keevlin	H16/60		Cork	Bridge St, Mallow
Thomas Kelly	H16/64			Native of Dublin
Ml Williams	H16/66	Family, Co. Laois	Cork	Ex-RIC. See NA 2007/56/11

Rutherford?	H16/70	Mrs Rutherford		Belfast
Dunne	H16/71	Martin Dunne	Dunmanway?	Ex-RIC?
Wm Leeson	H16/77			Native of Celbridge
J. J. Fitzsimon	H16/81		Tipperary?	Thurles
Ml Ewings	H16/82		Galway?	Ex-RIC
Patrick Doherty	H16/82		Galway?	Ex-RIC
David Wm Bracken	H16/83		Cork	
Patrick Keelan	H16/89			Kells, Co. Meath
Wm Cooney	H16/91			Mullingar
Thos Rose		Wife	Annamoe, Co. Wicklow	Dublin
Thos Manley			Cork	
D. Sheehan	H5/332		Cork?	

APPENDIX IV

Inquiries as to the Whereabouts of Missing Individuals 1923–28
(Department of Justice files: NA, H 229)*

Name	Origin of inquiry	File number	Other details
Walter Dennis	Walter Thornhill, Solicitors, Cork	H 229/30	Resident of Bantry
Udo de Baker	Garda Síochána	H 229/41	
John Hanrahan		H 229/74	Ballineen?
E. B. Dalton	DMP	H 229/81	
Mrs E. Diver	Husband (Co. Derry)	H 229/86	
George B. Reid	Wife (Scotland)	H 229/89	
Martha McNeill		H 229/91	Deceased
John Gore	Co. Galway	H 229/98	Deceased
Matthew Carson	Wife G. M. Carson (South Shields)	H 229/108	Member of Manchester Regiment?
John O'Reilly	Co. Limerick	H 229/117	
Mary Brett	Co. Roscommon	H 229/126	
James Doherty	Wife (Co. Derry)	H 229/139	
Julia Long	Dingle	H 229/149	
James Goulding		H 229/150	
T. J. Walsh	Co. Sligo	H 229/151	RIC man (Cork)
Blanchford Wiggins	IO (Cobh, Co. Cork)	H 229/156	American citizen
Andrew Cummins	Wife, Ann (Cork city)	H 229/158	Matthew Terrace, Ballintemple, Cork
Mr Gilbert	Wife, Mrs F. Gilbert (Manchester)	H 229/164	
Patrick Joseph Griffin	Dundalk	H 229/170	
Ed Ruby	Gardiner's Hill, Cork	H 229/180	Living with sister?
Wm McCarthy	Baltimore, Co. Cork	H 229/185	Emigrated to US?
Josiah Worthington	Sister	H 229/189	Last seen at Tralee boarding

			a train for Cork (1924)
John Charles Reynolds	Cork?	H 229/195	Ex-soldier
Capt. Arthur Cant		H 229/213	Disappeared having sailed from Cobh
Arthur and Helen Temperley	Murragh, Enniskeane, Co. Cork	H 229/217	
J. A. Smyth	King's County	H 229/223	
Sarah Moloney	Gardiner Street, Dublin	H 229/224	
L. V. Farquhar	Sligo	H 229/283	
James Berry		H 229/298	
Vladimir Murtagh	Relatives	H 229/308	
Albert J. White	USA delegation	H 229/335	
Thomas Hewson	USA	H 229/340	
David O'Connor		H 229/347	
Jack James	Dublin	H 229/348	
John Smee	Limerick	H 229/358	Missing since 1921
Sir William Waller	Limerick?	H 229/366	
R. Bazay		H 229/368	
Turner B. Brown	USA	H 229/384	
Eric Boden		H 229/390	
Wm F. O'Mahony	Skibbereen	H 229/401	Post Office official

*Files where individuals were located have already been released by the Department of Justice and can be accessed in H 229. Most of the above files have not been released.

APPENDIX V

Kidnappings/Illegal Arrests of Civilians
(September 1921 to January 1922)
(Only weeks where kidnappings are recorded as having taken place are included.)
Source: Weekly Surveys of the State of Ireland, PRO, CAB 24/-

Week ended	Total	For appearance before Sinn Féin Courts	To prevent appearance at assizes	Released	No record of fate of detainee
5/9/1921	1				1
12/9/1921	20	3		10	10
17/9/1921	2	1	1	1	1
15/10/1921	8	5	3	4	4
21/10/1921	20	7	7		20
28/10/1921	18	12	3	1 died	17
1/11/1921	10			6	4
14/11/1921	32		6	16	16
18/11/1921	18		3	7	11
28/11/1921	16			10	6
3/12/1921	23			14	9
10/12/1921	7		1	1	6
17/12/1921	6			2	4
30/12/1921	5			2	3
2/1/1922	3			1 + (1 deported)	1
9/1/1922	4			2	2
16/1/1922	6		3	2	4
23/1/1921	2				2
30/1/1922	12			4	8

APPENDIX VI

Property Transfers in the South-Eastern Quarter of Cork City, 1921–26

Address	Deeds transferred	Deeds not transferred	Total number of changes of occupancy
Douglas Road	17	39	56
Blackrock Road	12	21	33
Ballintemple and Ballinlough Road	8	23	31
Wallace's Avenue	7	28	35
Victoria Avenue			
Others*	4	19	23
Total	47 (26%)	131 (74%)	178

These figures were arrived at by comparing the total number of changes in occupancy in residential properties in these streets between 1921 and 1926, as given in Guy's Postal Directories for Cork city with the relevant transfers of deeds of property as recorded by the Registry of Deeds, Dublin, for the same period.

*Southern Road, Boreenmanna Road and part of High Street

APPENDIX VII

Attacks on Civilians and Others Reported to the IRA's Liaison Office, Cork City, January–March 1922*

January	Nature of attack	Other details
7	Kidnapping of R.S. Kay, *Times* reporter	Released
	Escape of civilian	
9	Interference with civilian	
10	Kidnapping of civilian	
11	Attack on civilian	
12	Interference with civilian	
14	Kidnapping of Major Hallinan, Mallow	Labour dispute: released
16	Assault on civilian	
	Threats to civilian	
17	Threats to civilian	
	'Arrest' of three civilians	
	Shooting of civilians	
18	Threat to civilian	
19	Interference with civilian	
21	Raid on civilian's residence	
	Raid/robbery at Bessborough	Pike residence, Blackrock
21	Alleged kidnapping of sailor	
25	Seizure of Hallanan's Mills, Mallow	Labour dispute
26	Kidnapping of Anthony Carroll, solicitor, Fermoy	To prevent him attending 'enemy' court: released
	Interference with civilian, Mallow	Probably related to labour dispute
30	Raid on Saunders, MacCurtain Street	

February	Nature of attack	Other details
4	Civilian, no more details	May be related to an attack on an RIC man
9	Death of Richard Savage	As a result of hold-up of General Higginson
10	Raid on Hanniford's, Ballintemple	Professor of Music: unharmed?
11	Commandeering of premises by Cork 1	
13	Attack on civilian, Ballyhooly	
	Civilian interference	
14	Flogging of RIC constables, Macroom	
15	Custody of civilian	St Marie's of the Isle, Cork 1
16	Interference with the Douglas Hunt	
17	Seizure of newspapers	
18	Shooting of enemy officer	Genochio
	Attacks on enemy constables	
	Comandeering of car and civilian	

Week ending 25/2   No kidnappings reported

March	Nature of attack	Other details
6	Hold-up of three enemy constables	
9	Shooting of enemy constable	
14	Civilian missing	
15	Civilian wounded	
16	Assault on civilian	
18	Threat to civilian	
	Civilian missing	
20	Threat to civilian, Newmarket	
25	Shooting of ex-constable	Arthur Gloster
30	Kidnapping of civilian	

* Truce Liaison Reports, Cork city, MA Truce Liaison Papers, LE/4/7.

APPENDIX VIII

Deaths, Resignations and Other Departures from Cork City
Freemason Lodges, 1920–26

(Source: Membership Rolls Grand Freemason Lodge of Ireland, 1900–30)

Lodge no.	Deaths	Resignations	Listed as 'left'	Struck off
1	5	19	0	0
3	7*	7	1	0
8	2	0	2	1
71	7#	22	0	28
95	7	8	0	3
209	1	4	0	0
Total	29	50	3	32

*Includes William L. Cooke and Edward Hawksworth

#Includes James C. Beal

APPENDIX IX

Members of Cork City Freemason Lodges Struck Off, 1920–26

Lodge 8	Frederick W. D. Leonard	ND

Lodge 71	Robert Cassidy	Cycle agent
	Edward Collingwood	Lithographer
	Walter Corrin	Artist
	Edward Sparks	Naval police sergeant
	Charles Wolfe	Merchant
	Wm B. Beamish	Land agent
	John Beecher	Retired RIC sergeant
	Stanley Hunt	Mill manager
	William Highet	Engineer
	Alfred Hennessy	Mechanical engineer
	George Storey	Lieut Royal Dublin Fusiliers
	John J. Carson	Chief petty officer
	Walter Roberts	Dentist
	Archibald Phillips	Staff sergeant RASC
	Lewis B. Jordan	Lieut of payments
	Frederick J. Moffett	Clerk
	Robert F. Beecher	Corporal, Canadian forces
	Victor H. Beecher	Soldier, Canadian forces
	John Cottrell	Accountant
	Nathaniel Todd	Chief steward
	Thomas J. Benson	Shop assistant
	Stanley Morgan	Varnish maker
	Thomas C. Morgan	Varnish maker
	John R. Hennessy	Accountant
	Francis McMahon	Accountant
	Eric Fleeton	Mechanical engineer
	John F. Moore	Accountant
	Thomas Bew	Commercial traveller

Lodge 95	Mungo J. Smith	Captain RFA
	Henry A. Harris	Gen. sec. YMCA
	Edward G. Owens	Clerk

APPENDIX X

YMCA members listed for 1920/21 but no longer listed for 1921/22 or thereafter*

J. Beecher
F. Cottrell
A. G. Creber
D. Dalton
W. Dalton
R. S. S. Gregg
E. Harvison
W. J. Hosford
W. Jennett
J. C. Johnston
H. Kenny
W. Kew
F. Leslie
T. F. Manly
J. McKenzie
W. McNeill
A. Monteith
H. Royce
W. Roycroft
W. Roycroft Jnr
M. W. Smith
J. A. Stokes
F. W. Vear Jnr
R. A. Warner
R. Williamson
U. A. F. Williamson

*This excludes anybody I was able to establish from other records as having lived in Cork subsequently. The actual list of departures is considerably longer than this.

APPENDIX XI

Cork City YMCA members present in 1921/22 but no longer listed as subscribers in 1922/23 or thereafter*

H. Ford
W. Gabriel
J. Gardiner
C. Geeve
R. Good
R. W. Graham
W. Hawkes
P. G. Holman
J. G. Kennedy
C. H. Lendrum
J. Leslie
G. H. Locker
J. Matthews
T. McDonald
J. McGuinness
P. McGurgan
J. J. Owens
S. Parsons
W. C. Pheasy
G. Pratt
G. Robinson
Wm Ross
A. E. Sikes
Isaac Taylor
G. H. Tully
E. Walsh
W. C. Warner
J. F. Williamson
A. J. Wolfe
R. Wolfe
V. Wolfe

*This excludes those I was able to establish from other records as having lived in Cork subsequently. However, this is by no means exhaustive and it is likely that some of these individuals continued to live in Cork.

NOTES

Chapter 1 (pp 2–4)

1. *Cork Examiner*, 25.2.1921.
2. Richard H. (Reggie) Tilson had been Deputy Lord Mayor (High Sheriff) during the mayorship of Henry O'Shea 1912–14 and was a Home Rule Protestant running under the banner of the All For Ireland League.
3. *Cork Examiner*, 25.2.1921.
4. Which is not the same thing as claiming that a wide range of IRA men did not claim that it did.

Chapter 2 (pp 5–9)

1. James Fitzgerald, *Foras Feasa na Paróiste*, Knockraha Macra na Feirme, 1977.
2. The remainder of the executions took place in Glounthaune, to the south, as will be made clear throughout much of this book.

Chapter 3 (pp 10–16)

1. Mick Murphy, BMH/WS 1547.
2. Roibeárd Lankford, BMH/WS 16.
3. Seán Moylan, *In His Own Words, His Memoir of the War of Independence*.
4. Lieut Colonel Hughes-Hallett, in William Sheehan, *British Voices from the Irish War of Independence 1918–1921*.
5. George Power, O'Malley, P17b/123.
6. Which is not to say they were blameless when it came to atrocities. Apart from sacking Fermoy and Mallow, they gunned down a group of railway workers in Mallow in January 1921 as a reprisal for the shooting of the wife of an RIC inspector, and drowned a man in the river at Fermoy.
7. Flor Crowley aka 'Raymond': 'Black and Tan Diary', *Southern Star*, 23.10.1971 and subsequent editions.
8. Peter Hart, *The IRA at War*.
9. Gerry White and Brendan O'Shea, *Baptised in Blood*.
10. The evidence linking Swanzy directly to the MacCurtain assassination is questionable. See Michael Feeley, BMH/WS 68.
11. See Peter Hart, *The IRA and its Enemies, Violence and Community in Cork 1916–1923*.
12. Kevin Girvin, *The Life and Times of Seán O'Hegarty*.
13. Connie Neenan in *Survivors*, ed. Uinseann MacEoin. Also Michael J. Crowley, BMH/WS 1603.

Chapter 4 (pp 17–18)

1. Tim Cadogan, *Cork County Council 1899–1999: A Centenary Souvenir*.

2. One such issue occurred when Tomás MacCurtain's son, also called Tomás, shot dead a policeman who had been following him. De Valera, so the story goes, wanted MacCurtain executed. Corry led a revolt in Fianna Fáil to prevent the execution. Dev had to back down because he had a small majority in the Dáil at the time. Corry was not able to save other east Cork republicans, however. For quotation see Dáil debates 11/3/1942 and 29/4/1938.

3. Dáil debates 29.4.1938 and 11.3.1942.

4. O'Farrell, *The Wit and Humour of Dáil Eireann.*

Chapter 5 (pp 19–21)

1. Cadogan, *op. cit.* Corry was rearrested in 1926 in connection with raids on Garda stations. He was probably innocent of the charge and subsequently released after a period in prison: NA, Department of Justice 2007 Series, 2007/56/034.

2. Michael Leahy Papers, CCM.

3. *ibid.*

4. O'Farrell, *Who's Who in the Irish War of Independence.*

5. O'Malley, *On Another Man's Wounds,* pp 302–3.

Chapter 6 (pp 22–24)

1. Peter Hart, *The IRA and its Enemies.*

2. This is in contrast with some of the literature on the period, where sources are often just plain wrong, misleading or selectively quoted.

3. Cadogan, *op. cit.*

4. *Cork Constitution,* 9.12.1920.

5. Fitzgerald, *Foras Feasa.*

6. *Cork Examiner,* 8.1.1921.

7. See Chapter 16.

8. Fitzgerald, *op. cit.* Connie Neenan in *Survivors,* ed. Uinseann McEoin; Martin Corry in O'Malley, P17b/112.

9. Fitzgerald, *op. cit.*

10. Martin Corry in O'Malley, P17b/112.

11. Richard English, *Ernie O'Malley: IRA Intellectual.*

Chapter 7 (pp 25–29)

1. Mick Leahy, O'Malley Papers, P17b/108.

2. Edmond Desmond, O'Malley Papers, P17b/112.

3. 2nd Battalion Notes 1921: *The 79th News,* the Journal of the Cameron Highlanders.

4. Mick Leahy, O'Malley Papers, P17b/108. The only Denis Lehane listed in the RIC records died in County Tipperary in 1919 as a result of the Great Flu epidemic. The last reason is the more likely scenario since the description Leahy gave to O'Malley is probably too detailed to have been made up. See RIC Records, HO 184 series.

5. Seán Culhane, O'Malley Papers, P17b/108.

6. Mick Murphy, O'Malley Papers, P17b/112.

7. Seán Healy, BMH/WS 1479.

8. The group carried out several high profile murders during 1922 (see *Cork Examiner,* 4.10.1922) and were still killing in Carrigtwohill as late as the summer of 1923. The German was probably a man called Peter Wahbrot, a sailor who disappeared from Cork during 1922. See Appendix III.

9.   MA, A/0535; MA, A/0649. Also see MA, DOD series, A/07360.

10. It has to be said that there are few recorded instances where torture was used by the IRA to extract information, though it was standard procedure by some elements on the British side. The IRA were amateur soldiers: torture did not come easy to most of them. However, local sources have it that a Midleton Volunteer was the resident torturer for the east Cork Battalion. And torture can take many forms. Patrick McGlynn, who worked for a solicitor in Midleton, was kidnapped, brought to Carrigtwohill and forced to walk the countryside barefoot for several nights in the height of winter before being released. He subsequently spent seven weeks in hospital, unable to walk, having had a toe amputated. He may even have been held in Sing Sing. Patrick McGlynn, CO762/148.

11. Seán Culhane in O'Malley, P17b/106. Also see the case of Sergeant O'Brien in Fitzgerald, *op. cit.*

12. O'Farrell, *The Wit and Humour of Dáil Eireann.*

13. MA, DOD, A/09690.

Chapter 8 (pp 32–38)

1.   Fitzgerald, *op. cit.*

2.   Mick Murphy in O'Malley, P17b/112.

3.   Florence O'Donoghue, *No Other Law.*

4.   *Cork Examiner*, 22.8.1921.

5.   *Cork Constitution*, 22.11.1920. It is also mentioned in several accounts of the war in the city.

6.   *Cork Examiner*, 5.11.1921.

7.   Fitzgerald, *op. cit.*

8.   See Chapter 29.

9.   Seán Healy, BMH/WS 1479.

10. As we'll see in Part VI, the real number of missing military personnel is much higher than the published official list suggests.

11. Peter Hart, *The IRA and its Enemies.*

12. Fitzgerald, *op. cit.*

13. Maurice Forde *et al*, BMH/WS 719. Also see Chapter 13.

14. Two women, allegedly informers, disappeared in Carrigtwohill. However, they may have fled when their menfolk were publicly shot by the IRA.

15. *Cork Weekly News*, 4.6.1921.

16. RIC County Inspector's Report Nov–Dec 1920, CO 904/113; Ml Kennedy, CO 762/185.

17. *Cork Examiner*, 22.8.1921.

18. See MA A/0535 for Horgan and A/0649 for Ray. For Coughlan, see Mick Leahy in O'Malley, P17b/112.

19. County Inspector's Report, May 1921 CO 904/115. Also see Edmond Desmond in O'Malley, P17b/112.

20. Peter Hart, *op. cit.*

21. See Table 2, Appendix III and Appendix IV.

22. Record of activities of the 6th Battalion, Cork 1, O'Donoghue, MS 31, 339.

23. Seán Healy BMH/WS 1479; Seán Culhane, O'Malley, P17b/108.

24. Fitzgerald, *op. cit.*

25. The execution of Parsons may have been more sadistic and less 'military' than this account from Corry suggests. See letter from 'A Sympathetic Mother' in DOJ, 2007/56/11 and *Sunday Independent*, 1.7.2007.

26.　Martin Corry, O'Malley, p17b/112.

Chapter 9 (pp 39–42)

1.　'Life in Cork', *The Times*, 18.5.1921.
2.　Foulkes Papers, 7/36.
3.　Colonel Sir Vernon Kell in Foulkes, 7/21.
4.　Michael Hopkinson, *The Irish War of Independence*.
5.　Hart, *The IRA and its Enemies*.
6.　Hart, *op. cit.*
7.　See Table 3.
8.　See Chapters 14 and 15.
9.　Moss Twomey in O'Malley, p17b/96 and 107; CCPO/Cork Boro and Cork County East Riding Court Registers.
10.　Jane Leonard, 'Getting Them at last: the IRA and Ex-Servicemen' in *Revolution? Ireland 1917–1923*, ed. David Fitzpatrick; Peter Hart, *The IRA and its Enemies*.
11.　1911 Census.
12.　I have been able to find only three women killed by the Cork IRA in the county as a whole, though, as Peter Hart has shown, women made up quite a large proportion of those who actually gave information. Half a dozen women were shot in Cork city during the Civil War, however.
13.　Seán Healy, BMH/WS 1479.
14.　Healy, *op. cit.*
15.　HQ Cork to GHQ, 10.10.1921; O'Malley, p7/A/26.

Chapter 10 (pp 43–50)

1.　Citation upon the investiture of MBE on Lieut A. R. Koe, Royal Hospital Kilmainham, Dublin, 12.7.1921, WO 35/181.
2.　Christopher Andrew, *Secret Service: The Making of the British Intelligence Community*. Also Keith Jeffrey, 'British Military Intelligence Following World War I'.
3.　Eunan O'Halpin, 'British Intelligence in Ireland 1914–1921'; O'Halpin, 'Collins and Intelligence 1919–1923'; Tim Pat Coogan, *Michael Collins*.
4.　Andrew, *op. cit.*
5.　Hopkinson, *op. cit.*
6.　Paul McMahon, *British Spies and Irish Rebels*.
7.　CI's Report Nov/Dec 1920, CO904/113.
8.　Seán Culhane in O'Malley, p17b/108.
9.　Richard Abbott, *op. cit.*
10.　*Cork Examiner*, 22.3.1921.
11.　Though, as we'll see, they sometimes managed to do so.
12.　Hart, ed., *British Intelligence in Ireland 1920–1921*.
13.　Julian Putkowski, 'The Best Secret Service Man We Had'. Also see Hopkinson, *op. cit.* and Coogan, *Michael Collins*.
14.　Hopkinson, *op. cit.* Also see Ormonde Winter, 'A Report of the Intelligence Branch of the Chief of Police, Dublin Castle, from May 1920 to July 1921', in *British Intelligence in Ireland 1920–1921*, ed. Peter Hart.
15.　Winter, *op. cit.*

16. Frank P. Crozier, *Ireland For Ever.*

17. Hopkinson, *op.cit.*; Coogan, *op. cit.*

18. For detailed accounts of the shooting of Quinlisk, see the RIC's List of Sinn Féin and Republican Suspects, CO 904/213/359–379. Also see Mick Murphy, BMH/WS 1547.

19. See the lists of officers put forward by the Irish Command for decorations for bravery in WO 35/181, WO 141/42 and WO 141/54.

20. Hart, ed., *British Intelligence in Ireland 1920–1921.*

21. The list of Sinn Féin and republican suspects collated by the RIC illustrates the very dated nature of RIC intelligence by 1920. The list shows the continued obsession with Sinn Féin as against the more serious activists in the IRA, CO 904/211.

22. Florence O'Donoghue, *No Other Law.*

23. Borgonovo, *Spies, Informers and the Anti-Sinn Féin League.*

24. Mick Murphy, BMH/WS 1547.

25. Hart, ed., *British Intelligence in Ireland 1920–1921.*

26. *ibid.*

27. *ibid.*

28. *ibid.*

29. Seán Moylan in his account of his capture states that while two NCOs visited his cell and gave him 'a good drubbing, I feel it right to say that he [a British Intelligence Officer] used no violence, intimidation or threat.' Seán Moylan, *Seán Moylan: In His Own Words.*

30. Hart, ed., *British Intelligence in Ireland 1920–1921.*

31. The local Centre for Cork city was Lieut A. R. Koe, whose medal citation is given at the head of this chapter.

32. *ibid.* This in all likelihood refers to either Major A. E. Percival or Captain (later Major) J. O. C. Kelly.

33. *ibid.*

34. Anderson to Macready, 7.3.1921, CO 904/188.

35. Confession of spy Saunders, Mulcahy P7/A/20.

36. Liam de Roiste Diary, 10.6.1920, quoted in Borgonovo, *Spies, Informers and the Anti-Sinn Féin League.*

37. Hart, *op. cit.*

38. Hart, ed., *British Intelligence in Ireland 1920–1921.*

39. *ibid.*

40. Patrick Collins, BMH/WS 1707.

41. Hart, ed., *op. cit.*

42. Frank O'Connor, *My Oedipus Complex and Other Stories.*

43. Hart, ed., *op. cit.*

44. O'Donoghue, *No Other Law.*

45. Meda Ryan, *Tom Barry: IRA Freedom Fighter.*

Chapter 11 (pp 51–57)

1. Michael Hopkinson, *The Irish War of Independence.*

2. *The Times*, 18.5.1921.

3. The Florence O'Donoghue Papers, taken as a whole, give a fascinating insight on how this system operated. Also see Borgonovo, *Florence and Josephine O'Donoghue's War of Independence.*

4. Donal Kelly, 'Ordeal By Fire', in *Rebel Cork's Fighting Story*. Its members were Jeremiah O'Brien, Bob Ahern, Michael Kenny, Jim Fitzgerald, Denis Hegarty and Frank O'Mahony.

5. Florence O'Donoghue to Minister for Defence, 13.7.1936 in Michael Kenny, IRA Pension Application.

6. Collins to O'Donoghue, 8.3.1921; see Borgonovo, *op. cit.*

7. Michael Kenny, IRA Pension Application.

8. Hart, ed., *British Intelligence in Ireland 1920–1921*.

9. Bob Ahern, *op. cit.* The BMH witness submissions contain many examples of how local IRA companies carried out the killings for Brigade Intelligence. See, for instance, Jerry Keating, BMH/WS 1657, Patrick Collins, BMH/WS 1707. For killings by the ASU see Danny Healy, BMH/WS 1656.

10. Danny Healy, BMH/WS 1656

11. See Keating, Collins, Healy, *op. cit.*

12. For an extensive and detailed analysis of the operations of IRA intelligence in Cork city, see Borgonovo, *Spies, Informers and the Anti-Sinn Féin League*.

13. Bob Ahern, BMH/WS1676.

14. See Mick Murphy, Jerry Keating and Patrick Collins, BMH witness statements.

15. G. White and B. O'Shea, *The Burning of Cork*. The O'Donoghue Papers contain many lists of names of British officers who resided in the city, as well as the names of prominent RIC men, including the names and addresses in Britain of many Black and Tans and Auxiliary officers. See O'Donoghue Papers, MS 31, 227 and MS 31, 228.

16. Kelly, whose proper name was Captain J. W. O'Kelly, was promoted to the rank of major as a result of his work in Cork. He also received an OBE in 1921.

17. Florence O'Donoghue in O'Malley, P17b/95.

18. O'Donoghue Papers, MS 31, 202.

19. Borgonovo, *op. cit.*

20. Tribute to Ernie Sorenson, in Borgonovo, *Spies, Informers and the Anti-Sinn Féin League*.

21. See the shooting of Sergeant O'Donoghue in Hart, *The IRA and its Enemies*, pp 1–18 for one example of an unauthorised killing.

Chapter 12 (pp 58–62)

1. Anne Dolan, 'Killing and Bloody Sunday', November 1920.

2. John Borgonovo, *Florence and Josephine O'Donoghue's War of Independence*.

3. Josephine lived in Wales from 1911 to 1916. For some of this time she lived with the Brown family but 'this was an unhappy experience in which I had many difficulties and hardships'. Coleridge Brown had converted to Catholicism in order to marry Josephine. However, when he died, he stipulated in his will that the boys be raised in the Protestant faith. She claimed they [the Browns] were hostile to Catholics and did not wish a Catholic in the house. 'Mother's Story', Borgonovo, *Florence and Josephine O'Donoghue's War of Independence*, pp 112–15.

4. Many of these documents can be found in the Collins Papers, MA, A/0413 and A/0622. Most of this documentation deals with matters relating to the British garrison in Berehaven and County Kerry, suggesting that Mrs Brown worked in an office dealing with these. Their military value appears to have been somewhat exaggerated as they deal with relatively routine matters.

5. Seán O'Callaghan, *Execution*.

6.   Florence O'Donoghue, *No Other Law.*
7.   Florence O'Donoghue, *Tomás MacCurtain—Soldier and Patriot.*
8.   O'Donoghue, MS 31, 124(2). There is more than an element of military snobbery here. MacSwiney looked as good in uniform as anyone else.
9.   Borgonovo, *Florence and Josephine O'Donoghue's War of Independence*, p. 56.
10. *ibid.*
11. Note in O'Donoghue, MS 31, 124(3).
12. It appears that MacCurtain had been a member prior to 1916 but resigned thereafter.
13. Hopkinson, *op. cit.*
14. Kevin Girvin, *The Life and Times of Seán O'Hegarty.*
15. Though that did not prevent him from travelling to Gravesend in east London early in 1921 in an attempt to assassinate one of the Victoria Barracks IOs who was on leave. 'Anonymous' (Connie Neenan) account in O'Donoghue, MS 31, 337.

Chapter 13 (pp 63–69)

1.   Jane Leonard, 'Getting Them at Last, The IRA and Ex-Servicemen'.
2.   Peter Hart, *The IRA and its Enemies.*
3.   Seán O'Callaghan, *Execution.*
4.   MA, A/0649.
5.   I was told this story by a very reliable source. See also Jim Cronin, *Making Connections: A Cork GAA Miscellany.*
6.   GHQ Dublin, 18.10.1921, Mulcahy Papers, P7/A/26.
7.   Cork Borough Electoral Register, 1913, in CCPO Records, NA.
8.   GHQ Dublin, 18.10.1921, Mulcahy Papers, P7/A/26.
9.   Julian Putkowski, 'A2 and the Reds in Khaki', *Lobster 94: Journal of Parapolitics*, No. 27 (April 1994). I am grateful to Julian Putkowski for sharing additional information on the infiltration of the Sailors, Soldiers and Airmen's Union and thereby the London Trades Council and a range of left-wing groups. Infiltration of the IRA was also attempted through the Irish Self-Determination League in London.
10. *Cork Examiner*, 22.2.1921.
11. Connie Neenan in O'Malley, P17b/112.
12. Cork Borough Criminal Injuries Book, 14 Feb 1921–12 June 1921, CCPO Records, NA.
13. 'Anonymous' (Connie Neenan), O'Donoghue, MS 31, 337.
14. *Cork Examiner*, 22.2.1921.
15. There are many accounts of the 'career' of McDonald as a spy. For instance, see Connie Neenan in O'Malley, P17b/112 and Mick Murphy, BMH/WS 1547.
16. Connie Neenan, *op. cit.*
17. Cork Borough Criminal Injuries Book, 14 Feb 1921–12 June 1921, CCPO Records, NA.
18. British records are quite frank about Connors. There is an intriguing account of his activities in *A Record of the Rebellion in Ireland* (6th Division), WO 141/93.
19. Patrick J. Twohig, *Green Tears for Hecuba*. It appears that the main reason for the failure of the ambush was that O'Hegarty and Sandow Donovan got fed up waiting for the British to arrive so they 'conceived the idea of sending a man into Macroom to let the enemy know we were waiting for them'. The enemy, forewarned, were heavily armed and proceeded with the utmost caution. The fleeing ambush party was then lucky to avoid encirclement by another detachment of British troops coming from Killarney. Dan Harrington, BMH/WS 1532.

20. Danny Healy, BMH/WS 1656.
21. *Daily Mail*, 15.4.1922. For substantial detail on the case, see the *New York Times*, 15.4.1922.
22. See correspondence on the execution of Herlihy in Mulcahy, P7/A/24.
23. O'Callaghan, *op. cit.* See also Hart, *The IRA and its Enemies*, Chapter 1.
24. This account is based on that given to Seán O'Callaghan by Frank Busteed (O'Callaghan, *Execution*). The details may not be entirely accurate, though Busteed was present at the execution, for there are suggestions that at least two other unknown suspects were picked up and executed as a direct result of the Broad Lane episode, with one of these killings taking place in the Lee Fields west of the city.
25. Pat Margetts, O'Malley, P17b/111.
26. Hart, *op. cit.*
27. See report of the Military Court of Inquiry into Walsh's death, *Cork Examiner*, 21.2.1921.
28. J. O'C. Kelly to QMG, 21.2.1921, O'Donoghue, MS 31, 223(1).
29. See Siobhan Lankford, *The Hope and the Sadness*.
30. *Cork Examiner*, 21.2.1921.
31. Hart, ed., *British Intelligence in Ireland 1920–1921*.
32. *Cork Constitution*, 22.2.1921. It is interesting to note that several other ex-servicemen shot and wounded by the IRA as spies were subsequently treated in the military hospital. These include Monkey Mac, Thomas Goulding and P. J. Poland, WO 35/180A. Walsh and Mohally, on the other hand, were treated in civilian hospitals, suggesting that, despite IRA claims, they may not have been spies.
33. HOC Debates, 21.3.1921, Vol. 139, c2246—in Borgonovo.
34. Jane Leonard, *op. cit.*

Chapter 14 (pp 72–80)

1. Peter Hart, *The IRA and its Enemies*; Peter Hart, *The IRA at War, 1916–1923*.
2. Contrary to most accounts of the killing, Herbert Woods was not the husband of Hornibrook's daughter, Matilda. He was rather a nephew of her husband Edward Woods. Edward Woods was a Cork city businessman who ran a wine and spirits shop in Patrick Street. Herbert Woods, who had been reared as one of the family by Edward Woods and his wife, had been a captain during the Great War and had been decorated for bravery. For details on Woods's character, see Alice Hodder letter, *Conditions in Cork*, CO 739/16.
3. Meda Ryan, *Tom Barry: IRA Freedom Fighter*.
4. This is in contrast to east Cork where a section of the IRA was expelled for extortion and drunkenness (Hart, *The IRA and its Enemies*) and north Cork where members were deported for embezzling IRA funds (Meda Ryan, *Liam Lynch*).
5. Alice Hodder letter, *op. cit.*
6. And also in loyalist Irish newspapers such as *The Irish Times* and the *Cork Constitution*. The events at the Hornibrook house, however, went unreported at the time.
7. *Cork Constitution*, 25.1.1921.
8. In some accounts the leader of the party is given as Jack Cody, a Volunteer from the city. However, it seems that two Tom Bradfields were tricked in this way, one in Enniskeane, the other near Bandon.
9. The gunmen were after his brother William, who had escaped. John, who was crippled from rheumatism, was not in a position to get away. He was shot through the neck and head.

10. *Cork Constitution*, 2.2.1921.

11. John D. Brewer, *The Royal Irish Constabulary: An Oral History.*

12. Hart, *The IRA and its Enemies.*

13. Hart, *op. cit.*

14. Art O'Brien Papers, 8428.

15. CO 904/168.

16. *ibid.*

17. IRA Casualty Lists, MA A/0437 and A/0438.

18. Bob Lankford's IRA Pension Application, quoted in Borgonovo, *Spies, Informers and the Anti-Sinn Féin League.*

19. Lieut W. S. Watts, Army Service Record, WO 374/72558.

20. The IRA has always claimed that the three officers were intelligence officers, but there is no evidence from British sources to suggest that they were. Contrast this to the case of Captain Thompson of the Manchester Regiment who was killed near Ballincollig around the same time, who was an intelligence officer and has always been referred to as such. Similarly two lieutenants captured and executed in north Cork at around the same time were stated to have worked in intelligence. *A Record of the Rebellion in Ireland 6th Division Report*, WO 141/93.

21. Lieut W. S. Watts, Army Service Record, WO 374/72558.

22. Manchester Regiment Record of Service, quoted in Hart, *The IRA and its Enemies*, p. 96. It is interesting to note that, though 22 others were captured at the pub, none was harmed.

23. *The History of the Manchester Regiment.* The boys were not aged 13 and 14 as is sometimes suggested. It was, none the less, one of the more pointlessly savage episodes in the conflict.

24. Murphy was also held responsible for the death of Captain Thompson, who was taken off a motor bike near Bishopstown and shot dead.

25. Brewer, *op. cit.*

26. Meda Ryan, *Tom Barry: IRA Freedom Fighter*; Kathleen Keyes-McDonnell, *There is a Bridge at Bandon.*

27. Meda Ryan, *op. cit.*

28. Put in place as a result of Tory and Unionist lobbying in the 1920s to compensate southern loyalists for losses incurred in the period after the Truce of July 1921.

29. Hart, *op. cit.*

30. HQ 1st Btn Cork 3, 22.2.1922, MA A/0960.

31. HQ Cork 3 to Div Adj 1st s. Div., 4.3.1922, MA A/0960.

32. Henry Forde to Arthur Griffith, 9.2.1922. MA A/0960.

33. 'Spy Farms in Cork', MA A/10876.

34. F. P. Crozier, *Ireland For Ever.*

35. Brig. Frederick Clarke in Sheehan, *British Voices*, 2005; Crozier, *op. cit.*

36. *Cork Examiner*, 25.1.1921.

37. 'Charlie' letter, 16.12.1920, O'Donoghue, MS 31, 226.

38. This is claimed mainly in Meda Ryan's biography of Tom Barry, but there have also been a number of articles and letters to the newspapers in the summer of 2006, in the wake of the release of the film *The Wind that Shakes the Barley.*

39. The contents of the diary were printed in *The Southern Star* over a number of succeeding issues, beginning on 22.10.1971.

40. The answer would be to make public the list of 'helpful citizens' and see how it compares with those killed.

41. Keyes McDonnell, *op. cit.*

42. See 'Enrolment of Civilians as Civil Guards', wo 35/66.

43. While both Reverends Harbord—his father, Rev. Richard Harbord, was rector at Murragh—
     stated that they were loyalists, neither claimed to have been a member of any clandestine
     Anti-Sinn Féin League or equivalent (Rev. Ralph Harbord, co 762/58, Rev. Richard Harbord,
     co 762/155). Both lived subsequently in west Cork and were not driven out, as was the case of
     the families of many 'convicted spies'. Tom Barry does, however, mention another Protestant
     minister who, he claimed, worked as a British agent and fled in the middle of the night when
     about to be assassinated. Tom Barry, *Guerrilla Days in Ireland*, p. 111. It should be pointed out
     that Rev. Ralph Harbord was only ordained to the ministry in the spring of 1922 and he was
     resident curate in Limerick at the time he was attacked. It appears he was on a visit home at
     the time. He was a seminarian during the period when he was supposed to be a 'spy'. See *Cork
     Weekly News*, 29.4.1922.

44. There *were* genuine loyalist vigilante groups patrolling and holding up suspected IRA men,
     but only in Ulster. See *Cork Examiner*, 12.11.1920 and also John McColgan, *British Withdrawal
     From Ireland: British Policy and the Irish Administration.*

45. 'Civilian Town Guards—Midleton', *Cork Constitution*, 14.2.1921.

46. *Southern Star*, 20.11.1971. Also see *Cork County Eagle*, 16.4.1921 for 'Civil Guards in Ballineen'
     and *Cork Constitution*, 15.2.1921 for Drimoleague.

47. RIC Daily Summary, 18.2.1921, co 904/144.

48. *Southern Star*, 20.11.1971.

49. Joseph O'Neill, *Blood-Dark Track.*

50. David Gray, a Cavan-born pharmacist in the town, was accused of being a 'Free Stater' by his
     assailants as he was being murdered. Gray was suspected because he was kind to children
     who came to his shop to have bandages put on cuts and bruises. One of Peter Hart's
     Protestant sources probably put his finger on it when he stated that David Gray and William
     Morrison were attacked because 'they went drinking with Black and Tans'. Hart, *The IRA and
     its Enemies.*

51. *The Irish Times*, 22.1.1921.

Chapter 15 (pp 81–90)

1.   ASFL notice sent to residents of Carraig an Suir, *Cork Constitution*, 22.4.1921.

2.   County Inspector's Report, November 1920, co 904/113.

3.   Michael Hopkinson, ed., *The Last Days of Dublin Castle: The Diaries of Mark Sturges.*

4.   Peter Hart, *The IRA and its Enemies.*

5.   To take one example, see the *Cork Weekly News* of 25.6.1921 for the almost casual shooting of
     one Michael Leahy in Cork city by undercover British agents in lieu of the 'real' Mick Leahy.

6.   John Miller Borgonovo, *Informers, Intelligence and the Anti-Sinn Féin Society, The Anglo-Irish
     Conflict in Cork City 1920–1921*, MA thesis, NUI Cork (1998). This has been published in book
     form: *Spies, Informers and the Anti-Sinn Féin League*, Irish Academic Press, 2007.

7.   Numerically, there were significantly more Catholic loyalists than Protestant loyalists, though
     that never appears to be taken into account.

8.   Florence O'Donoghue, as told to Donal O'Kelly in *Rebel Cork's Fighting Story.*

9.   Both reports are published in *British Intelligence in Ireland 1920–1921*, ed. Hart. It should be
     pointed out again that the intelligence reports do admit that one of the most useful players
     in the field was an organisation of ex-British officers—civilians in mufti who carried out

undercover 'jobs'—the ASFL again. See Chapters 41 and 42.

10. Lieut Gen. A. E. Percival in *British Voices*, ed. William Sheehan.

11. Eunan O'Halpin, 'British Intelligence in Ireland 1914–1921', in *The Missing Dimension*, ed. Andrew and Dilk, 1984.

12. O'Donoghue, MS 31, 223(1). This is a fascinating document, as it is in effect a list of the most loyal of the Irish Unionist establishment, or at least of those who lived around the coast during WWI. Paul McMahon dates it at 1915. McMahon, *British Spies and Irish Rebels*.

13. *Cork Weekly News*, 3.4.1920.

14. Liam de Roiste Diary, 17.7.1920.

15. *Cork Constitution*, 30.11.1920.

16. RIC *Weekly Summary*, 29.10.1920.

17. RIC *Weekly Summary*, 22.10.1920.

18. RIC *Weekly Summary*, 29.10.1920.

19. *Cork County Eagle and Munster Advertiser*, 25.11.1920, quoted in Borgonovo.

20. *Cork Examiner* and *Cork Constitution*, 13.10.1920.

21. *Cork Constitution*, 24.11.1920.

22. Florence O'Donoghue in O'Malley, P17b/95.

23. Olga Pyne Clarke, *She Came of Decent People*. Borgonovo prints Strickland's demands but neglects to mention Clarke's reply.

24. Borgonovo, *Spies, Informers and the Anti-Sinn Féin League*.

25. Borgonovo *op. cit.*

26. *New York Times*, 31.12.1920.

27. The record of the rebellion in Ireland concedes the point that British military men had little regard for Irish loyalists. 'Many Englishmen were inclined to regard the traditional Unionists as men calling themselves loyalists but who because they did not give information, were not really loyal. It must be admitted that the position of this class was particularly difficult.' A Record of the Rebellion in Ireland, unpublished section, Jeudwine Papers, IWM 72/82/2.

28. Hart, ed., *British Intelligence in Ireland 1920–1921*.

29. See Hansard, HOC Debates, 24.11.1920, 25.11.1920, 14.6.1921.

30. While there were assassinations by 'civilians' among these 19 killings (an example being the killing of Charlie Daly in the railway tunnel near Glanmire station on 1 March 1921), most were by raiding military units accompanied by IOs in disguise.

31. *Cork Weekly News*, 25.6.1921.

32. Patrick Ahern, BMH/WS 1003.

33. *Cork Examiner*, 11.4.1921.

34. See Chapters 41 and 42.

35. *Rebel Cork's Fighting Story*.

36. Cork East Riding Criminal Injury Book, Feb 1921–Oct 1921, CCPO Records, NA.

37. Register of Courts of Inquiry in lieu of Inquests, WO 35/163.

38. *Cork Constitution*, 15.2.1921.

39. *Cork Constitution*, 25.8.1920.

40. Kevin Girvin, *The Life and Times of Seán O'Hegarty*, MPhil Thesis (UCC).

41. Josephine Marchment Brown was adamant that this took place during the winter of 1920/21. See her IRA pension application, O'Donoghue, MS 31, 127.

42. There are many other reasons for believing O'Connor was the retired British Army officer

who contacted the military authorities on the movements of the IRA staff. O'Donoghue makes several references to it in his papers as occurring during the winter of 1920/21. Also all the HQ staff, except for O'Donoghue and O'Connor, had left the city from February. The key to the affair is the first attempt on O'Connor's life on 4 February 1921.

43. The other was Quinlisk. O'Donoghue Papers, MS 31, 124(2).
44. O'Donoghue Papers, MS 31, 124(2).
45. Coleman O'Mahony, *The Maritime Gateway to Cork: Passage West 1754–1942.*
46. *Cork Constitution*, 13.7.1921; *Cork Constitution*, 15.7.1921. Newspaper accounts suggest that up to 25 men were involved. The inquiry into his death, however, claimed that only seven men arrived to carry out the killing. Register of the Courts of Inquiry in lieu of Inquest, WO 35/163.

Chapter 16 (pp 91–94)

1. 1O Cork 1 to Adj Gen, 10.2.1922, MA A/0535.
2. *Cork Examiner*, 1.12.1920.
3. *Cork Constitution*, 1.12.1920.
4. O/C Cork 1 to Adj-Gen, 17.11.21, MA A/0535
5. George Horgan's mother gave her address as Ballintemple in her correspondence with the Irish government a year later. Indeed the family is also listed as living in Ballintemple in the 1911 Census. However, the Valuation books record that they were living at 62 High Street in 1920 and left some time in 1921. Valuation Lists Cork Boro, 5 A, B and C, South Ward, 1908–34, VO Dublin.
6. Comdt J. McCarthy to S. Command, MA A/0535.
7. CI Report, April/May 1921, CO 904/115.
8. Julian Putkowski, 'A2 and the Reds in Khaki', *op. cit.*
9. Letter from GHQ Dublin, 18.10.1921, Mulcahy, P7/A/26.
10. Seán Healy, BMH/WS 1479.
11. Connie Neenan in O'Malley, P17b/112.
12. Liam de Roiste Diary, 27.11.1920.
13. CO 905/15.
14. John F. Hayes, CO 762/7.
15. Official British Army report on the disappearance of Lieuts Watts, Chambers and Green, MA A 0435.
16. Seán Culhane, in O'Malley, P17b/108.
17. Lieut Gen. A. E. Percival in *British Voices*, ed. William Sheehan. Percival is often perceived as the commander of the Essex Regiment in Bandon. It is clear, however, from his own account in *British Voices* that he was chief intelligence officer and that, prior to 1921, his remit ran from Queenstown to Bantry.
18. In fact, suspicion of the garrison adjutant's office was justified, for the civilian working there, Con Conroy, was an IRA spy and probably provided the information.
19. Report on Watts, Chambers and Green, MA A/0435.
20. Michael Kennedy, CO 762/185.
21. Cork YMCA Annual Reports, 1918/19 and 1919/20.
22. *Cork Examiner*, 10.12.1920.
23. CI's Report, Nov/Dec 1920, CO 904/113.

Chapter 17 (pp 95–98)

1. Mick Murphy, BMH/WS 1579.
2. Jim Fitzgerald, *op. cit.*
3. Florence O'Donoghue, *Tomás MacCurtain*. Also Florence O'Donoghue in *Rebel Cork's Fighting Story*.
4. Mick Murphy in O'Malley, P17b/112.
5. Guy's Postal Directory of Cork 1920 and 1921.
6. Jerry Keating, BMH/WS 1657; Paddy Collins, BMH/WS 2998.

Chapter 18 (pp 100–107)

1. *The Nation*, 22.9.1928.
2. *Cork Constitution*, 24.10.1921.
3. See Mary Mulvihill, *Ingenious Ireland*, Chapter 11.
4. N. Marshall Cummins, 'The Great Irish Famine' in *The Cork Anthology*, ed. Seán Dunne, 1993.
5. Cork YMCA Annual Report 1918–1919.
6. Interestingly, Farrington polled around 2,254 votes, with his running mate Daniel Williams polling around the same number. This suggests that in 1918 Cork city Protestantism was evenly split between traditional unionism and a more pro-Home Rule position. See 1st Dáil, ElectionsIreland.org.
7. Liam de Roiste Diary, 3.3.1921.
8. *ibid.*
9. The PM, HOC Debate, 26 June 1922. In NA/Taoiseach s 1322. There were a number of meetings between Barry Egan and other senior Sinn Féin politicians and loyalist representatives mediating between the Sinn Féin and British government positions. See Midleton Papers.
10. *Cork Constitution*, 19.3.1921.
11. Certainly the city YMCA, the only branch for which I was able to find records, appears to make no reference to the others. They do not appear to have been sub-branches of the city organisation. The others seem to be more in the line of local Protestant and largely loyalist clubs.
12. For vast detail on these activities, see the YMCA Archive at Birmingham University.
13. *ibid.* Also see Dan Harvey and Gerry White, *The Barracks: A History of Victoria/Collins Barracks, Cork*.
14. World War I service medals, TNA Online.
15. *Cork Constitution*, 30.10.1920.
16. *Cork Constitution*, 3.5.1921.
17. Peter Hart, *The IRA and its Enemies*.
18. *Cork Constitution*, 30.10.1920.
19. Annual Minutes of the Irish Executive of the YMCA, December 1920, YMCA J7, BU.
20. Attendance at Burser's Meeting 1921, Cork YMCA Ladies Committee Year Book.
21. Guy's Postal Directories for Cork 1910 to 1925. James S. Parsons appears to have been a Dublin-based member of the YMCA who was present for that meeting along with a member of the Guinness family.
22. Cork YMCA General Committee Year Book 1904–42.
23. It should be remembered of course that this *rapprochement* was between loyalist and nationalist Ireland, not between loyalist and republican Ireland.
24. Cork YMCA General Committee Year Book 1904–42.

25. Cork YMCA Ladies Committee Year Book.

26. YMCA Annual Report 1920–21.

27. Cork YMCA General Committee Year Book 1904–1942, meeting of 22/6/1921.

28. John Borgonovo suggested that James Beal, whose second name was Charles, was a member of the YMCA. But that is to confuse him with Charles E. Beale, a member of the Cork Quaker family who *was* a member. Neither Beal nor the Blemenses ever appeared to have had any contact with the YMCA.

29. See the quotation at the head of this chapter. Taken from *The Nation*, quoted in Raids on Boy Scouts Camps, Department of Justice, H 280/37, NA. See also Gaughan, *Scouting in Ireland*.

Chapter 19 (pp 108–111)

1. Florence O'Donoghue, *No Other Law*.

2. Mick Murphy, BMH/WS 1547.

3. 'Ordeal by Fire', Donal O'Kelly in *Rebel Cork's Fighting Story*.

4. Pa Murray, BMH/WS 1584.

5. Mick Murphy, BMH/WS 1547.

6. Uinseann MacEoin, ed., *Survivors*.

7. Connie Neenan in O'Malley, P17b/112.

8. It has to be said that the military inquiries, while describing the killing of civilians—and often covering up the details of killings carried out by the military themselves—could do so only where a body was found. They did not deal with kidnappings.

9. See Foulkes Papers, 7/4 to 7/42, Liddell Hart.

10. *The Times*, 18.5.1921.

11. Peter Hart, *The IRA and its Enemies*.

12. They have recently been joined by John Borgonovo, who briefly mentions Parsons. Borgonovo, *Spies, Informers and the Anti-Sinn Féin League*.

13. The former is actually on the adjacent Victoria Road, suggesting that the latter is more likely to have been the place where the abduction took place.

14. *Cork Examiner*, 23.5.1921.

Chapter 20 (pp 112–115)

1. *Cork Constitution*, 1.12.1920.

2. *Cork Examiner*, 1.12.1920.

3. 1901 and 1911 Census Returns; Guy's Directories 1907–1921.

4. 1911 Census Returns.

5. World War I Campaign Medals, TNA Online.

6. Membership Rolls, Grand Masonic Lodge of Ireland.

7. Mick Murphy, O'Malley, P17b/112.

8. *Cork Examiner*, 19.2.1921 and 21.2.1921.

9. Finding of Military Inquiry, John Sullivan and Pat Sheehan, WO 35/159A. One of these was also a teenager.

10. Mick Murphy, O'Malley, P17b/112.

11. Mick Murphy, O'Malley, P17b/112.

12. Mick Murphy, BMH/WS 1547.

13. Josephine Marchment Brown, in the wake of the killing of the three officers at Waterfall, was under enormous stress. This is evident in many of her accounts. With O'Donoghue gone to

Wales at this time to spring young Reggie Brown, the stress was likely to have been even greater.

14. *Cork Constitution*, 6.12.1920; *Cork Examiner*, 6.12.1921.
15. *Cork Constitution*, 3.1.1921; *Cork Weekly News*, 8.1.1921.
16. *Cork Constitution*, 3.1.1921; *Cork Weekly News*, 8.1.1921.
17. O'Donoghue, MS 31, 213.
18. O'Callaghan, *op. cit.*
19. O'Callaghan, *op. cit.*
20. RIC CI's Report, Nov/Dec 1920, CO 904/113. Interestingly, while the CI mentions the Blemenses, he makes no mention of Downing or Horgan in his bi-monthly report, even though the Black and Tans were outraged at their disappearance and the evidence appears to support the idea that the latter may have been undercover agents.
21. The likely answer to that is that he was not living there at the time.

Chapter 21 (pp 116–119)

1. O'Callaghan, *Execution*; Connie Neenan, O'Malley, P17b/108.
2. Mick Murphy, BMH/WS 1547.
3. Jerry Keating, BMH/WS 1657; Patrick Collins, BMH/WS 1707.
4. Membership Lists of the Cork Masonic Lodges, Library of the Grand Masonic Lodge of Ireland.
5. Annual Reports of the Cork YMCA 1910–1921; *Cork Examiner*, 2.11.1920.
6. *Cork Constitution*, 12.2.1921 and 14.2.1921.
7. *Cork Constitution*, 14.2.1921. After his death, a bronze plaque was affixed to the organ in his memory. The last hymn he played before his death was 'Be Not Afraid'. R. Lee Cole: *A History of Methodism in Ireland*, Vol. 4.
8. *Cork Examiner*, 11.2.1921. Report of Military Inquiry, WO 35/157.
9. Liam de Roiste Diary, 19.2.1921.
10. These include the Cork Savings Bank, Cork Chamber of Commerce and the Cork Circuit Court.
11. Benjamin Haughton at Cork Assizes, *Cork Constitution*, 12.2.1921.
12. *ibid.*
13. Rev. J. W. Alley, Cork Methodist Minister at Memorial Service, *Cork Constitution*, 14.2.1921.
14. *ibid.*
15. *Cork Examiner*, 11.2.1921.
16. *Cork Constitution*, 10.2.1921.
17. Borgonovo, *op. cit.*
18. *Cork Constitution*, 9.2.1921.
19. *Cork Constitution*, 14.2.1921.
20. Rev. Alley, *Cork Constitution*, 14.2.1921.
21. Robert Kee, *The Green Flag, Ourselves Alone*, Vol. III.
22. William 'Sailor' Barry, BMH/WS 1708.
23. Report of Military Inquiry, WO 35/157.
24. When gunmen were ordered to carry out executions like this one, they were rarely given the exact reasons for it.
25. Their homes were less than half a mile apart in what was then largely a rural area, though it is now built up.

26. Criminal Injury Book Cork East Riding, Feb–Oct 1921, CCPO Records, NA.
27. They lived close to each other. O'Connor attended Reilly's funeral. Both deaths are mentioned in similar terms in the parish records of Douglas Church of Ireland parish, even though Reilly was a Methodist. Douglas parish records, RCB Library, Dublin.
28. Douglas Assizes in *Cork Constitution*, 15.2.1921.
29. Military Inquiry, WO 35/157.
30. Fines Book 1919–1922, Cork Court Records. Reggie Tilson had been fined for the same reason.
31. Mick Murphy, BMH/WS 1547.
32. O/C 1st S. Div to GHQ, 24.11.1921, Mulcahy Papers, P7/A/30.
33. See Chapter 1.
34. Antoin O'Callaghan, *The Lord Mayors of Cork*.
35. *Cork Constitution*, 14.2.1921.
36. Fines Book, CCPO Records, NA.
37. The most notable case was that of James Penrose Fitzgerald, who was driven out in May 1921.
38. MA A/0649.
39. Guy's Postal Directories 1921–1930.
40. MA A/0649.

Chapter 22 (pp 120–124)
1. Report of Military Inquiry, WO 35/1468.
2. Ironically, in later years Tom Barry lived in an apartment above Woodford Bourne in the very offices that Beal had worked in. It is now McDonald's.
3. It seems that Fred Blemens had also at one point worked at Woodford Bourne.
4. Mick Murphy, BMH/WS 1547.
5. Connie Neenan, O'Malley, P17b/108.
6. Jerry Keating, BMH/WS 1657.
7. Patrick Collins, BMH/WS 1707.
8. Report of Military Inquiry, WO 35/1468.
9. Jerry Keating, BMH/WS 1657.
10. Mick Murphy, BMH/WS 1547; Jerry Keating, BMH/WS 1657; Patrick Collins, BMH/WS 1707.
11. Frank Busteed in O'Callaghan, *Execution*; Jimmy Minihan in O'Malley, P17b/112.
12. Guy's Postal Directories, 1920–1930, Criminal Injuries Books, 1919–1922, Cork Borough and Cork East Riding, CCPO Records, NA.
13. YMCA Annual Reports, 1918–1930.
14. O'Donoghue, MS 31, 200 and MS 31, 227.
15. For example, see O/C 1st S. Div to C/S, 7.5.1921, Mulcahy, P7/A/20; also DI Cork 2 to O/C Cork 2, 11.4.1921, Lankford Papers, CAI U169.
16. Florence O'Donoghue, O'Malley, P17b/95.
17. O'Donoghue, MS 31, 124 (2).
18. List of Freemasons in O'Donoghue, MS 31, 227.
19. HQ 1st S. Div to GHQ, 7.5.1921, Mulcahy, P7/A/20.
20. Seán O'Callaghan's *Execution* is a detailed and harrowing account of the execution of Mrs Mary Lindsay and her chauffer James Clarke in mid-Cork. Along with the execution of Major Compton-Smith in the same area, it attracted a lot of unwanted attention to the Cork IRA's treatment of prisoners and the taking of hostages.

21. GHQ to 1st Div, May 1921, Mulcahy, P7/A/20.
22. 1st s. Div to GHQ, 10.6.1921, Mulcahy, P7/A/20.
23. Appendix 3 in Florence O'Donoghue, *No Other Law*.
24. This is a subject that deserves much more extensive analysis than can be made here. Its implications in the event of a resumption of hostilities are truly appalling and led the British to contemplate the forcible internment of the entire Protestant population for its own protection.
25. Membership of the Grand Masonic Lodges of Cork city, 1895 to date.
26. See Chapter 11.
27. *Cork Examiner*, 16.2.1921.
28. Report of Military Inquiry, WO 35/1468.
29. *ibid.*
30. J. S. Blemens to Michael Collins, 10.11.1921; J. S. Blemens/Matilda Blemens to Collins, 21.12.1921; Rev. Babington to Collins, 21.12.1922, MA A/0503.
31. *Cork Constitution*, 3.8.1921.
32. James and Matilda Blemens to Michael Collins, 21.12.1921, MA A/0503.
33. It was not uncommon for the relatives, particularly parents of victims, to die within a year or two of such killings. George Horgan's mother and Major O'Connor's wife died within two years; Finbarr O'Sullivan's father died within a few months of his son's death. The younger son James Blemens lived on in Cork until 1969, apparently finding great solace in his religious beliefs. There is a plaque by Seamus Murphy to his memory in St Finn Barre's Cathedral, Cork.

Chapter 23 (pp 125–131)

1. The County Inspector of the RIC reported that some loyalist business people were forced out of Cork city by IRS threats at this time. CI's Report, April/May 1921, CO 904/115. See also C/O 17th Infantry Brigade to HQ 6th Div, 7.3.1921, CO 904/188.
2. Guy's Postal Directory 1920–1921; VO Records, Dublin.
3. H. W. Higginson, C/O 17th Infantry Brigade to HQ 6th Div, 7.3.1921, CO 904/188.
4. See Peter Hart, *The IRA and its Enemies*. See also the RIC files, CO 904/168 and the hundreds of statements from west Cork Protestants, mostly farmers, in the Irish Grants Committee Papers, CO 762/-.
5. Higginson, *op. cit.*
6. CI's Report for April/May 1921, CO 904/115.
7. Criminal Injury Books: Cork West Riding, April 1921–Oct 1921, Cork East Riding, Oct 1920–Jan 1921 and Feb 1921–Oct 1921, Cork Borough, Sept 1920–Feb 1921 and Feb 1921–June 1922, CCPO Records, NA.
8. Criminal Injury Books: Cork Borough, Feb 1921–June 1922, Cork East Riding, Feb 1921–Oct 1921, CCPO Records, NA.
9. Liam de Roiste Diary, 19.2.1921.
10. James T. Mulligan, CO 762/4.
11. Thomas Stewart, CO 762/168.
12. Richard B. Baker, CO 762/19.
13. William Good Wood, CO 762/64. Wood, who lived in Skibbereen, had an office and second residence in Cork city. The kidnapping incident took place in west Cork.
14. Thomas Sheppard, CO 762/26.

15. Dobbin Ogilvie, CO 762/112 and Samuel Byford, CO 762/86.
16. Weekly Summary of the State of Ireland, 18.4.1921, CAB 24/124.
17. Rev. T. C. Day, CO 762/100.
18. *Cork Examiner*, 4.6.1921.
19. O'Donoghue, MS 31, 227.
20. He would not have needed specialist training if he were a mere transport officer.
21. Lieut G. E. Green, Service Record, WO 374/28927.
22. Green Service Record, *op. cit.*
23. See *Cork Examiner*, 10.6.1921 for the capture of the Crowleys. Green's Service Record states that he had 'not been selected for the recommended merit'. This, along with the fact that the military tribunal judging his own shooting overruled the evidence that drunken Auxiliaries were to blame, citing rather that Green had shot himself in the leg solely through his own carelessness, appears to have been a factor in his resigning his commission in December 1921. Green appears to have become a reluctant soldier after the shooting incident. WO/374/28927.
24. John Crowley disappeared on 24 June 1920, MA A/0535. Also see 'Raymond' for what is probably a reference to this event. *Southern Star*, 27.11.1971.
25. Sometimes referred to as Patrick Molloy (Peter Hart, *Mick: The Real Michael Collins*). His correct name, however, appears to have been Bryan Fergus Molloy, at least according to British Army Memorial Service Roll (MS) Dublin, 1922. I am grateful to Julian Putkowski who provided me with a copy of this list. The IRA's own lists of British Casualties, MA A/0437 and A/0438 refer to him as Fergus Bryan Molloy—'army perhaps'.
26. Julian Putkowski, 'A2 and the Reds in Khaki'; Peter Hart, *Mick: The Real Michael Collins*.
27. MA A/0437 and A/0438.
28. Interestingly, Josephine claimed to have taught the piano to the children of intelligence officers. Green had his wife with him when he was shot.
29. History of the 6th Division, Strickland Papers, IWM.
30. A Private Coe of the Essex Regiment was kidnapped in the city in November 1921 and 'every effort was made to get information out of him'. Clearly he was mistaken for Lieut Koe, who was Intelligence Centre for the city. Report of the COC Ireland, 3.12.1921, CAB 24/131/3537.
31. Undated memo, Strickland Papers, IWM, in Borgonovo, *Spies, Informers and the Anti-Sinn Féin League*.
32. Not surprisingly, the remaining Blemens family members found it safer to live on College Road on the western side of the city than beside O'Donoghue in the 4th Ward.
33. See Chapter 53 for an analysis of the likelihood of actual spying activities for given individuals.
34. Connie Neenan, O'Malley, P17b/112. While Neenan claims that the shoes were taken from the Blemenses, he may have been referring to another father and son who were later killed.
35. It has to be said that similar investigations were ordered into other cases of disappeared persons, at least into those whose relatives had the will to contact Collins or a minister of the Dáil on the matter.
36. c/s to o/c 1st s. Div, 8.10.1921, Mulcahy, P7/A/26.
37. o/c Cork 1 to the IRP, MA A/0649.

Chapter 24 (pp 134–139)
1. CI's Report for Jan–March 1921, CO 904/114.
2. History of the 6th Division, Strickland Papers, IWM.

3. Reports of the Military Court, *Cork Examiner*, 23–28.2.1921.
4. In fact both the Clogheen raid and the discovery of arms at Victoria Cross were based on information given by informers.
5. *ibid.*
6. *ibid.*
7. *ibid.*
8. *ibid.*
9. *ibid.*
10. *ibid.*
11. *ibid.*
12. Danny Healy, BMH/WS 1656.
13. *Cork Examiner*, 25.2.1921.
14. Peter Hart, *The IRA and its Enemies*.

Chapter 25 (pp 140–145)

1. Peter Hart, *The IRA and its Enemies*.
2. Mrs Bride McKay, CO 762/181.
3. Register of Births, Marriages and Deaths, GRO, Dublin.
4. Bride McKay, CO 762/181.
5. Also the reason why Henry Ford built his tractor factory in Cork.
6. A Record of the Rebellion in Ireland, 6th Division, WO 141/93.
7. Bride McKay, *op. cit.*
8. A Record of the Rebellion in Ireland, 6th Division, WO 141/93.
9. *ibid.*
10. A Record of the Rebellion in Ireland, 6th Division, WO 141/93.
11. Seán Moylan, *In His Own Words*.
12. *Cork Examiner*, 16.2.1921.
13. Bride McKay, *op. cit.*
14. Peter Hart, *The IRA at War, 1916–1923*.
15. RIC Sergeant Warren letter of support in Bride McKay's IGC application, CO 762/181.
16. They were incarcerated together on Spike Island and were fast friends for the rest of their lives. See Moylan, *op. cit.*
17. These statements and the quotation are to be found in her IGC application, Bride McKay, *op. cit.*

Chapter 26 (pp 146–147)

1. The Registers are available in the Courts Records in the National Archives, Dublin, CCPO, NA.
2. Criminal Injury Book, Cork Borough, 14 Feb 1921–12 June 1922, CCPO, NA.
3. Criminal Injury Book, Cork East Riding, Feb 1921–Oct 1921, CCPO, NA.

Chapter 27 (pp 148–151)

1. Collins to de Valera, 27.6.1921, DE 2/269, NA. This letter and its related correspondence, which condemns virtually everything that could be considered pro-British in administration terms, is an interesting prologue to the xenophobic nature of much of the public policy of the newly independent Ireland. It suggests that Collins would have pursued broadly similar policies to the de Valera and Cosgrave governments had he survived.

2. GHQ Memo to c/s 13/5/1921, Mulcahy, P/7/A/20; GHQ to A/General, 11.5.1921, Mulcahy P/7/A/23 and GHQ to D. Defence, 17.6.1921, Mulcahy, P/7/A/20.
3. CI's Report June–Sept 1921, CO 904/116.
4. *ibid.*
5. Chronological List of IRA Activities, Mulcahy, P/7/A/16.
6. See correspondence in Mulcahy, P/7/A/20.
7. GHQ to c/s, 13.5.1921, Mulcahy, P/7/A/20.
8. GHQ to M/Defence, 17.6.21, Mulcahy, P/7/A/20.
9. *ibid.*
10. Borgonovo, *op. cit.*
11. 1913 Divisional Electoral Register for Cork Borough, CCPO Records, NA.
12. 1911 Census.
13. Births, Marriages and Deaths Registers, GRO, Dublin.
14. 1911 Census.
15. BMD Records, GRO, UK.

Chapter 28 (pp 152–155)

1. IO Cork 1 to GHQ, July/Aug 1921, Mulcahy, P7a/7.
2. For detailed accounts of these, see Danny Healy, BMH/WS 1656 and Connie Neenan in O'Malley, P17b/112, respectively.
3. IO Cork 1 to GHQ, July/Aug 1921, Mulcahy, P7a/7. See Part IX for more on Stevens.
4. Those listed were the County Club, the City Club and Little Island Golf Course. Presumably, Douglas Golf Course would also have been included had it not been burned down in May as 'a nest of imperialists', as Mick Murphy called it.
5. Activity Reports of 1st and 6th Battalions Cork No. 1 Brigade for July 1921, Mulcahy, P/7/A/23.
6. *ibid.*
7. Activity Report of 6th Battalion Cork 1, July/Aug 1921, Mulcahy, P/7/A/23.
8. Annie Begley to M/D, 6.10.1922, DOD Series, A/07360.
9. Begley Correspondence in DOD, A/07360.
10. Connie Neenan, O'Malley, P17b/112.
11. Annie Begley to M/D, 6.10.1922, DOD Series, A/07360.
12. Borgonovo, *Spies, Informers and the Anti-Sinn Féin League.*
13. Hart, *The IRA and its Enemies.*
14. Borgonovo, *op. cit.* Borgonovo gives the date of his abduction as 7 June.
15. *Cork Examiner*, 14.7.1921.
16. The area around Annemount, Maymount, Friar's Walk and Summerhill South contained the families of scores of policemen. In fact, it might justifiably be described as an RIC ghetto, though it was quite salubrious by the standards of the time. See Guy's Directories.
17. His name appears as the signatory on large tranches of the 1911 Census gathered in the city.
18. CI Cork Report, July/Sept 1921, CO 904/116.
19. Pa Scannell, IRA Pension Application. I am grateful to Brian Scannell who provided me with a copy of this document.
20. In the first edition of *The Year of Disappearances* it was stated at this point in the text that a schoolboy called Edward Kenny was executed as a spy by the city IRA. While an alleged 'spy' called Kenny was executed, he was more likely to have been a member of the YMCA (see Appendix X). Edward Kenny, a schoolboy, was in fact shot (and merely wounded) in West Cork, not in the city.

Chapter 29 (pp 158–165)

1. CI's Report May/June 1921, CO 904/115.
2. Another Carrigtwohill man, 'Pablo Mullins', was held in Sing Sing for some nights before being released on the intervention of his sister: Fitzgerald, *Foras Feasa na Paróiste*. The German watch thief is likely to have been one Peter Wahbrot, a German national who went missing in Cork, probably in early 1922. The two women may have left, though there is no evidence of that. NA, DOJ 'H' series, H 16/3. Also see Appendix III.
3. *ibid.*
4. Martin Corry, O'Malley, P17b/112.
5. *Cork Constitution*, 9.12.1921.
6. Fitzgerald, *op. cit.*
7. I have decided to use the new name Cobh as it was officially renamed by the Sinn Féin town council in 1920. British records refer to it as Queenstown.
8. There were a number of assassinations of IRA men and others suspected of being in the IRA in east Cork at this time. On 5 May a Volunteer called Willie Bransfield was shot dead in Carrigtwohill; on 14 May Edward McNamara, a civilian, was shot dead by military forces in Midleton; and on 15 May Richard Flynn, Richard Barry and John Ryan were similarly shot outside Carrigtwohill. All were unarmed.
9. Undated Michael Burke letter, Seamus Fitzgerald papers, CAI PR6/39.
10. Seán Healy, BMH/WS 1479.
11. Fitzgerald, *op. cit.*
12. O'Farrell, *Who's Who in the Irish War of Independence*.
13. Letter from Evangeline Anderson and resulting correspondence, February 1922, MA A/0668.
14. NA, Department of Justice, H257/13.
15. *The 79th News*, the journal of the Cameron Highlanders and the Regimental Records of the Cameron Highlanders. I am grateful to Lieut Colonel A. M. Cumming OBE for copies of the relevant pages of these histories.
16. Records of the Cameron Highlanders, 2nd Battalion, 1920.
17. John McAuliffe, 'The Troubled Times in Cloyne', in *The Book of Cloyne*, ed., Padraig Ó Loinsigh.
18. My gratitude again to Katherine Boyce of the British Army Museum for looking up Mackintosh for me in the Army Lists. Also see World War I Campaign Medal Cards, WO 372/13.
19. Douglas Wimberly in *British Voices from the Irish War of Independence 1918–1921*, ed. William Sheehan.
20. Register of Courts of Inquiry, WO 35/162.
21. Michael Burke letter, Seamus Fitzgerald papers, CAI PR6/39.
22. See Chapters 41 and 42 for a more detailed assessment of the role of British undercover assassination squads.
23. NA, DOJ 2007 series, 2007/56/11. See also *Sunday Independent*, 1.7.2007.
24. Henrietta Williams's sworn statement claimed that he 'was not in any way concerned in and knew nothing whatever as regards the circumstances of the death of the Lord Mayor of Cork. Unfortunately, he happened to be in Cork city on the night [in question] in connection with the Services of Jurors Summons of the Cork Assizes. I was in service at Messrs Tyler and Co., Ltd in that city on the same occasion, and my brother, the said Michael Williams, stopped with me at my Lodgings on the night in question and did not go out at any time in the city upon that night.'

25. One witness at the inquest stated that 'Constable Williams arrived from Newmarket for the Assizes on 19th March'—the day before MacCurtain was killed. *Cork Examiner*, 9.4.1920.

26. Letter to Mrs Williams from 'A Sympathetic Mother', Williams file, *op. cit.*

27. Fitzgerald, *op. cit.*

28. Jim Fitzgerald interviewed several who were present at both executions. All agreed that it was Parsons who was hanged, while Williams was shot.

29. Garda Superintendent, Cobh, 31.1.1925, in Williams file, *op. cit.*

30. Closed file on Martin Corry, MA, DOD Series A/09690.

Chapter 30 (pp 166–169)

1. MA, DOD A/07304, MA; Collins Papers, A/0909; Mulcahy Papers, P7/B/21.

2. MA, A/0909.

3. The full list is called 'Pre-Truce Absentees from British Troops in Ireland' and can be found in the Department of Defence Papers, MA, DOD A Series, A/07304.

4. See Appendix 1.

5. Three of these, Lieuts Handy, Henderson and Dove were captured and executed near Macroom in May 1922, as was their driver, Private Brooks. The other 10, Lieut Genochio, was killed outside Cork city on 17 February 1922. The missing officers whose names were published in 1921 were Major Compton Smith, and Lieuts Rutherford and Brown, along with Chambers, Watts and Green.

6. Walsh and Ward, though Cameron Highlanders, were reported missing from Cork city; the others from Cobh.

7. They were subsequently released by a cousin of my mother's, who was given the job of executing them. Instead he bundled them into a pony and trap and brought them back to Cork.

8. The exception is Private Roughley, MA, A/07304. His body was recovered from a farm at Ovens, MA, A/0909.

9. Frank Busteed, O'Malley, P17b/112.

10. *ibid.*

11. O'Callaghan, *Execution*; Hart, *The IRA and its Enemies*.

12. Charlie Browne, BMH/WS 873.

13. P. J. Feeney, *Glory O, Glory O, Ye Bold Fenian Men.*

14. Busteed, *op. cit.*

15. See Chapters 56–59.

16. Feeney, *op. cit.*

17. Local lore has it that these were civilian 'spies'. They may also have been the Waterfall three who were in civilian attire.

18. Busteed, *op. cit.*

19. Patrick Collins, BMH/WS 1707.

20. Brigade Major to all Officers Commanding, 30.6.1920, MA, A/0341.

21. It is interesting to note that the Hampshire Regiment, the principal regiment based in Victoria Barracks which was responsible for most British successes against the IRA in the city and in east Cork, lost no men through 'disappearances'. This was despite the fact that its intelligence officers were the most effective on the British side, being responsible for Clonmult and several other IRA setbacks. Yet none of its men was kidnapped—other than Lieut Dove, who tracked down the column at Clonmult and was one of the three IOs

kidnapped and executed near Macroom in 1922. See Tom O'Neill, *The Battle of Clonmult*, 2006.

Chapter 31 (pp 170–173)

1. *Guy's Postal Directory for Cork City and County*, 1921.
2. *Cork Examiner/Cork Constitution*, 2/3.6.1920.
3. Cork YMCA Annual Reports, 1919–21; Guy's Directories 1919–21.
4. Cork YMCA Annual Reports, 1923–25. It is not listed in the Valuation Books for Cork city for that period, suggesting that it never came into operation. VO Records, Dublin.
5. British Army Telegraph Transcript 25.8.1921, O'Donoghue, MS 31, 230(1).
6. Weekly Survey of the State of Ireland, CAB 24/126/3151.

Chapter 32 (pp 176–180)

1. CO 905/19, CO 905/20 and CO 905/21. The card is in CO 905/20.
2. Records of the Governor General's Office, NA.
3. *Cork Constitution* and *Cork Examiner*, 25.3.1922.
4. *Cork Examiner* 5, 6 April 1922. See Fitzgerald, *Foras Feasa na Paróiste* for a description of Corry's part in the raid. Corry in this account greatly exaggerates the number of lorries commandeered, claiming that up to '126 lorries were lined up from Knockraha to Ballinagoul'.
5. Mick Murphy, BMH/WS 1547.
6. Mrs Joseph Parsons to the Duke of Devonshire, 29.4.1923, NA Department of the Taoiseach, S 3033. See also MA DOD Series, A/7431. The equivalent file in the Department of Justice has never been released.
7. Almost certainly a typing error and is likely to refer to Union Quay Barracks, the Republican HQ during this period.
8. Colonel Murphy to A/G, 24.5.1923, MA DOD Series, A/7431.
9. Colonel Murphy to Minister for Defence, 14.7.1923.
10. Mrs Parsons' letter.
11. O'Brien, whose real name was Ahern, also lived on High Street and was shot as a spy in April 1921. His 16-year-old brother may have suffered a similar fate. Cards on Michael Ahern, Isabella Ahern and John Ahern in CO 905/20.

Chapter 33 (pp 181–183)

1. *Cork Constitution*, 11.3.1922.
2. It is ironic that Frank O'Connor, a man who went on to champion free speech and expose the hypocrisies of independent Ireland, was one of the IRA censors working in the Cork newspapers around this time.
3. RIC Records, NA, MFA 24/1–21.
4. 1911 Census.
5. In his application to the RIC, Roycroft gave his birth date as 18.12.1897. However, his real birth date was 18.12.1902, suggesting that he added five years to his age in order to enrol. Births Records, GRO, Dublin.
6. William Roycroft, CO 762/170.
7. *Cork Constitution*, 10.4.1922.
8. RIC Membership Rolls, NA, MFA 24/1–21.

9.   William Roycroft, CO 762/190.
10. *ibid.*
11. *ibid.*

Chapter 34 (pp 184–187)

1.   I am grateful to Donal O'Flynn for this version of the Hornibrook affair.
2.   See list of JPS 1920/21, Guy's Postal Directory 1920/21.
3.   Peter Hart, *The IRA and its Enemies*. Also see the Courts Registers for Cork East Riding of 1920–23 for a catalogue of the intimidation suffered by the Hornibrooks. Cork CCPO Records, NA.
4.   Meda Ryan, *Tom Barry: IRA Freedom Fighter*.
5.   Ryan, *op. cit.*
6.   Free State Army report, 9 March 1923, DOD A/8274, quoted in Hart.
7.   Also see Part IX.
8.   Which goes to show the priority given to revenge in the period after the Treaty. Borgonovo, *Florence and Josephine O'Donoghue's War of Independence*, p. 83.
9.   Army lists, WO 338. See also Alice Hodder letter, CO 739/16.
10. Cork YMCA Annual Report 1920/21.
11. Edward Woods, CO 762/133.
12. Claims that Matilda Woods was no longer living in Cork at the time of her father's and brother's deaths are misleading. She is described as living in Cork as late as April 1923. *Cork Examiner*, 14.4.1923.
13. Registry of Deeds Records, Dublin, YMCA Annual Reports 1919–25. While it is tempting to speculate that Lacy may have been the spy 'harboured' by the Woods, he appears to have suffered no intimidation and attended most YMCA meetings in 1921. He did however have some sort of 'long illness' in 1922/23, suggesting that the stress he suffered began in 1922. YMCA records.
14. Edward Woods, CO 762/133.

Chapter 35 (pp 188–194)

1.   Hart, *The IRA and its Enemies*, p. 292.
2.   Interviews with local Protestant locals BF and BO by Hart. Hart, *op. cit.*; William Jagoe, CO 762/4.
3.   *Cork Constitution*, 27.3.1922. Interestingly, neither Revs Harbord appear to have been present.
4.   Ryan, *Tom Barry: IRA Freedom Fighter*.
5.   Barry, *Guerrilla Days in Ireland*.
6.   Rev. Ralph Harbord, CO 762/58; Rev. Richard Harbord, CO 762/155; *Cork Weekly News*, 6.5.1922.
7.   Kinneigh is on the back road from the Bandon valley to Cork which runs within a mile of the Hornibrook farm.
8.   Hart, *op. cit.*
9.   Hart, *op. cit.*
10. Thomas Nagle, CO 762/3.
11. *Cork Constitution*, 29.4.1922.
12. It appears that two Bradfield families were at the receiving end of this trick.
13. The only evidence we have that they were known is from the interviews with locals gathered by Peter Hart.

14. *Cork Constitution*, 30.4.1922.
15. Thomas Nagle, CO 762/3.
16. *Cork Constitution*, 29.4.1922.
17. Interviews by Hart. Hart *op. cit.*
18. See *Cork Weekly News*, 1.4.1922 for details of the presentations made to Rev. McKinley on his departure from Cork—his destination is not mentioned. I have not been able to prove conclusively that Gerald McKinley was related to Rev. McKinley. Nor have I been able to find anyone with that surname in the Ballineen/Enniskeane area at that time. Guy's Postal Directories 1914–21; 1911 Census.
19. *Cork Constitution*, 18.2.1922. Indeed, as we shall see in Part IX, the insertion of that notice into the *Constitution* on that date may itself be grounds for suspicion.
20. *Cork Weekly News*, 1.4.1922.
21. The records for Cork Grammar School for the years 1912–26 may well have been destroyed.
22. William Jagoe, CO 762/4; see also *Cork Constitution*, 30.4.1922.
23. *Cork Constitution*, 30.6.1921.
24. This was recalled by Pat Kenny, Michael Kenny's son, after he watched a recent television documentary on the west Cork killings. Source Dick Kenny.
25. *Cork Constitution*, 5.5.1922.

Chapter 36 (pp 195–198)

1. Many companies were more diligent. For the No. 2 Brigade area (north Cork) see the Siobhan Lankford Papers, CAI, U169, where several of these lists survive. The details gleaned on individuals are extensive and vary from whether they were regarded as friendly, neutral or hostile to how many acres of tillage they had and other farming details. I am grateful to my neighbours in Glenville, Paddy Forde and the late Bina Dunlea, for this story.
2. Relationships between Protestants and Catholics were good in most parts of the county. The only area where old animosities appear to have survived from the mid to early 19th century was Bandon and the surrounding districts. I have never seen evidence to suggest there was any mutual sectarian hatred in Cork city, for instance.
3. 10 Cork 4 to O/C 5th Btn, 31.1.1922. Lankford Papers, U 169, quoted in Hart, *op. cit.*
4. Set up in late 1919 by Michael Collins to raise money for the functions of the new State.
5. Hart, *The IRA and its Enemies*, pp 297/8. See also MA, A/0897.
6. For some lists of Cork Freemasons, see O'Donoghue Papers, MS 31, 200 and MS 31, 227.
7. See 'captured' list of Freemasons, O'Donoghue, MS 31, 227.
8. O/C 1st South Div to C/S, 4.5.1921 (Mulcahy Papers, p7/A/20); 1st South Div Intell Report, 15.11.1921 (O'Donoghue Papers, MS 31, 207); DI Cork 2 to O/C 2nd Btn 11, 11.4.1921 (Lankford Papers, U 169).
9. An extensive trawl through the relevant lists of British Freemasons failed to find Green's name. I am grateful to Martin Cherry, assistant librarian of the British Museum of Freemasonry, for this search.
10. Membership lists of the Cork city YMCA and Cork Masonic Lodges, Grand Lodge of Freemasons of Ireland records.
11. YMCA Annual Report, 1919/20; Guy's Postal Directory, 1921.
12. Some of these lists and letters, including the above quotation, can be found in O'Donoghue, MS 31, 200.
13. For background on Carrette's time at Bandon Post Office, see Tomás MacSeoin and Thomas B. Jones, 'Memories of Bandon Head Post Office', *Bandon Historical Society Journal*, NO. 13, 1997.

14. HQ Cork 3 to 10 1st s. Div, 27.1.1922, O'Donoghue Papers, MS 31, 246.
15. See next chapter and Part IX.

Chapter 37 (pp 199–202)

1. *Cork Examiner*, 23.8.1922; *Cork Examiner*, 1.9.1922.
2. Elizabeth Darkey Cooke, CO 762/59.
3. *Cork Examiner*, 1.9.1922.
4. *Cork Constitution*, 6.4.1922.
5. At least two others living within a hundred yards of Rockville Terrace were also targeted: Robert Parker who lived behind the Brown house was shot and wounded in May 1921 while there is reason to suspect that several merchants who lived on Blackrock Road may have disappeared in June 1922. See Chapters 55 and 56.
6. See Chapter 44.

Chapter 38 (pp 203–206)

1. John H. Bennett on the death of William Beale, from Trevor West, *Malting the Barley, John H. Bennett: The Man and his Firm.*
2. *Cork Examiner*, 17.3.1923; *Cork Examiner*, 22.4.1923; *Cork Examiner*, 23.4.1923.
3. Cork YMCA Annual Reports 1918–23.
4. *Cork Examiner*, 22.4.1923.
5. His name has been spelt in a variety of ways from 'Thomas Creevan' to 'Thomas James Creever' to 'Creeiber'. The correct spelling, however, is Creber, Theo Nicholas Creber, though it was pronounced *Creeber.*
6. This account of the killing is based on police reports. See Department of Justice Files, H5/925.
7. It should be pointed out that, in his submission for compensation to the IGC for the burning and subsequent deterioration of Kilcrenagh House, Pike suggested that Creber had been murdered by mistake and that the intended victim was Michael Twomey, the caretaker of the property (Ebenezer Pike, CO 762/200). This was one of the possibilities also suggested by the Civic Guard. However, the nature of the execution suggests that the killers knew who they were targeting. Superintendent Cork ER to Commissioner, 6.10.1923. NA, Justice H5/925.

Chapter 39 (pp 207–211)

1. In fact, he appears to have been more of a travelling organiser covering all of Munster. The Cork general secretary as named in the YMCA annual reports for Cork city was George Bird. However, Harris is referred throughout YMCA records as general secretary and appears to have been the one full-time officer assigned to Cork. Because of this I will refer to him throughout as the general secretary.
2. *Cork Constitution* 3.5.1921, Cork YMCA Annual Reports 1918/19 and 1919/20.
3. *Cork Constitution* 3.5.1921.
4. And Harris did move to Bristol. The East Bristol YMCA records name him as their general secretary for 1921/22.
5. *The Irish Times,* 26.3.1923 and 9.4.1923.
6. *Cork Examiner,* 21.4.1923.
7. *The Irish Times,* 9.4.1923. Curiously, this was not to be the only mystery in Boulogne with an Irish connection during that six-month period, for on 2 July an Irish American who went under the name of Mr F. Cash disappeared while going on a stroll from the Hotel Chatham

where he was staying. He never returned. Police on both sides of the Atlantic believed it was a political crime, though no further details were given. *The Irish Times*, 27.7.1923.

8.   Records of East Bristol YMCA, YMCA Special Collection, A95, BU; Minutes of the General Secretaries Association of the YMCA, YMCA Special Collection, H2, BU. I am grateful to Ivana Frlan of the Special Collections Department of the Library of Birmingham University who went to a lot of trouble looking up this material for me.

9.   See Chapter 51. Harris received his MBE for his work with the troops during the Great War. His name does not appear in the Honours Lists for 1921–23.

10. *Cork Examiner* and *Cork Constitution*, 3.5.1921.

11. *Cork Constitution*, 16.5.1921.

12. Liam de Roiste Diary, 3.3.1921.

13. Hopkinson, *The Irish War of Independence*, pp 173–4.

14. *Cork Examiner*, 7.4.1921. It is unclear if this refers to William Beale or another of the Beales. The most likely candidate is Alfred Beale, the family patriarch and president of the YMCA.

15. De Roiste was lucky to escape an attempt on his life in May. His house guest, Fr Seamus O'Callaghan, was not so lucky. Egan had to move to Paris for his own safety after the death of Terence MacSwiney.

16. For British military paranoia on the ACRI, see James B. Connelly, BMH/WS 849.

17. There is a file on these peace moves in Dublin Castle records, CO 904/232. One Southern unionist who tried to initiate peace moves through Thompson was Arthur Vincent of Muckross House, Killarney. B. Thompson to Sir John Anderson, 14 March 1921, CO 904/232.

Chapter 40 (pp 212–214)

1.   This may have been a second home, since it is merely a small terraced house. McNeill was able to buy a large house in Hampshire after moving there.

2.   William McNeill, CO 762/9; John Willis, CO 762/9.

3.   For a detailed discussion of the operation of the CDU and other similar groups, see Roisín McCarthy, BA dissertation, NUI Cork.

4.   Guy's Postal Directory 1919.

5.   William McNeill, CO 762/9.

6.   In fact, it petered out much earlier than that when Barrymore and other prominent Munster Protestants supported the Home Rule politics of William O'Brien's All For Ireland League in 1910. See Michael MacDonough, *William O'Brien*, p. 186.

7.   Earning the opprobrium of liberal Protestants such as Jasper Travers Wolfe. Jasper Ungoed-Thomas, *Jasper Wolfe of Skibbereen*, pp 72–77.

8.   John Willis, CO 762/19. On 3 February 1921 a cycle patrol of four RIC men was ambushed near Ballinhassig after collecting stores. Two were killed and one seriously wounded. Abbott, p. 198.

9.   John Willis, CO 762/9. It could be interpreted that the IRA were still after Willis long after the Truce. See 1st Brigade to IO 1st S. Div, 30.8.1921, O'Donoghue, 31, 212. However, this almost certainly refers to a Lieut Willis who was at the time on the 6th Division staff.

10. Though neither appears at any YMCA meetings for which I have seen minutes. (Cork YMCA General Committee Yearbook, 1904–42) They are reported as friends of the organisation in 1921; they were most likely associate members.

11. For another extraordinary case of a member of the ascendancy establishment routinely supplying information on IRA activities, see Harry Franks, CO 762/122.

Chapter 41 (pp 216–219)

1. Peter Hart, ed., *British Intelligence in Ireland 1920–1921*.
2. Captain R. D. Jeune in *British Voices*, ed. Sheehan.
3. Boddington was the officer who discovered the celebrated note from Andy Cope during a raid on Batt O'Connor's house in Dublin which indicates that high-level contacts were already in place between Collins and the British government as early as September 1920.
4. Boddington to Boyd, 2/1922, WO 35/180C. (The letter is dated January 1921, but it is clear from the context and replies that it was written in January 1922.)
5. Diary of 24–25.9.1920, quoted in Keith Jeffrey, *Field Marshal Sir Henry Wilson*.
6. 'My Dear Anderson', 29.1.1921, CO 904/232.
7. Diary of Sir Henry Wilson, 7.7.1920.
8. In July 1920 some 51 such officers were receiving 'civilian pay'. List of officers drawing civilian pay, Secret Service Accounts, HO 317/59.
9. Diary of Sir Henry Wilson, 23.9.1920.
10. Crozier, *Ireland For Ever*, p. 111.
11. F. P. Crozier, *The Men I Killed*. This of course is not strictly true. This was not the reason why Crozier resigned, but it is a useful insight from someone on the British side into the activities of these men.
12. Gough, like Wilson, was very much opposed to the 'outmurdering' policy.

Chapter 42 (pp 220–223)

1. The lady was a Mrs Seymour. She lived in Douglas just outside Cork city. Olga Pyne Clarke, *She Came of Decent People*.
2. Connie Neenan, Memoir, CAI PR7/7.
3. Connie Neenan Memoir 1916–1940, CAI PR7/7.
4. Weekly Survey of the State of Ireland, 14.3.1921, CAB 24/2735.
5. At least they were subsequently famous. See Owen Sheers in *The Guardian* Weekend Supplement, 20.10.2007. This has been chronicled by Sheers himself in his novel *Resistance* (2008) and by John Warwicker in *Churchill's Underground Army* (2008).
6. Peter Wilkinson and Joan Bright Astley, *Gubbins and SOE*. John Charles Francis Holland (1897–1956). In M. R. D. Foot, *Secret Lives*. In fact, Wilkinson and Astley's biography of Gubbins is dedicated to Holland. Holland, like Gubbins, greatly admired the technical and espionage skills of his Irish opponents and later copied them.
7. Peter Wilkinson and Joan Bright Astley, *Gubbins and SOE*. Many books have been written on the operations of SOE. Probably the most detailed and authentic is William Mackenzie's *The Secret History of Special Operations Executive 1940–1945*.
8. List of British Casualties 1921, MA A/0613.
9. Wilkinson and Astley, *op. cit.* Another senior secret service agent who served in Ireland during this period was Stewart Menzies, later to become head of MI6. Menzies had the nominal rank of Divisional Inspector, though he is not listed in RIC rolls.
10. Gubbins went on to write several pamphlets on the art of guerrilla warfare, based on IRA methods, which became part of the British Army's handbook for irregular warfare during World War II.
11. See Recommendations for Bravery, WO 35/42 and WO 35/54.
12. Probably the most complete list of those army personnel killed during the conflict is the nominal roll call for a memorial service held at the Royal Hospital Chapel, Kilmainham, on

21.11.1922: Memorial Service for Officers, NCOs and Men, Irish Command, 1920–22. Bare Papers, IWM. I am grateful to Julian Putkowski for letting me have a copy of this list.

13. Including Lieuts Rutherford and Brown, both RGA, who disappeared from outside Fermoy while dressed as civilians in late October 1920. See Record of the Rebellion, 6th Division, WO 141/93.

14. *Cork Constitution*, 5.11.1921. (Mitchell, it appears, was an Irishman.)

15. *The Red Triangle*, Vol. 4, No. 7, March 1921.

16. As distinct from retrospective recall by IRA men many years later.

Chapter 43 (pp 224–231)

1. Tom Kelleher, in *Survivors*, ed. Uinseann MacEoin.

2. Philip Orr, *The Road to the Somme*.

3. Frank Crozier, *Ireland For Ever*.

4. Tom Barry, *Guerrilla Days in Ireland*.

5. Tom Kelleher, *op. cit.*

6. Connie Neenan, interview transcript, CAI PR7/1.

7. Richard Russell, BMH/WS 1591; Court of Inquiry in lieu of Inquest, W. J. Peacocke, WO 35/157A.

8. *Cork Examiner*, 3.6.1921.

9. It should be pointed out that Kelleher was given to vast exaggerations of his role in the conflict.

10. RIC Daily Summary, 15.6.1921, CO 904/146.

11. *The Irish Times*, 2.6.1921.

12. *Cork Constitution*, 30.6.1921.

13. George Innes Webb, CO 762/51.

14. Previous editions of this book detailed how a Protestant teenager, Ed Olliffee, was abducted in Innishannon on the day of the Truce. He is listed as 'missing' both in RIC records (RIC Daily Summary, 16.7.1921, CO 904/146) and in the list of missing persons submitted to the newspapers on 22 August 1921 (*Cork Examiner*, 22.8.1921). He was not killed, however, but emigrated to the USA with his family in 1922. I am grateful to Barry Keane for discovering this.

15. Hart, ed., *British Intelligence in Ireland 1920–1921*.

16. The third register deals with the disposal of his estate.

17. Warren John Peacocke, Army Service Record, WO 339/14281.

18. See army telephone communications of 24.10.1921 and 4.11.1921, O'Donoghue, MS 31, 230.

19. Instructions on Distribution of Decorations, WO 35/181.

20. Ethel Peacocke, CO 762/200. Compare this with the case of Ebenezer Pike, who also claimed for pre-Truce damage and received nothing. Ebenezer Pike, CO 762/200.

21. Crozier, *op. cit.*

Chapter 44 (232–240)

1. Table 37, p. 304. Hart, *The IRA and its Enemies*.

2. June/July 1921. Letter on Sergeant Teehan: Department of Intelligence, Four Courts to IO 1st s. Div, 6.6.1922. O'Donoghue, MS 31, 212.

3. Tom Barry, *Guerrilla Days in Ireland*.

4. The exception was Dean Finlay, the rector of Swanlinbar, Co. Cavan. Finlay, who was 80 years of age, was murdered in June 1921, his family turned out in their night attire and the rectory burnt down.

5. Annual Synod of the Church of Ireland, Cork, Cloyne and Ross, *Cork Constitution*, 27.10.1921.

6. Flor Begley, O'Malley, P17b/111.

7. *Cork Weekly News*, 1.4.1922.

8. Admiralty to Captain Hall (undated), O'Donoghue, MS 31, 223(1). Interestingly, Rev. Hodges was never moved during the entire period, suggesting the IRA did not regard him as a threat and that the Admiralty patrols had long since ceased to be important.

9. These figures have been compiled from Guy's Directories 1920–23 and from Thom's Directories of the same period.

10. Including Girling. Annual Synod of the Church of Ireland Dioceses of Cork, Cloyne and Ross. *Cork Constitution*, 27.10.1921. Two others were to leave the city in the wake of the YMCA affair in 1922.

11. Rev. L. E. H. (Henry), Fin 1/1057. For examples of this in County Cork see Rev. Robert Parker, CO 762/65, Rev. J. A. Atkin, CO 762/196, Rev. Zebulon Miller, CO 762/144, Rev. T. C. Day, CO 762/100, Rev. W. M. O'Neill, CO 762/178 and Rev. W. A. Lamb, CO 762/150.

12. Cork Boro Criminal Injury Book, 30 June 1924–May 1933, CCPO Records, NA.

13. Rev. George Kell was based in Blackrock in 1921.

14. Cork YMCA Annual Report 1920/21. Mercer-Wilson was moved to London, *Weekly Irish Times*, 4.2.1922.

15. Also see R. Lee Cole, *A History of Methodism in Ireland*, Vol. 4.

16. Richard Kell, Introduction to his *Collected Poems 1962–1993*.

17. *Skibbereen Eagle*, 10.9.1921.

18. *The Irish Times*, 20.6.1923.

19. There were only 643 Methodists in the city in 1911, as against 6,576 Church of Ireland members and 912 Presbyterians: 1911 Census.

20. *Cork Constitution*, 14.2.1921.

21. Sunday Service Schedules, *Cork Constitution*, 5.2.1921 and 12.2.1921.

22. See Chapters 57–60. Kell does not appear to have been related to Vernon Kell, the head of MI5, who was, ironically, married in Cork in 1900. If they were related, it would of course strongly imply that Rev. Kell was a British spy because Vernon Kell frequently used family connections in the recruitment of agents. However, correspondence with genealogists working on the Kell family tree failed to find a connection. For Kell's transfer to Belfast, see *Cork Constitution* 2/7/1921.

23. And as many as a dozen more in 1922. See Part IX.

24. Rev. James M. Alley, 'Irish Methodism and Political Change' in *Irish Methodism in the Twentieth Century, A Symposium*, ed. Rev. Alexander McCrea, Belfast, 1931.

25. Michael McDonough, *William O'Brien*; Brendan Clifford, *The Cork Free Press*.

26. Michael McDonough, *William O'Brien*, p. 186.

27. Jasper Ungoed-Thomas, *Jasper Wolfe of Skibbereen*, pp 64–77.

28. R. Lee Cole, *op. cit.*

29. In fact, respectable Cork Protestants were as opposed to evangelical street preachers as were the Catholic mob since they feared they were lighting the fires of sectarianism in a city notable, by and large, for its absence. Matthew Kelly, *The Politics of Protestant Street Preaching in 1890s Ireland*.

30. Thom's Directory, 1919.

31. *Cork Constitution*, 24.1.1921.

32. Rev. R. B. Foster, 'Irish Methodism and War' in McCrea, *op. cit.*

33. Rev. R. B. Foster, 'Irish Methodism and War' in McCrea, *op. cit.*
34. R. Lee Cole, *A History of Methodism in Ireland*, Vol. 4.
35. Dan White, *The Musgrave Brothers: The 1st 125 Years*. Which meant, ironically, that the Imperial Hotel, rather than the Metropole, was favoured by the British Army officer class.
36. Tom Barry, *Guerrilla Days in Ireland*.
37. There are dozens of such attacks on Church property listed in the Criminal Injuries records of the Cork courts of 1921–24.
38. HOC Debate, quoted in *Cork Examiner*, 13.5.1921.
39. Cork Courts Registers—Cork Boro and Cork East Riding, 1922–33, CCPO Records, NA.
40. Rev. James M. Alley, 'Irish Methodism and Political Change' in *Irish Methodism in the Twentieth Century, A Symposium*, ed. Rev. Alexander McCrea, Belfast, 1931.
41. Alley, *op. cit.* The reference to entrapment refers to the killing of Tom Bradfield. This is confusing. There were two Tom Bradfields tricked and killed in this way, one near Bandon, the other in Enniskeane. While they were related, one was Church of Ireland, the other Methodist.
42. *The Irish Times*, 7.12.1922.
43. D. L. Cooney, *The Methodists in Ireland*. There are also reasons to believe that Methodists in Ballineen/Enniskeane may have paid a heavy penalty for that meeting. There are a surprising number of deaths in the community clustered around the last week of March 1922. Were these the 'six or seven' loyalist farmers marched to Rylane for execution?
44. Alley, *op. cit.*
45. Wm B. Hosford, CO 762/4.
46. *The Irish Times*, 17.6.1921.
47. *The Irish Times*, 19.2.1923.

Chapter 45 (pp 242–251)

1. If anybody doubts this, they should check out the courts records of the period, NA, Cork Crown and Peace Offices Files, 1921–33 which record scores of arson attacks not mentioned in newspapers.
2. Willie Kingston, 'From Victorian Boyhood to the Troubles: A Skibbereen Memoir'. Skibbereen and District Historical Society.
3. Guy's Postal Directories 1921–26. I chose 1926 as the reference year to allow time for the transfer of ownership/deeds. The reality is that most of these people left in 1922. In some instances, one Protestant family was replaced by another one, as there was significant immigration into the city by Protestants from more isolated areas, particularly from west Cork. This partly explains why this anomaly has not been picked up by historians comparing the 1911 and 1926 censuses.
4. One of these died. Several may have been murdered. These figures were taken from Guy's Directories and, again, most of the departures took place in 1922.
5. These figures are borne out by Valuation records.
6. The exact figures are 49.8% and 40.4%, respectively: 1911 and 1926 census statistics, National Library of Ireland.
7. Valuation List No. 6, Blackrock, Co. Cork, 1908–34, VO Dublin.
8. Cork Borough and Cork East and West Riding, 1922–1930, CCPO Records, NA.
9. And for many years afterwards. Tom Barry shot up the Masonic Hall in the 1930s. No less moderate a man than Seán McEntee was still claiming in the 1950s that Cork city was being run by a cabal of 50 Freemasons.

10. Lists of Freemasons, O'Donoghue, MS 31, 200 and MS 31, 227.

11. Lendrum states in his IGC submission that this was October 1920, but it is clear from the rest of the sentence and the context as a whole that he is referring to October 1921. Charles H. Lendrum, CO 762/129. Lendrum shared a practice with Frederick W. Wynne. The company represented many military personnel in court. Frederick Wynne mysteriously ceased to function as a solicitor in 1922, though the company continued to operate subsequently.

12. Charles H. Lendrum, CO 762/129.

13. Charles Geeve, CO 762/169.

14. Samuel C. Beamish, CO 762/125.

15. Criminal Injury Book, Cork East Riding, Feb 1922–Mar 1924, CCPO Records, NA.

16. George Bird, YMCA Divisional Secretary, in Henry Chamney, CO 762/191.

17. *Cork Examiner*, 12.9.1922.

18. CCPO Records: Cork Co. Register, 30 June 1922–Nov 1922. See Appendix II. In previous editions of this book, a Cork doctor, Edward Hawksworth, was described as also having been shot by the IRA during September 1922. It appears, however, that he died of a heart attack as a result of shots being fired in his vicinity rather than because he was actually shot. I am grateful to Barry Keane for establishing this.

19. Wm G. Williams, accountant, listed in Guy's Directory 1921.

20. Henry Chamney, CO 762/191.

21. Walter Hailes, CO 762/6.

22. *Cork Examiner*, 10.10.1922. This was probably a case of simple revenge. In 1920 O'Gorman had fired on an IRA party raiding his house for arms. Patrick Ahearn, BMH/WS 1003.

23. *Cork Examiner*, 6.12.1922 and 23.12.1922.

24. *Cork Examiner*, 20.1.1923.

25. *Cork Examiner*, 3.2.1923.

26. Criminal Injury Book, Feb 1922–Mar 1924, CCPO Records, NA.

27. *Cork Examiner*, 5.7.1922; Weekly Summary, 13.10.1921, CAB 24/129/3404; Jasper T. Wolfe, CO 762/54.

28. *Cork Examiner*, 18.12.1922; William Wolfe, CO 762/147.

29. See H16/- in the Department of Justice original register, H/Series. These include W. E. Parsons, William Nolan and Michael Williams. See Appendix III. See Appendix IV for another list of over 40 missing persons and Appendix IX for a list of probable disappeared.

30. See letter from 'Warner' to Mrs Willliamson, CAI, Lankford Papers, U 169. According to Ned Murphy, Williamson was one of many north Cork loyalists who were 'cleared out' and had his house burnt down. Ned Murphy in O'Malley, P17b/111.

31. British Army telephone transcript of 1.11.1921. O'Donoghue, MS 31 230 (2).

32. Also see Appendix II, Appendix III and Appendix IV.

33. See the *Freeman's Journal* of 27.7.1922 as an example of particularly prejudiced reporting and editorial line.

34. Mick Murphy in O'Malley, P17b/112.

35. YMCA Annual Reports, 1920/21 and 1921/22.

36. Connie Neenan in O'Malley, P17/b112. The Seaman's Bar was a public house down the quays from City Hall and was owned by a man called Markham. While it was a quayside pub, it was also the closest hostelry to the largely Protestant Victoria and Blackrock Roads.

Chapter 46 (pp 252–254)

1. Connie Neenan memoir, CAI PR7/7.
2. P. J. Feeney, *Glory O, Glory O.*
3. Sir Alfred Dobbin, CO 762/96.
4. Stan Barry, O'Malley, P 17b/103.

Chapter 47 (pp 255–258)

1. See Weekly Summaries of the State of Ireland, Jan–June 1922, CAB 24.
2. See Macready's report of 23 July 1921 for an insightful portrait of Barry's obduracy at this time. CAB 24/126/3175.
3. Weekly Survey, 1.10.1921, CAB 24/128/3366.
4. It is possible that the 20 'arrests' that occurred during the first week of September 1921 can be accounted for by ten Protestant boys who were taken in Shankill, Co. Dublin, and Bray, Co. Wicklow, held for three days and then released. Three teenagers were also taken in County Tipperary in connection with alleged criminality and there was one kidnapping in Cork of a man who was subsequently released. Two ex-soldiers also disappeared in Dublin. This leaves only four cases unaccounted for. See *The Irish Times* and *Cork Constitution*, 7–15.9.1921. However, it is also possible that only two of the Bray/Shankill abductions had taken place before 12 September when Macready filed his report, since *The Irish Times* mentions only two of them by 13 September—the rest are reported on 15 September. That would mean that, instead of four unaccounted-for abductions for the first week of September, the real number may well be as high as 12.
5. See 'Removal of Certain Officers From Ireland', WO 35/180C.
6. Truce Liaison Reports, Cork city. Truce Liaison/Evacuation Papers, MA LE/4/7. See Appendix VII.
7. See Chapter 56.
8. Letter from 'Corkonian', *Cork Examiner*, 24.3.1922.
9. Three youths were kidnapped in south County Tipperary on 12 September, allegedly for theft. *The Irish Times*, 13.9.1921.
10. Four youths from Cappamore, Co. Limerick, were 'kidnapped on the night of 24 August and taken to an unknown destination. They are charged, it is stated, with stealing from an orchard.' *The Irish Times*, 29.8.1921. A total of five of these youths (from Limerick and south Tipperary) appear to have disappeared entirely. British Army Telegram, 18.11.1921. O'Donoghue, MS 31, 230(2).
11. This went on right into the Civil War and beyond. Six Protestant youths were almost snatched from an orphanage in County Galway in July 1922 to be 'done in' for having a pro-British stance. When the matron refused to identify them, the orphanage was burned to the ground and the inmates had to be rescued by the Royal Navy. *The Irish Times*, 27.7.2009.

Chapter 48 (pp 259–262)

1. Liam de Roiste Diary, 18.3.1922.
2. Connie Neenan interview, Belt 7, CAI PR7/1.
3. Connie Neenan Memoir, CAI PR7/7.
4. British Army Telegraph Transcript 25/8/1921; O'Donoghue, MS 31, 230 (1).
5. John Borgonovo, *Spies, Informers and the Anti-Sinn Féin League.*
6. *Cork Constitution*, 15.9.1921, RIC Daily Summary, 14.9.1921, CO 904/147.

7. Cork YMCA General Committee Meeting, 9.9.1921, Cork YMCA General Committee Year Book, 1904–1942.

8. *Cork Constitution*, 17.9.1921.

9. RIC Daily Summary, 25–26.9.1921, CO 904/147.

10. See Borgonovo, *Spies, Informers and the Anti-Sinn Féin League*, pp 169–170.

11. To judge by other telegraphs, this one came from the army's Intelligence department. British Army Telegraph Transcript 24/10/1921, O'Donoghue MS 31, 230(1); RIC Daily Summary, 23.11.1921, CO 904/147.

12. British Army telegram, 12.12.1921. O'Donoghue, MS 31, 230(3).

13. British Army telegram, 17.12.1921. O'Donoghue, MS 31, 230(3).

14. Guy's Directories 1921, 1922, 1923 and 1926. Two other Boy Scout troops disappear off the postal directories after 1922. One was the Cork Hibernian Boys' Brigade at Morrison's Island. The other was Na Fianna.

15. 6th Division to GHQ, O'Donoghue, MS 31, 230(2). The telegram ends with the words 'I was talking to Grimsdale about Donnell, Cork.' A Sergeant O'Donnell was serving with the RIC in Cork at the time.

16. Cork YMCA Annual Report 1920/21.

17. On his visits to Ireland Baden Powell was adamant that the Boy Scouts were not a military or sectarian movement. Some scout troops were attacked by the IRA and had to be given discreet police protection. J. Anthony Gaughan, *Scouting in Ireland*.

Chapter 49 (pp 263–265)

1. Connie Neenan Memoir, CAI PR7/7.

2. Internal military inquiry, quoted in McMahon, p. 71, *op. cit.*

3. See *Cork Examiner*, *Cork Constitution* and *The Irish Times* of 18–21.2.1922.

4. Truce Liaison Department, Cork, Truce Liaison Papers, LE/4/7, MA.

5. See intercepted British military transcripts in O'Donoghue, MS 31, 230(1), where several well-known IOs are mentioned as living in civilian quarters and even given the designation of Mr, as distinct from their military rank.

6. Weekly Surveys of the State of Ireland, 20.3.1922. CAB 24/134/3855. It is very possible that Macready was merely reflecting the newspaper reporting on the case.

7. *Cork Examiner* and *Cork Constitution*, 10.3.1922.

Chapter 50 (pp 266–276)

1. Connie Neenan Interview, Belt 7, CAI PR7/1.

2. Liam de Roiste Diary, 18.3.1922.

3. *Cork Examiner, Cork Constitution, The Irish Times*, 18.3.1922.

4. *The Irish Times*, 21.3.1922. The *Morning Post* of 18.3.1922 mentioned the kidnappings, suggesting they must have taken place on the night of 16/17 March.

5. *Cork Examiner* and *Cork Constitution*, 21.3.1922.

6. *Cork Constitution*, 21.3.1922.

7. *Cork Constitution*, 21.3.1922.

8. It should be pointed out that two IRA officers who had applied for positions in the newly formed Gárda Síochána were also kidnapped in Cork around this time, as were three pro-Treaty election agents in Fermoy on 4 April. See Liam de Roiste Diary entries of 18.3.1922 and 5.4.1922.

9. See Appendix VII.

10. *Cork Examiner*, 21.3.1922.

11. *Cork Examiner*, 27.3.1922.

12. *Weekly Irish Times*, 1.4.1922.

13. Later to die on hunger strike during the Civil War.

14. *The Irish Times*, 28.9.1922.

15. Thomas L. Telford, CO 762/136.

16. Rita Curran, CO 762/120.

17. Letter from 'MD', Blackrock, *Cork Examiner*, 24.3.1922.

18. Connie Neenan, O'Malley, P17b/112.

19. See Appendix IV. The Department of Justice has already released those files for which there is an innocuous outcome, i.e. when persons had been traced. See NA, DOJ, H229.

20. See Appendix III.

21. Or at least I have not been able to find any.

22. This reluctance to provide any information on attacks on the Protestant community was to continue into the 1930s, when another spate of intimidation and attacks took place, particularly in Dunmanway. Those attacked would provide the police with no information lest it lead to even worse retribution. See Department of Justice papers, Jus/2008/-. Also see *Sunday Independent*, 22.2.2009.

23. They could, of course, have been caught on the basis of information extracted from Roycroft. However, Roycroft was most probably shot for being a Black and Tan, or else in lieu of his brother. Besides, no IRA man seems to remember him, let alone connect him to the YMCA.

24. Weekly Survey, 13.3.1922, CAB 24/135/3855. That the Protestant farmers were taken that week is based on a curious number of wills on unregistered deaths in the Bandon valley during that week.

25. Frank Busteed in O'Malley, P17/b/112.

26. Weekly Survey, 20.3.1922, CAB, 24/135/3889.

27. Statements were made by Protestant communities in Limerick, Carrigmacross, Kilmanagh, Co. Kilkenny, Tarbert, Roscrea, Tralee, Fermoy, Cork and Tullamore during the first two weeks of April. *The Irish Times*, 4–17.4.1922.

28. *The Irish Times*, 5.4.1922. Was Waller himself later to disappear? See H229/366 in Appendix IV.

29. *The Times*, 21.3.1922, Conclusions of Cabinet meeting, 5.4.1922, CAB 23/30.

30. This is the text of the statement printed in *The Irish Times* of 5.4.1922. For a full list of signatories of this statement, see the *Cork Constitution* of 6.4.1922 and *Cork Weekly News* of 8.4.1922.

31. *The Irish Times*, 1.5.1922.

32. *Cork Constitution*, 1.5.1922; *Irish Times*, 28.4.1922.

33. *Cork Constitution*, 5.5.1922.

34. See Orders No. 1 and 2. Appendix 1 in Survey of the State of Ireland, 18.4.1921. CAB 24/123/2867. This ban was fiercely resisted by Irish businessmen and manufacturers such as Jacobs the biscuit makers, which saw the obvious implications of a counter-ban on their products selling into British markets. At least one of the businessmen who appeared to have disappeared in Cork at this time ran an important export trade as well as importing materials from abroad. Quotation from Humphrey Murphy O/C Kerry Brigade, *Morning Post* 31/3/1922.

35. See Chapter 51.

36. Frank Busteed, in O'Malley, P17b/112.

37. *The Irish Times*, 8.4.1922.
38. *Cork Weekly News*, 2.4.1922.
39. YMCA General Committee Meeting, 9.2.1923; Cork YMCA General Committee Year Book, 1904–1942.
40. Such as postal directories, death records, will and probate records and valuation books.
41. These were Wm Warner, Wm H. Atkins, Anthony Fox, Arthur Dalton, Wm Neill, Michael D. Spillane, Henry Lord, Jasper Drury and Wm E. Williams. (Warner, Atkins, Fox and Spillane were merchants.) Valuation Book No. 6, Blackrock, Co. Cork, 1918–34, VO; Guy's Directories, 1921–24.
42. One exception is Thomas Hornibrook.
43. FOD Diary 1922, O'Donoghue, MS 31, 184.
44. Interestingly, however, the 'whereabouts' list does contain a Baker and a White. See Appendices III and IV.
45. Valuation Book No. 6, Blackrock, Co. Cork, 1918–34, VO; Guy's Directories, 1921–24.
46. Rev. James Alley, 'Irish Methodism and Political Changes', in *Irish Methodism in the Twentieth Century,* ed. Rev. William McCrea.
47. *Cork Examiner*, 28.3.1922.

Chapter 51 (pp 277–283)
1. Connie Neenan, O'Malley, P17b/112.
2. These are Stephen J. Cottrell (1923), Robert G. Donaldson (1924), Allen Ferguson RASC (1920), William Harwood (1922), Herbert Smellie (1922), Alexander Roche (1924) and Albert E. Strickland (1924). Some of these may have died in England or elsewhere.
3. Report of the secretary of the Munster Lodge, Grand Lodge of Freemasons Annual Report 1921.
4. Report of the secretary of the North and South Munster Lodges, Grand Lodge of Freemasons Annual Reports 1922 and 1923.
5. The burning in Clonakilty took place after the shooting of Robert Nagle at the end of April 1922.
6. 1st Div I Report, Cork No. 3 Brigade, 15.11.1921, O'Donoghue, MS 31, 207(1).
7. Hart, *The IRA and its Enemies*, p. 302.
8. Walter Hailes, CO 762/6.
9. See Appendix VIII and Appendix IX.
10. Two may have been merely struck off: Robert Cassidy and Archibald Phillips. A Robert Cassidy died in Cork in 1941, while a man called Archibald Phillips is registered as having died in Youghal in 1927. Cassidy's address, however, is listed in Guy's Directory as having been taken over by his wife in 1924, so they may not have been the same person.
11. See Appendix VIII and Appendix IX.
12. *Cork Examiner*, 3.5.1921.
13. His name was Richard Foott. He was a doctor aged 59, and died on 1 May 1922. R. E. Foott, Death Certificate.
14. Jerry Keating, BMH/WS 1657.
15. O'Donoghue, MS 31, 200.
16. The other lists are in MS 31, 227.
17. There are many reasons for coming to this conclusion: some of those listed were too young to be Masons in the early 1920s and were not Masons then—though they became Masons

later. One businessman, George Tolerton, a former member of Cork Chamber of Commerce, is described as being 'deceased'. He in fact died in 1928. Charles Lendrum is described as living at the farm in Sussex that he bought after he had to flee in the autumn of 1922. Several others are given the address they had in the late 1920s rather than where they lived in 1920/21. It could not have been compiled later than 1934 because Dr Dowse, the Bishop of Cork, who is listed, died in 1934. There are several other such anomalies in the list, all of which suggests the date of compilation to be sometime between 1928 and 1934.

18.   *Cork Constitution*, 29.5.1922.
19.   The first quotation is from his papers, MS 31, 124(2); the second can be found in *Rebel Cork's Fighting Story*.

Chapter 52 (pp 284–289)

1.   See Maps 1 and 2.
2.   There is a very detailed and colourful account of the tracking down of McDonald in the Neenan Memoir, CAI PR7/7. See also 'Anonymous' (Neenan) letter, O'Donoghue, MS 31, 337.
3.   Seán Healy, BMH/WS 1479.
4.   Alexander Stevens, CO 762/46.
5.   See Ernest Ince Allen, CO 762/4 and Joseph Northridge, CO 762/37 for examples of this.
6.   RIC Daily Summary, 11.9.1921, CO 904/147.
7.   British Army Telegraph Transcripts, O'Donoghue, MS 31, 230.
8.   O'Donoghue, MS 31, 184 and MS 31, 186.
9.   Mrs Stoker of Douglas Road was one of those expelled from Cork in 1921 or 1922.
10.   O'Donoghue Diary Feb–April 1922, MS 31, 186.
11.   Liam de Roiste Diary, 22.3.1922.
12.   Connie Neenan Memoir, CAI P7/7.
13.   Connie Neenan Memoir, CAI P7/7. He may have been the spy known as Bracken. A David William Bracken is on one of the missing lists, Appendix III.
14.   The operation of this squad is another fascinating if rarely mentioned subject. See MA A/10135.

Chapter 53 (pp 290–296)

1.   After the 1970s TV series of that name: 'And all the trains and banks they robbed, they never shot anyone.'
2.   A Record of the Rebellion in Ireland: 6th Division, WO 141/93.
3.   Undated newspaper cutting from April 1922, probably from the *Daily Mail*, in Mulcahy P7/B/199.
4.   'A Record of the Rebellion in Ireland: The Development and Organization of Intelligence in British Intelligence in Ireland 1920–21', in *British Intelligence in Ireland 1920–1921*, ed. Hart.
5.   GOC, CIC Ireland, Report to Cabinet, 11.6.1921, CAB 24/126/3062.
6.   A Report on the Intelligence Branch of the Chief of Police, in Hart, ed. *British Intelligence in Ireland, op. cit.*
7.   See the register of cases, CO 905/15.
8.   Memo on 'Criminal Injustices to the Person' pertaining to the Compensation (Ireland) Commission, T160/184.
9.   CO 905/15.
10.   Florrie O'Donoghue in Borgonovo, *Florence and Josephine O'Donoghue's War of Independence*, p. 84.

11. A Record of the Rebellion in Ireland, 6th Division, wo 141/93; *Cork Examiner*, 28.5.1921. Sullivan's family accepted British liability. Was he forced into being a British agent after losing his job in the barracks?

12. Pat Margetts, O'Malley, P17b/111.

13. Connie Neenan Memoir, CAI PR7/7.

14. The rump of the Dublin Castle administration put in a series of claims to the Cork courts for the 'personal effects' of nine men, including such items as a camera, a shotgun and two bicycles 'stolen' during the first week of April 1922 in Cork city and East Riding. These were Crown employees of some sort who could not appear in court—they assigned their claims to the applicant, in this case Sir Mark Sturges, as he was by then. It suggests that these were individuals who had to get out in a hurry and leave their belongings behind. Most got out between 1 and 10 April and were almost certainly evacuated with military and naval assistance. Cork Boro Criminal Injury Book, 30 June 1924–May 1933, Cork East Riding Criminal Injury Book, Feb 1922–March 1924, and Cork Criminal Injury Book (Mallow), June 1921–Oct 1922. Cork CCPO Records, NA.

Chapter 54 (pp 298–304)

1. Warning received by William Ludgate, editor of the *Cork Constitution*, after he had described the killing of Alan Bell as a 'Brutal Deed by Human Brutes', 30.3.1920. CO 904/148.

2. Nos 60, 61 and 61B High Street were officially occupied by Constables Young, Cooke and Kelly in 1921. Cork Boro Valuation Book 5, A, B, C, South Ward 1908–34, VO Dublin. They are not listed in *Guy's Directory* though.

3. See claim for compensation by John Murphy and John Daly, *Cork Examiner*, 7.4.1921.

4. Mrs Rose Ronayne to Canon Hodges, 6.12.1929, in Sherrard Ronayne, CO 762/119.

5. This seems to be impossible, as both of Wilson's killers were Londoners. While this reads like a piece of colourful paranoia, Mrs Ronayne's husband states elsewhere in the IGC correspondence that while living in London at the time of Wilson's murder his wife swore she recognised one of his killers from the evening paper as being one of the two men who had accosted her a year earlier. This was probably a case of mistaken identity. However, Patrick O'Sullivan, brother of Joe O'Sullivan, one of Wilson's assassins, fought with the Cork IRA and appears to have arranged for the disappearance of John Sullivan Lynch in a dispute over a back garden (MA, A/0649), so Mrs Ronayne may have been correct. (See also Timothy Herlihy, BMH/WS 810.) It should also be pointed out that Sherrard Ronayne had earlier refused to drive a group of IRA men and had tried to prevent them from stealing his car. After returning from Waterford that week he reported the entire affair to the police and was advised to leave the country immediately. However, his reporting to the police happened *after* the intimidation, not before it. Sherrard Ronayne, CO 762/119.

6. Frankfield House was burnt out by the IRA on 4 February 1923. Cork Criminal Injury Book, Cork East Riding, Feb 1922–March 1924, CCPO Records, NA.

7. *Cork Constitution*, 21.2.1920.

8. CO 905/15.

9. One James O'Shea disappeared somewhere south of the city on 16.6.1921, CO 905/15.

10. Report of GOC Ireland on the Situation in Ireland, 30.4.1921, CAB 24/123/2911.

11. Frankfield House had previously been the residence of Dr A. W. Sandford, District Commissioner of the Boy Scouts organisation in Cork.

12. Including the man who told the story, but only after everyone else connected with it was dead.

13. Apart from Corry and Busteed there were several others among the ranks who would not have baulked at such an execution. For instance, there appears to have been at least one IRA killer who specialised in slitting people's throats. At least four such apparent 'suicides' were reported in the press which had all the hallmarks of a knife-wielding killer: Charles Murphy, stabbed by two men, *Cork Constitution*, 22.4.1921; Denis Long, an ex-soldier who 'while under the influence of drink tried to slit his own throat', *Cork Constitution*, 12.5.1921; William Murphy, throat cut/wounded in abdomen at Fort Street, *Cork Constitution*, 9.12.1921; and Frank Beale, a clerk in the Provincial Bank, found in the bank's toilet with his throat slit, *Irish Independent*, 19.5.1922. George Tilson in London and veterinary professor Edward Hoare also died as a result of throat-cutting suicides, though these were probably genuine.

14. Entry on A. W. Sandford in Cadogan and Falvey. Senior officers of the Boy Scouts who were landowners usually made their lands available for the scouts for use. See Gaughan, *Scouting in Ireland*.

Chapter 55 (pp 305–314)

1. FOD to JOD, 12.5.1921, in Borgonovo, *Florence and Josephine O'Donoghue's War of Independence*.

2. 'Life in Cork', *The Times*, 18.5.1921.

3. Despite claims to the contrary, there is no proof that the 'mysterious individual' was 'some bastard of an Englishman'. Wilfrid Ewart, who witnessed the abduction, later expanded on this in his book *A Journey Through Ireland* (1922). What he actually wrote was: '"No Irishman did that," caught my ear as I passed; "it's some bastard of an Englishman,"' which is not quite the same thing. What else would a Corkman say in the middle of the War of Independence?

4. *Cork Examiner*, 23.5.1921.

5. See card in compensations card index, CO 905/22. Parker received £200 'for injury'. Also see list of claimants in NA, Fin 1/707.

6. Of course, the Cookes may also have witnessed it or were believed by the IRA to have witnessed it.

7. This correspondence has been lovingly reproduced by John Borgonovo in his recent book of O'Donoghue's writings. Borgonovo, *op. cit.*

8. Mick Murphy, in O'Malley, P17b/112.

9. Peter Hart suggests that several teenagers were abducted along Blackrock Road at this time. Hart, *The IRA and its Enemies*.

10. In addition to the raids listed here, Pier View pub in Blackrock and a number of other pubs in the area were also raided during April. *Cork Examiner*, 15.4.1921.

11. Cork East Riding Court Register, Feb–Oct 1921, CCPO Records, NA.

12. CI's Report, April 1921, CO 904/115.

13. FOD to JOD, 12–16.5.1921. Borgonovo, *Florence and Josephine O'Donoghue's War of Independence*.

14. Florence O'Donoghue to Josephine O'Donoghue, 17.6.1921, in John Borgonovo, *Florence and Josephine O'Donoghue's War of Independence*, p. 173.

15. FOD to JOD, 20.6.1921, Borgonovo, *op. cit.*

16. The boating article referred to by O'Donoghue occurred near Blackrock and was reported by the *Cork Examiner* on 20 June 1921.

17. As can be heard in tape recordings of Martin Corry made by Jim Fitzgerald in the early seventies. I am grateful to Jim Fitzgerald for access to these recordings.

18. Adj 1st S. Div to GHQ (undated), in Mulcahy P7/A/20.

19. 'Dear 'G', D. O'Donovan to Josephine O'Donoghue, 17.8.1945, Florence O'Donoghue, MS 31, 340(10).

20. The bodies of at least two others were dumped in the harbour: Michael Finbarr Sullivan and John Coughlan, who died in IRA captivity in Aghada in east Cork.

21. Cork YMCA General Committee meeting, 18.5.1921, Cork YMCA General Committee Year Book, 1904–42.

22. 6th Division Weekly Intelligence Summary, 17.5.1921. Florence O'Donoghue, *No Other Law*.

23. Weekly Survey of the State of Ireland, 9.5.1921, CAB 24/125/2937.

24. *Cork Examiner*, 18.5.1921.

25. Weekly Survey of the State of Ireland, 16.5.1921, CAB 24/125/2945.

26. *Cork Examiner*, 18.5.1921.

27. O'Donoghue, *No Other Law*.

28. O'Donoghue got the report from Lieut Colonel John MacCarthy who captured it from a downed plane in east Limerick in 1921. The copy of the report in *No Other Law* is the same as that in MacCarthy's BMH witness statement, suggesting that O'Donoghue did not personally doctor the document. J. M. MacCarthy, BMH/WS 883. O'Donoghue stated to Ernie O'Malley that both he and Seán O'Hegarty were mentioned in the original report though they are not in this version. O'Malley, P17b/96.

29. Weekly Survey of the State of Ireland, 16.5.1921, CAB 24/125/2945.

30. Thomas E. Wolfe, a seed merchant and a member of the Church of Ireland, was a member of the well-known Wolfe family of Cork and a distant relative of Jasper Wolfe. There is no evidence that he was ever targeted by the IRA or harmed in any way. He lived on at Citadella until his death in the 1940s.

31. YMCA Annual Reports, 1921–23, and Valuation Book No. 6, Blackrock, Co. Cork, 1918–34, VO, Dublin.

32. This story was told to me by Dick Kenny, Michael Kenny's son. His father remembered many years later meeting a member of the Watson family on a train. They too remembered the episode.

33. Jimmy Brennock, BMH/WS 1113. Ginn was deported on 7.6.1921, CO 904/15. See also the parallel experience of his brother Henry, Henry Ginn, CO 762/145.

34. Begley, clearly a decent man, shows surprising sympathy for his former enemy: 'He lives with a brother and sister. No one speaks to him, not even the children of the place. He does not go to Mass in the parish church but goes into Cork. He is a fine-looking man but of course no girl would have him now. He is a kind of living dead, poor fellow.' Flor Begley, O'Malley, P17b/111.

35. O'Donoghue, MS 31, 127.

36. Three men called at his house looking for him, but he had been warned three days earlier by the local priest. Capt R. W. Cooper, CO 762/120.

37. See 'G' letter quoted above.

38. O'Donoghue, MS 31, 127.

39. As we have seen, the three taken at Waterfall were not IOs. Two intelligence officers were wounded in the city: Holland on 8 January 1921 and Lieut Frederick Anderson, who partially lost his hearing in an attack on a combined police and army patrol on Parnell Bridge on 4 January 1921.

Chapter 56 (pp 315–323)

1. John H. Bennett Diary, 29.5.1921, CAI B609/9/A/42.
2. Frank Hynes, BMH/WS 446.
3. Denis Kennedy to Florrie O'Donoghue, O'Donoghue, MS 31, 340(8).
4. DI RIC report for June 1921, CO 904/116.
5. GO, CIC Ireland Report to Cabinet, 11.6.1921, CAB 24/126/3052.
6. The ss *Rostellan*, owned by the Blackrock and Passage Railway Company, was boarded by such a party on 25.6.1921. In this case nothing was taken and no damage ensued. DI RIC Cork report for July–Sept, CO 904/116. It had also been boarded on 17 June and quantities of provisions for Spike Island thrown overboard. RIC Daily Summary, CO 904/149.
7. Minutes of the meeting of 17.6.1921, Cork YMCA Ladies Committee Year Book.
8. GHQ General Order 22 June 1921 in O'Donoghue, *No Other Law*, Appendix 3. Also see Barry, *Guerrilla Days in Ireland*, O'Malley, *On Another Man's Wound* and Moylan, *In His Own Words*.
9. Connie Neenan, in *Survivors*, ed. Uinseann MacEoin.
10. See Chapter 9.
11· O'Donoghue, *No Other Law*.
12· HQ 1st S. DIV. to GHQ, 4.5.1921, Mulcahy P/A/20.
13. C/S to OC 1st S. DIV, 7.5.1921, Mulcahy P7/A/20.
14. O/C 1st S. DIV to C/S, 20.5.1921, Mulcahy P7/A/21.
15. HQ 1st S. DIV to C/S, 5.7.1921, Mulcahy P7/A/21.
16. William Sheehan, *A Hard Local War* (2011).
17. Staff Note on Internal Morale of Enemy, Mulcahy P7/A/42.
18. Offensive against Internal Morale of the Enemy, Mulcahy P7/A/42.
19. 1st Southern Division Memo, May 1921, Mulcahy P7/A/18.
20. HQ 1st S. DIV to C/S, 5.7.1921, Mulcahy P7/A/21. This does not refer to reprisal burnings which were an entirely separate issue.
21. Memo by the Secretary of State for War to the Cabinet, 24.5.1921, CAB 24/2965.
22. Florence O'Donoghue to Josephine O'Donoghue, 17/5/1921, in John Borgonovo, *Florence and Josephine O'Donoghue's War of Independence*.
23. Florence O'Donoghue to Josephine O'Donoghue, 20.5.1921, Borgonovo.
24. Florence O'Donoghue to Josephine O'Donoghue, 17.6.1921, op. cit.
25. Florence O'Donoghue to Josephine O'Donoghue, 27.7.1921, op. cit.
26. Florence O'Donoghue to Josephine O'Donoghue, 15.6.1921, op. cit.
27. *Irish Times*, 17.6.1921.
28. It is almost certain that they would not be allowed back—nor would they choose to come back in such circumstances. The change of occupier of their residences would not have been picked up by the Valuation records until the following year. So people who appeared to have left in 1922 had in fact departed in 1921.
29. Cork YMCA, Annual Report, 1920/21. This is the only year where a statement like this was made, with one exception—1922—when a similar statement was made about 'departed' adults.
30. Chief Liaison Officer to o/o Brigade, 23.7.1921, Mulcahy Papers, P7/A/22.

Chapter 57 (pp 324–330)

1. Alice Hodder letter, 28.5.1922. 'Conditions in Cork', co 739/16.

2. See Appendix x and Appendix xi.

3. These figures were arrived at by comparing the changes of residency as listed in Guy's Postal Directory between 1921 and 1926 with the number of times such changes were accompanied by the transfer of deeds during the same period (Registry of Deeds, Dublin). The year 1926 was chosen as a cut-off point because it would allow for changes of address (and deeds) to filter through into the postal registers and into the Registry of Deeds. See Appendix vi.

4. In fact, one way to identity at least some of those who disappeared in 1922 is to check up the instances where a property was transferred by a family member other than the departed (or disappeared) owner.

5. Valuation Books, Blackrock, No. 6; Cork North East 3A, 3B; Bishopstown, Gurteenaspig (all 1908–35), vo Dublin.

6. Guy's Directories 1921 and 1924. See also the case of 'Mr x' in Clarke, p. 53, *op. cit.*

7. See Admiralty correspondence concerning the evacuation of orphans from Clifden, Co. Galway, May–July 1922, ADM 116/2135.

8. Telegram, Admiral Queenstown to Admiralty, 1.5.1922, ADM 116/2135.

9. ss *Puma* was owned by the Burns and Laird Line of Glasgow and sometimes carried the Royal Mail run between Glasgow and Dublin. During the spring of 1922, however, she appears to have been chartered by the military for the evacuation of troops out of Ireland, travelling daily between Cork, Rosslare and Fishguard. *Cork Examiner*, 29.4.1922.

10. Alice Hodder, *ibid.*

11. A study of Guy's Directory suggests that in some cases actual next-door neighbours moved in.

12. *Notes From Ireland*, February 1924.

13. O'Donoghue in O'Malley, P7/B/96.

14. Doak left for Trinity, Glynn to Belfast. For Fleeton see *Examiner*, 6/6/1923. This is not as outrageous as it seems. The IRA had earlier tried to poison Cruxy Connors while he hid out in Victoria Barracks. It is incorrect to say that Cork Grammar School records are patchy. In fact, only records covering 1912–26 are missing.

15. *The Irish Times*, 2.6.1922. The article goes on to list the groups targeted, all of which are accurate. The writer then suggests that the targets of the intimidation—business people, professionals, Post Office officials, large landowners as well as ex-security forces personnel—are evidence of Bolshevik influences on the part of the republican movement. It is easy to see why the disappearance of businessmen might be seen as evidence of Bolshevik tendencies, though it is quite at odds with the views of the vast majority of republican activists.

16. Weekly Survey of the State of Ireland, 27.2.1922. CAB 24/132/3803.

17. HOC Debate, 10.5.1922, Hansard, Vol. 153, CC2294–339; *Cork Constitution*, 15.5.1922.

18. IO 1st s. Div. to all Brigades, 26.4.1922, O'Malley, P7a/91.

19. Members of the 1st Battalion were to remain at large for much longer and were to be the core of the Anti-Treaty IRA in the city during the Civil War. Hart, *The IRA and its Enemies.*

20. Even to the extent of reporting that 'the Jerries are on the Shannon' with reference to the Ardnacrusha hydroelectric plant that was being built in the late 1920s. *Notes From Ireland*, November 1928.

21. *Notes From Ireland*, November 1924.

22. ibid., August 1923.

Chapter 58 (pp 331–335)

1. See correspondence relating to the IRA pension application of Agnes McCarthy, O'Donoghue, MS 31 340(10).

2. There were usually three or four sales staff from various areas of the Cork hinterland.

3. Letter from FO'D to Minnie Murphy, O'Donoghue MS 31, 340(10).

4. John Borgonovo, *Florence and Josephine O'Donoghue's War of Indepencence*, pp 47–48.

5. T. Ryan letter in Ml Nolan, CO 762/147. Also see Tim Herlihy, BMH/WS 810 for the shooting of Murphy by 10s.

6. Ex-Sgt Thos Flynn to IGC, Michael Nolan, CO 762/147.

7. Borgonovo, *op. cit.*, p. 49. This is in the same city which a few years earlier O'Donoghue found was 'unquestionably pro-British. I never at the time heard a note of doubt or protest or anything but admiration for England and hatred for Germany.'

8. Fr Domnic to Seán O'Hegarty, 15.12.1921. Seán O'Hegarty Papers, CAI.

BIBLIOGRAPHY

Abbott, Richard, *Police Casualties in Ireland* (Dublin 2000).

Ainsworth, John, *The Black and Tans and Auxiliaries in Ireland: Their Origins and Legacy* (Queensland History Teachers' Association, 12 May 2001).

Andrew, Christopher, *Secret Service: The Making of the British Intelligence Community* (London 1985).

Barry, Patrick, *By Bride and Blackwater* (Cork 1944).

Barry, Tom, *Guerrilla Days in Ireland* (Dublin 1981).

Barton, E. C., *Let the Boy win his Spurs: An Autobiography* (London 1976).

Beecher, Seán, *The Story of Cork* (Cork 1971).

Begley, Diarmuid, *The Road to Crossbarry: The Decisive Battle of the War of Independence* (Cork 1999).

Bence-Jones, Mark, *Twilight of the Ascendancy* (London 1987).

Bennett, Richard, *The Black and Tans* (London 2000).

Bennett, Richard, 'Portrait of a Killer', *New Statesman* (24 March 1961).

Borgonovo, John, *Florence and Josephine O'Donoghue's War of Independence: A Destiny Shapes our Ends* (Dublin 2006).

Borgonovo, John, *Spies, Informers and the Anti-Sinn Féin League: The Intelligence War in Cork City 1920–21* (Dublin 2007).

Breen, Dan, *My Fight for Irish Freedom* (Dublin 1924; Tralee 1964).

Brennan, Niamh, 'A Political Minefield: Southern Loyalists, the Irish Grants Committee and the British Government 1922–31', *Irish Historical Studies* xxx, 119 (May 1997).

Brewer, John D., *The Royal Irish Constabulary: An Oral History* (Belfast 1990).

Browne, Charlie, *The Story of the 7th* (Macroom n.d.).

Bullock, John, *M.I.5: The Origins and History of the British Counter-Espionage Service* (London 1963).

Butler, Ewan, *Barry's Flying Column* (London 1971).

Cadogan, Tim, *Cork County Council 1899–1999: A Centenary Souvenir* (Cork 1999).

Cadogan, Tim and Jeremiah Falvey (eds), *Cork: A Biographical Dictionary* (Dublin 2006).

Clarke, Olga Pyne, *She Came of Decent People* (London 1985).

Clifford, Brendan, 'The Historical Significance of the All For Ireland League' in Cadogan, *Cork County Council 1899–1999: A Centenary Souvenir* (Cork 1999).

Clifford, Brendan (ed.), *Reprints from the 'Cork Free Press': An Account of Ireland's Only Democratic Anti-Partition Movement* (Cork 1984).

Coakley, D. J., *Cork: Its Trade and Commerce: Official Handbook of the Cork Chamber of Commerce and Shipping* (Cork 1919).

Cole, R. Lee, *A History of Methodism in Ireland*, Vol. 4 (Belfast 1960).

Coogan, Tim Pat, *Michael Collins: A Biography* (London 1990).

Cooney, Dudley L., *The Methodists in Ireland: A Short History* (Dublin 2001).

Cork Defence Union, *Boycotting in the County Cork* (Cork 1886).

Cronin, Jim, *Making Connections: A Cork GAA Miscellany* (Cork 2005).

Crowley, Flor ['Raymond'], 'Black and Tan Diary', *Southern Star* (23 Oct–27 Nov 1971).

Crowley, J. S., R. J. N. Devoy, D. Linehan and P. O'Flanagan, *Atlas of Cork* (Cork 2005).

Crozier, Frank P., *Ireland For Ever* (London 1932).

Crozier, Frank P., *The Men I Killed* (London 1937).

d'Alton, Ian, 'Keeping Faith: An Evocation of the Cork Protestant Character 1820–1920' in P. O'Flanagan and C. G. Buttimer (eds), *Cork: History and Society* (Dublin 1993).

Deasy, Liam, *Brother Against Brother* (Cork 1982).

Dickson, David, *Old World Colony: Cork and South Munster 1630–1830* (Cork 2005).

Dolan, Anne, 'Killing and Bloody Sunday, November 1920,' *The Historical Journal* (2006), 49, 3, pp 789–810.

Donnelly, James, *The Land and the People of 19th Century Cork* (London 1975).

Duff, Douglas V., *The Rough with the Smooth* (London 1940).

Dunne, Seán (ed.), *The Cork Anthology* (Cork 1993).

English, Richard, *Ernie O'Malley: IRA Intellectual* (Oxford 1998).

Fedorowich, Kent, 'Reconstruction and Resettlement: The Politicization of Irish Migration to Australia and Canada 1919–1929', *English Historical Review* (November 1999).

Feeney, P. J., *Glory O, Glory O, Ye Bold Fenian Men* (Dripsey 1996).

Fitzgerald, James, *Foras Feasa na Paróiste, Knockraha Macra na Feirme* (Knockraha 1977).

Fitzgerald, James, *Cnoc Ratha: History and Folklore* (Knockraha 2005).

Fitzgerald, Seamus, 'East Cork Activities 1920', *Capuchin Annual* (1970).

Fitzpatrick, David (ed.), *Revolution? Ireland 1917–1923* (Dublin 1999).

Foley, Conor, *Legion of the Rearguard: The IRA and the Modern Irish State* (London 1992).

Foot, M. R. D., *Secret Lives* (Oxford 2002).

Gaughan, J. Anthony, *Scouting in Ireland* (Dublin, 2006).

Girvin, Kevin, *The Life and Times of Seán O'Hegarty*, MPhil. Thesis, UCC (2003).

Gleeson, James, *Bloody Sunday* (London 1962).

Guy's Postal Directory of Cork City and County (1910–1926).

Hart, Peter (ed.), *British Intelligence in Ireland 1920–1921: The Final Reports* (Cork 2002).

Hart, Peter, 'Class, Community and the IRA in Cork' in P. O'Flanagan and C. G. Buttimer (eds), *Cork: History and Society* (Dublin 1993).

Hart, Peter, *Mick: The Real Michael Collins* (London 2005).

Hart, Peter, *The IRA and its Enemies, Violence and Community in Cork 1916–1923* (Oxford 1998).

Hart, Peter, *The IRA at War, 1916–1923* (Oxford 2003).

Harvey, Dan and Gerry White, *The Barracks: A History of Victoria/Collins Barracks, Cork* (Cork 1997).

Herlihy, Jim, *The Royal Irish Constabulary: A Short History and Genealogical Guide* (Dublin 1997).

Herlihy, Jim, *The Royal Irish Constabulary: A Complete Alphabetical List of Officers and Men 1816–1922* (Dublin 1999).

Hopkinson, Michael, *Green Against Green: The Irish Civil War* (Dublin 1998).

Hopkinson, Michael, *The Irish War of Independence* (Dublin 2002).

Hopkinson, Michael (ed.), *The Last Days of Dublin Castle: The Diaries of Mark Sturges* (Dublin 1999).

Jeffery, Frederick, *Methodism and the Irish Problem* (Belfast 1973).

Jeffery, Keith, *Field Marshal Sir Henry Wilson: A Political Soldier* (Oxford 2008).

Jeffery, Keith, 'British Military Intelligence Following World War 1' in K. G. Robertson (ed.), *British and American Approaches to Intelligence* (London 1987).

Kee, Robert, *Ourselves Alone: The Green Flag*, Vol. III (London 1989).

Kell, Richard, *Collected Poems 1962–1993* (Belfast 2001).

Kelly, Matthew, 'The Politics of Protestant Street Preaching in 1890's Ireland', *The Historical Journal*, 48, 1 (2005), pp 101–25.

Keyes-McDonnell, Kathleen, *There is a Bridge at Bandon* (Cork 1972).

Kingston, Willie, 'From Victorian Boyhood to the Troubles: A Skibbereen Memoir', *Journal of Skibbereen Historical Society*, Vol. 1 (2005).

Lankford, Siobhan, *The Hope and the Sadness* (Cork 1980).

Leonard, Jane, 'Getting Them at Last: The IRA and Ex-Servicemen' in D. Fitzpatrick (ed.), *Revolution? Ireland 1917–1923* (Dublin 1999).

Linge, John, The Royal Navy and the Irish Civil War', *Irish Historical Studies* XXXI, 121 (May 1998).

Lord, Cliff and Graham Wilson, *The Royal Corps of Signals: Unit Histories 1920–2001* (London 2003).

Mac Donough, Michael, *The Life of William O'Brien* (London 1920).

MacEoin, Uinseann (ed.), *Survivors* (Dublin 1980).

Mackenzie, W. J. M., *The Secret History of Special Operations Executive 1940–1945* (London 2000).

MacSeoin, Tomás, and Thomas B. Jones, 'Memories of Bandon Head Post Office in the 1920s', *Bandon Historical Society Journal*, 13 (1997).

McAuliffe, John, 'The Trouble Times in Cloyne' in Padraig O'Loingsigh (ed.), *The Book of Cloyne* (Cork 1977).

McCarthy, Kieran and Christensen, Maj. Batt, *Cobh's Contribution to the Fight for Irish Freedom* (Cobh 1992).

McCarthy, Roisín, *The Landlords' Defences: Organized landowner counter-reaction to agrarian agitation, land reform and the Home Rule Movement 1879–1914*, BA Dissertation, UCC (2004).

McColgan, John, *British Withdrawal From Ireland: British Policy and the Irish Administration* (London 1983).

McCrea, Rev. Alexander (ed.), *Irish Methodism in the Twentieth Century, A Symposium*, Belfast 1931.

McMahon, Paul, *British Spies and Irish Rebels* (London 2008).

Micheau, Edward, 'Sectarian Conflict in Monaghan' in D. Fitzpatrick (ed.), *Revolution? Ireland 1917–1923* (Dublin 1990).

Moylan, Seán, *In His Own Words: His Memoir of the Irish War of Independence* (Millstreet 2004).

Mulvihill, Mary, *Ingenious Ireland* (Dublin 2002).

Neeson, Geraldine, *In my Mind's Eye: The Cork I Knew and Loved* (Dublin 2001).

Nicholson, David and Philip Mackeown, *The Story of Woodford Bourne* (Cork 2005).

O'Brien, John, 'Population, Politics and Society in Cork 1780–1900' in P. O'Flanagan and C. Buttimer (eds), *Cork: History and Society* (Dublin 1993).

O'Callaghan, Antoin, *The Lord Mayors of Cork* (Cork 2000).

O'Callaghan, Seán, *Execution* (London 1974).

O'Connor, Frank, *My Oedipus Complex and Other Stories* (London 2005).

O'Day, Alan and John Stevenson, *Irish Historical Documents Since 1800* (Dublin 1992).

O'Donoghue, Florence, *No Other Law: A Biography of Liam Lynch* (Dublin 1986).

O'Donoghue, Florence, *Tomás MacCurtain—Soldier and Patriot* (Tralee 1971).

O'Donovan, Donal, *Kevin Barry and his Time* (Dublin 1989).

O'Farrell, Padraig, *The Ernie O'Malley Story* (Dublin 1983).

O'Farrell, Padraig, *The Wit and Humour of Dáil Eireann* (Dublin 1986).

O'Farrell, Padraig, *Who's Who in the Irish War of Independence* (Cork 1980).

O'Halpin, Eunan, 'Collins and Intelligence 1919–1921' in G. Doherty and D. Keogh (eds), *Michael Collins and the Making of the Irish State* (Dublin 1998).

O'Halpin, Eunan, 'British Intelligence in Ireland' in C. Andrew and D. Dilks (eds), *The Missing Dimension* (Illinois 1984).

O'Hegarty, P. S., *The Victory of Sinn Féin* (Dublin 1924).

Ó Loinsigh, Pádraig, *The Book of Cloyne* (Midleton undated).

O'Mahony, Colman, *The Maritime Gateway to Cork: Passage West 1754–1942* (Cork 1986).

O'Malley, Ernie, *On Another Man's Wound* (Dublin 1979).

O'Malley, Ernie, *The Singing Flame* (Dublin 1992).

Ó Maoileoin, Seamus, *B'Fhiú an Braon Fola* (Dublin 1958).

O'Neill, Joseph, *Blood-Dark Track* (London 2001).

O'Neill, Tom, *The Battle of Clonmult: The IRA's Worst Defeat* (Dublin 2006).

Orr, Philip, *The Road to the Somme* (Belfast 1987).

Pinkman, John A., *In the Legion of the Vanguard* (Dublin 1998).

Pochin Mould, Daphne D. C., *Discovering Cork* (Dingle 1991).

Proctor, Tammy M., 'Family Ties in the Making of Modern Intelligence', *Journal of Social History* (Winter 2005).

Putkowski, Julian, 'A2 and the Reds in Khaki', *Lobster 94: Journal of Parapolitics*, 27 (April 1994).

Putkowski, Julian, 'The Best Secret Service Man We Had', *Lobster 94: Journal of Parapolitics*, 28 (February 1995).

Rebel Cork's Fighting Story (Tralee n.d.)

Ryan, Meda, *The Real Chief: The Story of Liam Lynch* (Cork 1986).

Ryan, Meda, *Tom Barry: IRA Freedom Fighter* (Cork 2005).

St Leger, Alicia, 'Fota's Family: The Smith Barrys', Fota House and Gardens Pamphlet (Cork 2002).

Sheehan, Tim, *Execute Hostage Compton-Smith* (Dripsey 1993).

Sheehan, Tim, *Lady Hostage: Mrs Lindsey* (Dripsey 1990).

Sheehan, William (ed.), *British Voices from the Irish War of Independence 1918–1921* (Cork 2005).

Sheehan, William, *A Hard Local War: The British Army and Guerilla War in Cork 1919–1923* (Stroud 2011).

Sheers, Owen, 'Guerrillas in Waiting', *The Guardian* (20 October 2007).

Sheers, Owen, *Resistance* (London 2008).

Somerville Large, Peter, *Cappaglass* (Dublin 1984).

Stanley, Alan, *I Met Murder on the Way* (Carlow 2007).

Townshend, Charles, *The British Campaign in Ireland 1919–1921* (Oxford 1980).

Townshend, Charles, 'The IRA and the Development of Guerrilla Warfare 1916–1921', *English Historical Journal* (1979).

Twohig, Patrick J., *Green Tears for Hecuba* (Ballincollig 2004).

Ungoed-Thomas, Jasper, *Jasper Wolfe of Skibbereen* (Cork 2008).

Warren, Rev. Thomas, *A History and Genealogy of the Warren Family* (Dublin 1904).

Warwicker, John, *Churchill's Underground Army: A History of the Auxiliary Units in World War II* (London 2008).

Watergrasshill Old IRA Comrades Association Notebook.

West, Trevor, *Malting the Barley: John H. Bennett, The Man and his Firm* (Cork 2006).

White, Dan, *The Musgrave Brothers: The 1st 125 Years* (Cork 2001).

White, Gerry and Brendan O'Shea, *Baptized in Blood: The Foundation of the Cork Brigade of the Irish Volunteers* (Cork 2005).

White, Gerry and Brendan O'Shea, *The Burning of Cork* (Cork 2006).

Wilkinson, Peter and Joan Bright Astley, *Gubbins and S.O.E.* (London 1993).

Woodcock, Caroline, *An Officer's Wife in Ireland* (Dublin 1994).

INDEX